B O O K

The Philip E. Lilienthal imprint
honors special books
in commemoration of a man whose work
at University of California Press from 1954 to 1979
was marked by dedication to young authors
and to high standards in the field of Asian Studies.
Friends, family, authors, and foundations have together
endowed the Lilienthal Fund, which enables UC Press
to publish under this imprint selected books
in a way that reflects the taste and judgment
of a great and beloved editor.

The publisher and the University of California Press Foundation gratefully acknowledge the generous support of the Philip E. Lilienthal Imprint in Asian Studies, established by a major gift from Sally Lilienthal.

Japan

Japan

History and Culture from Classical to Cool

NANCY K. STALKER

University of California Press

University of California Press, one of the most distinguished university presses in the United States, enriches lives around the world by advancing scholarship in the humanities, social sciences, and natural sciences. Its activities are supported by the UC Press Foundation and by philanthropic contributions from individuals and institutions. For more information, visit www.ucpress.edu.

University of California Press
Oakland, California

Library of Congress Cataloging-in-Publication Data

Names: Stalker, Nancy K., author.
Title: Japan : history and culture from classical to cool / Nancy K. Stalker.
Description: Oakland, California : University of California Press, [2018] |
    Includes bibliographical references and index. |
Identifiers: LCCN 2017058048 (print) | LCCN 2017060303 (ebook) |
    ISBN 9780520962835 () | ISBN 9780520287778 (pbk. : alk. paper)
    Subjects: LCSH: Japan—History.
Classification: LCC DS806 (ebook) | LCC DS806 .S83 2018 (print) |
    DDC 952—dc23
LC record available at https://lccn.loc.gov/2017058048

Manufactured in the United States of America
25 24 23 22 21 20 19 18
10 9 8 7 6 5 4 3 2 1

Contents

Preface

While at the University of Texas at Austin, I taught a course called *Introduction to Japan* for over a dozen years. It is a gateway class, intended to entice students into deeper studies by providing a survey of a millennium's worth of Japan's cultural, social, and political highlights. Searching for a textbook for the course brought the story of Goldilocks to mind—this one focused too much on elite and premodern culture or was too expensive, that one minimized gender or religious matters or lacked illustrations—but unlike the girl in the fairy tale, I have never found one that was "just right." The opportunity to present my own version of "Japan" arose when Reed Malcolm at the University of California Press, at the suggestion of Professor Peter Duus, invited me to submit a proposal for an introductory textbook on Japanese history and culture. I am deeply grateful to Reed, Zuha Khan, and other members of the UC Press staff for their support of this project.

I had several goals for the text. As a historian, I knew that providing a basic historical narrative was important for helping students understand the context of cultural developments and see important continuities and discontinuities over time. I would devote significant attention to the visual and literary arts and to material culture, because aesthetics and tradition occupy a central role in modern Japanese national identity, to a degree seemingly unparalleled among the world's wealthiest nations. I would also occasionally attempt to relate problems of the past to present situations, as students tend to relate well to contemporary examples. While an introductory text can never be truly comprehensive, the development of colonies under the Japanese empire, everyday consumer culture, religious modernity, gender norms, and cultures of protest would receive some of the coverage they warranted. Postwar and contemporary art and popular culture would not be relegated to a brief afterthought. The resulting work admittedly reflects my own biases, but it also addresses areas that, I have found, most fully engage students.

The chapters are arranged both chronologically and thematically, resulting in some historical overlap. Thus, chapters 6 and 7 both cover the Edo period (1600s to mid-1800s), but chapter 6 addresses the Tokugawa shogunate's systems of governance, along with intellectual and religious developments of the era, while chapter 7 is focused on the flourishing of new forms of urban culture. Similarly, chapters 9 and 10 both address the first four decades of the twentieth century, with the former devoted to discussion of domestic modernity and the latter focused on Japan's expansion abroad as an imperial power.

At the conclusion of each chapter, I've provided a list of ten to twelve suggestions for further reading, which does not begin to include all the works I have drawn upon in writing this book. Instead, these sections provide readers an eclectic combination of classic works and cutting-edge scholarship. Each is followed by a brief selection of recommended films, including features, documentaries, and animated works. These lists, too, are idiosyncratic, reflecting available works on the period (more scarce for pre-Heian eras) along with my own preferences.

I am indebted to numerous experts in diverse fields of Japanese studies, on whose scholarship this text is based, and to several thoughtful reviewers who provided important insights and corrections. Any remaining errors and omissions are my responsibility alone.

NOTES ON CONVENTIONS

Names are provided in Japanese order, with family name preceding given name. Many names in the earlier chapters include the possessive pronoun "no," such as Sugawara no Michizane, meaning Michizane of the Sugawara family.

Macrons are used to indicate a drawn-out vowel sound in the pronunciation of some Japanese names and terms, such as Prince Shōtoku, the Ryūkyū Islands, or wartime *tokkōtai* attack squads. In names of the main islands and major cities, however, and in words that have become familiar in English—such as shogun, Shinto, and daimyo—macrons have been omitted.

1   Early Japan

GEOGRAPHY AND CLIMATE

Japan is an archipelago that consists of four large islands and over six thousand smaller islands, mostly uninhabited. Together, the islands are roughly the size of California or Italy. The four main islands, from north to south, are Hokkaido, Honshu, Shikoku, and Kyushu. Among the smaller islands, Okinawa, in the Ryūkyū chain to the south, and Sado, off the coast of northern Honshu, are two of the most populous. For this island nation, proximity to the seas has strongly influenced culture and society, as an important source of food, a factor in influencing climate, and a barrier to easy contact with nearby countries. The distance to China is five hundred miles, while the closest nation, Korea, is 125 miles away. If Japan were located farther from these Asian nations, it might not have absorbed Chinese civilizational influences, such as the writing system, Buddhism, and Confucianism, which were transmitted to Japan through migrants from the Korean Peninsula. If it were closer to the powerful Chinese empire, it might not have developed its own distinctive language and material culture.

Mountains cover about 80 percent of Japan's land surface and are surprisingly heavily forested. These mountains include many volcanoes, both dormant and active, so thermal hot springs are abundant and earthquakes occur frequently, up to one thousand tremors per year. Mount Fuji—Japan's tallest mountain, at 12,388 feet—is a volcano that last erupted in the eighteenth century. It was particularly active from the eighth to twelfth centuries, when it was perceived as an angry deity, but today represents an important and scenic symbol of national identity. Only about one-quarter of Japan's land is considered habitable, and settlement is concentrated densely

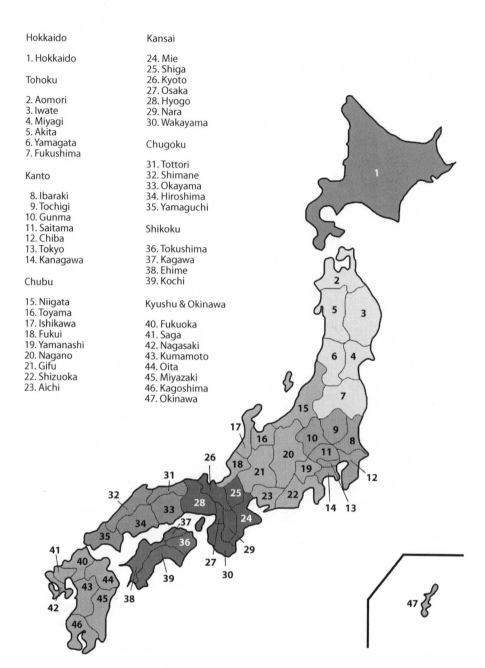

Hokkaido

1. Hokkaido

Tohoku

2. Aomori
3. Iwate
4. Miyagi
5. Akita
6. Yamagata
7. Fukushima

Kanto

8. Ibaraki
9. Tochigi
10. Gunma
11. Saitama
12. Chiba
13. Tokyo
14. Kanagawa

Chubu

15. Niigata
16. Toyama
17. Ishikawa
18. Fukui
19. Yamanashi
20. Nagano
21. Gifu
22. Shizuoka
23. Aichi

Kansai

24. Mie
25. Shiga
26. Kyoto
27. Osaka
28. Hyogo
29. Nara
30. Wakayama

Chugoku

31. Tottori
32. Shimane
33. Okayama
34. Hiroshima
35. Yamaguchi

Shikoku

36. Tokushima
37. Kagawa
38. Ehime
39. Kochi

Kyushu & Okinawa

40. Fukuoka
41. Saga
42. Nagasaki
43. Kumamoto
44. Oita
45. Miyazaki
46. Kagoshima
47. Okinawa

MAP 1. Regions and prefectures of Japan.

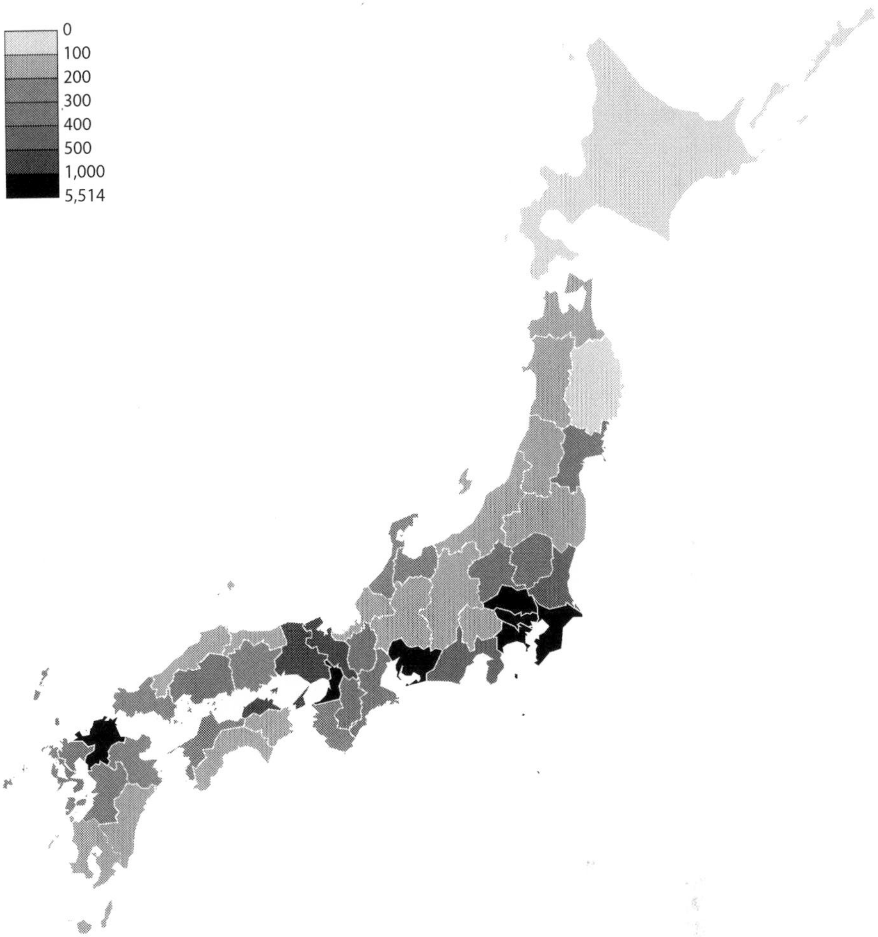

MAP 2.   Population density by prefecture, Japan (number per square kilometer).

along the coastlines of the Pacific Ocean, Japan Sea, and Inland Sea, in river valleys, and on the occasional plains, most notably the Kanto plain in northeastern Honshu, where Tokyo is located, and the Kinai plain in central Japan, where the cities of Kyoto, Nara, and Osaka are located. Today, over three-quarters of the population live in crowded urban areas in these places, while rural regions are much less densely populated. Before modern transportation, travel was difficult in the mountainous land, giving rise to distinctive regional differences in dialects, lifestyles, produce, and animal life.

Climate varies along the extensive archipelago, ranging from the harsh, snowy winters in the north and along the northwest coast of Honshu to the mild winters and subtropical summers of Okinawa. The capital city, Tokyo, is at roughly the same latitude as Los Angeles. Summers there are hot and humid, with a rainy season in June and July. Typhoons bring violent, destructive rainstorms to the islands beginning in September. The most pleasant seasons are the spring and fall, when many venture out to view blossoming cherry trees or colorful maple foliage. Such distinctive seasonal changes have been celebrated in Japanese arts and poetry for centuries.

PREHISTORIC JAPAN

Who were the ancestors of the Japanese? What were their origins, and when did they begin to inhabit the islands that we call Japan? The earliest inhabitants were likely from the Pacific islands or Southeast Asia, but there are no written records of these distant ancestors. The earliest Japanese chronicles, the *Kojiki* (Record of ancient matters) and *Nihon shoki* (Chronicles of Japan, also known as *Nihongi*), tell of the mythological origins of the islands but were written much later, in the early eighth century, and are unreliable sources for much early history. In order to investigate the sources of prehistoric Japanese culture, we must therefore rely on the findings of archaeologists. Archaeology is an extremely popular field of study in Japan, because of the thousands of readily accessible archaeological sites throughout the nation. Excavations indicate that the archipelago has been inhabited for about fifty thousand years and that a rich Paleolithic culture existed in the islands.

Japan's prehistoric era, before the existence of local written records, is generally divided into four phases: Paleolithic, from approximately 35,000 to 15,000 B.P.; Jōmon, from approximately 15,000 B.P. to 900 B.C.E.; Yayoi, from 900 B.C.E. to 250 C.E.; and Kofun, from 250 C.E. to 600 C.E. Each phase has distinguishing characteristics, yet there are also strong continuities running through these eras. Over many thousands of years, there were gradual transitions from Paleolithic (or "Old Stone Age") culture to the pottery-making, hunting, and gathering culture of the Jōmon era; to the metal use and agriculture of the Yayoi; and finally to an era characterized by enormous burial mounds, called *kofun*, which indicate that local rulers possessed the power to draft tens of thousands of laborers to build such monuments. It is important to remember that these eras are not clearly distinct. There was significant overlap between the periods—techniques for making ceramics and salt and for building structures, initiated in the Jōmon period, persisted long after the introduction of metal and advanced agricultural technologies in the Yayoi period.

Until the 1990s, archaeologists generally believed that Japan's modern inhabitants were largely descended from Jōmon stock. Now, however, DNA evidence from skulls and teeth has convinced most that the Japanese population has a dual structure, including both the ancestors of the Jōmon, who came from the south, and a later wave of immigrants with different characteristics who intermingled with the Jōmon during the Yayoi era. Most modern Japanese are genetically closer to the later immigrants, but characteristics of Jōmon people can still be seen among Okinawans and Ainu, the indigenous residents of Hokkaido.

JŌMON-ERA DEVELOPMENTS

Some time around 15,000 B.C.E., the inhabitants of the northern and eastern sections of the archipelago mastered the techniques of coiling clay to form vessels and figurines, then baking their work in open fires in order to harden it. The resulting pottery allowed the people of the Jōmon era to cook food more easily, to store food they had gathered, and to live farther from immediate sources of water. They could make salt by boiling seawater in the pots, allowing preservation of foods. The Jōmon period is very long—over ten thousand years—so there is a great deal of variety in the shapes and decorative markings among the pots; they differed over time and by region. From the prehistoric era to contemporary society, ceramics have remained an important aspect of Japanese art and culture.

The period takes its name from the distinctive earthenware pottery produced throughout the period. The word *jōmon* means "cord-mark"; many pieces of pottery were decorated with patterns made by pressing cords or branches into the soft clay before firing. Jōmon pottery is generally classified by age: Incipient, Early, Middle, and Late. Incipient pots are the earliest clearly dated pottery found so far in the world, dating from around 11,000 to 5000 B.C.E. They typically have rounded or pointy bottoms, and archaeologists believe they were mainly used for cooking outdoors, with stones or sand to keep the vessel upright. By the Early Jōmon period (5500–3500 B.C.E.), flat-bottomed pots had become customary, which suggests that they were now being used more indoors, set on floors. Different styles of ornamentation are found in different regions. In northeast Honshu and Hokkaido, cord markings are common, whereas

FIGURE 1. Middle Jōmon pot, British Museum. Photo by Morio, via Wikimedia Commons.

in Kyushu a herringbone style of decoration was dominant. Middle Jōmon pottery is especially striking. Many vessels have wild, abstract, decorative shapes, suggesting things like leaping flames or snakes heads. These pots were not standardized—each was a unique work of creative art. Archaeologists believe that the imaginative design of the pots indicates they were used for ritual as well as functional purposes. In the Late Jōmon period (2500–1500 B.C.E.), pots with thinner walls were made in a greater variety of shapes and sizes.

Much of what we know about Jōmon society, including the pottery, comes from the excavation of garbage mounds, or middens. Huge mounds of shells near settlement areas preserved remains of the diet, daily life, and burial practices. The high calcium and alkaline content of shell middens slowed decay, allowing archaeologists to examine food remnants, tools, and other evidence of Jōmon society. The mounds indicate that the people survived through a hunting-and-gathering lifestyle—living on nuts, fruit, roots, fish, shellfish, and animal flesh. Shell mounds contain deer, boar, and bear bones; the bones and shells of dozens of different kinds of fish and shellfish; stone and wooden tools; bows and arrowheads; fishhooks and harpoon heads; oars and net fragments; and personal ornaments like lacquered hair combs and shell earrings. American zoologist Edward Sylvester Morse first discovered the shell mounds in 1877. Morse had been hired by the new Meiji government to help modernize the education system and spied a large mound while looking out a window on a train between Yokohama and Tokyo. In September 2016 the world's oldest fishhooks, around twenty-three thousand years old and made from the shells of sea snails, were found in a cave in the Okinawan islands.

Archaeological excavations have uncovered semipermanent settlements, consisting of a small cluster of pit dwellings, with floors dug well below ground level and hearths in the center, each housing five or six people. Sometimes these clusters also contained a large ring of tall stones, which may have been used for village rituals related to hunting or fishing. Jōmon communities probably tried to be self-sufficient, but there is evidence of trade: salt from coastal regions has been found in mountain settlements, and obsidian and stone from the mountains, used for tools, have been found at coastal locations. They also engaged in simple, small-scale farming, probably using slash-and-burn techniques to raise beans, melons, and grains like barley and millet.

Graves were small and simple holes into which bodies were inserted. Dwellings and gravesites in the settlements appear to be undifferentiated, leading scholars to suggest that Jōmon society did not make social distinctions according to class or wealth. They theorize that there was simply not enough surplus food to support elites who did not perform labor.

Among the most striking artifacts from the Jōmon period are stone and clay figurines, known as *dogū*. These become increasingly elaborate in the northeastern part of the country during Middle and Late Jōmon. The clearly anthropomorphic dogū are characterized by bulging eyes, sometimes called "coffee-bean eyes" or "goggle eyes" because they resemble the snow goggles used by northern peoples. Some appear to be pregnant females with prominent breasts, and others seem to be intentionally broken.

FIGURE 2.   Late Jōmon *dogū,* Tokyo National Museum. Photo by Rc 13, via Wikimedia Commons.

Archaeologists have suggested that healers used the figurines in rituals to facilitate childbirth or to cure injuries or diseases.

YAYOI DEVELOPMENTS

The introduction and diffusion of organized agriculture and other technologies enhanced the daily life of the inhabitants of the islands. Wet rice cultivation, metal technologies, weaving, and new pottery techniques greatly improved the material quality of life. The Yayoi period is named for the area in present-day Tokyo where a new style of pottery, less earthy and organic than Jōmon pots and characterized by smooth lines and surfaces, was first found. Yayoi people had apparently begun using a potter's wheel and advanced firing techniques to produce vessels of greater delicacy, more elegant and more carefully finished than those of the Jōmon era. While Jōmon pots emphasized flamboyant decoration, Yayoi pottery focused on form and function. Many had no decoration at all; others had simple geometric designs. They demonstrate that pots were being specialized for different uses, including cooking, storage, and ritual offerings. Pottery was also used in burial rituals. Large jars, which could only have been made by specialist potters, were set mouth to mouth, for use in human burial. Other methods of burial also existed, including stone coffins and rectangular mounds, the precursors of the great tombs of the fourth and fifth centuries. In contrast with Jōmon gravesites, which demonstrate little social distinction in burial, Yayoi grave goods—including bronze mirrors, semiprecious beads, personal ornaments, and weapons—seem to indicate evidence of social rank.

The introduction of wet rice cultivation had far-reaching social implications, requiring a coordination of labor that set a pattern that continues to influence Japanese rural life and culture today. Farmers in China had grown rice since at least 5000 B.C.E., and farmers on the Korean Peninsula since around 1500 B.C.E. Migrants or traders from the Asian continent likely carried the crop to western Japan. The earliest rice-growing sites were swampy natural wetlands. Seed was broadcast over these sites, and the farmers relied on rainfall for a successful crop. Over time, rice farming became more systematic. Farmers began constructing paddy fields, which they flooded using artificial irrigation channels. They raised seedlings separately and transplanted them into these fields in careful rows to better manage weed control. They created specialized tools such as wooden rakes, iron hoes and shovels, mortars and pestles for pounding rice, and stone axes and reaping knives. As control over irrigation improved, rice sites and settlements were constructed at higher elevations. Paddy cultivation was labor intensive, requiring cooperative efforts to prepare fields, organize irrigation, and harvest the crop. But rice was a worthwhile crop, rich in calories and capable of sustaining larger populations than gathered foodstuffs. Because of the demands of intensive agriculture, the Japanese formed permanent farming communities in the lowlands. From that time forward, rice became a main staple of the economy, although other grains, such as millet and buckwheat, played a larger role in rural daily diets until the twentieth century.

One can visit several restored Yayoi village sites in Japan. Among the best-known is an excavation site called Toro in Shizuoka prefecture, discovered in 1943. The village is on low ground near the mouth of a river and contains twelve dwellings and two storehouses to the north, rice fields to the south, and evidence of elaborate irrigation and drainage systems. Like Jōmon dwellings, the houses had thatched roofs supported by four heavy posts, sunken floors, and hearths in the center of the dwelling. They are oval in shape, with around 160 square feet of floor space. Some food was stored in jars, but by mid-Yayoi, special wooden storehouses with floors raised a few feet off the ground were constructed to protect crops from insects, rodents, and rot. Many well-preserved artifacts of village life are on display at the Toro museum. The raised storehouse, an important building for the community, was represented in clay figures and in designs of early bronze bells. It later became a motif in shrine and palace architecture.

Metallurgy also enriched social and aesthetic aspects of life. Japan began using iron and bronze around 300 B.C.E. Both metals had been employed for a long time in China and Korea, and migrants brought the technologies together to Japan. All iron, copper, and tin used in the era were imported from the Asian continent. Iron, forged on anvils, was more utilitarian, used for tools and practical weapons. Bronze, an alloy of copper and tin, was cast in molds for swords, mirrors, and bells known as *dōtaku*, usually as ritual symbols of power. The bells were initially copied from continental models, but as the Japanese improved casting techniques, the bells grew larger and had more intricate designs. Later models featured extensive decoration and such thin walls that they probably didn't actually function as bells, but as symbols of allegiance to some political authority. This theory is supported by the fact that bells made from the same mold have been found at widely scattered sites.

The increase in the quality and number of weapons made possible by metallurgy brought a sharp increase in warfare, as armies under local chieftains battled to extend or consolidate control over larger territorial units. By the end of the Yayoi period, we can discern stratified communities, with

FIGURE 3.   Yayoi-era *dōtaku* bronze bell, The Metropolitan Museum of Art, New York, Rogers Fund 1918 (18.68). Source: ARTstor Images for Academic Publishing.

the gravesites of chieftains and their families demarcated from ordinary cemeteries and containing caches of mirrors, jewels, swords, spears, and bells from different parts of Japan. Some of the bodies buried at the elite gravesites wore armbands that restricted the size of their biceps, symbolizing their status as rulers rather than ordinary manual laborers.

THE ERA OF GREAT TOMB MOUNDS

The innovations introduced in Yayoi-period agriculture, metallurgy, pottery, and burial practices continued to spread and evolve over the next few centuries. While new technologies enabled greater surplus in society, daily life for ordinary villagers did not experience radical changes, although the rulers grew steadily wealthier and more powerful. From the third to seventh centuries, they built increasingly elaborate kofun that became a defining characteristic of the era. Around ten thousand such tombs have been found, often in clusters in northern Kyushu, along the coasts of the Inland Sea and Japan Sea, and especially in the Kinai plain. The largest tomb mounds are found in the Nara basin at the eastern end of the Inland Sea, known as the Yamato region.

The earliest tombs were built into the side of an existing hill. Later large tombs consisted of extensive mounds built over stone burial chambers, entered from the side through stone passageways. Shapes varied from round to square to combinations of both. The most characteristic were keyhole-shaped tombs with a square front and round back, recalling the shape of dōtaku bells. Massive keyhole tombs surrounded by moats were built during the fourth and fifth centuries. The Nintoku tomb, outside the city of Osaka, is the most famous, considered a great monument that rivals the pyramids in terms of the amount of resources and labor needed for its construction. There are no verifiable accounts of the ruler Nintoku, but the *Nihon shoki* claims that his reign lasted ninety years. Nintoku's tomb is over 1,600 feet long and nearly 115 feet high. Surrounded by three moats, it covers more than eighty acres. The tomb features stone burial chambers with painted walls containing inscribed sarcophagi and precious grave goods.

One distinctive art form of the Kofun period is known as *haniwa*, or rings of clay. Clay cylinders, three to four feet in height, were modeled into figures of humans, animals, and objects and placed on the slopes of the mounds. Their initial purpose may have been to keep the mounds in place, but they evolved into a rich art form that expressed many aspects of daily life of the era. Haniwa include figures of young warriors, old men, priestesses, mothers with children, horses, boats, and storehouses. Many have a

FIGURE 4.   Kofun-era *haniwa* warrior, Tokyo National
Museum. Source: Wikimedia Commons.

charming quality of openness and candor. At some tombs, the haniwa seem to be laid out in ritual order, as if they were a procession to welcome the dead and surround them with familiar people and objects. The thousands of haniwa needed for a large tomb like Nintoku's were likely made by specialized craftspeople. The *Nihon shoki* claims that in earlier times, attendants were buried alive with deceased rulers and that Suinin—another legendary king, said to have reigned from 29 B.C.E. to 70 C.E.—prohibited this practice, substituting the clay images for live people.

Unfortunately, we cannot see the Nintoku tomb or others connected to the imperial family because they are under the control of Japan's Imperial Household Agency, which severely restricts access and prohibits excavation. The reasons for these restrictions lie in current politics and international relations. The grave goods of many tombs contain evidence of a horse-riding culture, including stirrups, saddle decorations, and the bones of horses. The obvious existence of a horse-riding aristocracy gave rise to the theory that Japan was invaded by a horse-riding people from the Korean Peninsula during the fourth century. Official acceptance of this theory would mean acknowledgment that the ancestors of the imperial house were from Korea, a former colony and current rival, and this is unacceptable to the Imperial Household Agency and conservative politicians and bureaucrats. In 2001, however, Emperor Akihito publicly acknowledged that the mother of Emperor Kanmu (737–806) was Korean.

It is misleading to think of Japan and Korea in the Kofun era as separate, rival entities with fixed boundaries. Within East Asia, China was considered the source of civilization and models of governance. Chinese philosophy and material culture generally reached Japan via the Korean Peninsula, which was divided into three kingdoms in 400 C.E.: Silla, Paekche, and Koguryō. In addition, there was a cluster of confederated small states, known as Kaya or Mimana, at the southern tip of the peninsula, dominated by migrants from Japan. There was steady, fluid migration from China to the Korean Peninsula to the archipelago, which was critical for Japan's economic, social, and political development. Migrants of many classes and with many different skill sets arrived in Japan from Korea. Legends describe how the scholar Wani was sent by the king of Paekche in 405 to introduce the Chinese writing system to the Japanese court. Wani's descendants became a caste of official court scribes. Many of the powerful Japanese clans, or *uji*, had close ties to the Asian continent and brought over new industries or technologies, such as sophisticated iron work that allowed the fabrication of body armor, better spears and pikes, and nonporous stoneware fired in closed kilns. Hereditary occupational groups attached to uji clans, known as

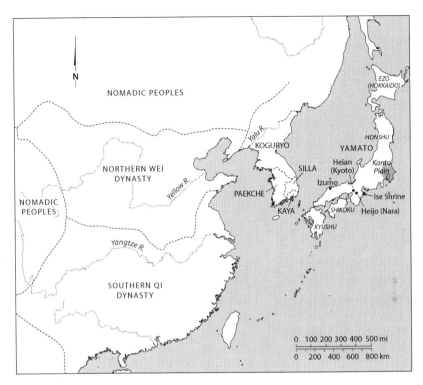

MAP 3. Ancient kingdoms of East Asia.

be, often consisted of immigrants and served in diverse positions, including scribes, diplomats, horse grooms, silk weavers, papermakers, weavers, and potters. Elite uji clans with strong ties to the peninsula, such as the Soga, maintained practices that originated in Korean kingdoms. Soga-commissioned temples and palaces imitated Paekche style. Fragments of murals and paintings from the seventh century depict the Japanese court in Koguryō-style dress.

YAMATO SOCIETY

There are no written Japanese chronicles from the Kofun period, but the number, size, and distribution of the tombs, along with other artifacts found during excavations and legendary accounts, have led scholars to surmise that society was organized in states of different sizes and strengths, controlled by chieftains of local uji clans. These clans were part of a larger confederation dominated by a dynasty based in the Yamato region, whose descendants became the Japanese imperial family. The Yamato rulers—who claimed descent from Amaterasu, the Sun Goddess—distributed goods such as bronze mirrors, swords, and bells, many from China or Korea, to uji chieftains who submitted to Yamato power. Allied chieftains also built themselves Yamato-style tomb mounds that contained the gifts bestowed by the central regime. The uji clans that submitted to Yamato rule were allowed to continue ritual worship of their own local deities and ancestors, but they were considered subordinate to Amaterasu.

Chinese dynastic official histories, an important source of written information about Japan before the sixth century, help confirm this account. Envoys from China traveled to Japan, identified as the kingdom of Wa, as part of efforts to record the conditions in nearby barbarian lands. These histories provide information on both political configurations in the archipelago and the practices and beliefs of the people of Wa. Envoys noted details of everyday Wa life, for instance that people subsisted on raw vegetables, ate with their fingers, and went barefoot. They remarked on Wa devotion to purity and cleanliness and their reverence for mountains. The accounts noted that, although Wa men often had more than one wife, there was a lack of distinction in male and female deportment. Many such observations likely stemmed from visible differences with Chinese norms. Accounts also noted religious and ritual practices, such as divination through reading the cracks in heated animal bones, and death practices that included mourners' abstention from meat and the covering of graves with dirt mounds.

In the first Chinese accounts, from around the first century, Japan is described as a land with more than a hundred tribal communities. Some tribes sent emissaries to China to obtain recognition of their supremacy over other tribal communities. The first detailed account was written in 297 for the Wei dynasty (220–65). Some of the most intriguing passages of the Wei chronicles address a queen named Pimiko (or Himiko) who ruled a kingdom called Yamatai. Pimiko used shamanic powers to unite and rule thirty warring clans. She was unmarried and lived in a heavily guarded palace, served by a thousand female attendants. She rarely appeared in public; her younger brother communicated her orders to others. In 238, Pimiko sent an embassy to the court of the Chinese emperor to deliver a tribute of "four male slaves and six female slaves, together with two pieces of cloth with designs, each twenty feet in length."[1] In turn, she was officially recognized as "Queen of Wa, Friendly to Wei" and presented with a golden seal. When Pimiko died, she was interred in a "great mound" and more than one hundred attendants were reportedly sacrificed and buried with her.

Following her death, she was succeeded by a king, but he was unable to maintain peace, so a thirteen-year-old relative of Pimiko, a girl named Iyo, was appointed ruler instead.

The first Japanese historical chronicles mention neither Pimiko nor Yamatai, and the location of the kingdom has been a topic of hot debate among historians. Some believe that Yamatai was located in northern Kyushu, others in the Kinai region. The Japanese histories, written many centuries later with the objective of rationalizing and promoting Yamato rulers, may have omitted Pimiko because she was outside of the Yamato lineage that eventually succeeded in extending control over the islands.

Pimiko's story highlights important aspects of political leadership in early Japan. An ancient word for government, *matsurigoto*, reflects that leaders were equally responsible for political rule and religious worship, and that they should obey the will of the gods in matters of state. Important responsibilities for rulers such as Pimiko included communicating with deities of the community, often through divination or spirit possession, and conducting rituals to worship or pacify those deities. Shamans who possessed these abilities were usually female, so rulers were often women. In many cases, they ruled in a pair with a male, usually either their husband or a male relative. The female ruler was generally responsible for ritual aspects of governance, while the male handled statecraft. Later empresses such as Suiko (554–628), Jitō (645–703), and Kōken (718–70) also followed this pattern. If the ruling pair was not husband and wife, the female was generally senior to her partner. Such gendered ruler pairs were also found in Silla and in China. Gender complementarity is also apparent in Japan's mythology, in couples such as Izanagi and Izanami, the progenitors of the Japanese islands. Beginning in the eighth century, however, women were rarely appointed to serve as monarch, because of increasing emphasis on Confucianism and Chinese models of statecraft, along with other factors.

Another Chinese account of conditions in Japan, written in 513, highlights interactions between Wa and neighboring kingdoms on the Asian continent. It describes how four different Wa rulers sought permission by the Chinese court for control of territories on the Korean Peninsula, as well as over Wa. One king, known as Bu (or Nu), asked for recognition to lead an army into the Korean kingdom of Koguryō. The Chinese emperor passed an edict naming Bu "King of Wa and Generalissimo Who Maintains Peace in the East Commanding with Battle-Ax All Military Affairs in the Six Countries of Wa, Silla, Imna, Kala, Jinhan, and Mokhan" and gave him a golden seal that named him "King Nu of Wa, vassal of Han." In 1784 an elaborately carved seal with this inscription was found in northern Kyushu but was initially considered a forgery. Experts now believe it is actually the seal described in the Chinese account.

RELIGIOUS FOUNDATIONS: SHINTO— THE WAY OF THE KAMI

Both archaeological evidence and the Chinese accounts testify to the importance of religious rituals in prehistoric Japan. The indigenous religion of Japan is known today as Shinto, or the Way of the Kami. The word *Shinto* came into use to distinguish indigenous beliefs from Buddhism, officially introduced to Japan in the sixth century. Shinto has no founder, no official sacred scriptures in the strict sense, and no fixed dogmas. It is a polytheistic and animistic faith intended to mediate relationships between humans and *kami,* or divinities. Kami are very different from the conceptions of "God" shared by many monotheistic faiths. For one, they can take many forms. Humans who were powerful in life are often considered kami after their deaths. Some kami represent formidable forces of nature, such as storms or earthquakes; others are associated with elements of the landscape, such as mountains, waterfalls, or trees. Unlike most gods of monotheistic faiths, kami are not transcendent, omnipotent, or omniscient. Furthermore, kami are not perfect—they make mistakes and behave badly. There is no absolute separation between kami and humankind; they inhabit the same natural world that we do, and feel and think in the same ways that we do. Over the course of centuries, under the influence of imported religions such as Buddhism and Taoism, the Japanese began to consider kami as anthropomorphic spirits, with names, lineages, and human characteristics and authority.

Amaterasu, purportedly the ancestress of the imperial family, is enshrined at Ise Grand Shrine, Shinto's holiest and most important shrine, established in the fourth century. The high priest or priestess of the shrine must be a member the Japanese imperial family. Every twenty years, the two main buildings of the shrine are reconstructed according to blueprints over a thousand years old, and the old shrine buildings are dismantled. The reconstruction is exorbitantly expensive, requiring specially raised timbers and eight years of preparation. The most recent reconstruction, the sixty-second iteration, was begun in 2013.

Japan's second most sacred shrine, the Izumo Grand Shrine, is its oldest and is dedicated to the kami Ōkuninushi. The chief priests of Izumo are also said to be descendants of the gods, tracing their lineage to a son of

Amaterasu. The mythological account of Izumo's establishment reflects the state-building efforts of the ruling Yamato clan, who sought to subdue and control local chieftains but allowed them to maintain their local kami, who would be subordinated to Amaterasu in a hierarchy of divinities. According to mythological accounts, Ōkuninushi was a gifted chieftain who had united many neighboring lands, building a strong polity. Amaterasu wanted him to turn control of these lands over to her and sent her son Amenohohi to deliver this message, but Amenohohi was impressed by Ōkuninushi's talents and decided to serve him instead. Many years of struggle between Amaterasu and Ōkuninushi ensued, but the Sun Goddess prevailed in the end. She promised him a shrine that reached all the way to heaven, which would be maintained by the descendants of Amenohohi. When originally constructed (date unknown), Izumo was the largest wooden structure in Japan, believed to host an annual gathering of millions of Shinto kami. Around 1200, however, the main building was significantly reduced in size.

Rather than doctrine or individual belief, Shinto religious life is focused on rituals and seasonal festivals (*matsuri*) dedicated to kami enshrined at each locality. While there is little dogma, two interrelated values, sincerity (*magokoro*) and purity (*seijō*), are very important. One must demonstrate these characteristics in order to attract the attention and favor of the kami. Sincerity entails doing one's best in life, including in one's work and in relationships with others. Purification, both physical and spiritual, is needed to achieve this sincerity. Certain conditions, including death, illness, sin, and misfortune, create ritual impurities that must be cleansed before approaching the kami. The practice of reconstructing Ise Grand Shrine every twenty years reflects this Shinto preference for purity and cleanliness, as well as its abhorrence of decay and pollution.

Rites of purification include cleansing agents like water, salt, and paper. Before entering sacred grounds, visitors must rinse their hands and mouths with water. Standing under a waterfall or bathing in the sea or at the mouth of a river are considered particularly powerful cleansing rituals. Salt is used to purify the land in groundbreaking ceremonies or before moving into a new home. Sumo wrestlers throw salt before entering the ring, considered a sacred space. After returning from a funeral, people sprinkle themselves with salt to counter pollution from death. Paper is used in zigzag streamers (*shide*) on sacred ropes (*shimenawa*) that demarcate sacred sites and on special wands (*gohei*) that Shinto priests wave over people or objects as a form of blessing. All such rites remain very common in contemporary Japanese life.

SHINTO MYTHOLOGY

Shinto mythology is recorded in the *Kojiki* and *Nihon shoki*, which were compiled from oral traditions in the early eighth century by order of Emperor Gemmei. One reason for creating the chronicles was to enhance the legitimacy of the Yamato clan's claim to the throne by documenting its divine lineage. Around the seventh century, the Japanese adopted the use of the Chinese title Emperor (Tennō) for the monarch, rather than King (Ō or Okimi), a title also used by some uji chieftains. The core of the mythology consists of tales about Amaterasu and how her direct descendants unified the Japanese people under their authority. The *Kojiki* describes the creation of the world and birth of the kami and provides the lineages of the noble families. The *Nihon shoki* also explains the origin of kami, but it is mainly concerned with historical events in the establishment of the Yamato kingdom and extends through events of the eighth century. It is considered a relatively reliable historical source from about 660 forward. Highlights from the myths given below demonstrate Shinto values, such as the need for purification and abhorrence of death and pollution.

In the myth of creation, the first gods summoned two divine beings into existence, the male Izanagi and the female Izanami, and charged them with creating the first land. Standing on the bridge between heaven and earth, the pair churned the sea below using a spear decorated with jewels. When drops of water fell from the spear, they formed an island. The couple descended to the island and began a mating ritual that involved walking in opposite directions around a large pillar. In their first attempt, Izanami spoke first in greeting, but this displeased Izanagi, who claimed that, as a man, he should be first to speak, and he ordered that they circumambulate the pillar again. This time he spoke first, inquiring:

> "In the body is there aught formed?"
>   She answered and said, "In my body there is a place which is the source of femininity."
>   The male deity said, "In my body again there is a place which is the source of masculinity. I wish to unite this source-place of my body to the source-place of thy body." Hereupon the male and female first became united as husband and wife.[2]

The two children born of their first consummation, however, were deformed and could not be considered proper gods, so they were put into a boat and set out to sea. Izanagi and Izanami mated again and gave birth to the islands of Japan and various kami, but Izanami died giving birth to the kami of fire.

The grieving Izanagi journeyed to the land of the dead, covered in eternal darkness, to ask his wife to return. He found Izanami but could not see her in the deep black shadows. She told her husband that since she had already eaten the food of the underworld, she could no longer return to the land of the living, but Izanagi refused to depart. He took out the wooden comb that bound his long hair and set it alight to see his beloved but was horrified to discover that his wife was now a maggot-ridden, rotting corpse. Screaming in terror, he began running back to the land of the living. Izanami, insulted and angered by his reaction, pursued him, accompanied by other hags of the underworld. Izanagi hurled objects behind him to slow their advance: his headdress became a bunch of grapes that the pursuers paused to consume, his comb became an obstructive clump of bamboo. He urinated against a tree, creating a river that blocked their path. Finally, he reached the entrance to the underworld and pushed a large boulder across the cavern's mouth to seal in his pursuers.

Wishing to purify himself after his descent to the underworld, Izanagi undressed to bathe. As he removed adornments from his body, each item that dropped to the ground transformed into a kami. More powerful deities came into being when he entered the water to wash himself. When he washed his face, the most important were created: the Sun Goddess, Amaterasu, was born from his left eye; the Moon God, Tsukuyomi, from his right eye; and the God of Storms, Susanoo, from his nose. Izanagi divided the world between them: Amaterasu would control the heavens, Tsukuyomi the moon and the night, and Susanoo the seas.

One day the siblings Amaterasu and Susanoo engaged in a competition to see who could produce the most offspring using a possession of the other. Amaterasu used Susanoo's sword to make three women, while Susanoo made five men from Amaterasu's necklace. Both declared victory, Amaterasu insisting that she had won because her necklace had produced the greater number. Her claim drove Susanoo into a rage and he began a campaign of malicious acts against his sister. He smashed the walls of her carefully constructed rice paddies and secretly defecated in her palace in order to defile it. Finally, he threw a dead pony, an animal sacred to Amaterasu, into her weaving hall. Angry and frightened, she fled and hid in a cave. As the Sun Goddess disappeared, darkness covered the world. All of the kami tried to coax her out but she ignored them, so they devised a plan to lure her out. First, they placed a large bronze mirror and hung a jewel in a tree facing the cave. Then the female kami Ame-no-Uzume began to perform a bawdy striptease atop an overturned washtub, prompting roars of laughter from the other kami. Amaterasu became curious and peeked outside, allowing a ray of light to escape from the cave and reflect in the mirror, leaving her dazzled. A strong male kami then quickly pulled her from the cave, returning light to the world, and the mouth of the cave was sealed with a sacred rope.

Susanoo, exiled from heaven for his naughty deeds, traveled to the land of Izumo, where he encountered an old man and his wife sobbing beside their daughter. The couple explained that they originally had eight daughters, and the others had been devoured one by one, each year, by a terrible dragon with eight heads. Their daughter Kushinada was the last of the eight. Susanoo offered his assistance in return for the beautiful girl's hand in marriage. The parents accepted, and Susanoo transformed Kushinada into a comb and hid her safely in his hair. He built a large fence with eight small entrances around the house and placed an open cask of sake before each of the entrance gates. When the dragon arrived, he found his way blocked by the fence. He smelled the sake, which he loved, but the fence stood in the way. If he simply smashed the fence down, it would knock over the sake; if he used his fiery breath to burn the fence, the sake would evaporate. The only solution was to stick each of his eight heads through a gate. At last, he could begin to drink. As he finished the casks, Susanoo launched his attack on the drunken beast, decapitating each of the heads in turn. When he began to dismember the dragon's carcass, he found a magical sword in the tail, which he presented to Amaterasu and which became one of the three sacred imperial treasures, the others being the jewel (called a *magatama*) and bronze mirror that were used to lure her out of the rock cave.

Amaterasu ordered her grandson Ninigi to descend from the heavens and rule the earth. She gave him the three sacred treasures, which each represented virtues required by rulers, to help in his task: the sword symbolized courage; the mirror, wisdom; and the jewel, compassion. Ninigi and several companions descended to the earth, where he built a large following. According to legend, his great-grandson Jimmu became the first emperor, born in 711 B.C.E. and dying at age 126 in 585 B.C.E. There are no reliable historical records to confirm Jimmu's existence, and it is not until the eighth-century reign of Emperor Kammu, reportedly the fiftieth ruler of the Yamato dynasty, that verifiable records are available.

The legends about Japan's origins recounted in the *Kojiki* and *Nihon shoki* are strikingly different from the founding myths of China in the Confucian *Book of Documents* (also known as *Classic of History*), which depicts human sage-kings who wield political and moral authority to forge a civilization. By contrast, the capricious and fallible gods of Japanese myth engage in creation and procreation to establish lands and other gods. They are sometimes sly, vindictive, boisterous, or frightened. In short, they are all-too-human.

RELIGIOUS FOUNDATIONS—BUDDHISM AND THE EARLY JAPANESE STATE

Buddhism was officially introduced to Japan in the mid-sixth century from the kingdom of Paekche, which sent a Buddhist statue and scriptures to the Yamato court with the note "This doctrine is amongst all doctrines the most excellent.... Every prayer is fulfilled and naught is wanting."[3] The issue of whether or not to accept Buddhism sparked a larger debate over national reform within the Japanese court.

Buddhism was at least a thousand years old by the time it entered Japan. It had emerged in northern India with the teachings of Gautama Siddhartha, the historical Buddha (563–483 B.C.E.), also known as Sakyamuni, meaning the sage of the Sakya clan. He became known as the Buddha after attaining enlightenment and teaching others the path to enlightened lives. The essence of the teachings is known as the Four Noble Truths. The first truth is that all of human life is characterized by dissatisfaction, unhappiness, frustration, and suffering. The second is that this dissatisfaction arises because of desire, craving, and acquisitiveness. The third truth reveals that release from this dissatisfaction can be achieved if one understands and controls one's desires, thus attaining enlightenment. Finally, the fourth truth provides an "eightfold path" to achieving the control of desire through right views, right intention, right speech, right action, right livelihood, right effort, right mindfulness, and right concentration.

The Buddha drew upon existing Indian beliefs about rebirth and the law of karma, which states that for every action or thought there is a reactive effect. Good thoughts, deeds, and words will generate good karma, allowing reincarnation in positive conditions and vice versa. He explained that humans were trapped in cycles of desire and suffering and had to live through countless painful cycles of death and rebirth due to the laws of karma. The ultimate spiritual goal was not a better rebirth but to escape the cycle by achieving enlightenment, or nirvana. The Buddha offered an ethical program that involved respect for all living beings, honesty, and compassion to achieve this escape. Among his earlier followers, ethical goals were thought to be best achieved in a monastic lifestyle combining meditation, celibacy, vegetarianism, and abstinence from alcohol to allow one to accumulate good karma and eventually obtain release from the cycle of suffering.

Accounts of the Buddha's life were not written down until several centuries after his death. There is very little verifiable biographical information available about him. According to the legendary biographies, Gautama

Siddhartha was born through a miraculous birth to a royal family and brought up in luxury. In his opulent surroundings within the palace, he never saw human suffering. On a trip outside the palace at age twenty-nine, however, he was shocked when he encountered the human realities of sickness, old age, and death for the first time. He abandoned his wife and his royal lifestyle to seek deeper spiritual understanding of the causes of human suffering. For six years he subjected his body to severe austerities, as many holy men from South Asia did, but he then renounced this path as too harsh and embarked on a more moderate path focused on meditation, which he called the "middle way." One night, while meditating under the Bo tree, he attained enlightenment, or perfect understanding of the nature of existence. He spent the remainder of his life wandering and teaching a growing group of disciples, who became the earliest communities of Buddhist monks and nuns. After his death, his disciples continued to spread and enlarge his teachings, known as Dharma. Later followers compiled an extensive collection of tales of the virtuous lives the Buddha had led before he was incarnated as Prince Siddhartha, in a work called the *Jataka*. In these morality tales the future Buddha may appear as an animal, a king, or a beggar, but in each life he demonstrates ethical and compassionate qualities that ensure he will one day achieve rebirth as the Buddha.

The teachings of the Buddha, initially transmitted orally, were recorded around 100 B.C.E. Within a few centuries, kings and wealthy patrons provided resources to establish monasteries where monks and nuns could live, study, meditate, and conduct rituals communally. Buddhism spread from South Asia to Southeast, Central, and East Asia. As it traveled over the centuries, it became an increasingly complex, universalistic religion with diverse sects that embraced doctrines far removed from the original teachings of Gautama. The prevailing sect in Southeast Asia was Theravada Buddhism, which continued to emphasize striving for one's own enlightenment in monastic settings. In East Asia, a new branch of Buddhism known as Mahayana, or "the great vehicle," developed around the first century. Mahayanists broadened the teachings to draw in people who were unable or unwilling to lead a monastic life. They added devotional practices and stressed that salvation was available for all laypeople, not just monks and nuns. Mahayana Buddhism included a pantheon of Buddhas besides the historical Gautama, such as the Buddha of the Western Paradise, known in Japanese as Amida (Sanskrit: Amitahba); Yakushi, the Buddha of Medicine and Healing (Bhaisajyaguru); Dainichi, the Cosmic Buddha (Vairocana); and Miroku, the Buddha of the Future (Maitreya). Over the centuries, different sects of Buddhism would arise that centered on one or more of these Buddhas. Another group of popular deities, known as *bodhisattvas,* shared the goal of bringing all sentient beings to enlightenment. The widely revered and beloved Kannon (Avalokitesvara, or Guanyin in Chinese) is the bodhisattva of compassion. The Dalai Lama of Tibet is considered an incarnation of this bodhisattva by Tibetan Buddhists.

When first introduced to the Yamato court, Buddhism was regarded by most as a source of powerful magic for healing, avoiding disaster, guaranteeing harvests, and protecting Yamato and uji clan interests. Many were awed by Buddhism's material culture, including its sculptures, paintings, and temple architecture. They regarded Buddhism as a carrier of higher civilization and therefore highly desirable. According to traditional accounts, when the king of Paekche first sent Buddhist artifacts to the Yamato court in the mid-sixth century, the uji clans adopted polarized positions on whether to accept the religion. Several powerful and conservative uji led by the Nakatomi, responsible for conducting Shinto rituals, and the Mononobe, who were military specialists, wanted to reject the foreign gods. Other uji, led by the Soga, a powerful immigrant clan, advocated accepting the new religion, hoping that the promotion of Buddhism would decrease their rivals' influence and improve their own position in the court.

According to legend, Emperor Kinmei allowed the Soga to worship the Buddha statue as a family kami. Shortly afterward, a terrible epidemic broke out and the Nakatomi blamed the epidemic on Buddhism, saying that it had angered native kami, who caused the epidemic in response. The statue was thrown into a canal. But the Soga clan, led by its powerful chieftain Soga no Umako, persisted and gained power through marriage politics, providing consorts and wives to the ruling Yamato. Umako's niece Suiko became ruler after the death of her Yamato husband. The new power of the Soga paved the way for greater acceptance of Buddhism; monks, nuns, scribes, architects, and artists arrived from the Asian continent in increasing numbers. When new plagues and epidemics broke out, the proponents of Buddhism now argued that they were caused by angry Buddhas who had to be placated and venerated.

While it seems that the clans adopted Buddhism for its magical powers and as a tool in court power struggles, it is important to remember that Buddhism made important contributions to Japanese culture. In terms of spiritual development, it offered ideas about moral behavior, karma, and personal salvation not available in Shinto. Intellectually, Buddhism offered a sophisticated philosophical tradition, although deep understanding was limited to a very small body of elite, educated monks. Buddhism's temples and monasteries contrasted impressively with the natural, simple style of the Shinto shrines and native architecture; its art and statuary were without parallel in early Japan. The idea of professional monks and nuns was also new to Japan.

Buddhism quickly came to assume functions in society not provided by early Shinto, such as services for the dead and for the pacification of angry spirits. Another set of functions revolved around obtaining practical benefits, including relief from sickness, ease of childbirth, a male heir, or rain in times of drought, through prayer or practices such as copying Buddhist scriptures, known as *sutras*. Providing protection for the nation and its rulers constituted a third important function. The Buddhas were seen as protective deities, and state-sponsored monks and nuns were expected to pray and work for the needs of the state as much as for their own enlightenment.

After the initial tension between leading clans over Buddhism, it settled into a complementary relationship with the indigenous Shinto. Early Shinto could not match Buddhism philosophically, textually, or in terms of art, but devotion to native kami was deep and would not be easily abandoned. As in most Asian nations, the result was a melding of Buddhist and local religious practices. In Japan, local Shinto kami were said to be native manifestations of universal Buddhist deities. Most large religious complexes contained both Buddhist temples and Shinto shrines.

In summary, early Japanese civilization and culture reflected numerous influences, both indigenous and imported. Geography shaped the location of human settlements; together with climate, it directed how people could live and what they could eat. Indigenous Jōmon peoples learned how to make pottery and tools for fishing and hunting. They developed a wide variety of primitive cults that worshipped objects of nature and ancestors as kami. Later immigrants and settlers brought more advanced agricultural and pottery techniques to the islands and introduced metal technologies. As settlements stabilized, their material culture began to reveal social stratification. The chieftains who led their clans traded and warred with others; eventually the Yamato clan dominated the islands of Kyushu, Shikoku, and most of Honshu, becoming the ancestors of Japan's imperial family. Their cult centered on the Sun Goddess, who was subsequently acknowledged by defeated clans as the preeminent native deity. When Buddhism was introduced to the Yamato court, it was recognized as the product of the more advanced civilizations of the continent, and elites adopted Buddhist deities, in addition to continuing their worship of native kami, in order to further support and legitimize their rule.

FURTHER READING

Ashkenazi, Michael. *Handbook of Japanese Mythology.* New York: Oxford University Press, 2008.

Breen, John, and Mark Teeuwen. *A New History of Shinto.* London: Blackwell, 2010.

Como, Michael. *Weaving and Binding: Immigrant Gods and Female Mortals in Ancient Japan.* Honolulu: University of Hawaii Press, 2009.

Farris, William W. *Sacred Texts and Buried Treasures: Issues in the Historical Archaeology of Ancient Japan.* Honolulu: University of Hawaii Press, 1998.

Habu, Junko. *Ancient Jōmon of Japan.* New York: Cambridge University Press, 2004.

Hudson, Mark J. *Ruins of Identity: Ethnogenesis in the Japanese Islands.* Honolulu: University of Hawaii Press, 1999.

Kidder, J. Edward, Jr. *Himiko and Japan's Elusive Chiefdom of Yamatai: Archaeology, History and Mythology.* Honolulu: University of Hawaii Press, 2007.

Mizoguchi, Koji. *An Archaeological History of Japan, 30,000 B.C. to A.D. 700.* Philadelphia: University of Pennsylvania Press, 2002.

no Yasumaro, Ō. *The Kojiki: An Account of Ancient Matters.* Translated by Gustav Heldt. New York: Columbia University Press, 2014.

Piggot, Joan R. *The Emergence of Japanese Kingship.* Stanford, CA: Stanford University Press, 1997.

RECOMMENDED FILMS

Himiko. 1974. Feature film directed by Shinoda Masahiro. Imagines the life of Queen Himiko.

Hi no tori, also known as *Firebird: Daybreak Chapter.* 1978. Feature film directed by Kon Ichikawa. Combines mythology and history, centering on the struggles of the Yamatai kingdom, with its Queen Himiko and Prince Susanoo.

Phoenix (Hi no tori), "Yamato chapter." 1986. Anime series based on manga by Tezuka Osamu illustrating lessons about karma and rebirth. This episode depicts ending the practice of burying servants alive with the ruler's burial mound.

Spirited Away. Studio Ghibli, 2001. Animated feature film directed by Miyazaki Hayao. This Oscar-winning anime features an assortment of kami of different forms who congregate in a bathhouse of the gods.

2 Forging a Centralized State

550–794

By the end of the Kofun period, the Yamato lineage had consolidated ruling power and stood at the apex of a hierarchy of other leading uji clans. From the mid-sixth through the eighth century, the Yamato embarked on programs to further strengthen their position, creating institutions, bureaucracies, religious support, and capital cities that would further legitimize and symbolize their power. These new tools of state were often modeled after those of China's powerful Sui (581–618) and Tang dynasties (618–907) and those employed by Paekche and Silla, but adapted to fit Japan's circumstances.

The first permanent capital city, Heijō-kyō (now Nara), was established in 710. It was modeled on the Tang capital Chang'an (now Xian) and remained the seat of government until 794, when the new capital was established in Heian-kyō (now Kyoto). Nara became Japan's first large, urban center, with a population of over two hundred thousand. It hosted a massive court bureaucracy, with between seven and ten thousand government workers. During this era, Nara also developed into an impressive and important nucleus of Buddhism in Japan, epitomized by the building of the massive Tōdaiji Temple. The state continued to sponsor projects that legitimized the Yamato as the ruling lineage of a centralized state, commissioning the writing of the first national histories, the *Kojiki* and the *Nihon shoki*, along with the first anthologies of poetry, the *Kaifūsō* and the *Man'yōshū*. During the eighth century, however, severe epidemics of smallpox and other diseases, along with famine, plagued Japan, killing 25–35 percent of the population between 735 and 737 alone. The radical decrease in the productive population resulted in a major decline in imperial revenue.

POLITICAL, SOCIAL, AND RELIGIO-CULTURAL DEVELOPMENTS

The mid-sixth to late eighth centuries are often subdivided into several different periods. The Asuka period begins with the official introduction of Buddhism from Paekche in 552 and extends to 645, when rulers inaugurated an era of great reform (Taika), designed to further enhance and consolidate Yamato power over the uji clans. The Asuka era witnessed the strengthening of diplomatic and cultural exchanges with Korean kingdoms and Sui dynasty China. The period is named after the Asuka region, where the ruler, Suiko, located her court. Prior to the establishment of Heijō-kyō, the palace of the ruler was considered the capital. Each time he or she died, the entire court moved to a newly built palace for the new ruler. The old palace was abandoned to avoid pollution associated with death and because of the belief that the spirit of the deceased ruler might remain within the palace and threaten a new regime.

In the late sixth century, the Soga clan, who were likely of Korean ancestry, dominated court politics, increasing their influence by marrying daughters to members of the imperial family. Soga territories were in the Asuka region, located in the Kinai plain. Empress Suiko (554–628), a niece of powerful uji chieftain Soga no Umako, was the official consort of Emperor Bidatsu (538–85). After he died, struggles over the imperial succession arose between the Soga and Mononobe clans. Suiko was appointed reigning empress in 592 and served in this role until her death in 628. She appointed her nephew Shōtoku (574–622, also known as Umayado) as her regent. Achievements of their joint reign included official recognition of Buddhism in 594, opening of diplomatic relations with China's Sui dynasty in 600, the adoption of a system of court ranks in 603, and the promulgation of a seventeen-article "constitution" in 604.

Together Suiko and Shōtoku sought to transform the Yamato kingship into a more powerful centralized state modeled on Chinese ideals of imperial governance. Wishing to clearly elevate the position of the Yamato ruler above clan politics, they introduced a system of twelve court ranks, designated by caps of different colors and with different styles of feathers. Similar ranking systems were in place in Paekche, Koguryō, and Sui dynasty China. The cap rank system was intended to allow for some promotions based on individual merit, not heredity alone, thus containing the potential to weaken the power of the uji clans. In practice, however, the wealthiest and most powerful clans dominated positions within the top ranks.

The details of Shōtoku's life are found in legends; the primary source of information on his achievements is the *Nihon shoki,* completed a century after his death. He is said to be the first to officially refer to the Yamato state as Nihon, as Japan is known today. In 607, he reportedly sent a letter to China's Sui court with an impertinent address: (from) "The Child of Heaven in the Land of the Rising Sun to the Child of Heaven in the Land of the Setting Sun."[1] One legend claims that he met Bodhidharma, known as Daruma in Japan, the fifth-century monk who transmitted the Ch'an (Zen) school of Buddhism from India to China. Daruma was disguised as a beggar but Shōtoku offered him food and clothing, demonstrating his compassion and wisdom in recognizing a holy man. As a side note, Daruma remains prominent in contemporary culture because of the popularity of the Daruma doll, a round, red figure depicting a bearded man with blank eyes. These dolls are symbols of good luck and perseverance. One makes a wish or sets a goal, painting in one eye, and paints in the second eye when the aim is achieved. The shape and function of the doll reflect grisly legends about Daruma, who sat in meditation for nine years, causing his limbs to atrophy. After falling asleep during meditation, he angrily cut off his own eyelids to prevent a second occurrence.

Shōtoku is most celebrated for authoring Japan's first "constitution," a document with seventeen clauses or articles that primarily reflected Chinese Confucian law and institutions but melded these with both Buddhist philosophy and native traditions of governance that stressed discussion and consultation in order to reach consensus. The document overall emphasizes the principles of loyalty, harmony, and dedication to government as ideals for political life. The first clause critiques the factionalism in Yamato society, stating: "Harmony is to be valued, and contentiousness avoided. All men are inclined to partisanship and few are truly discerning. . . . But when those above are harmonious and those below are conciliatory and there is concord in the discussion of all matters, the disposition of affairs comes about naturally."[2] The desire to elevate the ruler above clan factions, as the Chinese emperor was elevated above his ministers, is apparent in the third clause, "When you receive the imperial commands fail not to scrupulously obey them. The lord is heaven. The vassal is Earth."[3] Other clauses urge officials to be impartial, diligent, trustworthy, and fair to the people they govern. Buddhist thought is reflected in a clause that counsels against anger, stating that what is right and what is wrong are not absolute, but relative perspectives. To contemporary eyes the document may seem to be a collection of simple maxims, but it was quite revolutionary,

representing the first official statement on the need for ethical government in Japanese history.

Shōtoku is also revered as one of Buddhism's most important early scholars and patrons, said to have authored several commentaries on Buddhist sutras. Over the centuries, he became the center of a cult of worship for the protection of Buddhism, the imperial family, and the nation. Important religious figures in later centuries, including Saichō (see chapter 3) and Shinran (see chapter 4), claimed to have experienced visions of Shōtoku. With Soga patronage, just fifty years after Buddhism was officially introduced to the court, there were over forty temples and nearly fourteen hundred ordained monks and nuns. Over the sixth and seventh centuries, six schools of Buddhism, imported from China and Korea, were established in Nara: Hossō, Kegon, Risshū, Sanron, Kusa, and Jōjitsu. These sects were largely focused on complex metaphysical philosophies of existence. The schools competed to attract elite patronage, and high-ranking monks increasingly attempted to meddle in court matters.

The earliest Buddhist temples were built by the Soga in the late sixth century but haven't survived. Common features of early temples included a large entrance gate, a roofed gallery that enclosed a rectangular compound, a hall housing the primary artifacts of devotion, and a pagoda—a tall, multistoried tower modeled after Indian stupas, said to contain a relic of the historical Buddha. Among temples still standing, the oldest is Hōryūji near Nara, originally commissioned by Shōtoku and dedicated to the Buddha of Healing, Yakushi Nyorai. It contains the oldest wooden building in the world, believed to have been completed in 607. In addition to the features described above, the Hōryūji compound contains an octagonal building known as the Yumedono, or Hall of Dreams, constructed in 739 to appease the spirit of Shōtoku. Hōryūji is a UNESCO World Heritage site, containing numerous sculptures and artifacts designated National Treasures in Japan.

Some of the art of the Asuka era was produced by Korean and Chinese craftsmen and reflects links between court families and the continent. Extant artworks demonstrate a variety of artistic styles found in Silla, Paekche, Koguryō, and Northern Wei China. The official style of Suiko's reign, however, was the school of Tori Busshi, a seventh-century sculptor descended from a clan of Chinese saddle makers who had migrated to Japan. Tori's statues have a geometric, front-oriented design and combine aspects of Northern Wei and Koguryō sculpture, but with a greater sense of softness and tranquility.

One representative work at Hōryūji, the *Sakyamuni Triad,* is a bronze sculpture depicting the historical Buddha Gautama in the center, flanked by two bodhisattva attendants. Gautama's robes drape over the platform below in a two-dimensional "waterfall" style. His hands are in mudras, special positions of Buddhist iconography conveying fixed messages. Here, the right upraised hand symbolizes the Buddha's fearlessness and blessing, and the open left palm symbolizes charity. The central figure is surrounded with a flaming halo depicting his previous incarnations. His attendants wear tall crowns and stand on lotuses, important symbols of purity in Buddhism because they flower above the muddy waters, paralleling the ability of humans to overcome desire and achieve enlightenment. Lotuses also symbolize the multidimensional Buddhist universe, each of their petals representing a different world.

Other Hōryūji treasures include the Tamamushi shrine, a portable wooden structure from the mid-seventh century, named for the beetle whose iridescent wings were originally inlaid in the pedestal. The lacquered wood panels of the shrine contain oil paintings illustrating tales of the Buddha's previous lives. In one, a prince offers his body to feed a starving tigress and her cubs, a compassionate act that ensures he will become a Buddha in a future life. The six-foot-tall, gilded wood *Guze Kannon* statue is housed in the Yumedono and supposedly represents Shōtoku, resembling portraiture of the prince and standing at the same height. Considered sacred, the statue is seldom viewed and remains in excellent condition, as it

FIGURE 6. *Sakyamuni Triad*, 623 C.E., Hōryūji Monastery, Nara, Japan. Source: Wikimedia Commons.

is stored wrapped in over five hundred yards of cloth. It had not been seen for many centuries until Ernest Fenollosa (1853–1908), an American professor hired by the Meiji government who became involved in efforts to preserve Japan's art treasures, demanded that it be unwrapped.

Despite Suiko and Shōtoku's efforts to stimulate governmental reform, there was little real effect since the uji clans continued to have complete autonomy over their lands and its inhabitants. After Shōtoku's death in 622, the powerful Soga became the primary opponents of major reforms that concentrated power in the hands of the Yamato rulers. In 644, an anti-Soga faction, including Naka no Oe (626–72, later known as Emperor Tenji) and Nakatomi no Kamatari (614–69, head of a powerful clan of Shinto ritualists), led a coup against the Soga, slaughtering chieftain Soga no Iruko and his followers at a banquet for a visiting Korean dignitary. Following this coup, Nakatomi was bestowed with a new clan name, Fujiwara, and became the ancestor of one of the most illustrious families in Japanese history, one that would intermarry with and dominate the imperial line for centuries.

The period between the coup and the establishment of the capital at Nara in 710 is known as the Hakuhō period. It is characterized by continuing efforts to centralize and bureaucratize government; the rapid expansion of Buddhism among leading clans, witnessing major developments in Buddhist art and architecture; and the development of the writing system and calligraphy. Japan was still largely decentralized, but during the seventh century the Yamato court faced pressure to construct a strong, centralized state to defend themselves against the expansionist Tang empire, which allied with Silla to conquer Koguryō and Paekche, a Yamato ally. Fearing invasion, the Japanese needed to marshal national economic and defensive resources. They were aided in their efforts by Paekche refugees, including members of the royal house, who fled to Japan in larger numbers after they were defeated by the Tang-Silla alliance in 660. By the mid-700s, a network of roads connected every region from northern Honshu to southern Kyushu to the center of power in the Kinai plain, enabling greater trade and commerce along with an infrastructure for defense.

In 646 the new emperor, Kōtoku (596–654), proclaimed an era of "great change," announcing major reforms planned in an edict. The Taika reforms aimed to recover power for the imperial family and reduce the influence of the clans by creating a system of centralized government using Chinese imperial models. The Taika edict contained four articles. The first declared that private ownership of land would be abolished; all land would henceforth be considered public (i.e., belonging to the emperor) and would be allocated fairly among farmers, based on their family size. Another clause announced that new government and military institutions, emulating those of China's powerful Tang dynasty, would be established in both the capital and the provinces. A third edict declared the establishment of a new tax system, with the populace paying taxes in kind through goods such as rice, textiles, and horses and through unpaid labor on roads and other imperial construction projects. Taxes were needed to support the planned expansion of the bureaucracy and military. The final edict ordered a national census in order to help determine land distribution, taxes, and manpower available for military conscription.

The old uji clan aristocracy remained, but the authority and income of clans and their chieftains would now be derived from their position as officials of the court and central government. Unlike ordinary farmers, uji clans received special, large land grants that enabled them to retain their privileges and wealth. Members from the powerful clans staffed the many developing government departments and councils of state. Positions quickly became hereditary.

The planned "great changes" were far too extensive to be realized overnight, but they provided a blueprint for the transformation of the government according to Chinese models, and reforms proceeded steadily in the seventh and eighth centuries. A fully Chinese-style state, however, was never achieved, for two primary reasons. For one, the Chinese used an examination system to choose its bureaucratic leaders according to merit. Although the Japanese also adopted an examination system for officials, those qualified to take the exams were limited to court families. Some lower-ranking court members had the possibility of advancement, but it was rare, and the Japanese bureaucracy remained a hereditary system that preserved the privileges of the aristocrats. Another difference from the Chinese model was the concept of the emperor. The Chinese emperor had a divine mandate, known as the Mandate of Heaven, which could be revoked if he or his dynasty proved to be unvirtuous or ineffective leaders. In Japan, the imperial family's divine mandate was claimed via direct descent from the Sun Goddess, Amaterasu. It was thus irrevocable and not associated with the virtue or merit of the ruling family.

The Hakuhō period, from 645 to 710, was a time of vigorous reform, directed by members of the imperial family itself. Some of the most powerful emperors in Japanese history ruled during this period, each furthering the structures needed to create a strong, centralized state. Emperor Tenmu (631–86), who reigned from 673 until his death in 686, ruled with his consort Jitō (645–703). He is considered the first monarch to be addressed as Emperor (Tennō) within his own time. Tenmu's achievements included revision of the cap rank system to reflect closeness and loyalty to the imperial throne, strengthening of military institutions under the fear of invasion, the commissioning of national histories, and the compilation of a seventeen-volume code that specified penal *(ritsu)* and administrative *(ryō)* law; the Taihō code became the legal basis of the *ritsuryō* state, which prevailed in Japan until the late tenth century.

The ritsuryō system incorporated patriarchal Chinese legal, philosophical, and social norms and attitudes. It assumed that all power was derived from the monarch, who was above the law. The system established two realms of government. The Department of Divinity (Jingikan) handled all ritual and spiritual matters, including court ceremonies, divination, astrology, and geomancy; the Department of State (Dajōkan) dealt with secular and administrative matters through eight ministries, such as Military, Justice, Taxation, and Treasury. The penal portion of the Taihō code specified sanctions for hundreds of different types of crimes, from beating with a light or heavy rod to exile to death. Elite offenders rarely faced corporal punishment; they could forfeit grades of rank or make payment as restitution for their misdeeds. The administrative portion of the code scrupulously defined the qualifications, duties, and prerogatives of each official appointment. It divided the country administratively into sixty-six provinces, with governors appointed by the court. Provinces were subdivided into districts, administered by local officials responsible for collecting taxes, keeping population and land registers, and maintaining the peace.

Tenmu is often recognized as the first ruler to officially sponsor Buddhism as a protector of the country and the imperial family. Before this time, individuals like Shōtoku or clans like the Soga patronized Buddhism; but under Tenmu and his successors, the construction of great Buddhist temples and monasteries was sponsored by the state. Their role was to pray and conduct rituals for the protection and prosperity of the state. During the eighth century, Japanese monks produced or copied more than a hundred thousand volumes of Buddhist texts to this end. The court's favoring of Buddhism was usually based less on deep understanding of metaphysical philosophy than on obtaining practical benefits through magical powers. Practices to obtain health and prosperity included the worship of Buddhist images and copying sutras. A focus on health and healing, likely prompted by the epidemics that plagued the era, is seen in the popularity of the Buddha of Healing, Yakushi Nyorai.

Following the death of Tenmu, Empress Jitō ascended the throne and ruled from 686 to 697, continuing to carry out administrative reforms that strengthened imperial family power. The law code initiated by Tenmu was actually promulgated under Jitō, and it was during her reign that plans for Japan's first permanent capital city were initiated.

THE FIRST PERMANENT CAPITAL

As the Japanese built their Chinese-style system of government administration, the central bureaucracy grew rapidly, requiring a more permanent and spacious capital with a great palace surrounded by government buildings. The court moved to the newly built city of Heijō-kyō in 710 and remained there until 784, abandoning the practice of shifting the capital each time an emperor died. Nara was designed as a smaller version of the

Tang capital at Chang'an. It was laid out in an orderly fashion, with the palace in the center, to the north, and offices, temples, markets, and residences of the nobles to the south. A grand boulevard ran from the palace to the city's main entrance in the south, and a checkerboard grid of smaller streets ran north–south and east–west. For the 1,300th anniversary of the city in 2010, the former palace grounds, which had been used as rice fields for over a thousand years, were partially reconstructed. Visitors marveled at the massive scale, many times the size of existing imperial palaces.

The site for construction was chosen through Chinese geomancy, the art of selecting a suitable location based on the arrangement of surrounding hills, wind, and water, known popularly today as *feng shui*. Nara was Japan's first truly urban center, with a population of two hundred thousand and with a cosmopolitan outlook that reflected the influence of Tang China, then the greatest empire in the world. The Nara court adopted the practices of the Tang and Silla courts, placing high value on performance of elegant music *(gagaku)* and masked dances as ritual means to maintain peace and harmony in the realm. Tang Buddhist art, emulated by the Japanese, had a variety of world influences, not just from India but from Persia, Greece, and the Byzantine Empire, all in contact with China by means of the overland trade route known as the Silk Road. Many art objects preserved in Nara came from these exotic locales. The courts of eighth-century Japan welcomed visitors from throughout South and Southeast Asia and beyond. In the following centuries Japan would become much more insular, and such cosmopolitanism would not be seen again until the sixteenth century and the modern era.

Nara civilization reached a peak with the reign of Emperor Shōmu (701–56) from 724 to 749. He was the first emperor whose official consort, Kōmyō, was not of the royal family, but rather a member of the Fujiwara clan. Shōmu is remembered as a devoutly Buddhist emperor. In 741, following a series of national disasters and epidemics, he decreed that state-supported temples, monasteries, and nunneries be constructed in every province to pray for the health and protection of the state. He is best known for commissioning the Daibutsu, a fifty-three-foot-high statue of the Buddha Dainichi, which was to be housed in a new temple known as Tōdaiji, the Great Eastern Temple. It was mammoth in comparison to earlier temples such as Hōryūji, spreading over a huge tract of land. Shōmu urged the entire population to contribute to the effort, even if only a twig or handful of dirt if they had nothing else to give. Fundraisers were sent to the provinces to collect contributions and to generate support for the project among the populace.

At this time, Buddhism was largely limited to the elite; the court discouraged Buddhist monks from proselytizing among the people, afraid that

FIGURE 7.   Scroll painting depicting the dedication of the Daibutsu at Tōdaiji Temple, Nara, Japan, 1536. Source: Wikimedia Commons.

popular preachers might use magical abilities to attract large followings, which could result in turmoil. The state monitored and restricted the numbers of monks and nuns ordained and ensured that their lives were closely regulated. Nevertheless, some became itinerant priests in defiance of the law. One such individual, Gyōki (668–749), began to travel widely around the country to preach Buddhism to commoners and to help the poor through charitable works. During his lifetime, he built forty-nine monasteries that also served as community centers—providing medical facilities for the poor, helping to organize public works projects, and teaching farmers to build better irrigation systems. He is also recognized as the first individual to construct a map of Japan. Through the efforts of such itinerant priests, the basic teachings of Buddhism, such as the idea of karmic retribution (i.e., that good actions bring good results and evil actions eventually bring misfortune) began to gradually diffuse through the population. The people venerated Gyōki as a living bodhisattva, but the government persecuted him and his followers for their illegal activities. When he proved to be effective at recruiting labor and contributions for Tōdaiji, however, he earned a pardon and was given the highest Buddhist rank possible.

Shōmu's orders to construct the giant Buddha statue and massive temple, far from strengthening and protecting central rule, exhausted national supplies of bronze and precious metals. These expensive ventures—in the face of epidemics, natural disasters, and intra-court strife—were likely a major factor in the decline of national administration over the next century and a half. Tōdaiji, however, became the greatest Buddhist establishment in Japan and the focal point for Nara culture. At the great Buddha's eye-opening ceremony, a priest from India, the motherland of the faith, painted in the pupils of the statue's eyes to provide it with symbolic life. Ten thousand Buddhist priests and visitors from many distant lands attended the ceremony, the largest and most elaborate in early Japanese history.

Tōdaiji statuary included a new method of sculpture that used dry lacquer over a clay base, allowing artists to achieve a remarkable degree of realism. Lifelike detailing can be seen in the statue of Ganjin (668–763), a blind Chinese monk who founded the Risshū school of Nara Buddhism and helped raise the funds to build Tōdaiji from among the populace. Ganjin had been invited to Japan to teach and made five attempts at the arduous voyage across the East China Sea. During one, he lost his eyesight to infection. He finally succeeded on his sixth attempt in 754, joining a Japanese diplomatic mission returning home. The following year, he constructed Japan's first official ordination platform at Tōdaiji. Another outstanding example of dry lacquer technique is the Asura, one of the eight types of Buddhist guardian deities, housed at Nara's Kōfukuji Temple. The slender, three-headed, six-armed figure—sometimes known as Japan's *Venus de Milo*—differs from the muscular, martial figures of other types of guardian deities. The Asura's two side faces display stern expressions befitting a guardian deity, but the front-facing countenance is more complex, revealing both concern and steadfastness.

The Tōdaiji complex also contains a remarkable treasure house called the Shōsōin, which contains more than ten thousand precious items, including the personal belongings of Emperor Shōmu and his wife Kōmyō, ritual objects used in the Buddha statue's eye-opening ceremony, maps, documents, medicines, musical instruments, and masks used for performing court dances. The objects came from all corners of the world: Southeast and Central Asia, India, Arabia, Persia, Assyria, Egypt, Greece, and Rome. They included a vast variety of fabrics, glass, ceramic ware, paintings, and statuary that have been preserved in excellent condition for over a millennium. This is due to the fact that the Shōsōin was constructed using special techniques that allowed the log walls to expand and contract in order to maintain steady temperature and humidity conditions. Furthermore, it was very rarely opened over the centuries.

In 749, after a twenty-five-year reign, Emperor Shōmu abdicated the throne, prostrating himself before the great Buddha statue and taking the tonsure, the first retired emperor to become a Buddhist monk. Since he lacked an appropriate male heir and his nonroyal consort Kōmyō could not

FIGURE 8.   Asura, 734 C.E., Kōfukuji Temple, Nara, Japan.
Source: Wikimedia Commons.

accede to the throne, he appointed his unmarried, twenty-one-year-old daughter Abe as heir. She would reign twice, as Empress Kōken (749–58) and as Empress Shōtoku (766–70). Many in the court were critical of this appointment; in 757, over four hundred and fifty courtiers mounted an unsuccessful rebellion against the empress. Kōken stepped down the following year, passing the throne to Tenmu's grandson and her adopted heir, who became Emperor Junnin (733–65). Unlike males of the royal families, who could take the daughters of court families as wives or consorts, royal females were required to marry within the family. Kōken had no children of her own.

In 761, the retired empress was cured of illness by a charismatic monk named Dōkyō, scion of an elite provincial family. Later that year, she took the tonsure, shaving her head and donning Buddhist robes. She began to feud with the sitting emperor, Junnin, accusing him of disloyalty and unfiliality, and announced that she would reassume key powers of the throne. Junnin's allies, led by Fujiwara no Nakamaro, attempted another coup against the retired empress, but Kōken successfully reascended as Empress Shōtoku in 766. Her critics claimed that a nun was not qualified to hold the position of sovereign, but she dismissed such detractors, reminding them that her father, Shōmu, had advised her to deal harshly with any who obstructed her imperial will.

Shōtoku proceeded to reorganize court government, appointing Dōkyō head of the Department of Divinity. Although many monks had advised the throne in the past, none had been appointed to such high court rank. He was proclaimed the Prince of the Law (Hōō) and given broad authority in spiritual and secular matters. The empress responded to critical members of the court as follows: "Although my head is shaved and I wear Buddhist robes I still must govern the realm. As the Buddha declared, 'Kings who ascend the throne receive the ordination of a bodhisattva.' Such words show that there can be no objection to rule by one who has taken orders. Furthermore, since the reigning monarch has taken the precepts, it is fitting that the grand minister should also be a monk."[4]

In 769 the court received an oracle from a shrine in Kyushu stating that peace and prosperity could be maintained in the realm only if Dōkyō was enthroned as sovereign. An official sent to Kyushu to investigate returned with a second oracle advising that wicked pretenders who attempted to usurp the throne from the imperial line should be ousted from the court. Dōkyō was exiled; the empress died five months later, succeeded by Emperor Kōnin, the great-grandson of a seventh-century emperor, Tenji. For the past century the throne had been occupied by the descendants of Tenmu, the brother of Tenji. With Kōnin, a new royal lineage emerged, with the throne passing next to his son, who ruled as Emperor Kammu, and to Kammu's subsequent progeny.

Historians have debated the question of who was responsible for the first, forged oracle in the Dōkyō scandal: some point to the monk himself, while others believe that the priest of the Kyushu shrine sought to curry favor with him, and still others claim that the empress herself devised the scheme. An alternative theory holds that the entire story was fabricated. It was recorded in the *Shoku nihongi* (completed in 797, the second of six national histories following the *Nihon shoki*), commissioned by Kammu. Historian Joan Piggott suggests that the compilers aimed to enhance Kammu's legitimacy and lineage by casting aspersions on Kōken, part of the Tenmu lineage replaced by his father.[5]

Unlike earlier emperors, who drew their wives and a small number of consorts from leading clans like the Soga and Fujiwara, Kammu had sixteen empresses and consorts, so that no clan could claim undue influence over him. He was an active emperor who deployed military campaigns to suppress the Emishi people of Ezo (northern Honshu and Hokkaido), believed to be descendants of the Jōmon and ancestors of Hokkaido's indigenous Ainu. The Emishi (a disparaging Japanese term meaning "toad barbarians") had battled Yamato armies in northern Honshu for centuries. They were skilled in horse-mounted archery and engaged in guerrilla tactics that proved effective against the slower, infantry-based imperial armies. Kammu appointed Sakanoue no Tamuramaro to the office of *Sei-i Taishōgun* (popularly abbreviated as *shogun*), or "barbarian-quelling generalissimo," to defeat the Emishi. Sakanoue changed the Imperial Army's battle strategies, adopting the enemy's techniques, and succeeded in driving the barbarians north to Hokkaido.

From the sixth through the eighth century, empresses and gender-complementary pairs of rulers were not unusual. Among the most notable of the gendered pairs were Empress Suiko and her nephew Shōtoku in the Asuka period; Emperor Tenmu and his consort Jitō in the Hakuhō era; and Emperor Shōmu and his consort Kōmyō, and Empress Kōken and her Buddhist monk adviser Dōkyō, both during the Nara period. By the end of the eighth century, however, the notion of male dominance and rulership prevailed over ideas of gender complementarity. One key reason for this shift was the increasing acceptance of Chinese Confucian texts and norms, which were embedded within the codes of law and administration produced by the Japanese state in the early eighth century. As a result, succession to the throne was limited to males; female members of the court, including consorts and officials, began to experience a long, broad decline in their authority and status that continued throughout the following centuries.

The question of whether females can inherit the throne poses controversy in Japan today. The current Crown Prince Naruhito and his wife, Crown Princess Masako, have only one child, their daughter Aiko, who was born in 2001. The Imperial Household Act of 1947 decreed that only males could be named to the imperial succession, but given that members of the imperial family had not produced a male heir for over forty years, many Japanese believe that the law should be amended to allow a firstborn daughter to ascend to the throne before younger brothers and cousins. Conservatives have advocated against Aiko's succession, however, arguing that the selection of early empresses offered only temporary solutions, compromises to avert conflict over succession. They charge that Empress Kōken was a weak sovereign, infatuated with and victimized by a Rasputin-like monk, concluding that the instability of her reign provided court members with the rationale to exclude royal females from acceding to the throne. Since the 2006 birth of a male heir to the crown prince's younger brother, Akishino, it has become far less likely that the law will be changed to allow women to inherit the throne.

NARA LANGUAGE AND LITERATURE

The development of Buddhist visual art during the early centuries of the centralized state was accompanied by the first great blossoming of Japanese poetry. Since the court had no written language of its own, the functioning of the state depended on the use of Chinese ideographic characters for official texts, codes of law, proclamations, and recording of national histories. Non-governmental forms of written communication, such as Buddhist sutras and poetry, also relied on written Chinese. Spoken Chinese differs radically, however, from spoken Japanese. Chinese is monosyllabic, tonal, and does not employ tense, while Japanese is polysyllabic, nontonal, and highly inflected. Classical Chinese, which used *kanji* characters for their meaning, was employed in most official communications, but in the eighth century a method of employing these ideographs phonetically, like letters, enabled writers to express the spoken Japanese language using Chinese characters. The phonetic use of these characters is known as *man'yōgana*. This approach was used by the first national history, the *Kojiki*, and by the poetry anthology known as the *Man'yōshū*. Standard classical Chinese prevailed for the majority of official and religious texts, including another, more standardized national history, the *Nihon shoki*, and a Chinese-style poetry anthology, the *Kaifūsō*.

Around the ninth century, the method of using Chinese characters to express Japanese sounds evolved into a native syllabary of about fifty symbols called *kana*. Although the Japanese were then able to write their language exclusively in kana, many Chinese words had entered the vocabulary and continued to be written using their kanji characters. Ultimately, the Japanese came to write in a mixture of Chinese characters and kana, which is why it is among the most complex written languages in the world today.

The *Kojiki*, Japan's earliest extant literary work, completed in 712, and the *Nihon shoki*, completed in 720, were introduced in chapter 1 as the sources of Japanese mythology. They were commissioned by Emperor Tenmu in the 670s to legitimize and glorify the Yamato reign, in the manner of early Chinese dynastic histories. These works combined genealogical records of the imperial family with myths, legends, songs, and poetry. The

Kojiki, which combined man'yōgana and classical Chinese, was more difficult to read and less systematic than the *Nihon shoki*, which better reflected
the style and patterns of Chinese dynastic histories and included more references to Confucian and Buddhist ideas taken from Paekche and Chinese
sources. The *Nihon shoki* is considered to be a fairly reliable historical
source from about the sixth century forward. Both works reflected the
court's ambition to assert a level of civilizational development relatively
equal to that of China and Korea. At the same time, the histories convey a
sense of ethnocentrism, depicting Japan as the center of the world and the
Sun Goddess as the world's most powerful deity. In the eighteenth and
nineteenth centuries, nativist scholars such as Motoori Norinaga and Hirata
Atsutane used these texts as a basis to chauvinistically assert Japan's superiority over other nations (see chapter 6).

Poetry was a central component of the cultural life of the Nara court; the
ability to compose poetry was usually required for official positions. The
Kojiki and *Nihon shoki* contain numerous poems and simple songs, but
the first efforts at issuing anthologies occurred in the mid-eighth century
with the *Kaifūsō* (Fond recollections of poetry), compiled in 751, and the
Man'yōshū (Collection of ten thousand leaves), compiled sometime after
759. The *Kaifūsō* contains 120 verses in classical Chinese. Most are full of
allusions to Chinese literature and history, demonstrating elite esteem for
and desire to emulate the higher civilization of the continent. The
Man'yōshū, a collection of around 4,500 poems contained in twenty volumes, is often considered the true beginning of a Japanese poetic tradition
and is among the most revered works of Japanese literature. Throughout
subsequent centuries, this work has served as a reference point for poets,
writers, and artists.

Japanese literature and poetry are often described in contrast with
Western literature and poetry; the latter are said to emphasize ideas, action,
and morality, while the Japanese emphasize emotion, beauty, and reflections
upon nature and seasonal change. Such broad contrasts support stereotypes
of Japanese national character but are rooted in the different styles and subject matters of respective texts. Many Japanese poets favored expressive
lyricism over pedantic verses about virtue. Two frequent subjects of classical
Japanese poetry were romantic love and nature. Poets especially celebrated
the ephemerality of beauty in nature—the transient splendor of natural
phenomena that mark the seasons. Poetic words and images evoking spring
included mist, the songs of frogs and nightingales, and, of course, cherry
blossoms. Wisteria, lotus, and cicadas are among the tropes signaling sum-

mer; the harvest moon and crimson foliage of maple trees evoke autumn; cold, bleak landscapes and bare trees recall winter months. These and other seasonal tropes are still widely used today. The sensitivity to change and to the passage of time represented by such seasonal discernment reflected Buddhist sentiments about the transience and cyclicality of life.

Early poems often followed the Chinese practice of composing verses to commemorate public rituals, ceremonies, and events, such as the death of monarchs, visits by foreign envoys, or journeys and pilgrimages made by court members. In comparison to the *Kaifūsō*, the poems of the *Man'yōshū* are relatively free of Confucian ideals and Chinese conventions and allusions. During the ninth and tenth centuries, court poetry would evolve to strictly follow rules and forms and could address only a limited range of topics and emotions. The often unrefined and emotionally direct poems of the *Man'yōshū* are often said to represent the first true record of early Japanese sentiment. Nationalist scholars have claimed that this anthology demonstrates the pure, sincere, or primeval character of the early Japanese that existed before contamination by Chinese philosophy, religion, and literature. Such judgments are difficult to sustain, however, given that the earliest extant works already demonstrated deep Chinese influence.

The poems in the *Man'yōshū* are arranged chronologically, beginning with poems improbably attributed to figures in remote antiquity and ending with works composed in the eighth century. Most fit into categories including poems about love and longing, grief and lamentation, travel, and nature. The vast majority of the entries, over four thousand, are short poems *(tanka)*, with five lines in a 5-7-5-7-7 syllable pattern. This genre would remain dominant for many centuries, but the anthology also contains 265 long poems *(chōka)*, rarely found in later anthologies of classical poetry.

One often-noted feature of the *Man'yōshū* is that many poems appear to have been written by people from different classes, including peasant farmers, frontier guards, and beggars, alongside those penned by emperors and other aristocrats. Such works address the difficulties of poverty or the loneliness of soldiers posted in the provinces, nostalgic for their homelands. Others employ rustic phrases or rural dialects. Modern scholars believe that they were actually written by courtiers posing in these roles, because members of other social classes generally lacked the necessary education to compose poetry. Nevertheless, the nonaristocratic perspective expressed in these works distinguishes them from later imperial anthologies.

The gifted poet Yamanoue no Okura (660–730), a court member of embassies to Tang China who is believed to be of Paekche origin, authored several poems describing a life of poverty. His long poem "Dialogue between Poverty and Destitution" begins as follows:

> On nights when rain falls
> Mingling with the blowing wind,
> On nights when snow falls,
> Mingling with the pouring rain,
> I have no choice
> But to endure the cold.
> I eat lumpy salt,
> Keep nibbling away at it,
> Drink *sake* dregs,
> Keeping sipping away at them,
> Snuffle the snot in my nose,
> Keep running my hand
> Over my skimpy beard,
> Boast to myself,
> "Where is there to be found a better man?"
> But I'm cold all the same. . . .[6]

Another of Okura's verses poignantly depicts the predicament of a poor family when the main breadwinner has fallen ill:

> By my pillowside
> My father and my mother crouch,
> And at my feet
> My wife and children; thus am I
> Surrounded by grief
> And hungry, piteous cries.
> But on the hearth
> No kettle sends up clouds of steam
> And in our pot
> A spider spins its web.
> We have forgotten
> The very way of cooking rice;
> Then where we huddle
> There comes the voice
> Of the village chief with his whip,
> Standing, shouting for me,
> There outside the place we sleep.[7]

Poems about love and romance often feel surprisingly contemporary, concisely capturing human feelings such as passion, longing, and regret, shared across time and space. An eighth-century poem attributed to a Princess Hirokawa describes being swept away by a new affair after experiencing the devastation of heartbreak:

I thought there could be
No more love left anywhere.
Whence then is come this love,
That has caught me now
And holds me in its grasp?[8]

An anonymous poem pleads for a visit from an indifferent lover, offering a view of the garden as enticement:

That you like me not
It may well be—
Yet will you not come
Even to see the orange tree
Abloom in my dooryard?[9]

A peasant farm girl awaits a nighttime rendezvous with her elite lover in the following short poem:

My hands, so chapped from
rice pounding
Tonight he will hold them
again, sighing,
my young lord of the mansion.[10]

An anonymous poem attributed to a frontier guard describes how the early winter season brings recollection of time spent with his wife:

I will think of you, love,
On evenings when the grey mist
Rises above the rushes,
And chill sounds the voice
Of the wild ducks crying.[11]

The most well-known and celebrated poet of the *Man'yōshū* is Kakinomoto no Hitomaro, a court poet of middle rank who served three sovereigns from around 680 to 700. He is considered one of the "Thirty-Six Immortals of Poetry," a list of the most accomplished Japanese poets from the sixth to eleventh centuries. Hitomaro contributed nineteen long and seventy-five short poems to the *Man'yōshū*. He demonstrated a great range of subject matter, from commemorating activities of the imperial family to intimate expressions of romantic love. One of his finest poems in the collection, excerpted below, is the awkwardly titled "On Seeing the Body of a Man Lying among the Stones on the Island of Samine in Sanuki Province." This moving verse recounts the experience of a typhoon in the Inland Sea and the speaker's identification with, and pity for, one of the storm's victims:

O the precious land of Sanuki,
Resting where the seaweed glows
    like gems! . . .
Having rushed our ship upon the breakers
    From the port of Naka,
We came rowing steadily until the wind
    That rises with the tides
Stormed down from the dwelling of
    the clouds. . . .
We sought haven on rugged Samine,
    The isle so beautiful in name.
Erecting a little shelter, we looked about,
    And then we saw you:
Pillowed upon your shaking beach,
    Using those wave-beaten rocks
As if the coast were spread out for
    your bedding;
    On such a rugged place
You have laid yourself to rest.
    If I but knew your home,
I would go tell them where you sleep;
    If your wife but knew this place,
She would come here searching for you,
    But knowing nothing of the way—
The way straight as a jeweled spear—
    How must she be waiting,
How anxiously now longing for you,
She so dear who was your wife.[12]

In summary, this period marked the consolidation of a centralized Japanese state that simultaneously drew upon continental models of kingship while developing its own indigenous conventions. Successive generations of the Yamato ruling clan attempted to strengthen their rule by adopting the norms of Chinese dynastic rule, such as court rank, a permanent capital, codified systems of penal and administrative law, and bureaucratic examinations. Native traditions, however, tempered reform attempts: hereditary privileges were preserved for uji elites, and the notion of a revocable divine mandate for the imperial family was rejected. Another route for strengthening authority was through the patronage and official sponsorship of Buddhism as protector of the imperial family and nation, resulting in a broad network of temples, including Nara's impressive Tōdaiji. The poetry and historical chronicles of the era also reflect the duality of indigenous and continental influence, with the *Kojiki* and *Man'yōshū* written in the native tongue, using Chinese characters as a phonetic medium only, while the *Nihon shoki* and *Kaifūsō* were composed in classical Chinese.

FURTHER READING

Batten, Bruce L. *Gateway to Japan: Hakata in War and Peace, 500–1300.* Honolulu: University of Hawaii Press, 2003.

———. *To the Ends of Japan: Premodern Frontiers, Boundaries and Interactions.* Honolulu: University of Hawaii Press, 2003.

Carr, Kevin G. *Plotting the Prince: Shotoku Cults and the Mapping of Medieval Japanese Buddhism.* Honolulu: University of Hawaii Press, 2012.

Como, Michael. *Shōtoku: Ethnicity, Ritual, and Violence in the Japanese Buddhist Tradition.* New York: Oxford University Press, 2008.

Farris, William W. *Daily Life and Demographics in Ancient Japan.* Ann Arbor: University of Michigan Center for Japanese Studies, 2009.

———. *Population, Disease, and Land in Early Japan, 645–900.* Cambridge, MA: Harvard University Press, 1985.

Hall, John W. *Government and Local Power in Japan, 500–1700: A Study Based on Hizen Province.* Princeton, NJ: Princeton University Press, 1966. Reprint, Ann Arbor: University of Michigan Center for Japanese Studies, 1999.

Lurie, David. *Realms of Literacy: Early Japan and the History of Writing.* Cambridge, MA: Harvard University Asia Center, 2011.

Ooms, Herman. *Imperial Politics and Symbolics in Ancient Japan: The Tenmu Dynasty 650–800.* Honolulu: University of Hawaii Press, 2008.

Piggott, Joan R. *Capital and Countryside in Japan, 300–1180: Japanese Historians Interpreted in English.* Ithaca, NY: Cornell East Asia Series, 2010.

RECOMMENDED FILMS

Phoenix (Hi no tori), "Karma chapter." 1986. Anime based on manga by Tezuka Osamu, illustrating lessons about karma and rebirth. This episode includes an account of the construction of Todaiji in a story about rivalry between a sculptor and an ex-bandit turned sculptor.

Horyuji. 1958. Film directed by Hani Susumu. Short documentary on the treasures of Hōryūji Temple and techniques of conservation.

3 The Rule of Taste

Lives of Heian Aristocrats, 794–1185

The Heian period, from 794 to 1185, is named for the new imperial capital established at Heian-kyō (later called Kyoto). That city would remain the imperial capital of Japan until 1868, when the young Meiji emperor moved his court to Tokyo to stand at the head of a new system of government and a new nation-state. Heian is known as Japan's classical period, a time when aesthetics and court culture attained a high degree of refinement. Around the year 1000, there was a flowering of distinctively Japanese aristocratic culture centering on the court, while imported Chinese cultural practices, from poetry to geomancy, also continued. It was an age of great creativity in literature, the arts, and religion. The lives of Heian elites were filled with aesthetic cultural practices. Cloistered and idle in the capital city, courtiers obsessed over their appearance, love affairs, cultural pastimes, and ceremonial rites. This chapter focuses on such activities among the aristocracy. It is important, however, to remember that these elites constituted only a small minority, numbering several thousand men and women in a population of around 5.5 million persons. The rich written record of courtly life—including diaries, poetry, and novels produced by noblemen and noblewomen—describes a lifestyle that no member of the lower classes could dream of attaining.

POLITICAL AND SOCIAL DEVELOPMENTS

In early Heian, courtiers and aristocrats, led by vigorous emperors, continued to actively assimilate Chinese administrative and cultural models introduced under Nara-era reforms. Emperor Kammu (737–806) moved the capital from Nara to Heian-kyō in 794 in order to escape the influence of powerful Buddhist monastic institutions and to locate the palace closer to his allies, powerful clans of immigrants from the Korean Peninsula. Kammu

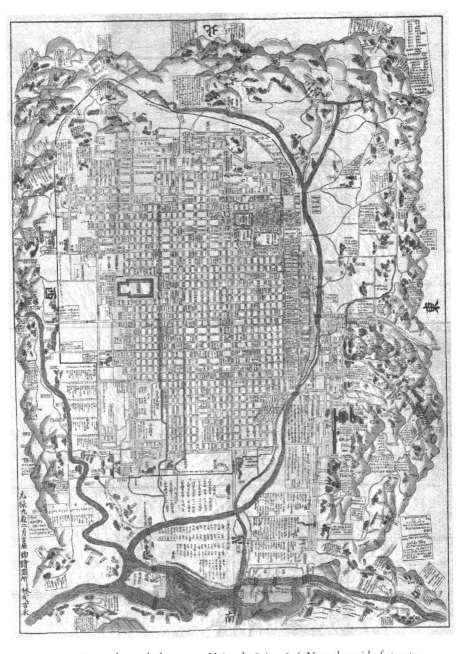

MAP 4.   Kyoto, formerly known as Heian-kyō, in 1696. Note the grid of streets and the geomantic setting. From James Murdoch and Isoh Yamagata, *A History of Japan during the Century of Early Foreign Intercourse (1542–1651)* (London: Kegan Paul, Trench, Trübner & Co., 1926).

attempted to maintain many of the centralized practices of government established in Nara but abolished conscription. The site for the new capital was selected through geomancy, with surrounding mountains and waterways that served to protect the court. As in Nara, the streets were laid out in a rational grid.

After a half-century, however, imperial authority and the centralized ritsuryō state waned as a court-centered polity emerged. One particular clan, the Fujiwara, used marriage politics to gain influence over the imperial household and effectively controlled the office of the emperor for over two hundred years. This established a pattern we will see repeatedly over the course of the following centuries, with emperors and other symbolic leaders who reigned but did not rule. That is, actual political power was in the hands of another, pulling the strings behind the throne. In this case, the hand that wielded power was a Fujiwara regent; in later years it would be a retired emperor or the shogun. Emperors were not eliminated—throughout history they remained a powerful symbol of authority and national identity, based on the myth of divine descent from the Sun Goddess, Amaterasu. The centralized state eroded under the Fujiwara, estates were increasingly reprivatized, and clan influence increased. With the crumbling of the Tang empire, in 838 the court stopped sending official embassies to China, the source of knowledge for developments in government, religion, and culture, although Buddhist priests continued to travel between Japan and the continent. Turning away from the all-inclusive borrowing from China in the Nara period, native forms of classical culture emerged. This shift from a phase of intensive cultural borrowing to one of introspection or isolation, with the Japanese absorbing and adapting foreign forms but creating more indigenous practices, would emerge as another important pattern in Japanese history. We will see it again in the sixteenth century, with the arrival of Catholic missionaries—the Japanese first eagerly adopted their fashions and guns, then prohibited foreign visitors and Christianity—and again in the nineteenth century, with frenzied borrowing from Western institutions and cultures under the new Meiji government, followed by the growth of nationalism and xenophobia that, among other factors, led to the Pacific War.

During the tenth and eleventh centuries the Fujiwara—a powerful clan descended from Nakatomi no Kamatari, who helped launch the Taika reforms—dominated the court. They excelled in marriage politics, maneuvering their daughters into the position of wives or consorts of the emperor in order to give birth to male children who might succeed the monarch. Boys with Fujiwara mothers were raised in the maternal home, allowing

Fujiwara grandfathers and uncles to exert influence over imperial successors. After ascending the throne, they took Fujiwara wives and consorts—usually their cousins or aunts—and when the union resulted in a son, the emperor was persuaded to abdicate, with a Fujiwara acting as regent *(sesshō)* for the child and exercising actual political control. The first to take power in this way was Fujiwara no Yoshifusa (804–72), who appointed himself regent to his grandson, the eight-year-old emperor, ruling on behalf of the monarch until he reached maturity. Yet when the boy reached adulthood, another Fujiwara, Mototsune (836–91), continued as a type of regent in the newly established position of chancellor *(kanpaku)*. The Fujiwara continued to control the throne without actually occupying it for two hundred years, reaching the apex of their power in the tenth and eleventh centuries under Michinaga (966–1027), who was effectively head of state for three decades, using his daughters to control three emperors. Michinaga's era coincides with what is considered the golden age of classical culture, and he is said to be the model for Genji in the renowned *Tale of Genji*, although one scholar suggested that the novel's main character is actually the "anti-Michinaga," sensitive and beautiful rather than crudely powerful.

Fujiwara dominance was sometimes opposed by other members of the court. There were occasional periods without a Fujiwara regent, when rival courtiers or other members of the imperial family attempted to gain control over the throne. In the late ninth century, the gifted statesman, scholar, and poet Sugawara no Michizane (843–903) gained the favor of Emperor Uda (867–931) and rose through court ranks to the position of minister of the right *(udaijin)*, one of the emperor's two closest advisors. His two daughters became imperial consorts, and for a few years Michizane exercised Fujiwara-like power over the court. Rivals conspired against him; they falsely accused Michizane of plotting against the emperor, and he was sent into exile at Dazaifu in Kyushu, where he died of homesickness. Before departing the capital, he sorrowfully composed a poem addressed to the precious plum tree he would leave behind:

> When the east wind blows,
> Send me your perfume,
> Blossoms of the plum:
> Though your lord be absent
> Forget not the spring.[1]

After Michizane's death, his enemies met mysterious ends; the capital was plagued with fires, storms, and diseases; and the imperial palace was struck repeatedly by lightning. These calamities were blamed on Michizane's vengeful spirit, which was posthumously appeased by restoring his titles and building the Kitano-tenmangu Shrine in the capital in 987. Michizane was the first Japanese subject to be enshrined as a kami by imperial decree, and he became known as the deity Tenjin, associated with literature and learning. Today, children taking school entrance examinations visit Tenjin shrines throughout the nation to request his help with their studies. The plum tree at the Tenmangu Shrine in Dazaifu is called the "flying plum" *(tobi-ume)*, and legend claims that it missed its master so much that it flew to his place of exile. The Michizane legend became a staple of popular culture. In the fifteenth century, it became the basis for the Nō play *Raiden*, and in the eighteenth century the story was adapted for the puppet theater and Kabuki as *Sugawara and the Secrets of Calligraphy*.

Emperor Shirakawa (1053–1129) also managed to wrest power from the Fujiwara. He did not have a Fujiwara mother, and in 1086 he abdicated and nominally retired to a Buddhist monastery, symbolically shaving his head—while actually continuing to exercise power behind his four-year-old son, Emperor Horikawa (1078–1107). This pattern, known as the "retired emperor system" *(insei)*, continued under the next two emperors, allowing the paternal line (the imperial family) to regain authority over the throne and restore a degree of their earlier wealth and power, sapped by Fujiwara privatization of estates. But the late Heian period—the eleventh and twelfth centuries—was an era of decline for court authority overall. Violence became more prevalent throughout the country; there were revolts in the provinces, piracy was rampant, and monk-warriors led massive raids on the capital city. Leisured aristocratic life continued in the capital, but the nobility became more dependent on warrior chieftains to maintain order on their estates in the provinces. By the mid-twelfth century, some of these provincial warrior clans began to compete with the courtiers of the capital for wealth and power, leading to the establishment of dual governments in the Kamakura period (see chapter 4).

The economic power of the elite rested on the privatization of rights to land and income from private estates, called *shōen*, that supported the lavish lifestyles of courtiers, supplying necessities and luxuries like rice and silk, lumber and building materials, swords and horses, lacquer and wax, ink and brushes, and fish and poultry. Surplus produce from estates was transported by land and water to be traded at markets in the capital. Under the official imperial system established in Nara, all productive land was to be treated as taxable imperial property, which the emperor could parcel out to court families, shrines, and temples as tax-exempt shōen. In addition, estates created by noble families who reclaimed wild lands for agricultural purposes were also exempted from taxes, and thus there was heavy competition between families to reclaim lands and lure peasants from public lands to work on their private estates.

Another way to accrue income was through the process of commendation, in which a small landholder gave control of his holdings to a more powerful landlord, such as a court noble or a shrine or temple, in order to receive protection and tax immunity while retaining a share of income. The new landlord might, in turn, commend the land to an even higher-ranking member of court. Commendations resulted in a formal system of rights to a percentage of income or produce from land. These rights, known as *shiki*, were divisible, salable, and heritable. In this system, there were four or five levels of individuals entitled to proceeds from the land, over and above the peasants who cultivated it: local proprietors who had controlled the land prior to commendation, estate officials who managed estates for absentee proprietors in the capital, those central proprietors, and the principal patron. Each got a slice of the income from the estate.

Official appointments provided another source of income, generally dependent on rank. Heian aristocracy was divided into nine ranks that determined the positions one could hold within the court. The top three ranks, occupied by around twenty clans, had the power to dictate central court policy and amassed the greatest wealth. The bottom four ranks were occupied by professionals of lineages that specialized in law, medicine, geomancy, or other areas; they had little opportunity for advancement into the higher ranks. Junior court officials and governors of the provinces occupied the middle ranks, which held the potential for advancement in court.

THE CULTURE OF ARISTOCRATIC LIVES

Heian courtly life has been called "the rule of taste," because the written record suggests that court society valued style and aesthetic experience as much as or more than the moral principles embodied in Chinese scholarship. The literary record of the era suggests that aristocrats were less interested in abstract, philosophical studies than in appreciating beauty and culture. With the rare exception, courtiers engaged in one or more of the arts. The "rule of taste" applied not only to the formal arts but also to nearly every aspect of the lives of the upper class. It was central to Heian Buddhism, making religion into an art and art into a religion. It was critical in conducting romantic liaisons. Even in the conduct of government, male officials were expected to perform stylized dances as part of their duties. *Miyabi*, or an appropriate level of refinement and sophistication, was an important elite aesthetic standard. Another term used in later centuries to describe Heian aesthetics is *aware*,

FIGURE 9.   Scene from an illustrated hand scroll of *The Tale of Genji,* twelfth century, Tokugawa Art Museum, Nagoya, Japan. Source: Wikimedia Commons.

indicating sensitivity to beauty or pathos in the sights or sounds of nature or in the conditions of human life. Throughout the centuries, the avid pursuit of a cult of beauty in all aspects of art, nature, and society has continued to play a critical role in the perception of Japan's national aesthetic identity.

The leisure supplied by income from the shōen estate system allowed elites to indulge in minutely detailed cultivation of taste. Sensitivity to seasonal changes and their reflections in nature were especially important qualities in aristocratic taste. Their aesthetic code applied to the smallest details, such as selecting an appropriate seasonal blossom to attach to a letter; its shade must also exactly complement the paper chosen. The range of colors in use was so wide that we cannot precisely translate some of their names. Furthermore, there was specific vocabulary for the color effects created by layering fabrics *(kasane),* such as producing the violet of the aster flower by layering a pale gray over blue, or producing a pale pink with white over scarlet. These color considerations were particularly important in women's clothing. Feminine formal court clothing was elaborate and cumbersome. Known as the "twelve-layered garment" *(jūnihitoe),* it consisted of an unlined robe worn over loose crimson trousers, over which there were a number of colorful lined robes, a luxurious silk top robe, and a pleated train, all topped with a short coat. The hems and sleeves of the many robes were arranged to display colorful bands of silk.

A woman's skill in selecting attractive and original color combinations was seen as a critical guide to her character and an expression of her aesthetic response to seasonal change. Literature and diaries often recorded the details of these ensembles. Murasaki Shikibu (978–1014?), the author of *The Tale of Genji*, noted in her diary: "The Empress was wearing the usual scarlet robe, under which she had kimonos of light plum, light green and yellow rose. His Majesty's outer robe was made of grape-coloured brocade; underneath he had a willow green kimono and below that, one of pure white, all most unusual and up to date in both design and colour."[2] The ugly, reverse side of the Heian appreciation of elegance and beauty was the intense pressure to have one's own sense of elegance recognized, as seen in the many competitions that occupied the Heian elites, described at the end of this chapter. Courtiers cruelly gossiped about those who made aesthetic faux pas; artistic insensitivity could even be fatal to one's career at court. Heian diaries and literature contain copious examples of snide remarks and criticisms over another's lack of taste. The excerpt from Murasaki's diary quoted above goes on to note how a court lady has made an error in her color combinations—one of the robes was "a shade too pale." Sei Shōnagon (966–1017?), author of *The Pillow Book* (discussed below), was a master of sharp barbs, skewering others for ugliness, awkwardness, and self-importance, or for behaving inelegantly, such as by snoring, blowing one's nose, or leaving doors open.

Court life was highly gendered. Binaries of male/female, public/private, and Chinese/Japanese often overlapped. Thus, public buildings associated with male domains, such as government offices or Buddhist temples, were usually built using Chinese elements, like tiled roofs with curved eaves and tile or stone floors, according to Chinese geomancy; private residences where women were sequestered featured wooden floors and thatched roofs. Masculine and feminine aesthetic and emotional ideals are conveyed in the rich literary and visual record. Male beauty was represented by a round, white-powdered face with a tiny mouth, narrow eyes, and a wisp of beard. Men generously scented their hair and clothing with incense. Literature informs us that ideal men should also be sensitive to beauty and unafraid to cry when parting from their loved ones or when moved by the beauty of nature. By contrast, hairy and muscular men were considered unattractive. Feminine beauty had many of the same ideals, favoring plump white faces and delicate round mouths. White skin was a sign of aristocratic birth; powder was used to produce the right degree. Over this base, women usually applied rouge to their cheeks and lips. Heian women also painted their eyebrows into large, black, rectangular blocks (see fig. 9). They blackened their teeth with a dye of iron and vinegar, a practice called *ohaguro* that was adopted by married women and courtesans in later eras. Those who failed to attend to these toiletries were thought hideous, with teeth that gleamed horribly. Hair was an important aspect of female attractiveness. It should be straight, glossy, parted in the middle, and very long, ideally reaching the ground. The glimpse of a fine head of hair was often enough to interest a potential lover. In an episode from *The Tale of Genji,* a character becomes hopelessly infatuated with a girl he has only glimpsed from behind.

In the Heian period, aristocratic women enjoyed a relatively high degree of independence and security not often seen in Japanese history: they possessed the legal right to inherit and keep property, so daughters of the elite usually had independent incomes and were entitled to maintain their own houses. As seen in Fujiwara marriage politics, many principal wives lived in their natal home during marriage, escaping the tyranny of mothers-in-law. Daughters were desired, because marriage politics made them useful as tools for advancement in court. There was fierce rivalry for the hand of attractive girls of high birth who would produce attractive daughters. In comparison to noblemen, who still had to occasionally tend to official duties, noblewomen had more free time to devote to literary and artistic pursuits. As a result, nearly every noteworthy author at the height of Heian culture was a woman. Furthermore, men sometimes adopted the personae of women in their poems and diaries, such as in *The Tosa Diary (Tosa nikki),* in which the author Ki no Tsurayuki (872–945) pretended to write as a woman in his traveling entourage.

One probable reason for such a ruse was that women were free to use the kana phonetic script, known as the "women's hand" *(onnade),* allowing them to express their thoughts and feelings more freely in their native tongue. "Serious writing," by contrast—including matters of state, religion, and philosophy—was composed in classical Chinese by male scholars, priests, and officials. In order to be able to write in their native language, Heian women used the kana syllabary derived from simplified Chinese characters, although many women were also literate in classical Chinese. Chinese calligraphy can be classified into three styles: *shin,* with extremely formal and angular characters; *sō,* with curvy, loose, elegant characters; and *gyō*—somewhere in between. The cursive *sō,* or grass style, eventually evolved into kana, which could be used to express oneself clearly in one's mother tongue. (Note that these three style types are also widely used in other Japanese spatial designs, such as in gardens and flower arrangement.) A variety of texts were written in kana by men and women alike, including poetry; diaries like *The Tosa Diary, The Gossamer Years,* and *The Diary of Murasaki Shikibu;* collections of miscellaneous jottings, exemplified by *The Pillow Book of Sei Shōnagon;* vernacular tales; and long fictional narratives, most notably *The Tale of Genji,* described in greater detail later in this chapter.

While Heian women enjoyed a degree of status and independence, according to Confucian and Buddhist doctrine there was no question about male supremacy and female inferiority. Buddhist teachings claimed that no matter how virtuous, a woman could not be reborn as a higher being without first being reborn as a man. Confucianism's "Three Obediences" subordinated women to their fathers, brothers, and husbands. Despite the privileges she enjoyed, an elite woman who was not in active court service led an immobile and sedentary existence. At home, when not with immediate family or servants, she was hidden behind a screen or curtains, although she might display her elegant taste to visitors by letting her sleeves peek out from behind the screen (see fig. 9). She could rarely leave the house, and when outside she always needed to be protected from the eyes of strangers. If embarking in a carriage, she was also hidden by screens; if on foot, she draped a thin robe over her hair and head, securing these with a deep, broad-brimmed hat. Surrounded by servants, Heian elite women were free of domestic duties, including looking after children, and spent their days practicing poetry, calligraphy, or music and waiting for letters or visits from their husbands and lovers.

The literature of the time depicts elite women obsessed by their relations with men, their very existence seemingly governed by the latter's romantic attitudes. Like most aspects of Heian society, elite courting and marriage customs were prescribed. Heian society was polygamous, with three main types of relationships. Principal wives were chosen by the bridegroom's family according to social, political, and economic considerations. Since the number of suitable candidates was limited to those of equal court rank, marriages between cousins or between aunts and nephews were acceptable. On average, girls were betrothed at age twelve and boys at fourteen; wives were often several years older than their husbands. Principal wives lived with their natal family; the husband either visited her while continuing to live with his parents (a living arrangement known as "duolocal") or sometimes moved in himself ("uxorilocal"). When the husband's father died, the principal wife would normally move into her husband's residence.

Secondary wives, or concubines, were officially recognized and received the same courting and marriage rituals (described below) as principal wives. Rules about class and rank were less rigid but would not fall outside the general aristocracy—it was inconceivable for a nobleman to take a peasant girl as an official concubine. If the principal wife failed to produce offspring, she would normally adopt a child of the concubine. The third type of relationship, and the most commonplace, was the casual affair, in which the woman was usually a court lady-in-waiting or from a far lower class. The parties might be married to others. Chastity was not particularly considered a female virtue, and unattached noblewomen, many with their own houses, could sleep with whomever they liked, refuse a man's favors, or terminate the relationship. Nevertheless, because women were required to remain at home, they were stuck waiting for the men to arrive. Thus, jealousy was an emotion commonly recorded in the literature, sometimes driving women to hysteria and insanity. Jealousy was closely tied to the idea of public humiliation—that the scorned woman would lose status in the eyes of others. In *The Tale of Genji*, such jealousy drives one of Genji's lovers to travel as a spirit and murder one of her rivals. *The Gossamer Years*, a journal of the unnamed secondary wife of powerful court noble Fujiwara no Kaneie (929–90), records her misery and humiliation over his many affairs as she waits anxiously at home, not knowing when or whether he will visit. The author cruelly celebrates when one of her rivals, who has recently given birth, also loses the favor of Kaneie when the child dies: "Now she was abandoned. The pain must be even sharper than mine. I was satisfied."[3]

Formal love affairs, for principal and secondary wives, were conducted according to ritual. After a man or his family learned of a suitable woman through a matchmaker, he would write a poem expressing conventionally romantic sentiments. This called for a prompt reply, composed either by the woman or, more usually, by the most capable member of her family or entourage, under her name. The man would scrutinize the reply carefully, examining the calligraphy and poetic skill for signs of the woman's character and charm. If she passed muster, he arranged to visit her secretly on the first convenient night. Generally the woman's family knew this was happening; besides, the architecture of mansions, with sliding paper doors and screens to separate rooms, did not allow for real secrecy. On this first night, by custom, the man should express sadness at the first sign of dawn, dragging himself away. Returning home, he would immediately compose his "next morning letter," adding a love poem. When the messenger arrived with the letter at the woman's house, he would be given wine and gifts along with the reply. On the following night a second visit was paid, with another exchange of letters. The third night was the most important. On this occasion, small rice cakes known as "third night cakes" were prepared and placed in the room. The appearance of the cakes was a central marriage rite that placed a religious sanction on the union. At that time the woman's father sent the man a formal letter of approval. After a few days, there would be a small social event with wine and food, in which a priest conducted rituals and the couple exchanged cups of sake. Now that they were openly wed, the man could visit the woman's house at any time and stay until late in the morning.

Even casual liaisons often called for poetry in establishing communications between the parties. In *Tales of Ise,* while on a hawking trip to a village outside of Nara, Ariwara no Narihira (825–80) approaches a local beauty he has spied through a fence with this poem:

> Seeing such blooming beauty,
> Fresh as the *murasaki* of Kasuga Moor,
> Like this passion-plant pattern,
> The passion in my heart
> Knows not any limit.[4]

Poems could also express disappointment in a lover. Later in *Tales of Ise,* while Narihira is on a falconing expedition, he has a tryst with a shrine priestess but is unable to meet her the following night because of required attendance at an all-night banquet. The following morning she sends a simple poem that indicates her displeasure:

> Shallow our union,
> Shallow as the inlet
> One walks unwetted.[5]

Literary Arts

Poetry was indeed central to court life; composing, exchanging, and quoting poems were critical means of communication, and perhaps no other society in the world has attached such importance to poetic skills. Elite Heian life was punctuated with poetry from beginning to end, and no important event was complete without it. Birth was attended by congratulatory verses; poetic exchanges were integral parts of both formal and informal rites of courting; and when death approached, parting poems would be composed. Poetry was often the best way to achieve a romantic conquest or to obtain a promotion at court. Those who weren't very skilled at poetry were often ridiculed. For instance, *Tales of Ise* includes an awkward poem sent to a lady-in-waiting by an admirer, about which the narrator remarks, "What a shabby and ignoble poem!"[6]

Poems were judged by the appropriate use of nature imagery, the ability to use and allude to other famous Chinese and Japanese poems, and the subtlety or nuance of their expression. One should be obscure and use allusion rather than being direct or too explicit. For example, in *The Pillow*

Book, when Sei Shōnagon fears that she has fallen out of favor with the empress, she receives a letter from Her Highness with nothing written on the paper itself. Instead it encloses a single yellow petal from a mountain rose on which the words "He who does not speak his love" are written. Shōnagon recognizes the words from a classical poem and understands, from this obscure hint, that she is still in the empress's favor. There were many occasions in daily life—a visit to the country, the first snowfall of the year—when failure to compose an appropriate poem immediately was considered a faux pas. Also, when one received a poem, it was mandatory to send a prompt reply using the same imagery.

The most popular form of Heian poetry was the *tanka,* written in Japanese rather than classical Chinese. These poems consisted of a verse of five lines with thirty-one syllables following the pattern 5-7-5-7-7. Fine examples of poetry were collected in twenty-one imperial anthologies, beginning with the *Kokinshū* (Collection of ancient and modern poems) in 905. The *Kokinshū* contained around eleven hundred poems that fell into two main categories echoing the interests of Nara poets: poems about love and those about the seasons and nature. Smaller groupings included poems about travel, congratulations, and laments. The *Kokinshū* was highly influential in dictating the proper form, format, and topics of Japanese poetry until the late nineteenth century. In its often-quoted preface, one of the main compilers, Ki no Tsurayuki, claims:

> Japanese poetry has the human heart as seed and myriads of words as leaves. It comes into being when men use the seen and the heard to give voice to feelings aroused by the innumerable events in their lives. The song of the warbler among the blossoms, the voice of the frog dwelling in the water—these teach us that every living creature sings. It is song that moves heaven and earth without effort, stirs emotions in the invisible spirits and gods, brings harmony to the relations between men and women, and calms the heart of fierce warriors.[7]

Exchanging or completing famous verses was a common aspect of festive Heian gatherings. Poetry contests were fiercely competitive: topics were announced well in advance, and participants came armed with well-polished poems. Entries were recited in pairs by official readers and recorded for posterity. The judge's decisions and reasoning were also recorded. Thus, these were no casual games, but battles in which a person's reputation could be made or broken. Another type of poetry contest placed men and women on opposing teams. One team member delivered a love poem, and the other had to promptly recite an appropriate response using similar imagery and tone. Such poetic games have remained popular throughout Japanese history. Even today, some families play a card game during the New Year's holidays that requires players to complete the second half of famous verses from a collection of a hundred poems from a hundred poets called the *Hyakunin isshu*.

The sister art to poetry in Heian Japan, as in China, was calligraphy. Much of the enjoyment that people derived from poetry and literature depended on the actual handwriting. Bad handwriting was as fatal to your reputation as bad poetry—handwriting was regarded as the mirror of the soul. People waited anxiously for the first letter from a potential lover because poor calligraphy was sure to disqualify them from favor. This is illustrated in *The Tale of Genji* when Genji is reading a note from one of his admirers and Murasaki is curious less about the content than about the calligraphy. As she looks at the envelope, she sees that the penmanship conveys the sensitivity and elegance of the most refined ladies at court. Later, when Murasaki has a new rival in the young girl who has become Genji's official wife, she is anxious to view the girl's handwriting and feels reassured when she sees the childish, unpolished style, even feeling sorry for the girl because her hand is shameful for someone of her rank.

Poetry and calligraphy combined in the art of letter writing, another area that held high critical standards. Sending a letter involved a great deal of preparation. First one had to choose paper of the proper thickness, size, design, and color to suit the emotional mood one wanted to suggest, as well as the season and the weather on that particular day. Paper might also be decorated with metallic flakes or pre-imprinted with designs. A single sheet might also be a collage, made by tearing or cutting different papers diagonally and joining them together to provide a rainbow of hues. Letters were sometimes inscribed on fans or other materials. The calligraphy was at least as important as the message, and the writer made several drafts with different brushes to produce the exact effect wanted. The centerpiece of the letter was usually a poem with a central image of some aspect of nature that delicately symbolized the occasion. After finishing the letter, the writer would scent the paper appropriately and carefully fold it in one of the accepted styles. The next step was to select the proper branch or blossom to attach, depending on the season, mood, and imagery of the letter and the color of the paper. Finally, the writer would summon an attractive messenger and give him instructions about delivery. In Heian diaries and literature, messengers constantly shuttle between aristocratic mansions, day and night, delivering these tasteful missives.

Turning to narrative, the literary classic *The Tale of Genji* is undoubtedly a treasure of world literature. Written from around 1000 to 1012 and attributed to court lady-in-waiting Murasaki Shikibu, it quickly became popular in elite circles, and hand-copied manuscripts were distributed throughout the provinces. *Genji* has been called the world's first novel, the first modern novel, the first psychological novel, and the earliest novel still considered a classic. It has key elements found in the modern novel: a well-developed central character, a large cast of other major and minor characters, and a sequence of events over a period of time covering the central character's lifetime and beyond. The work does not have a specific plot; over the course of fifty-four chapters, characters grow older, develop relationships, and experience events, much as in real life. One complication for readers is that characters are rarely given an explicit name, instead referred to by their function or role (e.g., Minister of the Left), an honorific (e.g., His Excellency), or their relation to other characters (e.g., Heir Apparent), which may change as the novel progresses. This lack of names may stem from a court preference for ambiguity that made it overly blunt to specifically mention a character's name, or it may have been a tactic used by Murasaki to maintain a fictionalized veneer and avoid offense to members of the court.

Through the years, *Genji* has remained extremely influential in Japanese literature, drama, and visual arts. Well-known episodes or chapters have been adapted numerous times in Nō, Kabuki, and Bunraku (puppet theater) plays. In modern times, several versions have been made for TV and film, the most recent in 2011. Allusions to *Genji* are abundant in later poetry, prose, and fiction. It is also parodied, such as in Ihara Saikaku's *The Life of an Amorous Man* from the Edo period (see chapter 7). The original tale centers on the life and many loves of the "shining prince" Genji, a handsome and gifted example of the aesthetic sensitivity and talent idealized for Heian male courtiers. Genji is the son of an emperor and his beloved, if low-ranking, concubine who died when the boy was just three years old. Although the emperor wishes to name the boy as his heir, Genji's low birth makes this impossible. Instead, Genji is removed from the royal lineage and given the surname Minamoto, which will allow him to obtain court ranks and official appointments. As a young man he marries Aoi, the daughter of a powerful courtier. They are not well matched, and Genji finds solace in love affairs with other women of all stations. His father, the emperor, takes another official wife, Fujitsubo, who resembles Genji's dead mother. Genji becomes obsessed with his stepmother, and she eventually succumbs to his amorous attention. Their liaison results in a child, whom others believe was sired by the emperor. Genji is also captivated by Fujitsubo's young niece Murasaki; he brings her to his palace to be raised and groomed as his ideal lover. One of Genji's affairs leads to a scandal at the court and he subsequently becomes exiled. After his eventual return, Genji ascends to the pinnacle of court power and works to advance the careers of his children and grandchildren. When his son with Fujitsubo becomes emperor, he receives the unprecedented title Honorary Retired Emperor. The last third of the text deals with Genji's grandson Niou and his best friend Kaoru, who engage in rivalry over women.

Another form of Heian literature is the collection of miscellaneous observations, gossip, and opinions *(zuihitsu)*, epitomized by *The Pillow Book of Sei Shōnagon*. The sharp wit, keen eye, and aesthetic sensibility of the author, a court lady-in-waiting and rival to Murasaki Shikibu, are visible in the many lists scattered throughout the work. For example, "Unsuitable Things" include "ugly handwriting on red paper" and "a handsome man with an ugly wife"; "Elegant Things" include "a rosary in rock crystal" and "plum blossoms covered in snow"; and "Rare Things" include "a servant who does not speak badly about his master."[8] Some of the views Shōnagon expresses feel surprisingly modern, especially those concerning human relationships. Many of us today can relate to some of the items in the following list.

EMBARRASSING THINGS

While entertaining a visitor, one hears some servants chatting without any restraint in one of the back rooms. It is embarrassing to know that one's visitor can overhear. But how to stop them?

A man whom one loves gets drunk and keeps repeating himself.

To have spoken about someone not knowing that he could overhear. This is embarrassing even if it be a servant or some other completely insignificant person.

To hear one's servants making merry. This is equally annoying if one is on a journey and staying in cramped quarters or at home and hears the servants in a neighboring room.

Parents, convinced that their ugly child is adorable, pet him and repeat the things he has said, imitating his voice.

An ignoramus who in the presence of some learned person puts on a knowing air and converses about men of old.

A man recites his own poems (not especially good ones) and tells one about the praise they have received—most embarrassing.

Lying awake at night, one says something to one's companion, who simply goes on sleeping.

In the presence of a skilled musician, someone plays a zither just for his own pleasure and without tuning it.

A son-in-law who has long since stopped visiting his wife runs into his father-in-law in a public place.[9]

Visual Arts

It was not only the literary arts that flourished and were indigenized during the Heian period; native styles of painting, architecture, and decorative arts also emerged. *Yamato-e,* or Japanese pictures, which depicted familiar landscapes and the activities and circumstances of the elite courtiers, formed a contrast to Chinese-style painting *(kara-e),* typically of Confucian sages, Chinese legends, and imagined landscapes, although both were popular. Yamato-e are further divided into feminine painting *(onna-e)* and masculine painting *(otoko-e),* depending on subject matter, techniques, and where the work was displayed. Onna-e are more decorative, using combinations of dyed papers embellished with gold leaf. Calligraphy in feminine works was invariably in kana. They paid close attention to the details of costume and interior and have been invaluable in providing information on the material culture of elites, depicting clothing, architecture, and furnishings. A pictorial technique, the "blown-away roof" *(fukinuki yatai),* provided a bird's-eye view of the interiors of homes (see fig. 9). Mansions of courtiers were vast but contained minimal furniture. Furnishings in use, such as painted sliding doors and curtained room dividers, folding screens, and tatami mats bordered in brocade, were highly decorative. Useful items such as lacquered containers, trays, and armrests were richly embellished, featuring elegant paintings or inlays of gold, silver, or mother-of-pearl. While interiors, costumes, and hairstyles were rendered in detail in onna-e, the faces of individuals were rather generic, using a technique known as *hikime kagibana* (slit eyes, hook nose). Masculine paintings contained historical or religious content and will be further discussed in the next chapter.

Both masculine and feminine styles were painted on sliding doors and folding screens and included in long, illustrated hand scrolls *(emakimono).* These horizontal scrolls combined illustration, poetry, and text to tell a story, joining together pieces of paper or silk and rolling these around a cylinder, which allowed one to unroll the tale a bit at a time (around one to two feet) to follow the narrative. One story could result in many scrolls, as with a twelfth-century set prepared for *The Tale of Genji* with an estimated twenty scrolls totaling over 450 feet, containing over one hundred paintings and over three hundred sheets of calligraphy created by teams of artists. Sadly, only fragments of these *Genji* hand scrolls have survived. The scrolls themselves were luxurious items; their cylinders were made with precious materials like jade and ivory, and their covers were made of beautiful brocades. They were commissioned by, and circulated only among, court aristocrats. Another famous set of picture scrolls illustrates the eleventh-century tale "Yoru no Nezame" (Wakeful at night), a tragic story of the unhappy love affairs of its heroine Nezame, who becomes pregnant by her sister's husband and is unwillingly pursued by the emperor.

Performing Arts

Music and dance were also central to court life, and courtiers spent a good deal of time practicing their songs, dances, and instruments. An imperial department of music had been established as early as 701, staffed by teachers and performers specializing in styles of music or dance imported from Koguryŏ, Silla, and Tang China or in native Japanese styles. The official song and dance repertory contained around 120 pieces. Gagaku (elegant music) was the name for all styles of court music. It employed a pentatonic scale and was played using a variety of wind, string, and percussion instruments. Among the best known of these are the *hichiriki,* an oboe; the *shō,* a mouth organ; the *biwa,* a four-stringed lute; and the *tsuzumi,* an hourglass-shaped drum. Dance performances by courtiers and officials were an important aspect of court ritual. *The Tale of Genji* describes how the hero is rewarded with a promotion in rank after his particularly moving performance of a dance called *Seigaiha* (Waves of the blue ocean).

Other categories of Heian performers included *asobi* and *shirabyōshi,* professional women who provided both entertainment and sexual services for Heian elites. The asobi were distinct from common prostitutes, literate and accomplished traveling performers who worked along roads and river routes from the capital, often staging their songs and dances on small boats. They were particularly known for singing modern songs, known as *imayo,* rather than the classical repertoire found at court. Patrons praised their talents, seductive skills, elegant attire, and beauty in poetry and prose. In the fictional tale "Shinsarugakuki," Fujiwara no Akihira (989–1066) describes an asobi as follows: "Her vigor in soliciting lovers, her knowledge of all the sexual positions, the merits of her lute strings and buds of wheat and her mastery of the dragon's flutter and tiger's tread techniques—all are her endowments. Not only that, she has the voice of a bird in Amida's paradise, as well as the face of an angel."[10]

Shirabyōshi, female dancers who wore men's attire and danced with swords, became popular in the late Heian period. They were known for their slow, rhythmic performances and, like the asobi and later eras' courtesans and geisha, were both generally well educated and available for sexual services to their elite customers. Some became the concubines of famous individuals and were celebrated in literature, like Shizuka, the lover of Minamoto no Yoshitsune (1159–89), a popular hero in *The Tale of the Heike,* or Giō and Hotoke, concubines associated with Taira no Kiyomori (1118–81) (see chapter 4).

Games and Pastimes

In addition to literary and performing arts, Heian elites engaged in a wide variety of competitive games and contests. Men gambled at the chess-like board game of Go (see fig. 9), backgammon *(sugoroku),* and dice. They played a game of football known as *kemari,* where the objective was to prevent a leather ball from touching the ground. Kemari was played in a circle, on a square field with a tree planted at each of the four corners: a willow, a cherry, a pine, and a maple. Imperial guards and provincial warriors of the elite class competed at archery and horsemanship.

"Comparison games" were a popular form of leisure, played with a certain category of items—like seashells, flowers, or birds—instead of with poems. Players were divided into two teams, and pairs from opposing sides would pit their entries, along with an appropriate poem, against each other. A panel of judges compared the items submitted in terms of beauty and/or rarity. For example, in the small-bird comparison, members of each team brought songbirds they had raised at home, which were compared in terms of plumage, color, and voice. Other popular pastimes involved incenses and perfumes. The names of Genji's heir, Niou, and his friend, Kaoru, both refer to scent, demonstrating its critical importance in daily lives. Elites used incense to scent their clothing, hair, and living quarters, often creating their own secret, signature scents through combinations of different woods like sandalwood and pine, spices like clove and cinnamon, musks, resins, and other substances, ground together with iron mortars and bound with honey. An episode in *The Tale of Genji* describes an incense-blending contest and its accoutrements—beautiful containers and jars, censers, and boxes. Incense-based games included one in which a player burned one kind of incense and the next player burned a fragrance that would combine pleasantly with the first. In another game, participants tried to create the atmosphere of a particular poem from the *Kokinshū* by combining incenses. Like most Heian social occasions, all such games were accompanied by plenty of wine, music, and flirtation.

HEIAN RELIGION AND BELIEF

Religion and supernatural belief pervaded classical society. For the Heian aristocrat, hardly a day passed without performing some rite with religious or supernatural implications. Tendai and Shingon, two schools of Buddhism introduced in the era, provided structured paths for the elite to gain merit in pursuit of spiritual development. Details of their daily lives, however, were often guided by popular beliefs and practices, such as geomancy and divination, as much as or more than by institutional Buddhism. Everyday life was governed by beliefs about taboos, auspicious and inauspicious days and directions, and pollution and ritual purification.

Over the course of the Heian period, Buddhism began to move out of the monasteries and into the residences of the aristocracy, where it could be seen in performance of pious tasks intended to accumulate good karma, such as copying sutras, building statues, and commissioning temples and artworks. In 804, Emperor Kammu, who had moved the capital to Heian-kyō to escape the influence of the powerful Nara Buddhist schools, sent two young monks to China to find alternative schools of Buddhism that might be brought back to Japan to protect the new capital. The monks were part of the same diplomatic mission to Tang China but traveled on different boats. The monk Saichō (767–822) made a direct passage, but the boat of the second monk, Kūkai (774–835), was blown to the south. As a result, they studied and brought back very different forms of Buddhism.

Saichō remained in China for around a year, studying a variety of Buddhist teachings and approaches at a monastery on Mount Tiantai. The Tendai school of Buddhism he established in Japan advocated a mix of monastic discipline, meditation, and orthodox teachings based largely on *The Lotus Sutra*, considered the Buddha's supreme teaching, reconciling all other schools in a comprehensive synthesis and containing everything necessary for salvation. Tendai stressed that intellectual and contemplative approaches to religion were like the two wings of a bird—one needed both teachings and meditation to achieve enlightenment. Overall, Tendai focused on *exoteric* teachings and practices—those that are open, publicly available, and attributed to the historical Buddha—rather than the *esoteric*, secret teachings and rituals associated with the Buddha Dainichi, which were emphasized by Shingon, the religion established by Saichō's competitor Kūkai.

Returning to Japan in 805, Saichō established a monastery and temple complex called Enryakuji on Mount Hiei, to the northeast of the capital, considered the most unlucky direction. The temple would protect the capital from evil emanating from that direction. Saichō's Buddhism was strongly oriented toward protection of the state and loyalty to the ruler. Tendai received a great deal of patronage from emperors and the court, allowing the Enryakuji complex to eventually grow to over three thousand buildings. In order to establish independence from the older sects of Nara, Saichō insisted that Tendai monks be ordained at Mount Hiei with a set of vows and monastic rules and precepts much simpler than those for monks ordained at Tōdaiji in Nara, and reflective of norms in China. He developed a plan to rigorously train monks for twelve years. The best students would remain on Mount Hiei as religious leaders; others would be sent to the provinces, either as teachers or as functionaries assisting provincial governors in projects such as land reclamation and bridge construction.

Like the great Nara temples, Enryakuji received tax-free estates from the court. By the twelfth century, Enryakuji had hundreds of shōen estates scattered throughout the provinces, supporting a large network of provincial branch temples. All of the powerful monasteries during this era built up private armies of monk-soldiers *(sōhei)* to protect their interests and landholdings. When Tendai temples felt their interests were in jeopardy, the warrior-monks of Enryakuji would swarm down the mountain to threaten the capital. Rivalry between monastic armies from the Nara monasteries and Enryakuji, and between Enryakuji and private warrior bands protecting the estates of court families, contributed to the violence and turmoil in the late Heian period. One eleventh-century emperor reportedly remarked that there were three things in the world that he could not control—the floods of the Kamo river, gambling, and the monks of Mount Hiei.

The other monk on the 804 diplomatic mission was the brilliant young Kūkai, one of the most revered figures in Japanese religious history. Legends credit Kūkai with developing the Japanese kana script and with the ability to locate hot springs and other bodies of water through divination. Japan's most famous pilgrimage route links eighty-eight temples associated with Kūkai on the island of Shikoku. The 750-mile route is still undertaken today by around a hundred thousand pilgrims annually. It takes thirty to sixty days to complete on foot, but the majority of pilgrims today take buses.

Like Saichō, Kūkai sought a universal and unifying Buddhist tradition more appropriate to Japan's needs than the abstract doctrines of the Nara schools. He studied at the Tang capital Chang'an, where the Chinese Buddhist master Huigo initiated him into esoteric teachings and rites that would eventually become known in Japan as Shingon (true word or mantra). Shingon emphasized the transcendent or all-embracing cosmic Buddha

Dainichi, believing that other Buddhas and bodhisattvas were manifestations of the cosmic Buddha.

Shingon's esoteric teachings could not be fully understood through textual study alone; practitioners embodied the words, actions, and thoughts of Dainichi through mantras, mudras, and mandalas. Mantras were secret incantations composed of sacred syllables that were chanted and repeated; the name Shingon comes from this practice. Mudras represented the actions of Dainichi through sequences of stylized hand gestures, each with a specific meaning, just as in Buddhist statuary. And mandalas were paintings that practitioners meditated upon, representing Dainichi's central position in the universe and his transformation into myriad forms and beings. Kūkai brought two mandalas back from China: the Mandala of the Diamond Realm, symbolizing the unchanging principles of the Buddha; and the Mandala of the Womb Realm, depicting the active manifestations of the Buddha. In addition to being objects of meditation, the mandalas were used to select a patron Buddhist deity (like a guardian saint) for initiates, who were blindfolded and instructed to throw a flower on one of the mandalas. Its landing place helped determine the initiate's tutelary deity.

The secrets of the Shingon teachings and the meanings of the mantras, mudras, and rituals had to be imparted orally by a master directly to a disciple. In this sense, Shingon was probably the first Japanese tradition to stress the importance of the direct transmission of secrets from master to disciple. In later years, this practice would spread from Japanese religion to arts and even business, where different schools and houses jealously guarded their own secrets.

Because Shingon rituals and practices were complex, colorful, and artistic, they naturally held a deep appeal for Heian courtiers, who valued aesthetic sophistication. Kūkai proved very popular among the elite, and he was appointed by the emperor to be head of two great temples, Tōdaiji in Nara and Tōji in Heian-kyō. Secure in his ties to the capital, Kūkai established his own monastery far to the south of Heian-kyō (present-day Kyoto) at Mount Kōya. It rivaled Enryakuji for religious, political, and economic influence.

During the mid-Heian period, a new devotional practice began to develop within Tendai, offering hope for salvation that didn't require intense study and meditation. The new movement centered on the Buddha Amida and offered salvation in his Pure Land of the Western Paradise. Rebirth in the Pure Land was available if one simply placed one's faith in Amida, expressed in a short prayer called the *nembutsu* that said simply, "Praise to the Buddha Amida" (Namu Amida Butsu). Thus, the practice offered ordinary

FIGURE 10.   Mandala of the Womb Realm, ninth century, Tōji, Kyoto, Japan.
Source: Wikimedia Commons.

men and women, and not just monks and nuns, access to the Pure Land that
was not too difficult to obtain. These practices eventually evolved into Pure
Land Buddhism and its offshoot True Pure Land Buddhism, which is the
largest sect of Buddhism in Japan today (see chapter 4).

Amida became a popular subject of art commissioned by courtiers.
Paintings of Amida descending to earth on a purple cloud, accompanied by

FIGURE 11. *Welcoming Descent of Amida and Bodhisattvas,* fourteenth century. Courtesy of The Metropolitan Museum of Art, New York.

bodhisattvas and other divine beings, known as *raigō*, were part of Heian death rituals. Raigō were brought to the houses of persons nearing death so that Amida might welcome them to the Pure Land.

One of the reasons for the emerging popularity of Amida devotion was the belief that, in the eleventh century, Japan had entered the Latter Age of the Buddhist Law, known in Japanese as *mappō*, which early Buddhist texts predicted would begin two thousand years after the passing of the historical Buddha and would last for ten thousand years. Texts claimed it would be an age of decadence and the decline of Buddhism, a pessimistic and gloomy era. Saichō claimed that "in the Latter days of the Law, there will be none to keep the Buddha's commandments. If there should be such, they will be as rare as a tiger in a market place." During mappō, one could not rely on one's own efforts alone for salvation or good rebirth and had to have faith in the power of compassionate Buddhas, like Amida, who could guarantee salvation.

When it came to the details of their daily life, Heian aristocrats usually relied more on popular belief and practices than on the doctrines of institutional religion. Nevertheless, many such beliefs were often related to larger philosophical traditions, like Taoism and Buddhism. In turn, popular practices influenced the rites performed by institutionalized Buddhist sects, as seen in *The Tale of Genji*, which records how Buddhist priests often performed exorcisms and divinations.

The court's Bureau of Divination was responsible for astrology, discerning good and evil omens, and other activities to help shape state policies in accord with the universe. Their findings also shaped everyday lives; court members limited their movements and activities according to calculations of lucky and unlucky days and directions. Some taboos were permanent and some temporary. The northeast was permanently the unlucky direction, but at different times other directions were considered unlucky (e.g., when one was sixteen years old, the northwest was inauspicious). One must not repair gates during the summer or water wells during the autumn, because kami were believed to reside there during those seasons. Taboos were also based on the Chinese cycle of sixty years, and calculations were made to determine when it was essential to stay indoors, or when to cut one's hair or fingernails.

Ritual pollution, especially from illness or death, applied to all members of the household of the afflicted, who were "infected" by association. Their houses were off-limits to visitors, and special tags were hung on the shutters to keep others away. If a nobleman from a polluted household was required to venture outside because of official duties, he would attach a tag to his headdress to keep people at arm's length.

FIGURE 12.   Statue of a *tengu* dressed as a *yamabushi* mountain wizard. Photo by WolfgangMichel, via Wikimedia Commons.

The world of Heian was also heavily populated with goblins, demons, spirits, and other supernatural beings. *Tengu* were bird-like beings with beaks and wings that lived in the mountains and forests and had magical powers. In later centuries, depictions of tengu changed and they were represented as red-faced, long-nosed goblins. Foxes were closely associated with the supernatural. They could bewitch and possess individuals and could assume human forms, luring gullible young men into their power by appearing as a beautiful girl. *Tanuki* (Japanese raccoon dogs, sometimes called badgers) were also shapeshifters capable of possessing humans, but they were considered more mischievous than the devious foxes.

While tengu and foxes were visible, there were even more invisible spirits and demons who could cause all kinds of misfortune. Vengeful spirits of the dead who felt they had been wronged or treated badly in life could cause illness, death, or other disasters, as illustrated in the case of Sugawara no Michizane. Even the spirits of the living could travel and wreak havoc. In *The Tale of Genji*, the spirit of Rokujō, tormented by jealousy, travels outside of her living body to attack and kill a rival for Genji's affections. People kept troublesome spirits from their houses by means of charms, spells, and incantations. Special precautions were taken around the emperor's palace. At regular intervals, the imperial guards twanged their bowstrings to scare off evil spirits lurking in the air.

One of the main treatments for illness was to drive out evil spirits causing the malady through exorcism, conducted by shamans or Buddhist priests. People spoke of "catching an evil spirit" in the same way we talk about catching a cold today. In one episode from *Genji*, Kumoi blames her husband for their child's illness. After returning home from a late-night romantic excursion, he had opened the windows and let in all the evil spirits who made the child ill. The husband accepts this explanation and apologizes.

To treat illness through exorcism, the priest or shaman recited incantations to drive the spirit into a medium, usually female. If this was successful, the spirit would then identify itself and the exorcist would drive it out of the medium. Heian literature is full of dramatic accounts of such practices, like this one noted by Sei Shōnagon in *The Pillow Book*:

> When the girl had sat down next to the priest in front of a small three-foot curtain of state, he turned round and handed her a thin, highly polished wand. Then with his eyes tightly shut he began to read the mystic incantations, his voice coming out in staccato bursts as he uttered the sacred syllables. It was an impressive sight, and many of the ladies of the house came out from behind their screens and curtains and sat watching in a group. After a short time the medium began to tremble and fell into a trance. . . .
> She lay there groaning and wailing in the most terrible way. . . .
> Meanwhile it was announced that the patient was a little better. Some young attendants were sent to the kitchen to fetch hot water and other requisites. They wore pretty unlined robes and formal skirts whose light mauve color was as fresh as on the day they were dyed—it made a most charming effect.[11]

Even in such dramatic circumstances, Heian elites managed to maintain their fashion sense.

In summary, Heian elites engaged in marriage politics and intrigue in order to gain power and wielded aesthetics to enhance their reputations. The proceeds of private estates supported their lavish lifestyles, allowing men and women of the court to cultivate literary, musical, and artistic talents that they displayed through competitive games, and to obsess over their frequent love affairs. They developed detailed aesthetic standards for everyday material culture, such as clothing, interior décor, and correspondence.

In contrast with the Nara period, when the imperial family had acted as the primary patrons of Buddhist monasteries, Buddhist art and practice associated with newly imported sects entered the private homes of courtier families. Their daily decisions were guided by popular belief in the supernatural, including geomancy, astrology, spirits, and omens.

Heian courtiers prized daughters for their potential to improve family standing through marriage to powerful men. Elite women, often cloistered at home awaiting husbands and lovers, produced much of the best literature of the era. Although they were considered inferior to men, women enjoyed economic rights and sexual liberties that would erode over the centuries as the patriarchal warrior class, which practiced primogeniture, ascended in power.

FURTHER READING

Adolphson, Mikael, Edward Kamens, and Stacie Matsumoto, eds. *Heian Japan: Centers and Peripheries.* Honolulu: University of Hawaii Press, 2007.

Emmerich, Michael. *The Tale of Genji: Translation, Canonization, and World Literature.* New York: Columbia University Press, 2015.

Goodwin, Janet. *Selling Songs and Smiles: The Sex Trade in Heian and Kamakura Japan.* Honolulu: University of Hawaii Press, 2007.

Heldt, Gustav. *The Pursuit of Harmony: Poetry and Power in Early Heian Japan.* Ithaca, NY: Cornell East Asia Series, 2008.

Hurst, Cameron G. *Insei: Abdicated Sovereigns in the Politics of Late Heian Japan, 1086–1185.* New York: Columbia University Press, 1976.

LaMarre, Thomas. *Uncovering Heian Japan: An Archeology of Sensation and Inscription.* Durham, NC: Duke University Press, 2000.

Shikibu, Murasaki. *The Tale of Genji.* Translated by Royall Tyler. New York: Penguin, 2001.

Shirane, Haruo. *Japan and the Culture of the Four Seasons: Nature, Literature, and the Arts.* New York: Columbia University Press, 2012.

Wallace, John R. *Objects of Discourse: Memoirs by Women of Heian Japan.* Ann Arbor: University of Michigan Center for Japanese Studies, 2005.

Winfield, Pamela D. *Icons and Iconoclasm in Japanese Buddhism: Kūkai and Dōgen on the Art of Enlightenment.* New York: Oxford University Press, 2013.

RECOMMENDED FILMS

Onmyōji: The Yin Yang Master. 2001. Feature film directed by Takita Yōjirō. Depicts popular belief in magic and spirits centered around court astrologer Abe no Seimei, who, according to legend, possessed mystical skills.

Rashomon. 1950. Feature film directed by Kurosawa Akira. An account of the murder of a court noble and the rape of his wife, told through four different witnesses' perspectives. Considered a masterpiece of world cinema.

Tale of Genji: A Thousand Year Enigma. 2011. Feature film directed by Tsuruhashi Yasuo. Latest film version of the classical tale.

Tale of Princess Kaguya. Studio Ghibli, 2013. Animated feature film directed by Takahata Isao. Relates the folktale of a bamboo-cutter who finds riches and a tiny girl, originally from the moon, in a bamboo grove and moves his family to the Heian capital to raise the girl as a noblewoman.

The Tale of Genji. 1987. Animated film directed by Sugii Gisaburo. A well-done adaptation of the classic.

4　The Rise and Rule of the Warrior Class

12th–15th Centuries

The late twelfth to the late sixteenth century is considered Japan's medieval age. Over these centuries the warrior class accumulated power and wealth and was able to gain a large degree of independence from the court. The transfer of power from the court to the warrior elites began in the late twelfth century with the establishment of the first warrior government, the *bakufu* (tent government) or shogunate, established by Minamoto no Yoritomo (1147–99) in the eastern city of Kamakura in 1185. Yoritomo earned the warrior class the ability, granted by the court, to tax all public and private estates in return for keeping law and order. By receiving the title of Shogun from the emperor, he was designated the military protector of court privileges. Nevertheless, the warrior class began to siphon off the wealth and privileges of both the court and the Buddhist monasteries.

The Mongol invasions of the thirteenth century, however, impoverished the Kamakura regime and disrupted its authority, leading eventually to the establishment of the Ashikaga shogunate, also known as the Muromachi bakufu, in Heian-kyō (hereafter referred to as Kyoto, its current name) during the fourteenth and fifteenth centuries. The idea of vassalage emerged under these warrior governments. *Bushi*, or *samurai*, a term derived from the verb meaning "to serve," were warriors who fought in return for material reward and personal advancement—in essence, mercenaries. The Minamoto extended their powers by offering military families lucrative posts or control over land. Vassals did not follow their leaders out of an abstract sense of loyalty or honor, but for concrete benefits.

As the warrior elite ascended within the social and political order, they sought to develop religious and cultural capital in keeping with their status as rulers. They became patrons of Zen Buddhism, which in turn influenced the aesthetics of different art forms that emerged during the medieval era.

Other Buddhist sects that emerged during these centuries effectively extended the message of salvation, previously limited to the elites in Nara and Kyoto, to all classes of people in all regions of Japan.

POLITICAL AND SOCIAL DEVELOPMENTS

During the Heian period, while the court enjoyed luxurious pastimes, the provinces slowly slipped into lawlessness and rebellion. Imperial courtier families had little taste for military campaigns and were reluctant to leave the amusements of the capital, so they increasingly relied on deputies to govern their shōen estates and landholdings. Many courtiers sold their appointments to these men, who proved willing to reside in the provinces in order to recoup their investment. Deputies reclaimed lands, extending the reach of tax-free estates, and made alliances with local warrior families, many of which had aristocratic origins. As the product of numerous illicit love affairs, many of the children of nobility could not be appointed to high court ranks and were instead given commoner names and settled into provinces as subjects, where they were left to fend for themselves. They devoted themselves to increasing their wealth in land and to practicing martial skills. The arts of war were limited to the rural elite, as they called for costly equipment like swords and armor, bows and arrows, and stables of horses. Large regional leagues of warriors clustered around two rural clans that claimed imperial ancestry: the Taira, also known as the Heike, claimed descent from Emperor Kammu; the Minamoto, or Genji, claimed to be descendants of Emperor Seiwa (850–78). The rivalry between these two great military families is described in one of the greatest works of premodern Japanese literature, *The Tale of the Heike,* discussed later in this chapter. Members of these clans acquired land and followers in different areas of Japan, forming independent Taira and Minamoto branch families.

During the tenth and eleventh centuries, these clans and branches grew in size, especially in eastern Japan, but none was powerful enough to seriously challenge the power of the court—they could only control their immediate domains. Occasionally rebellions occurred in the countryside, such as the 939 revolt of Taira no Masakado, who took control of eight provinces. A chronicle of his career, *Shōmonki,* claims that Masakado launched his campaign after receiving an oracle announcing that he would be the new emperor. Lacking any military power to control such uprisings, the court relied on the provincial warrior clans to quash the rebels. The Minamoto became known as the "claws and teeth" of the Fujiwara. Warrior families agreed to serve courtiers in return for land and immunity from taxes and for court honors and appointments, which they valued because of their aristocratic origins. Even though they had become a provincial military class, warrior families continued to seek the legitimation and cultural capital associated with the imperial court.

By around 1100, there had been a significant shift in the position of the military class. While the court remained the source of honors and awards, and central officials continued to pass edicts, outside the capital actual control over land mattered more than court titles; military force was more effective than law. As the Taira and Minamoto built their wealth and power, they were increasingly called upon by different factions in Kyoto, like the retired emperors or the Fujiwara, to intervene in court-related matters such as imperial successions. In 1159, a succession dispute between a cloistered and a reigning emperor resulted in the Hōgen and Heiji rebellions, pitting the military clans directly against one another. Taira no Kiyomori (1118–81), leader of the Taira clan, which had developed extensive ties with China's Song dynasty, emerged victorious and assumed a position of control over the court, taking the title of chief minister in 1167 and settling his vassals into the capital. Kiyomori forced his critics and rivals to resign from government posts and engaged in Fujiwara-like marriage politics, coercing the emperor to marry his daughter and to abdicate the throne in favor of his grandson, who was named Emperor Antoku in 1180.

Courtiers resented the boorish upstarts who had invaded their capital and usurped their privileges and began to search for alternative sources of military power that might oust the Taira. The Minamoto leader Yoshitomo and his eldest sons were killed in the Heiji rebellion, but Kiyomori had spared his younger sons Yoritomo, Noriyori, and Yoshitsune. From his stronghold in Kamakura, Yoritomo mustered the remnants of Minamoto strength in the eastern provinces and launched the Genpei War (1180–85), a campaign to drive the Taira from the capital. In 1183, the Minamoto set fire to the Taira palace in Kyoto and forced them to flee to their ancestral homelands around the Inland Sea. The Minamoto achieved final victory in the battle of Dan-no-Ura, one of the most famous in Japanese history, in which most of the Taira were slaughtered and the child emperor Antoku was forced to commit suicide by jumping into the sea along with his grandmother, the widow of Kiyomori, and the women of the Taira court.

Establishment of Kamakura Bakufu

The Minamoto had long been building their own institutions of warrior rule in Kamakura, a city in the eastern Kanto plain. Under Yoritomo, the age of warrior government—the medieval period of Japanese history—was set to begin. There were three shogunates in Japanese history: the first established by the Minamoto in Kamakura; the Muromachi bakufu established by the Ashikaga shoguns in Kyoto during the fourteenth and fifteenth centuries; and the Tokugawa bakufu, which ruled from the seventeenth to the mid-nineteenth century from the city of Edo (now Tokyo). The source of bakufu authority, however, remained the imperial court. As noted above, the title of Shogun made Minamoto no Yoritomo the military protector of court privileges. The court accepted the bakufu as an agent concerned with maintaining discipline in the warrior order, headed by Yoritomo and his vassals.

Because his control of military vassals and allies relied on the ability to provide them with material rewards (e.g., confiscated lands) for their services, Yoritomo had to strike a balance, obtaining new prizes to distribute to followers while maintaining and protecting enough of the court's privileges for them to retain him as their shogun. Thus, he didn't attempt to replace the existing system of court governance but added another layer to meet the needs of the rising warrior class. Yoritomo sent his army to the capital to "request" that the court establish two new official posts: a military governor for each province *(shugo)* and a military steward for each of the great private shōen estates *(jitō)*. These officials were in control of all military and police affairs in the province or estate and were entitled to collect a tax for the service. The tax was assessed on all cultivated land, whether public or private. This radical step meant that no longer were there estates completely immune from taxes, and the warrior class could begin to siphon off the wealth of the noble families and temples.

Yoritomo appointed his most trusted vassals to these posts. Over time these officials increased their own duties and powers. They collected not only the military tax due to the bakufu, but all taxes due on lands under their charge, remitting the proceeds to the owners after subtracting a portion for themselves. They also carried out land reclamation, supervised roads and post stations, arrested criminals, and judged lawsuits. In this way, they slowly replaced the officials and authority of the civilian governors appointed by the court. In Kamakura, Yoritomo established three main branches of government: the military, the administrative, and the judicial, each headed by trusted vassals. These offices were responsible for dividing war booty among vassals, handling disputed claims, administering justice, and maintaining law and order. The judicial branch was particularly noteworthy for its scrupulous examination of evidence and precedents in deciding claims, which were often complicated by the system of dividing the proceeds of estates among numerous holders of *shiki,* or rights to income.

Yoritomo died in 1199 and was succeeded by his two sons, Yoriie and Sanetomo, but they were dominated by Yoritomo's wife, Hōjō Masako, a formidable woman who had taken Buddhist vows after the death of her husband and became known as the "nun shogun." For more than a hundred years, Hōjō regents controlled the titular shogun, just as the Fujiwara regents had controlled the emperors. Under the Hōjō, the shoguns themselves were of little importance. After the end of Yoritomo's line, Masako adopted a Fujiwara baby to be appointed shogun. Thus, in the thirteenth century, Japan's government structure was quite convoluted—a dual polity in which an emperor reigned in Kyoto, but his little remaining authority was actually controlled by retired emperors, while real power was exercised by a shogun in Kamakura, who was actually controlled by a Hōjō hereditary advisor. The Hōjō were, however, competent administrators who compiled a practical and effective formal code of law and believed in efficient government, strictly supervising their military constables and stewards. They established a branch of the bakufu in Kyoto to keep the court under surveillance and intervened in court matters like the imperial succession. The Hōjō also assumed authority in foreign affairs, organizing the defense of the country in the face of Mongol invasions in 1274 and 1281.

One feature of the early Kamakura regime was its simplicity and austerity. Founder Yoritomo kept his headquarters in Kamakura, far from Kyoto, because he believed the luxurious lifestyles and expensive cultural pursuits of the capital were a waste of resources. Minamoto vassals were encouraged to be frugal and industrious. As puppet shoguns were appointed from court families and moved to Kamakura, however, they brought courtly tastes that didn't correspond with the austere military virtues idealized by Yoritomo. As arts and culture became highly valued in the shogun's household, they also began to spread among the warrior elite.

The court, seeing more and more of its authority and income slip away to the warriors, made several attempts to recover their power. In 1221, retired emperor Go-Toba trained some of his own troops and proclaimed the Hōjō rebels, but he was easily crushed and banished to a remote island. This victory gave the Hōjō new powers over the court; they could now punish or exile nobles and even emperors, and they assumed full control over the imperial succession. They confiscated over three thousand estates from the ex-emperor and his supporters, which allowed them to appoint and reward more of their vassals to official positions.

The Mongol Invasions

In the mid-thirteenth century, the Mongols controlled an empire that stretched from Korea to Europe. They seized control of China, and their leader, Kublai Khan (grandson of Genghis Khan) claimed the title of emperor, establishing the Yuan dynasty (1280–1368), the first alien dynasty to rule China. Korea docilely accepted Mongol vassaldom, and the Khan expected Japan to similarly submit to his rule. In 1268, he sent a letter to the "king of Japan," delivered to both the Hōjō in Kamakura and the emperor in Kyoto. The letter threatened war if Japan did not consent to Mongol rule. The bakufu refused to answer and continued to ignore increasingly menacing dispatches sent over the next five years. In 1274 the Mongols sailed from Korea with a fleet of around 450 ships manned by Mongolian and Korean troops. They sailed to Kyushu, capturing the islands of Tsushima and Iki en route. Local warriors tried to defend their shores but suffered heavy losses. Fortunately for the Japanese, a huge typhoon destroyed much of the Mongol fleet, and the remaining ships retreated to Korea. But Kublai Khan had not abandoned his desire to rule Japan. He summoned the Japanese again, demanding that they pay him homage at his court. The bakufu responded by beheading the Khan's messengers. For the next several years the Mongols were preoccupied with their own affairs in China, and the bakufu used this opportunity to prepare for the next invasion by building fortifications at potential landing points, installing a coastal watch, and shoring up loyalty among its vassals, promising rewards to all who fought and threatening severe punishment for those who refused.

The Mongols launched their second attack in the spring of 1281, sending two separate forces totaling 140,000 troops on a fleet of over four thousand ships. The Japanese defense forces were heavily outnumbered, but their intensive preparations helped them battle the Mongols for two months. The weather, once again, proved Japan's ally; another massive, two-day typhoon arose in Kyushu in August, wrecking the bulk of the Mongol fleet. The storms that had saved the Japanese were thought to be a gift from the gods—a *kamikaze*, or divine wind, a term later used for World War II pilots who sacrificed their lives in suicide missions against enemy ships in order to protect the nation.

The Mongol war impoverished the bakufu. Heavy expenditures were needed to build and maintain fortifications. Vassals and military supporters who fought the Mongols expected material rewards, but the bakufu had gained no new sources of income, as it was a defensive campaign. When the

FIGURE 13. Scene from the Mongol invasions on an illustrated scroll, thirteenth century. Source: Wikimedia Commons.

Hōjō failed to deliver on their promises, many warrior families became disgruntled. Court nobles spied a potential opportunity to plot against Kamakura using these dissatisfied warrior families.

Kemmu Restoration and Muromachi Bakufu

In 1318, Go-Daigo (1288–1339) ascended to the imperial throne and made clear that he intended to overthrow the shogunate and regain imperial prerogatives. He enlisted the support of several disgruntled warrior families in the east and west, including the Ashikaga clan. In 1333, Go-Daigo's allies captured and burned the city of Kamakura. Regent Hōjō Takatoki and more than two hundred of his vassals killed themselves rather than surrender. In this series of events, referred to as the Kemmu Restoration, Japan returned to direct imperial rule, with Kyoto once again acting as the single seat of the government. This situation, however, didn't last long; in just three years, the warriors turned against the emperor for failure to properly reward their services. Ashikaga Takauji (1305–58) assumed the title of Shogun and forced Go-Daigo to flee Kyoto, installing in his place Emperor Kōmyō, a member of the rival imperial lineage. Go-Daigo and his supporters established a Southern Court in the mountains of Yoshino, near Nara, ushering in fifty years of ideological battle over whether Go-Daigo's Southern Court or the Northern Court backed by the Ashikaga was the legitimate source of imperial authority.

The new Ashikaga shogunate (1336–1573) established its headquarters in Kyoto rather than Kamakura. It is also known as the Muromachi bakufu, named for the neighborhood in which the third Ashikaga shogun, Yoshimitsu (1358–1408), built his stronghold, the poetically named Palace of Flowers. In contrast to the Kamakura bakufu, which coexisted with the court in a balance of power between the warriors in the eastern part of the country and the courtiers in the west, the Ashikaga took over court privileges in Kyoto. The capital was thronged with soldiers, and the military elites immersed themselves in the culture of the court, aspiring to emulate its elegance, while treating the courtiers themselves with contempt. The Ashikaga shoguns thus lived in luxury, supporting the arts and the intricacies of court hierarchy rather than concentrating on affairs of state. Kamakura shoguns had been satisfied with modest court ranks, but the Ashikaga took the highest offices of court and lived in keeping with this position. When Yoshimitsu abdicated in 1395, he retired to his luxurious villa, known today as the Golden Pavilion (Kinkakuji), where he continued to rule behind the scenes, just like the cloistered emperors of earlier years.

After the fall of the Mongol dynasty, Yoshimitsu reestablished regular embassies to China's new rulers, the Ming. China once again became a model for cultural emulation, as well as a source of Ashikaga income from controlling trade with the Ming. The bakufu built many new seaports to support China-related trade and commerce. Nevertheless, the Ashikaga grip on national power was never as firm as that of their Kamakura predecessors, because they possessed neither extensive landholdings nor their own significant military power. They had to rely instead on the cooperation and loyalty of the shugo constables they appointed to govern the provinces. Many of these shugo began to exercise power autonomously within their landholdings. A chronicle of this period called the *Taiheiki* said of the constables: "Now all matters great and small were determined by the Shugo, who was master of the fortunes of his province, treated the (Bakufu) stewards and vassals like servants, and forcibly took over the manors of shrines and monasteries using them as a source of military supplies."[1]

Strong Ashikaga shoguns could dominate the coalition of warriors, but under the weaker shoguns the local warriors competed among themselves to extend their local power bases, resulting in nearly constant warfare. In 1467, war erupted between rival leagues of shugo constables supporting different candidates for the shogunal succession. The Ōnin War was a ten-year conflict that laid much of Kyoto to waste and escalated into a nationwide war, ushering in a century of sporadic warfare known as Sengoku jidai (the age of warring provinces), to be discussed in chapter 5.

RELIGION IN MEDIEVAL JAPAN

From the late twelfth century onward, revivals within different sects of Buddhism increasingly extended the promise of salvation beyond the elites to the masses. Reform and revival were championed by monks critical of the established Buddhist sects for catering to the elite, breaking vows, and engaging in commerce. They believed in mappō, the idea that the world had entered a stage of spiritual decline, and thought this could be seen in the degeneration in monastic life. In the age of mappō, the old paths to religious salvation by self-effort through meditation, textual study, and good works would not be enough even for monks to attain salvation. Buddhist reformers sought new and easier paths to salvation that might benefit all of society.

A long autobiographical essay from 1212, *Hōjōki* (An account of my hut, or The ten-foot-square hut), illustrates how some individuals responded to living under mappō; it is considered a masterpiece of Japanese literature. The author, Kamo no Chōmei (1153–1216), began his career as a poet at the imperial court. In the *Hōjōki*, he describes the advantages of a life of isolation and tranquility compared to the turbulence, hazards, and upheavals of life in the capital. The essay provides both historical and philosophical perspectives on life in thirteenth-century Japan. Historically it describes a series of disasters that hit the city of Kyoto in rapid succession: a great fire, a whirlwind, a famine, and an earthquake, all while the war between the Taira and Minamoto clans was plaguing the capital. In the midst of such chaos, the author decides to renounce the world; but rather than entering a Buddhist monastery, he becomes a hermit living in a small hut in the wilderness, where he contemplates nature and the seasons, writes, plays music, and reads Buddhist texts. The *Hōjōki* elegantly celebrates the pleasures and virtues of this simple life, away from the turmoil in Kyoto. It is deeply infused with Buddhist ideas about the impermanence of life and the need to renounce worldly attachments to escape from the sufferings that characterize all of human existence. The opening lines of the *Hōjōki* are among the most familiar in Japanese literature:

> The flow of the river is ceaseless and its water is never the same. The bubbles that float in the pools, now vanishing, now forming, are not of long duration: so in the world are man and his dwellings. It might be imagined that the houses, great and small, which vie roof against proud roof in the capital remain unchanged from one generation to the next, but when we examine whether this is true, how few are the houses that were there of old. Some were burnt last year and only since rebuilt; great houses have crumbled into hovels and those who dwell in them have fallen no less. The city is the same, the people are as numerous as

ever, but of those I used to know, a bare one or two in twenty remain.
They die in the morning, they are born in the evening, like foam on
the water.[2]

Buddhist reformers established new traditions and sects: Pure Land (Jōdo
Shū) and True Pure Land (Jōdo Shinshū), based on faith in Amida; Nichiren
(Nichiren Shū), based on faith in the *Lotus Sutra;* and Zen, which centered
on the practices of seated meditation and contemplation of paradoxical word
puzzles known as *kōan.* These new schools shared certain features. In contrast with Shingon and Tendai, which advocated blends of meditation, practices and rituals, and textual study, they tended to focus on a single, simple
practice said to be the best and only route to salvation. In addition, they
tended to reject traditional monastic life as an ideal in favor of the life of the
layman, embedded in the family and community ideal. This was most evi-
dent in the Pure Land movements. Zen, on the other hand, reaffirmed the
importance of the monastic community, although it also encouraged lay
practice. Another common characteristic of the new Buddhist schools was
the strong, charismatic personality of the founder. In many cases, the
founder did not intend to establish a new, separate sect, but after his death
his followers multiplied, establishing new religious institutions that, over
time, became as powerful as the older Buddhist sects in Kyoto and Nara.

Faith in Amida and the *Lotus Sutra* on one hand, and Zen on the other,
also characterizes two main streams in Japanese Buddhism, Other Power
(tariki) and Self Power *(jiriki).* Other Power is characterized by pure, devout
faith in a deity or sutra that will help humans in their hour of need. By
reciting a prayer or mantra, like the nembutsu "Namu Amida Butsu," one
can be reborn in the Pure Land or attain religious salvation. By contrast,
religions emphasizing Self Power believe that one must take individual
responsibility for one's life—that to depend on some external power is an
escape rather than true salvation. Zen epitomizes such an approach, focusing on personal cultivation rather than devotion to a deity. This idea of Self
Power is illustrated in a Zen fable about a monk who, facing the piercing
winter cold in an old temple, burned a wooden statue of the Buddha for
warmth. When criticized for his sacrilegious action, he pointed out that he
was cold and that the statue was nothing more than an ordinary piece of
wood. Adherents of Other Power religions such as Pure Land, however,
think that the idea of Self Power is an example of human arrogance and
egotism in a universe where much remains unexplained.

During the Heian period, belief in Amida's Western Paradise had been
one school of thought within Tendai. It was adopted by many court elites
who commissioned elegant statues, *raigō* paintings, and temple buildings as

testaments to their faith. In the medieval era, reformer-monks broke with Tendai, establishing schools dedicated solely to Pure Land devotionalism. They believed that faith in Amida was the singular route to salvation and should be open to all men and women, no matter how poor, uneducated, or sinful. Hōnen (1133–1212), who established the Pure Land School, believed that one must constantly chant the nembutsu as the surest way to salvation. As a Tendai monk at Mount Hiei, one day he read a passage from a Chinese Pure Land master that urged adherents to focus solely on the nembutsu; thinking of Amida during every waking moment was the surest path for obtaining rebirth in the Pure Land. Hōnen discarded all other Tendai beliefs and rituals for the sole practice of chanting the nembutsu. His revolutionary approach was strongly opposed by the other monks of Enryakuji, who thought they were being criticized for not meeting the needs of the mappō era. Hōnen left Mount Hiei and settled in Kyoto, where he began to gather followers. The powerful temples and monasteries tried to ban the nembutsu and persecute the new faith, but the simplicity of the practice attracted large numbers of both lay and monastic devotees.

Hōnen's disciple Shinran (1173–1263), also a Tendai priest, founded the True Pure Land school of Buddhism. Rather than his master's call to constantly chant the nembutsu day and night, he argued that one single, truly sincere invocation, expressing complete surrender of the self to Amida, was adequate for gaining rebirth in the Pure Land. Shinran also believed that in the time of mappō, Buddhist monks were unable to keep their vows. Meat consumption was common among the clergy, although forbidden by their vows. Monks evaded the prohibition by removing their outer robes before eating meat, but Shinran refused to even remove his robe. He also eschewed monks' vows of celibacy, marrying and fathering seven children. Shinran's attitudes foreshadowed Buddhist practices in modern Japan, with priests who commonly marry and pass their temples and positions on to their heirs.

Another monk of the Pure Land tradition, Ippen Shōnin (1234–89), established the Ji (Time) sect in the late thirteenth century. Wanting to ensure that the message of the Pure Land was carried to the ordinary people, he spent his life as an itinerant preacher, wandering throughout Japan with a band of monks and nuns. They distributed amulets to all they met and encouraged them to chant the nembutsu, often in group sessions that also involved ecstatic dancing. Female disciples were entrusted with the same tasks as the male, including the authority to conduct memorial services and run local practice halls. They and other Pure Land preachers delivered the message that women, not just men, could achieve salvation. Ippen's peripatetic life is the subject of one of the finest medieval scroll paintings, *The Life of Ippen the Holy Wanderer.*

Itinerant preachers extended Pure Land faith throughout remote regions and among all sectors of society from the thirteenth to the sixteenth century. Unlike the wealthy Buddhist institutions of Nara and Kyoto, Pure Land evangelists needed to proselytize directly among the commoners in order to solicit donations. In addition to chanting and dancing sessions, many delivered pictorial sermons *(etoki)*, using a pointer and large, highly detailed mandala paintings depicting Buddhist paradises and hells, or narrative paintings illustrating tales of Buddhist saints and miracles. By the sixteenth century, Pure Land sects were as firmly established as the earlier schools of Buddhism but drew their support from a larger cross section of society than the Nara and Heian sects that relied on elite and state support.

Another reformist school adopted the Tendai emphasis on the *Lotus Sutra*. Established by the monk Nichiren (1222–82), this school advocated chanting a different sacred invocation, "Namu Myōhō Renge kyō" (Hail to the Mysterious Law of the Lotus Sutra), as the only means to achieve salvation in the age of mappō. The sect he founded is Japan's only major Buddhist school that did not originate in China. Unlike other founders of medieval sects, Nichiren was not a member of the elite courtier or warrior classes. He was born in a remote eastern province to a family of fishermen. At age twelve, he entered a Tendai temple near his home and studied Pure Land teachings. At seventeen, he embarked on a tour of the famous temples in Kamakura and Kyoto but felt alienated by the grandeur of the elite-sponsored Buddhism he found there. Dissatisfied with Pure Land doctrine, Nichiren became a devotee of the *Lotus Sutra* instead and saw his mission as returning Tendai to its original advocacy of the *Lotus Sutra* as the ultimate vehicle of deliverance.

Nichiren was a fierce, controversial figure who attacked rival schools and criticized the court and bakufu for supporting other Buddhist institutions. Following a series of natural calamities from 1257 to 1260, Nichiren told the shogun that these were caused by the growing popularity of evil sects and prophesied that unless all people, from the ruling classes to the masses, paid homage to the *Lotus Sutra*, the calamities would continue. In 1268, when the bakufu received the first letter from the Mongols demanding Japan's submission, Nichiren claimed this was proof of his earlier prophecy. Because of such brash opinions, he was sent into exile on remote Sado Island. Unchastened and fearless, he built a devoted following among warriors and farmers throughout northern and central Japan. His followers shared his zealous, uncompromising stance. Rivalries developed between his devotees and followers of the Pure Land faith, resulting in battles between the two sides during the mid-sixteenth century (see chapter 5). Incidentally, Nichirenism is the forerunner of one of the largest Japanese religious movements today, Sōka Gakkai, established in 1938 and achieving massive growth in the 1950s (see chapter 11).

Meditation was already a part of many Buddhist traditions, but in Zen, intensive seated meditation *(zazen)* was believed to be the single most efficacious way to religious salvation—just as the nembutsu was for the Pure Land school and the *Lotus Sutra* was for Nichiren. The first advocates of Zen in Japan were Tendai monks who traveled to China in the twelfth century looking for a means to revitalize Buddhism in Japan. Chinese Zen (Ch'an) developed in a strict monastic setting that stressed intensive communal meditation as the core of monastic life and used aids to help achieve enlightenment, such as contemplating kōan. When these reformers returned, they met resistance from Tendai leaders, so they sought new patrons to give Zen an independent identity. Luckily, in the late twelfth and thirteenth centuries, the warrior class had come into power. They wished to establish their own source of spiritual authority, separate from the Buddhist sects patronized by the court. Thus, the shogunate and elite warrior families became the primary patrons of Zen, and Kamakura developed into an important Zen center.

Many warriors were attracted by the discipline and directness of Zen training, the rigor of meditation, and the possibility of personal enlightenment. In contrast with the Other Power of Pure Land or Nichiren, Zen taught that enlightenment could be attained here and now by one's own efforts. Achieving this was not helped by methodical, rational methods like studying sutras; the best path to enlightenment was through meditation, the means used by the Buddha himself. Intensive zazen meditation could break through the delusions of the senses and of the rational mind to grasp one's own Buddhahood directly and spontaneously.

Two main schools of Zen were established during Japan's medieval period. Rinzai, introduced by the monk Eisai (1141–1215), who is credited with popularizing green tea in Japan, emphasized "sudden enlightenment," centering on the use of kōan—stories, dialogues, or phrases that include absurd or contradictory statements, intended to force the mind to abandon rational thinking. Zen masters tested their disciples' progress through question-and-answer sessions using kōan. In the West, kōan are often characterized as unanswerable riddles; the best-known examples are "What is the sound of one hand clapping?" and "Does a dog have Buddha-nature?" Kōan study is better described, however, as a method for understanding the recorded sayings of past Zen masters or comprehending the world from an enlightened point of view. Progress in kōan study was a standardized process, following a set curriculum. Zen masters expected their students to deliver fixed, correct responses. Collections of and commentaries on kōan, such as the twelfth-century *Blue Cliff Record,* form an important body of Zen literature. The following example is from *The Gateless Gate,* a thirteenth-century collection of forty-nine kōan and commentary on them by a Ch'an master known in Japan as Mumon Ekai.

NANSEN KILLS THE CAT

The Case

Once the monks of the eastern and western Zen halls in Master Nansen's temple were quarrelling about a cat. Nansen held up the cat and said, "You monks! If one of you can say a word, I will spare the cat. If you can't say anything, I will put it to the sword." No one could answer, so Nansen finally slew it. In the evening when Jōshū returned, Nansen told him what had happened. Jōshū thereupon took off his sandals, put them on his head, and walked off. Nansen said: "If you had been there, I could have spared the cat."

Mumon's Commentary

What is the meaning of Jōshū putting his sandals on his head? If you can give a turning word concerning this matter, you will be able to see that Nansen's command was not meaningless. But if you can't, look out! Danger!

The Verse

Had Jōshū been there,

He would have given the command instead;

Had he snatched away the sword,

Even Nansen would have begged for his life.[3]

While this story may seem illogical, Zen adherents believe that it expresses obvious truths to those who have experienced true Zen realization. It was the responsibility of the Zen master, part of a lineage of teachers that could reportedly be traced to the historical Buddha, to gauge whether students had achieved such realization.

Under the patronage of shoguns and warriors, Rinzai Zen built up a system of several hundred officially sponsored monasteries in Kamakura, in Kyoto, and throughout the provinces. They became centers for the cultivation of Zen-related arts like landscape gardening, calligraphy and ink painting, and tea ceremony (described later in this chapter).

The other primary school of Zen is Sōtō, introduced from China by Dōgen (1200–1253), who emphasized that zazen meditation, which he called "just sitting," was the core of Zen practice. Dōgen rejected the official patronage that tied Rinzai to the ruling elite, and he established his temple Eiheiji in rural Fukui prefecture, far from the distractions of Kamakura and Kyoto. Development of meditative self-awareness in Sōtō was not limited to formal zazen sessions, but might also be pursued while engaged in the mundane activities of everyday life—working, eating, walking, and resting. In his work *Tenzo kyōkun* (Instructions for the cook), Dōgen explained the daily duties of monastery cooks in detail, emphasizing the opportunities for practicing mindfulness, such as in the following excerpt: "When washing the rice, remove any sand you find. In doing so, do not lose even one grain of rice. When you look at the rice see the sand at the same time; when you look at the sand, see also the rice. Examine both carefully. Then a meal containing the six flavors and three qualities will come together naturally."[4]

After Dōgen's death, Sōtō teachings and practices expanded to incorporate folk beliefs, prayers for material benefits, and elements of esoteric Buddhism, giving Sōtō more popular appeal among ordinary people than Rinzai. It spread widely among farmers and local samurai in northern Japan.

ARTS AND CULTURE OF THE WARRIOR CLASS

As the warrior class gained political power, it began to set the norms for society and culture. Warrior ideals were expressed in the concept of balance between *bun* and *bu*, the arts of peace and the arts of war. On one hand, elite warriors should be adept practitioners of bu—the martial arts, especially the way of the bow and arrow, but also including the sword. Idealized warrior ethics and behaviors, including heroism, loyalty, and willingness to die for your lord, were fostered and promoted in epic war tales like *The Tale of the Heike*, though not necessarily practiced among fighting men. The rising martial class patronized craftsmen who made weapons, armor, helmets, and horse trappings that reached sophisticated new technical and aesthetic levels. The blades of deadly swords and daggers were increasingly decorated with elaborate carvings; their fittings were luxurious, including sharkskin-wrapped handles and lacquered scabbards with special pockets for chopsticks and hair-arranging tools. Armor, traditionally made of leather and lacquer to withstand the weather, began to incorporate iron and steel plates to provide better protection from muskets.

On the other hand, elite warriors responsible for serving in official posts also had to master bun—the skills of governance and administration that involved literacy and cultural attainment. Rural, low-ranking samurai by

FIGURE 14.   Samurai armor and helmet, mid-fourteenth century, The
Metropolitan Museum of Art, New York, Gift of Bashford Dean, 1914. Source:
ARTstor Images for Academic Publishing.

no means possessed the time or resources to become literate and cultured, but as the military class rose in status, warrior elites learned to enjoy the cultural pastimes necessary for interaction with courtiers and high-ranking monks. They participated on equal terms in literary salons and became great patrons of artists and dramatists.

Nevertheless, the warrior class also held their own spiritual and cultural aspirations, modeled after, but divergent from, the court nobility. Older Buddhist sects in Kyoto, like Shingon and Tendai, were associated with the court, and the shoguns desired their own, separate forms of religious legitimation and power. Zen priests acted as their advisors, and Zen ideals, alongside those of Confucianism, deeply influenced many aspects of warrior society, including the arts. Many of the major arts associated with the medieval period, including ink painting, landscape gardens, Nō drama, and tea ceremony (discussed in chapter 5), are regarded as parts of a distinctive Zen culture governed by aesthetic tastes for abstraction, simplicity, and asymmetricality, along with a preference for things that look earthy, faded, or neglected *(wabi* or *sabi)*. A meditative aesthetic of stillness and mystery, or *yūgen,* found in Nō, was felt to inspire the eternal and the profound. Such tastes represented a departure from the aesthetic preferences of the Heian-era courtiers, who favored colorful, lavish decorative styles and more lighthearted entertainment. The age of warriors and warfare sharpened the sense of life's insecurities and sorrows, and the aesthetics valued in the era reflected this shift, from the luxury of courtiers to the spare, lean mode favored by warriors.

Zen Painting and Calligraphy

Zen masters patronized by the warrior class were often accomplished ink painters and calligraphers. In a sense, Zen ink paintings can be characterized as both impressionistic and expressionistic. While presenting abstract or idealized impressions of natural scenery, the medium of ink, which instantly creates an image that cannot be corrected, is thought to express the artist's inner self and spiritual energy, conveyed via the vitality or subtlety of his brushwork.

With renewed ties to China, monks traveled regularly between Japan and the continent, and Rinzai Zen monasteries became centers of Chinese learning and arts. The Japanese artists built upon the monochrome ink-painting *(sumi-e)* techniques they learned there, epitomized by the sumi-e masters of the Song dynasty (960–1279). The simplicity and austerity of paintings using only black ink appealed to both the Zen monks and their warrior patrons. Song painters used scant strokes on vertical scrolls to depict birds and plants like bamboo and orchids; their impressionistic land-scapes of pines and craggy cliffs are particularly impressive. The Japanese drew upon Song compositions but also executed their works in larger for-mats, on large folding screens *(byōbu)* or sliding paper doors *(fusuma)* enclosing entire rooms of villas and palaces (see chapter 5).

One of the greatest Japanese masters of ink painting was the fifteenth-century Zen priest Shūbun (?–1460), considered the founder of the Japanese-Chinese style of "mind-landscape" painting, depicting imagined visions of natural settings in China. This style features a distinctive use of space, eschewing the depiction of distinct foregrounds, backgrounds, and middle distances employed by Song masters in favor of a more abstract approach with an expansive sense of space, in which mountains, cliffs, trees, and other elements in the painting appear to float unanchored. Unfortunately, few of Shūbun's work are extant.

Shūbun's disciple Sesshū (1420–1506) became the best-known master of Japanese ink landscapes. Sesshū was also a Rinzai Zen priest and excelled in multiple styles and subject matter, including flowers, birds, and portraiture along with landscape. Sesshū's works employed the choppy, bold brush-work of Song ink painters and their structured compositions of space, rejected by his master. Nevertheless, he retained some of the abstract qual-ities of Shūbun's work. In *Winter Landscape,* strange, unidimensional shadows of mountains in the background contrast with the boldly drawn hills, trees, and castle in the foreground and middle ground, and an unex-plained, irregular black line dominates the center of the painting. Paul Varley observed that *Winter Landscape* is "an abstract mosaic of surfaces that looks startlingly like the work of a modern cubist painter."[5] Sesshū is also associated with a style known as "broken-ink" *(haboku sansui)* that uses explosive splashes of ink, washes, and free brushstrokes to create abstracted scenes of nature. His disciples Sōen (1489–1500) and Tōshun (1506–42) inherited and further developed the *haboku* landscape style.

Zen Gardens

The imperial palaces and the residences of Heian nobility were built around carefully designed gardens that included streams and ponds with fishing pavilions, where courtiers often composed their poetry, using the garden for inspiration. They sometimes floated their poems on the ponds and along the streams. During the medieval age, a new variety of garden evolved that used rocks, water, and plant life to depict a "nature-scape," a life-sized land-scape represented on a miniaturized scale. Zen gardeners experimented with new and abstract ways to use rocks and sand in dry landscape gardens

FIGURE 15. Sesshū, *Winter Landscape,* fifteenth century, Tokyo National Museum. Source: Wikimedia Commons.

(karesansui) where gravel, sand, moss, and stones replaced altogether not just water, but flowers, plants, and trees. Rocks of varying shapes and textures were used to represent both natural features, such as mountains and waterfalls, and man-made structures such as bridges. Sand, gravel, or pebbles were painstakingly raked into wavy and circular patterns that represented water.

The new approach to gardening was associated with the Rinzai Zen priest Musō Soseki (1275–1351), the abbot of Nanzenji Temple in Kyoto, reportedly the designer of the famous Moss Garden at Saihōji, which contains over 120 varieties of lush moss, and the renowned gardens of Tenryūji—both designated UNESCO World Heritage sites. Tenryūji's rock gardens are arranged so that visitors can enjoy changing scenery while walking around the central pond. Boulders and stones symbolize a waterfall cascading into the pond and carp within it. The views of two hills outside of the garden are incorporated into the overall design in a technique known as *shakkei* that integrates background scenery into the garden plan.

The most famous Zen dry landscape garden, thought to be the work of the artist Sōami (1472–1525), is located at Ryōanji Temple in Kyoto. This garden represents an ocean with islands protruding above the surface and consists of a flat rectangular surface of white gravel, raked into straight lines, with fifteen boulders scattered about singly and in clusters, surrounded by circles of raked gravel. The garden is meant to be viewed from a seated position on the adjoining veranda, and its stones are arranged so that one can view only fourteen of the fifteen from any given angle. Legend has it that one can view the final boulder only after attaining enlightenment. Sōami is also credited with the remarkable sand garden of the Silver Pavilion, shogun Ashikaga Yoshimasa's retirement villa. In this garden, alternate bands of raked and smooth sand and gravel lead to a carefully formed, massive pile of sand with a flattened top, thought to represent the sacred Mount Fuji.

Two fundamental principles in designing Zen gardens are the recreation of natural habitat and the attempt to appeal to the intuitive, less rational side of the viewer. The abstract nature of dry landscape gardens allowed visitors to engage their imagination in conjuring up the natural scene represented by the garden. Zen monks also considered dry gardens an aid in attaining enlightenment, gained not only through zazen meditation or by studying kōan, but also in the mindful performance of simple, daily tasks such as the peeling of vegetables for a monastic meal or the meticulous labor required to rake the sand and gravel in these gardens.

FIGURE 16.   Ryōanji Temple rock garden. Courtesy of JNTO.

Nō Drama

Another arena of artistic development related to Zen-based aesthetics is Nō, the oldest extant form of Japanese theater, originating in the fourteenth century. A Nō performance consists of solemn, highly ritualized dance, drama, and music centered on a masked main character *(shite)* who usually represents an incarnation or ghost of a past historical figure returning to a site of significance in his or her life. The shite harbors a powerful emotion such as jealousy, rage, or sorrow that prevents him or her from finding spiritual release after death. The main character's true identity is revealed over the course of the play. The stories presented in Nō dramas, drawn from multiple sources including folk tales, *The Tale of Genji*, and *The Tale of the Heike*, are suffused with Buddhist themes such as karma, rebirth, suffering, and impermanence.

The actors speak and sing in poetic verse, accompanied by a small chorus. Rhythm and pacing are very important, following a pattern of a stately introduction *(jo)*, mounting through the exposition of the play *(ha)*, and culminating in a fast, intense finale *(kyū)*. This jo-ha-kyū rhythm is a foundation of many other Japanese arts, from linked verse poetry *(renga)* to tea ceremony to martial arts like kendo. The dance, drama, and rhythm

FIGURE 17.   Nō performance. Courtesy of JNTO.

of Nō are heightened by the music of the flute and drums and by the chanting of the chorus.

Costumes and especially masks are critical elements of Nō performance. Masks denote character types and include men and women of different ages, holy men, gods, and demons or spirits, corresponding to the five categories of Nō plays: gods, warriors, women, demons, and miscellaneous. In many plays, the main character switches masks to reveal his true character. For example, in *Aoi no ue,* based on an episode from *The Tale of Genji,* the beautiful mask of the main character, Genji's lover Rokujō, is traded for that of a horned demonic spirit (Hannya) that expresses her jealousy and sorrow over his unfaithfulness. One of the actor's challenges is expressing emotion while masked. This is particularly true of the female masks, which wear blank or neutral expressions in comparison to those of warriors and demons. Masks are carved and painted by master craftsmen, who are able to construct them in a manner that allows a slight change in expression when the actor tilts his head. Costumes are bulky and luxurious, consisting of at least five layers of robes, the outermost of rich damask, brocade, or embroidered silk, along with wigs, hats, and other headpieces.

The costumes are opulent, but other aspects of Nō share the austerity and abstraction that characterize other Zen-related arts. Stage props like boats, carriages, and huts are seldom more than abstract outlines of the objects. An actor's fan may be employed to represent a cup of sake or a weapon. The gestures of the actors are also spare and highly stylized—for example, a hand lifted in a certain position in front of the mask represents weeping. Many of the actors' movements, such as their distinctive walk, barely lifting the feet from the floor, can be seen in traditional martial arts, the tea ceremony, and the decorum expected of Zen priests. These Nō props and movements embody the economy of means and the preference for suggestion over realism valued by Zen.

The origins of Nō are attributed to various sources, including masked dances performed at shrines as ritual prayers for peace or abundant harvests, rustic forms of music and dance performed during rice-planting season *(dengaku)*, and acrobatic dance performances *(sarugaku)*. Their transformation into an elite art form is often identified with the relationship between the shogun Ashikaga Yoshimitsu and the gifted actor and playwright Zeami Motokiyo (1363–1443). In 1374, Yoshimitsu, then seventeen, attended the play *Okina*, performed at a shrine by a sarugaku troupe led by the actor Kan'ami, with his eleven-year-old son Zeami in a minor role. The shogun fell in love with the beautiful boy actor, a not uncommon phenomenon among samurai elites who, like the ancient Greeks, sometimes demonstrated erotic preferences for male youths. Yoshimitsu became the patron of Zeami and his troupe, but some viewed the shogun's favored treatment of the youth with disdain. When Yoshimitsu constructed a special platform so that he and Zeami could watch the spectacular floats of Kyoto's annual Gion Festival together, one court noble wrote:

> The Shogun was accompanied by a boy, a Yamato *sarugaku* player, who watched the festival from the Shogun's box. The Shogun, who has for some time bestowed his affection on this boy, shared the same mat and passed him food from his plate. These *sarugaku* performers are no better than beggars, but because this boy waits on the Shogun and is esteemed by him, everyone favors him. Those who give the boy presents ingratiate themselves with the Shogun. The daimyos and others vie to offer him gifts, at enormous expense. A most distressing state of affairs.[6]

In his twenties, having succeeded to the headship of his troop, Zeami began to attract acclaim for his acting skill. In his thirties, he began to author plays, including many of the most beloved classics of the Nō repertory, along with critiques and treatises on acting techniques. In these works he extolled yūgen, an aesthetic style characterized by mystery and depth, as the highest ideal of perfection in all arts, including Nō. To achieve yūgen in performances, Zeami urged actors to study poetry and costuming and to make certain that all of their visual and aural expressions were beautiful. After the fall of the Ashikaga bakufu, Nō remained a potent means for warriors to display their cultural patronage. At the end of the sixteenth century the great unifier Toyotomi Hideyoshi (see chapter 5), born a peasant, decided that studying and performing Nō was the best avenue for proving that he was not culturally inferior to nobles and priests. Other warrior elites were obliged to study Nō in order to stay in Hideyoshi's good graces. The founder of the third and last shogunate, Tokugawa Ieyasu, was also a patron and performer of Nō.

Other Literary and Visual Arts

During the medieval period, poetry continued to be considered an essential practice for members of the court. Emperor Go-Toba commissioned the eighth imperial anthology of poetry, the *Shinkokinshū*, which is considered the greatest Japanese poetry collection after the *Man'yōshū*. Six courtiers, including one of Japan's greatest poets, Fujiwara no Teika (1162–1241), completed the anthology, which contained nearly two thousand works of verse. Entries were organized in remarkable linked sequences, using similarities of word or expression to connect poems on a given topic, such as the season of spring, the experience of travel, or the stages of love.

In his *Guide to the Composition of Poetry,* Teika advocated using the language of famous poets of earlier times, stating: "There are no teachers of Japanese poetry. But they who take the old poems as their teachers, steep their minds in the old style and learn their words from the masters of former time—who of them will fail to write poetry?"[7] Critics charged, however, that such sentiment resulted in works that lacked originality, used worn clichés, and evoked nostalgia, harkening back to the golden ages when courtiers enjoyed unquestioned dominance. Teika also compiled the *Hyakunin isshu,* an anthology of one hundred poems by one hundred different poets. This collection became the basis for a popular card game by the same name, still played by many Japanese during the New Year holiday.

The poems of the *Shinkokinshū* demonstrate a more melancholic and solemn tone than those of the Heian-era *Kokinshū*, which were more concerned with expressing elegance and wordplay. Two examples by the Buddhist priest Saigyō (1118–90), known for composing verse on long, solo journeys that later inspired Matsuo Bashō (see chapter 7), are particularly poignant:

In a tree standing
Beside a desolate field,
The voice of a dove
Calling to its companions—
Lonely, terrible evening.

Living all alone
In this space between the rocks
Far from the city,
Here, where no one can see me,
I shall give myself to grief.[8]

The most representative works of literature of the medieval period, however, are the war tales *(gunki mono)*, which provide much information on historical events and battles from the tenth to fourteenth centuries and relate the values and culture of the rising warrior class. Like the Greek epics *The Odyssey* and *The Iliad*, these tales were originally recited by blind monk-bards who memorized the stories and retold them with accompaniment on the biwa, a lute-like instrument. Most were not written down for many years after the actual events occurred. The best-known version of *The Tale of the Heike* was not recorded until 1371. War tales mixed historical fact and fiction; they were based on actual events but often embellished the exploits of individual warriors or introduced invented characters. In keeping with the shift toward warrior governance, the tales glorify courageousness and military valor, providing idealized and romanticized descriptions of warfare and accomplishments on the battlefield. They provide insights into the values of the rising warrior class, including the importance of loyalty to one's lord, to the extent of sacrificing one's family or one's own life to protect the lord. Tales valorize warriors who lead austere lifestyles, controlling their emotions and desires in the service of victory.

Such ideals would become the basis for the code of Bushidō—the way of the *bushi,* or samurai—which was not elaborated until centuries later, during a time of peace, as rationale for the status and privilege accorded a warrior class that no longer engaged in actual violence. War tales portrayed valiant warriors highly conscious of personal honor and status; when enemies encountered one another on the battlefield, each announced his lineage and accomplishments to determine whether he faced a worthy opponent. In reality, warfare was messier and more ruthless. Warriors readily engaged in deception and guerrilla tactics; they murdered the innocent and burned villages in pursuit of victory and reward.

The tales draw distinct portraits of the warrior and courtier classes. Since many tales were composed by courtiers, they offer unflattering comparisons between refined court manners and warrior brutality. This contrast is captured vividly in *The Tale of Hōgen*, which describes a one-night skirmish in 1156 between Taira and Minamoto forces called to Kyoto by Emperor Goshirakawa and retired emperor Sutoku to settle a dispute, resulting in the first warfare seen in the capital for three hundred years. In this tale, the warrior Minamoto no Tametomo describes his battle plan to Sutoku and his ministers, recommending a nighttime attack on Goshirakawa's palace, setting fire to three sides, and waiting to slaughter those who fled the fire from the fourth side. Minister of the Left Fujiwara no Yorinaga condemns the plan as "a crude scheme which is quite out of the question" because it is not fitting for a struggle between emperors to be settled by such underhanded and dishonorable tactics.[9]

The Tale of Heiji, recounting the 1159 Minamoto attack on Taira no Kiyomori's forces, then installed in the capital, provides an unusually graphic account of the warriors' wanton arson and slaughter of courtiers. Here, Minamoto no Yoshitomo engages in the very strategy Tametomo had advised, setting fire to the palace of Goshirakawa, now a retired emperor:

> The situation at the Sanjō Palace was beyond description. Soldiers were guarding all the gates, and flames were shooting up here and there. Wild flames filled the heavens, and a tempestuous wind swept up clouds of smoke. The nobles, courtiers and even the ladies-in-waiting of the women's quarters were shot down or slashed to death. . . . When they rushed out, so as not to be burned by the fire, they met with arrows. When they turned back, so that they would not be struck by the arrows, they were consumed by the flames. Those who were afraid of the arrows and terrified by the flames even jumped into the wells in large numbers, and of these, too, the bottom ones in a short time had drowned, those in the middle had been crushed to death by their fellows, and those on top had been burned up by the flames themselves. . . . How could anyone at all have saved himself?[10]

Warriors from the eastern provinces, associated with the Minamoto, were considered the fiercest—skilled horsemen able to draw the largest bows, capable of penetrating armor. Eastern warriors appeared especially battle-hardened when contrasted with the vassals of Taira no Kiyomori and the Ashikaga shoguns, who became soft from their pampered lifestyles in the capital. The difference between such "courtier-warriors" and their provincial opponents is poignantly illustrated in "The Death of Atsumori" episode of *The Tale of the Heike*, in which the young Taira commander Atsumori encounters Kumagai no Naozane, a Minamoto vassal. Atsumori is richly attired according to courtly tastes, "wearing a silk *hitatare* embroidered with cranes under delicately tinted green armor, a helmet with

FIGURE 18. Detail of a warrior and courtier from a scroll illustrating *The Tale of Heiji*, thirteenth century, Boston Museum of Fine Arts. Source: Wikimedia Commons.

spreading horns, a sword of gold fittings, and, on his back, arrows fletched with mottled feathers. He carried a lacquered, rattan-wrapped bow and rode a dappled gray with a gold-trimmed saddle."[11] Naozane roughly grabs Atsumori from his horse, pushing off his helmet to sever his head, but is taken aback when he sees a handsome youth with a powdered face and blackened teeth. He wishes to spare Atsumori's life but fears what the youth might suffer at the hands of his brutal comrades, so he beheads the boy himself with great regret. Among Atsumori's belongings is a flute that Emperor Toba had given to his grandfather; Naozane marvels that a warrior would bring such a refined possession to the battlefield. This episode was further immortalized in Zeami's classic Nō play *Atsumori*, in which the ghost of the young warrior appears to a priest, who is a reincarnation of Naozane, and declares that, though they were once enemies, they are now friends under Buddhist law.

The Tale of the Heike is the most renowned of the military tales. In the canons of premodern Japanese literature, it is considered second only to *The Tale of Genji*, and like *Genji*, its episodes have deeply influenced subsequent culture, serving as familiar material for Nō and Kabuki plays and for paintings and prints. In the modern era, these classics continue to inspire retellings in film, television, and manga comics. The epic spans many decades, providing a comprehensive account of the rise and fall of the Taira clan and their defeat by the Minamoto in the Genpei War. *Heike's* sympathies generally lie with the Taira. Although Taira no Kiyomori is portrayed as an arrogant tyrant and villain, the Taira as a whole are pitied as an aristocratic clan overpowered by the rough, provincial warriors of the Minamoto. Although the downfall of the Taira is presented tragically, as a military tale, *Heike* also extols martial values, lauding the Minamoto for their strategic skills, courage, and close ties between commanders and soldiers.

Heike is also deeply informed by religious beliefs. Important Buddhist motifs in the tale include karma and impermanence. The law of karma is especially illustrated through the figure of Kiyomori, whose hubris and evil acts lead to the ruination of his clan. Impermanence *(mujō)* is a notion crucial to both Buddhist belief and medieval Japanese values. It is the belief that human (and all) existence is transient, in a constant state of flux between growth and decay. Impermanence is illustrated in the rise and eventual downfall of even the most powerful of their day, as invoked in the famous opening passage of *Heike:* "The sound of the Gion Shōja bells echoes the impermanence of all things; the color of the *sala* flowers reveals the truth that the prosperous must decline. The proud do not endure, they are like a dream on a spring night; the mighty fall at last, they are as dust before the wind."[12]

The arts of portraiture and picture scrolls *(emakimono)* also made great strides during the medieval era. In the Heian period, individual features were portrayed generically rather than realistically, as too faithful a rendition might be considered rude. Around the twelfth century, however, portraits known as "likeness pictures" *(nise-e)* achieved greater fidelity to the features of their subjects. Fujiwara no Takanobu (1142–1205) specialized in large-scale portraits that not only captured the distinctive eyes, noses, and lips of his patrons, but imbued these with the very spirit of their subjects. His famous portrait of Minamoto no Yoritomo gave the shogun buckteeth and a somewhat bulbous nose, but there is no questioning the strength of Yoritomo's character behind his steely, focused gaze. Another artist, Bokusai, captured the likeness of the iconoclastic Zen master Ikkyū Sōjun (1394–1481) as tight-lipped, wary, and careworn but still exuding sharp intelligence. Artists often painted only the faces of their subjects, leaving the more generic clothing, bodies, and background to lesser craftsmen.

Hundreds of picture scrolls on a variety of subjects remain extant from the medieval era. Some, like the excerpts above from picture scrolls depicting the Mongol invasions and the Heiji rebellion, portray scenes of battle and warfare. These were known as masculine paintings (otoko-e) in contrast with the decorative feminine paintings (onna-e) described in chapter 3. In addition to such battle-centered narratives are picture scrolls based on

FIGURE 19. Fujiwara no Takanobu, *Portrait of Yoritomo*, thirteenth century, Jingoji Temple, Kyoto. Source: Wikimedia Commons.

episodes from popular novels or depicting a variety of religious topics, including the lives of religious leaders, the histories of famous temples and shrines, and the didactic paintings of Buddhist heavens and hells used by itinerant preachers. One of the most beloved picture scrolls is *Chōjū giga* (Pictures of frolicking animals), a set of four satirical ink monochrome scrolls depicting animals engaging in human behaviors, such as picnicking,

FIGURE 20. Detail from *Chōjū giga*, twelfth or thirteenth century, Kōzanji Temple, Kyoto. Source: Wikimedia Commons.

sumo wrestling, and engaging in religious rituals. These scrolls poke fun at the twelfth-century Buddhist clergy—in one scene a monkey priest chants in front of an altar of a Buddha, represented by a fat, bored-looking frog.

CHANGES IN ELITE WOMEN'S STATUS

During the Heian period, elite women were often quite powerful—they were educated and inherited property on par with their male counterparts, were able to hold land and office and operate independently from their husbands, and could pass on their inheritances to whomever they pleased. But rather than following the court custom of dividing property among sons and daughters alike, thus diluting a family's wealth over time, the new warrior elites engaged in primogeniture, selecting a single, male heir to inherent all of a family's property. By the fourteenth century, there was a marked decline in women's property rights.

Changes in patterns of marriage residence contributed to the decline in women's status. Among Heian courtiers, children traced their descent through their father's line but lived in the natal home of the mother. The father/husband might also reside there or might simply visit, but the maternal grandparents raised and controlled the children. Marriages among the powerful warrior houses were, by contrast, virilocal—that is, the couple lived in the natal home of the husband, where the bride was taken in as a daughter-in-law. In this way, the maternal natal family lost all control over the grandchildren and thus lost interest in maintaining a daughter's wealth, education, or other assets that might attract powerful husbands. By the sixteenth century, when elite warrior women married, they had no source of independent income, depending completely on the family of their husband for support; they no longer had the right to name an heir or take part in lawsuits.

Marriage ritual also underwent a fundamental change, from simple, domestic ceremonies—essentially the sharing of rice cakes at the hearth of the woman's house to formalize a sexual union—into an elaborate public arrangement between two houses. With the increase of virilocal residence among the warrior class, husbands' families began to dispatch palanquins, oxcarts, and bands of vassals to fetch the bride to their new home. Marriage ceremonies became increasingly elaborate. In the sixteenth century, Hōjō Ujimasa dispatched twelve palanquins, three thousand horses, and ten thousand vassals to retrieve his bride. Such marriage rituals were spectacles performed for an audience to demonstrate male success and power—they signaled that women were no longer relatively equal partners in the relationship, but pawns for political and military alliances between families. By the Tokugawa period (1600–1868), women in the ruling warrior class were economically, sexually, and ideologically subordinated to the males of their households. Under warrior rule, the perpetuation of the house *(ie)* through a line of male successors became the highest goal, making women useful primarily in a reproductive capacity, sometimes referred to dismissively as "borrowed wombs" valued primarily for their ability to produce male heirs. Among commoner classes such as farmers and artisans, however, women continued to work alongside their husbands and retained a greater degree of influence in household and family matters.

In summary, as the warrior class grew in power they usurped wealth and ruling prerogatives from the court. In 1185, the Minamoto established their own capital in Kamakura where shoguns and their regents ruled in a dual-polity system, with authority divided between themselves and the court. Sapped by the thirteenth-century Mongol invasions, the Minamoto regime was replaced by the weaker Ashikaga bakufu, based in Kyoto, who emulated courtiers' lives while the provinces descended into chaos and warfare, considered part of the age of mappō spiritual decline. In response to this ethos, several new schools of Buddhism emerged to meet the needs of the warrior and commoner classes by offering simple, direct methods for achieving salvation and enlightenment. As warrior elites became Zen patrons, aesthetic qualities associated with Zen, characterized by simplicity and solemnity, influenced many emerging forms of art and culture, including painting, drama, gardens, and poetry. The foremost military epic of the medieval age, *The Tale of the Heike,* idealizes warfare and martial values but infuses its episodes with Buddhist themes, such as karma and impermanence. In the subsequent era of civil war, values such as loyalty to one's lord were often disregarded in warriors' quests for more land and power.

FURTHER READING

Conlan, Thomas D. *From Sovereign to Symbol: An Age of Ritual Determinism in Fourteenth-Century Japan*. New York: Oxford University Press, 2011.

Farris, William W. *Heavenly Warriors: the Evolution of Japan's Military, 500–1300*. Cambridge, MA: Harvard, 1992.

———. *Japan's Medieval Population: Famine, Fertility, and Warfare in a Transformative Age*. Honolulu: University of Hawaii Press, 2006.

Goble, Andrew E. *Kenmu: Go-Daigo's Revolution*. Cambridge, MA: Harvard, 1996.

LaFleur, William R. *The Karma of Words: Buddhism and the Literary Arts in Medieval Japan*. Berkeley: University of California Press, 1986.

Mass, Jeffrey P. *The Origins of Japan's Medieval World: Courtiers, Clerics, Warriors, and Peasants in the Fourteenth Century*. Stanford, CA: Stanford University Press, 1997.

———. *Yoritomo and the Founding of the First Bakufu: The Origins of Dual Government in Japan*. Stanford, CA: Stanford University Press, 1999.

Oyler, Elizabeth, and Michael Watson. *Like Clouds or Mist: Studies and Translations of Nō Plays of the Genpei War*. Ithaca, NY: Cornell East Asia Series, 2013.

Payne, Richard K., ed. *Re-Visioning Kamakura Buddhism*. Honolulu: University of Hawaii Press, 1998.

Segal, Ethan I. *Coins, Trade, and the State Economic Growth in Early Medieval Japan*. Cambridge, MA: Harvard, 2011.

Souyri, Pierre F. *The World Turned Upside Down: Medieval Japanese Society*. New York: Columbia University Press, 2003.

Yiengpruksawan, Mimi H. *Hiraizumi: Buddhist Art and Regional Politics in Twelfth-Century Japan*. Cambridge, MA: Harvard, 1999.

RECOMMENDED FILMS

Gate of Hell (Jigokumon). 1953. Feature film directed by Kinugasa Teinosuke. Award-winning depiction of the tensions between courtiers and warriors under the reign of Taira no Kiyomori.

Mongol: The Rise of Genghis Khan. 2007. Feature film directed by Sergei Bodrov. Semi-historical epic about the early life of Genghis Khan.

Onibaba. 1964. Feature film directed by Shindō Kaneto. A horror film that depicts the travails of two women trying to survive amid the civil warfare surrounding the Kemmu Restoration.

Taira Clan Saga (Shin Heike monogatari). 1955. Feature film directed by Mizoguchi Kenji. Saga based on Yoshikawa Eiji's historical novel *Shin Heike monogatari,* by an iconic director.

Zen: Principles and Practices. 1986. Documentary film. Illustrates life in a Rinzai Zen monastery.

5　Disintegration and Reunification

1460s–Early 1600s

The years between 1467 and 1568 are known as Sengoku jidai (the age of warring provinces), a time of civil war, with battles fought at many levels of society. Around 1500, Japan was at the extreme of political decentralization; neither the imperial court nor the bakufu commanded national political authority or respect. Instead, more than 250 military strongmen, known as *daimyo*, ruled their own territories. Many of these daimyo had served as shugo constables in the provinces and converted these into domains under their control. During the latter third of the sixteenth century, after a century of warfare, an ambitious young daimyo, Oda Nobunaga (1534–82), began the process of reunifying the realm, a task carried on by his successors Toyotomi Hideyoshi (1536–98) and Tokugawa Ieyasu (1542–1616), the founder of the third and final bakufu. Each of these unifiers built on the accomplishments of their predecessors. This chapter describes the Sengoku era; policies undertaken by the three unifiers; and arts and material culture of the era, such as castle décor, tea ceremony, and flower arranging, that these military leaders cultivated to give their rule an air of legitimacy and civility. Many of these cultural pursuits retained connections to Buddhist philosophy and practice. The concluding portion of the chapter describes the arrival of the Europeans—first Portuguese and Spaniards who brought trade and Catholicism, then the Dutch and British. The intervention of Europeans deeply influenced the balance of power during Japan's age of civil war.

POLITICAL AND SOCIAL DEVELOPMENTS

The Ōnin War (1467–77), a decade-long conflict over shogunal accession that devastated the city of Kyoto and gutted the power of the Ashikaga bakufu, ushered in the century of warfare. The war was fought between eastern and western leagues of daimyo that descended upon Kyoto with tens of thousands of soldiers who ravaged the city, looting and setting temples and palaces ablaze. Courtiers and townspeople fled the chaotic capital, moving to provincial estates or to the strongholds of prominent daimyo, where they might be employed as artisans or instructors of courtly arts and culture. Remaining residents banded together to build fortifications around their neighborhoods. The conflict ended inconclusively and the Ashikaga bakufu remained nominally in power, although they were seriously weakened. Battles between daimyo and provincial warriors continued to rage in the countryside, and by 1500 the Ashikaga were shoguns in name alone, unable to control the capital city, let alone the provinces.

Toyotomi Hideyoshi described the Sengoku era as a time when "the country was divided, the polity disturbed, civility abandoned and the realm unresponsive to imperial rule."[1] During this era of insurrection, aristocratic or military lineage mattered less than martial and strategic skills; men of low birth overthrew their masters, peasants their landlords, and sons their fathers, to gain control over land in a phenomenon known as *gekokujō*, or "the lower-ranking overthrow the upper-ranking." The strongmen who ruled their local territories came from a variety of backgrounds and were called *daimyo* (big name), a title that continued into the third Tokugawa shogunate, designating the rulers of semiautonomous domains, or *han* (see chapter 6). Some daimyo had originally held court or shogunal appointments as local deputy governors, governors, or constables. They recruited bands of vassals from among the local warrior-landholder classes *(jizamurai)* who agreed to fight in return for protection of their own land rights, new rewards of land, or other compensation. Their forces pillaged, burned, and raped their way through enemy lands, but once the enemy was conquered, the daimyo sought to assert law and order and foster economic growth. They built military fortresses, often on bluffs and surrounded by moats, to secure and protect their territories.

Warfare was rampant, as daimyo fought over provincial domains and as petty local barons contended with each other and with the daimyo for territory. In Yamashiro, near Kyoto, the jizamurai ousted their daimyo, elicited peasant support through lower taxes, and held control of the province for a decade. Autonomous communes were built behind fortifications in other areas; residents refused to pay taxes and engaged in uprisings *(ikki)* and guerrilla warfare to protect their interests. Religious institutions maintained their militaries of monk soldiers *(sōhei)* and attacked daimyo or one another. Lay followers of the Ikkō (One Mind) sect of True Pure Land Buddhism engaged in large uprisings known as Ikkō ikki. Ikkō followers believed that all people were equal in the eyes of Amida, rejecting court and warrior hierarchies. They lived in a network of self-governing enclaves overseen by True Pure Land headquarters in Kyoto's Honganji Temple. In 1488, a league of Ikkō followers, composed of peasants allied with jizamurai and low-ranking clergy, seized control of Kaga province and ousted its governor—the first time in Japanese history that a province was controlled by commoners. Leaders promised non-follower peasants that they would lower rents and taxes in creating a new "estate of Buddha" *(Buppōryō)*, and the uprisings soon spread to neighboring areas. The urban version of the Ikkō ikki was found in Kyoto with the Lotus Leagues, militant groups of the Hokke sect of Nichiren Buddhism who provided security and support for commoners in the capital and demanded the abolition of taxes. Their more than twenty temple-fortresses, built in major cities, featured moats and embankments. They hoped to bring all of Kyoto under their control as the "Estate of the Lotus" but were defeated by a coalition between Enryakuji Temple on Mount Hiei and powerful daimyo from adjacent provinces. The campaign against the Lotus Leagues further ravaged large swaths of Kyoto and slaughtered many of its innocent residents.

The variety and complexity of Sengoku-era conflicts are illustrated by the Daishō Ikki (Big League–Little League War) of 1531, a civil war between two different factions within True Pure Land Buddhism, fighting for control of Kaga province. Neighboring daimyo, jizamurai, and believers from other provinces all participated in the conflict. The following year, the head temple, Honganji, was destroyed in Kyoto by an alliance of daimyo and the Lotus Leagues. The temple was reconstructed in Osaka as a powerful citadel from which the leader continued to issue calls for believers to rise against enemies of their faith.

Sengoku battles waged from 1490 to 1530 resulted in many large, self-governing domains headed by a daimyo clan. Over the next three decades these clans schemed, battled, and formed alliances to expand the territories under their control. The most common strategy for expansion had a dual character. Armies first engaged in scorched-earth tactics—burning, pillaging, murdering, and conscripting peasants in order to gain control over territory. Once this was achieved, however, lands were quickly pacified to return the populace to economically productive activity.

Villages began to develop their own defensive tactics against the rampant violence and robbery, building up barriers, increasing weaponry, and skillfully hiding crops and valuables. They played opposing daimyo sides against one another. One of director Kurosawa Akira's best-regarded films, *Seven Samurai* (1954), provides a fictionalized account of a sixteenth-

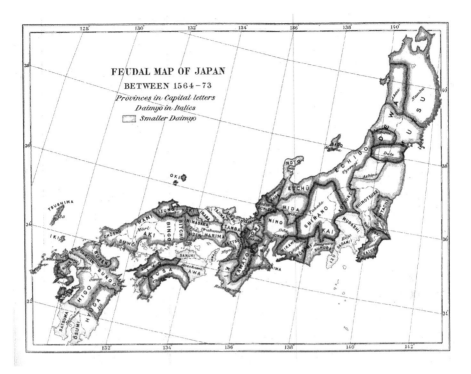

MAP 5. Sengoku daimyo domains in the mid-sixteenth century. From James Murdoch and Isoh Yamagata, *A History of Japan during the Century of Early Foreign Intercourse (1542–1651)* (London: Kegan Paul, Trench, Trübner & Co., 1926).

century farming village that hires a motley crew of masterless warriors *(rōnin)* to protect them.

By the 1550s, some of the most powerful clans—such as the Takeda, Go-Hōjō, and Mōri—could amass armies of fifty thousand or more and hoped to use regional victories in a drive for greater power over all of Japan. They watched for chances to take control of Kyoto, the imperial base from which they could assert control over central Japan. Tactical skill and strategic vision, not to mention military might, were required to gain the upper hand. The daimyo who first achieved such dominance over central Japan, however, was Oda Nobunaga, the young leader of the small province of Owari on the Pacific coast. Nobunaga proved himself a military genius in 1566 at the age of twenty-seven, defeating the much larger army of daimyo Imagawa Yoshimoto in battle. He created strategic alliances with powerful daimyos, such as Matsudaira Motoyasu (an earlier name for Tokugawa

Ieyasu) and Takeda Shingen, marrying his daughter to Shingen's son. Nobunaga dreamed of establishing a unified state, which he referred to as *tenka*, a word meaning "everything under heaven," referring to the entirety of Japan. His correspondence carried a vermilion seal with characters reading *"tenka fubu,"* or "the realm subjected to the military," and he viewed himself as the *tenkajin*, or person who ruled the realm. Nobunaga first gained national prominence by helping the fugitive shogun, Ashikaga Yoshiaki, back to power in Kyoto in 1568. There, Nobunaga generously restored the imperial palace for the near-destitute Emperor Ōgimachi, who had to rely on contributions from wealthy daimyo to hold coronation ceremonies; the emperor was reportedly reduced to selling examples of his calligraphy to raise funds. Yoshiaki, however, plotted with Nobunaga's secular and religious enemies to destroy the rising young warlord. In 1573, Nobunaga responded by surrounding Kyoto with a huge army and chasing the shogun into exile, putting a definitive end to the Ashikaga bakufu.

Nobunaga's road to mastering the realm was not easy; ambitious rival daimyo schemed to crush him. He disposed of them through tactical genius and technology, forging strategic military partnerships through marriage alliances and using weaponry recently introduced from Europe. Nobunaga seized two important arquebus factories to guarantee access to firepower and organized three-thousand-man gun brigades that rotated in three groups, allowing a volley to fire every ten seconds. His rivals, some still relying on mounted swordsmen and archers, were powerless in the face of such new methods of warfare.

Another obstacle Nobunaga encountered in his drive for national reunification was fierce resistance from religious institutions, including Buddhist monastic armies and Ikkō and Lotus Leagues of militant lay believers. In 1571, Nobunaga infamously burned the Tendai headquarters on Mount Hiei, Enryakuji, an important symbol of the power of institutional Buddhism. He slaughtered three thousand monks and laypeople in the vicinity and completely destroyed the massive complex of temple buildings. Court nobles, clergy, and even some warriors were appalled by this sacrilegious act, but Nobunaga was ruthless with his enemies and the assault on Enryakuji represented military retaliation for the temple's support of rival daimyo forces. An account of the assault by his vassal Ōta Gyūichi makes clear that Nobunaga acted to punish the monks for offering help to his enemies:

> Nobunaga then summoned the monk soldiers from the Enryakuji and promised, striking steel on steel, that if the monks were to give him loyal service on this occasion, he would restore all of the Enryakuji's

domains in the provinces under his rule with their original privileges intact. Moreover, he sent the monks a vermilion-seal document to that effect. But if their religious principles prevented them from supporting one side exclusively, he reasoned, they should not interfere at all. Nobunaga also made it clear to the monks that if they violated these conditions he would burn down the whole mountain.[2]

The monks, however, ignored this warning, continuing to take the side of other daimyo. The account goes on to describe the resulting carnage:

> Surging round in swarms, Nobunaga's troops in a flash set fire to a multitude of holy Buddhas, shrines, monks' quarters, and sūtra scrolls; they spared nothing. . . . How miserable it was to see it all reduced to ashes! At the foot of the mountain, men and women, young and old ran about panic stricken. . . . Soldiers shouting battle cries advanced up the mountain from all sides. One by one they cut off the heads of monks and laymen, children, wise men and holy men alike. They presented the heads to Lord Nobunaga, saying: "Here is an exalted prelate, a princely abbot, a learned doctor, all the men of renown at the top of Mt. Hiei". . . . Thousands of corpses lay scattered about like so many little sticks, a pitiful end.[3]

Although this act is persistently invoked as an example of Nobunaga's brutality, his ten-year campaign against the Ikkō ikki in Echizen and Kaga provinces, in which he butchered the combative members of True Pure Land's Honganji Temple by the tens of thousands, was much bloodier and more atrocious. Nobunaga's reign of terror ended through the betrayal of one of his generals, Akechi Mitsuhide. In June 1582, Mitsuhide defied orders to lead an army to the west, instead turning his forces to attack Nobunaga, who was resting at Honnōji Temple in Kyoto. Nobunaga and his heir and eldest son Nobutada were forced to commit suicide at Honnōji, a karmically fitting end for a warlord who had himself destroyed so many temples. There are many theories, but no certainty, about why Mitsuhide turned traitor: some claim he had been humiliated and kicked by Nobunaga, others that he sought revenge for his mother's execution or was manipulated by Hideyoshi or Ieyasu.

History has often depicted Nobunaga as a cruel despot, but he was also a great administrator and leader who stimulated economic development through reducing the power of monopoly guilds, issuing stable currency, building ships and roads, and supporting foreign trade. At the time of his death, he controlled thirty of the roughly sixty provinces in central Japan, including the cities of Kyoto, Osaka, and Sakai. The task of unifying the realm would be taken up by his vassal Toyotomi Hideyoshi.

Hideyoshi's origins are obscure, but he was probably the son of a peasant foot soldier from Owari province. He served as a menial attendant under Nobunaga, a sandal-bearer, but made a reputation for himself as a strategist and was quickly promoted to the position of general, conducting important military campaigns. By leading a rout against Mitsuhide's forces to avenge Nobunaga's death and then ordering a lavish funeral for his deceased lord, Hideyoshi confirmed his role as heir to the realm. He destroyed other Nobunaga vassals who resisted his assumption of power and made conquest after conquest, gaining control of the island of Shikoku by 1585 and subduing Kyushu by 1587. The provinces held by the Go-Hōjō of Odawara, the last great independent power of the eastern Kanto region, were captured in 1590. Hideyoshi gave control of these eastern hinterlands to his formidable ally and rival Tokugawa Ieyasu, who turned the small fishing village of Edo (present-day Tokyo) into his stronghold.

The last lands to unify lay in the far north, where vicious warfare persisted. Hideyoshi built a new road to the north, which he traveled with his great army of daimyo vassals. Local daimyo who agreed to submit were confirmed in their landholdings, and those who resisted had their lands confiscated. Daimyo had to agree to three conditions: to send their wives and children to live as hostages in Kyoto; to destroy all fortresses but one, which would become a castle for their residence; and to perform land surveys of their holdings. By forcing the northern daimyo to submit to him, Hideyoshi also made their respective vassals recognize that their daimyo's local authority was granted through his central power. Daimyo lost their character as independent, regional rulers and were integrated into a national realm.

Hideyoshi enforced several important policies to consolidate his power, including the Sword Edict of 1588 and the enforcement of new land and tax systems. These and other policies, such as the transfers of daimyo from one domain to another and the demolition of provincial forts, had been initiated on a limited scale by Nobunaga, but Hideyoshi implemented them across the realm. The second great unifier realized that his position would remain precarious if the jizamurai remained armed in their local areas. Some might rise and overthrow the daimyo who had sworn fealty to Hideyoshi. To prevent such occurrences, he removed warriors from the villages, forcing them to live in castle towns *(jōkamachi)* under the direct control of their daimyo. By decree, these samurai were prevented from leaving their status group as warriors or from changing their daimyo affiliation, keeping the forces for each of Hideyoshi's vassal daimyo intact. Although he himself had peasant origins, Hideyoshi froze membership within the elite warrior class, to be determined thereafter by birth into established samurai families. He also prohibited private quarrels that resorted to arms, to demonstrate that only the master of the realm had the authority to settle disputes throughout the land.

Those jizamurai who wished to remain in their village would be treated as farmers and confined to their village and fields. They were disarmed through a massive weapons roundup ordered in 1588; swords, daggers, bows, spears, firearms, and other kinds of weaponry were confiscated. Hideyoshi thus deprived the rural warrior-landowner class of the means for armed resistance and guaranteed that the bearing of arms became the exclusive privilege of the samurai class. In exchange, he promised the people peace, security, and happiness even in the life to come, as the scrap metal from their weapons would be fashioned into an enormous statue of the Buddha.

The separation of farmers from warriors was part of a larger classification of social status. Hideyoshi determined four social classes: samurai, peasants, artisans, and merchants, the latter two collectively known as *chōnin* (townspeople)—providing the blueprint for the even more rigid class system of the Tokugawa period. Like the farmers in their villages and samurai in their castle towns, the chōnin were confined to their cities and townships. In short, the possibilities for social mobility available in the free-for-all Sengoku environment were being fundamentally eliminated. The subsequent Tokugawa regime passed many more laws and codes restricting possibilities for each of these classes.

Hideyoshi's new tax system emerged as a result of extensive land surveys. Nobunaga had begun surveying fields with the aim of assessing the productive capacity within his realm, but Hideyoshi was more systematic, ordering land registers containing the annual rice yield *(kokudaka)* of all land and the registered cultivator of each field. Each village was required to pay a percentage of its total yield as an annual tax. All ranks within the samurai class, from daimyo to the lowest foot soldier, were provided a fixed salary paid in rice from their domain's rice tax yield. Based on all of this data, Hideyoshi clearly understood both the amount of taxable land he could rely on for economic support and the extent of military and labor power that he could mobilize. This rice-based taxation and remuneration method greatly simplified the complex patterns of landholding and income distribution under earlier estate and provincial systems and continued to be used for the next three hundred years. In order to generate more income for his regime, Hideyoshi also encouraged maritime trade with Southeast Asia, initiating a "red seal" system in 1592 that provided official permits to daimyo and merchants who wished to engage in foreign trade. To deter piracy, he promised to pursue any who brought harm to the red-seal ships.

A letter written by a Jesuit priest in 1594, excerpted here, astutely analyzed Hideyoshi's accomplishments:

> If he give his word of security to any after he has conquered a [province], they shall have no harm, which was not observed by Nobunaga, who never conquered any town or [province] but that he put all the governors thereof to the sword. . . .
>
> He has taken away all their private quarrels and questions, which gave always occasions of their farther risings and tumults. Whosoever is now found in any of these risings and tumults is sure to die therefore. . . .
>
> He will not suffer any of his soldiers or gentlemen to live in idleness, setting them [to] work with buildings and repairing of his forts . . . so as they have no time, nor leisure to procure or practice any treasons or rebellions.
>
> He uses [his power] to change the potentates of one [province] and place them in another far off.[4]

After achieving unification of the realm, however, Hideyoshi engaged in increasingly megalomaniacal behavior. Responding to a letter of congratulations on his feats from a Korean embassy, Hideyoshi ignored his humble origins and claimed a miraculous birth, that "the wheel of the sun" had entered his mother's womb, foretelling that his rule would extend "as far as the sun shines." He boasted of future conquests: "I shall in one fell swoop invade Great Ming" [i.e., China] in order "to introduce Japanese customs and values to the four hundred and more provinces of that country."[5] In 1592 he conscripted over 150,000 troops and launched his invasion, with Korea as the initial stage. His armies quickly defeated the Korean army, captured Seoul, and devastated the country all the way to Pyongyang but were stopped by Ming forces. After years of unsuccessful negotiations with the Ming, Hideyoshi relaunched the invasion in 1597, but he died the following year without attaining a decisive victory. His advisory board of five powerful daimyo allies, including Tokugawa Ieyasu, brought the Japanese troops home.

While many writers of the time glorified the invasion and war, Keinen, a True Pure Land priest serving as chaplain and doctor, recounted the horrors committed in the campaign. Keinen's diary, recording each day during seven months of the invasion, combines prose and poetry to provide a compassionate eyewitness account of the hellish events. The following entries begin in mid-September 1597 and cover the first days after he landed in Korea:

> Eighth Month, 4th Day (September 15, 1597). Everyone is trying to be the first off the ship; no one wants to lag behind. They fall over each other in trying to get at the plunder, to kill people. It is a sight I cannot bear to see.
>
> A hubbub rises
> As from roiling clouds and mist
> Where they swarm about
> In their rage for the plunder
> Of innocent people's goods. . . .
>
> VIII.6. The very fields and hillsides have been put to the fire, not to speak of the forts. People are put to the sword, or they are shackled with chains and bamboo tubes choking the neck. Parents sobbing for their children, children searching for their parents—never before have I seen such a pitiable sight.
>
> The hills are ablaze
> With the cries of soldiers
> Intoxicated
> With their pyrolatry—
> The battleground of demons. . . .
>
> VIII.8. They are carrying off Korean children and killing their parents. Never shall they see each other again. Their mutual cries—surely this is like the torture meted out by the fiends of hell. . . .[6]

A grisly reminder of the bloody campaign can still be found in Kyoto, where a shrine marks the Mimizuka, or ear mound, which contains nearly forty thousand ears and noses sliced off of Koreans and Chinese. Invading Japanese generals were rewarded according to the verifiable number of enemies killed, but entire heads were too heavy to ship home, so ears and noses were packed into barrels filled with brine. Only a small fraction of the total shipped are buried at Mimizuka.

Hideyoshi died begging his advisors, including Ieyasu, to ensure the succession of his five-year-old son, Hideyori. But Ieyasu gained the allegiance of many of the most powerful daimyo and generals. The great Battle of Sekigahara in October 1600 settled the question of who would rule Japan. With over 160,000 combatants, it was the largest gathering of samurai in history, pitting Hideyori supporters from the west against Ieyasu's eastern forces. After one powerful general on the western side switched allegiances, the Tokugawa eastern army achieved victory.

AZUCHI-MOMOYAMA CULTURE
Castles

Castles were a primary cultural symbol of the Sengoku era, reflecting the conquests and power of their masters with deep moats, huge walls, intricate courtyards, and soaring turrets. They were so important that the final phase of Sengoku, from the 1570s to 1600, is named after two such citadels, Nobunaga's Azuchi and Hideyoshi's Momoyama castles. Through these magnificent structures, the unifiers sought cultural expression of their new power.

Early castles were small, defensive, semipermanent fortifications built at the tip of steep mountain ridges, meant for war and not as enduring structures. To prevent enemy approach, two or three lines of such fortifications were built. With the constant warfare of the Sengoku era, daimyo wanted to build more permanent strongholds. They added watchtowers and moats to their own residences and located these on plains or low plateaus to command valleys and protect nearby rice fields. Around these castles there was space for towns to grow, and artisans and merchants, along with warriors, flocked to these new spaces for the opportunity to serve the daimyo. Jōkamachi evolved into large urban communities that served as the daimyo's administrative headquarters and became the domainal centers for commerce, trade, and craft production. They became the basis for further urbanization in later centuries and provided regional economic opportunities for an emerging merchant class.

While castles were designed to impress the populace with immense size and beauty, their primary function in the Sengoku period was military. They were built like labyrinths, designed to confront an attacking force with an intricate array of deceptive defenses. The moats, outer walls, and watchtowers were the first layer of protection. Once beyond these, attackers plunged into forking, maze-like passageways designed to confine and confuse them while castle defenders peppered them with musket fire and arrows. At the end of the maze stood the four linked towers of the castle keep *(donjon)*, with windows and chutes to drop boulders and boiling water or oil on the enemy. In case of siege, donjons had access to wells and to storage for weapons, rice, salt, and other provisions.

Himeji, known as the "white heron castle," is one of the most beautiful examples of this form in Japan. It was designated one of the first UNESCO World Heritage sites in Japan in 1993 and is Japan's most visited castle. It was also the largest castle complex, with eighty-three buildings and covering 576 acres—fifty times the area of Tokyo Dome stadium. The structure

FIGURE 21. Himeiji Castle. Photo by Bernard Gagnon, via Wikimedia Commons.

dates originally to the fourteenth century but was significantly reconstructed by Hideyoshi. According to legend, when Hideyoshi was building the castle keep, he ran out of boulders. An old woman who earned her living as a grain miller donated her only millstone, inspiring others to also offer stones to Hideyoshi, which allowed him to complete construction.

Architects employed the latest technology and design features to make Himeiji nearly impenetrable. Attackers would first have to cross a series of three large moats in Himeiji's outer precincts, preventing the enemy from rapid approach because of the time needed to unload and transport necessary supplies across the water. By the time the enemy had crossed the third moat, their strength and reserves would already be diminished. The white plaster façade that gives Himeiji its beautiful appearance was fire resistant, but if attackers employed arson on other structures, moat water could also be used to fight the fire. Himeiji's high, steeply sloping stone walls made it impossible for the approaching enemy to view the castle directly from the base of the walls. If they managed to scale the walls, they had to pass through eighty-four heavily fortified gates so narrow that only a few could pass through at one time, slowing their advance. Himeiji's defenses were never tested, however, as it never suffered a major attack.

Nobunaga's Azuchi Castle did not survive the Sengoku era. In 1575, he turned family affairs over to his eldest son and ordered the construction of a great castle fortress in Azuchi in Omi province, which would act as visible evidence of his new role as lord of the realm. Azuchi was strategically located on a hill, on the shores of Lake Biwa between the Sea of Japan and the Pacific Ocean, permitting rapid deployment of troops throughout central Japan. It was close, but not too close, to the imperial capital, some thirty miles away, because while Nobunaga wanted to dominate the court, he wished to avoid entanglements in all of its rituals and ceremonial affairs.

The great castles were not simply fortresses; they were living quarters for the daimyo and the centers of their administration. They gave the warlords who aspired to national leadership the opportunity to add to their legitimacy by wielding the kind of cultural capital that ruling classes had always possessed. In keeping with the interests of the court and Ashikaga shoguns, Azuchi Castle contained a Nō theater. Rather than being simply black or white, its exterior was colorfully painted with tigers and dragons. Its interiors were gorgeously decorated with wall paintings and screens replete with gold leaf and vivid color. Extensive use of gold and silver leaf, pounded paper-thin by skilled craftsmen, helped illuminate the dark interiors of castles. The unifiers lavishly patronized the painters and artisans who decorated their castles. Nobunaga employed Kanō Eitoku (1543–90), the most influential painter of the era, as master artist for Azuchi Castle. It was an immense project requiring Eitoku to organize large teams of painters for every level of the castle, each decorated with a different theme. On the top floor, sliding screen doors were covered with gold-leaf paintings of ancient Chinese rulers, symbolizing Nobunaga's aspirations to rule all of Japan. Lower floors were decorated with Buddhist themes, horses, falcons, birds and flowers, and landscapes.

Eitoku, the fourth-generation head of the Kanō school of painters, was also the master designer of Hideyoshi's palaces. He helped establish the Momoyama style, which retained some of the characteristics of Zen ink painting, but with more vibrancy through greater use of color and gold. The Kanō school was established in the fifteenth century when founder Kanō Masanobu was appointed court artist to the Ashikaga bakufu. He specialized in Chinese-style monochrome ink washes, but his son, Motonobu, blended that style with the more colorful *yamato-e* style of the Tosa school of painters. The hybrid style proved popular for the decorative folding screens *(byōbu)* and sliding doors *(fusuma)*, described below, that had long been used to partition the large open spaces of palaces and mansions. After Eitoku, the Kanō school continued to produce fine painters and to receive the patronage of powerful rulers, gradually developing an even more decorative, elegant style, transforming Chinese styles and themes to Japanese taste. Eitoku's adopted son, Sanraku, produced decorative bird and flower paintings that became the hallmark of the Kanō style.

The tower of Azuchi Castle was completed in 1579, when it became Nobunaga's official residence. Jesuit missionary Luis Frois left a detailed description of the castle's exterior and interiors, marveling that its "opulence, order and architectural design can compete with the noblest and most sumptuous in Europe . . . as immaculate and elegant as human industry alone could ever accomplish."[7] Following Nobunaga's death in 1582, the splendid castle was burned to the ground by unknown arsonists, leaving only ruins today.

Interior Architectural Décor

Japanese domestic architecture is renowned for its simple yet elegant designs and use of natural materials. Many of the most renowned European and American architects of the twentieth century, including Frank Lloyd Wright, Bruno Taut, Le Corbusier, and Walter Gropius, visited Japan and sought to inject the feelings of spaciousness and simplicity in Japanese architecture into their own designs, hoping to move away from the excessive decoration of the Victorian era and toward more minimal, modernist designs. Many innovations in interior design occurred during the Muromachi and Azuchi-Momoyama eras, displayed in the castles and mansions of elites and in Buddhist temples, resulting in an architectural style known as *shoin-zukuri*. Ashikaga Yoshimasa's Silver Pavilion is considered the oldest extant example of this style. Shoin-zukuri allowed the ruling warrior elite to gather large numbers of allies and vassals in vast, impressive reception areas.

The interiors of castles and mansions were spacious and open in order to allow cooling breezes to circulate and to accommodate large gatherings. They contained few fixed walls; large wooden pillars supported the roof and the ceiling, which were often decorated with colorful, lavish paintings. In order to use these large spaces flexibly, the Japanese created two key interior features that allowed them to divide space and create smaller private areas—byōbu and fusuma. Both are still widely used in Japanese domestic architecture and décor today.

Byōbu, literally "wind wall," are a highly portable form of screening, first introduced around the seventh century from Korea, but coming into maturity during the fourteenth to sixteenth centuries. Indoors, they provided protection from drafts, a lightweight means to provide a degree of privacy, or an elegant backdrop for formal occasions. Outdoors, they could be taken on picnics to block wind or discourage voyeurs. They came in a

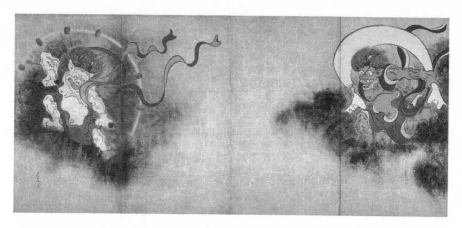

FIGURE 22.   Ogata Kōrin, *Fujin and Raijin* byōbu, seventeenth century, Tokyo National Museum. Source: Wikimedia Commons.

wide variety of heights and lengths, depending on the use for which they were intended, from two to eight panels in width and from a few feet to over ten feet high. The most popular format was a six-panel screen, approximately twelve feet long and five feet high. Panels are constructed by pasting handmade paper *(washi)* over a latticed bamboo frame and connected to each other using paper hinges, which allowed them to be folded in either direction. In earlier centuries, byōbu panels featured individual paintings framed with silk brocade. Artists soon realized that they might extend a single composition across all of the screens, enhancing the overall impact of their work. The styles and subjects of painting varied widely according to room function. Simple ink paintings were often employed in private quarters, while colorfully painted screens covered in gold leaf might adorn public areas. Byōbu were frequently produced in pairs, allowing the artist to represent two related images or concepts, such as a tiger and a dragon; different episodes from famous literature such as *The Tale of Genji;* or Raijin and Fujin, the kami of thunder and lightning and the kami of wind.

Fusuma are sliding doors installed between interior pillars and set into wooden tracks in the floor and in carved overhead transoms. They provided another effective method for partitioning large, open interiors; fusuma could be closed to create smaller spaces, pushed back to connect rooms, or removed altogether. Like byōbu, they were constructed by pasting layers of washi paper over a lightweight wooden or bamboo framework. While byōbu allowed artists to extend their design across several planes, fusuma enabled them to continue a single design around an entire room.

FIGURE 23. Kanō Sansetsu, *The Old Plum Tree*, fusuma, seventeenth century, The Metropolitan Museum of Art, New York. Source: Wikimedia Commons.

A third interior architectural feature that appeared in the late Muromachi period is the *tokonoma*, an alcove space that remains an essential element of interior décor. The tokonoma is the focal point of the room, differentiated by a raised and polished wooden base set above the *tatami* mat flooring. The tokonoma customarily contained a hanging scroll *(kakemono)* of ink painting or calligraphy, an incense burner, an arrangement of flowers *(ikebana)*, and sometimes a candleholder. It allowed elites to exhibit their cultural treasures, changing them regularly to match the seasons. The inclusion of tokonoma in interior architecture spread widely among commoners in subsequent centuries, allowing nonelites to also display their aesthetic tastes. Considered the hearth of a room, there are forms of ritual etiquette attached to the tokonoma. Stepping within it is forbidden, except when changing displays, when one must follow a prescribed set of instructions. The most important guest at a gathering should be seated with his back facing the tokonoma because it would be considered untoward if the host pointed his guest directly toward the alcove to show off his treasures.

The flooring material used for rooms, tatami, consists of thin, fragrant mats woven from rush, mounted on a base of straw bound with hemp threads and finished with cloth edgings that varied by the owner's rank, from plain cotton to elaborate brocades. The term *tatami* comes from the verb *tatamu*, to fold or pile. During the Heian era, the flooring of residences was constructed of wood; thin, foldable rush mats were piled up in layers on the floor for seating. During the Muromachi period, temples, castles, and mansions began to install fixed tatami matting across entire rooms, known as *zashiki* (sitting rooms).

Mats are of a standard size, approximately three feet by six feet (though this size varies slightly between regions), and the area of a given room is described in terms of the number of tatami mats it contains. This practice continues today, even though most rooms are no longer floored with tatami. Many typical rooms today are six to twelve mats in size, roughly one hundred to two hundred square feet. Rooms in castles and mansions, however, could be vast. The first floor of the main keep of Himeji Castle is sometimes referred to as a "thousand-mat room," although it only contained around 350, measuring around six thousand square feet.

By the late seventeenth century, tatami flooring was widely used in the homes of wealthy commoners; lower classes might cover earthen floors with a thin layer of foldable tatami mats. Today, most housing has few if any tatami-floored rooms, although it is not uncommon to have one "Japanese-style room," or *washitsu*, with tatami flooring, a tokonoma, and other elements of traditional architecture.

An alternative style of domestic architecture, *sukiya-zukuri*, also emerged during this period. *"Suki"* indicates refined, elegant taste, and the style was rooted in the aesthetics of a humble mountain hut, highlighting natural materials, rather than in the ostentatious grandeur of castle zashiki. Sukiya rooms were small and simple in ornamentation. In place of massive squared columns, pillars were constructed of slender, polished trunks, sometimes with bark still attached. Walls and ceilings were unadorned; walls were finished with a natural-colored earthen plaster. Sliding *shōji* screen doors were unpainted, consisting of wooden grids filled with translucent paper. The Katsura Detached Palace, an imperial villa in the outskirts of Kyoto constructed in the early seventeenth century, is considered one of the finest examples of sukiya-zukuri style and was especially admired by later European and American architects. The villa combines rhythmic repetition of rectangular elements, such as tatami mats, shōji screens, and paving stones, with the irregularity of natural shapes in wooden elements and the garden, which was seamlessly integrated with the interior spaces.

Arts of Power—Tea Ceremony and Beyond

Hideyoshi, lacking any traceable lineage, felt the need to claim legitimacy for his position even more acutely than Nobunaga, whose father was a daimyo from a priestly family. Thus, whereas Nobunaga refused to be entangled in the webs of the imperial court and Ashikaga shogunate, Hideyoshi eagerly sought access to the court and emperor, even though they had been shorn of any real authority. He insinuated himself into the position of regent *(kampaku)*, an office reserved for high-ranking court families, through forced adoptions, and compelled the emperor to grant court ranks to his top military supporters, transforming military leaders into an imperial aristocracy. This unsavory process, however, also had the effect of reviving the imperial order of governance. By giving daimyo court offices, Hideyoshi, like Taira no Kiyomori in the twelfth century, infused the court with actual power. The title of Regent, long meaningless, became synonymous with national authority again under Hideyoshi's domination of the court.

One forum through which Hideyoshi acquired cultural capital was *chanoyu*, or tea ceremony. Tea was introduced to Japan in the Heian period by Buddhist monks, who drank it for its medicinal and stimulative effects, but from the fourteenth to sixteenth centuries, rules and an art form developed around the practices of preparing, serving, and drinking tea, resulting in the tea ceremony, which remains a strong symbol of Japanese cultural ideals and traditional aesthetics today. Chanoyu is a composite art that brings together painting, calligraphy, pottery, landscape gardening, architecture, and other traditional arts into a single experience. It is not simply accumulating and displaying the necessary components. The host must carefully select each required item—including a hanging scroll and flower arrangement for the alcove, tea bowls, tea caddy, and incense burners—according to the season, place, and guests involved. Thus, the tea ceremony became the ultimate forum for demonstrating one's connoisseurship and cultural mastery, an area the new warrior elite desperately wished to cultivate.

Over two centuries, the tea ceremony evolved from a Chinese-oriented form, in which guests sat in upright chairs and the host displayed exquisite, costly Chinese wares in a party setting, to a more solemn and spiritual form, conducted in a small, hut-like room and adding Japanese and Korean pottery and implements that appeared irregular and unrefined to elegant Chinese pieces. The new enthusiasm for local pottery represented both a form of nativist reaction against widespread reverence for Chinese art and an opportunity for merchant-class tea practitioners to assert their own aesthetic values, but it was not embraced by all tea enthusiasts. Throughout the tea ceremony's subsequent history, there have been two different styles: one, favored by the very wealthy, ornate and relatively free of rules; and another, more rigidly defined, based on aesthetic preferences for rusticity, austerity, and quietude. This latter aesthetic, known as *wabi* or *sabi*, had a philosophical component; it was thought to embody Buddhist concepts like transience and imperfection. Tea master Takeno Jōō (1502–55) tried to convey the essence of wabi tea through the following poem by Fujiwara no Teika, which expresses a sense of muted colors and humble, sincere settings:

FIGURE 24.   Seto-ware tea jar, Muromachi period. Source: Wikimedia Commons.

As far as the eye can see
No cherry-blossom
No crimson leaf:
A thatched hut by a lagoon,
This autumn evening.[8]

Japanese pottery from ancient kilns in Bizen, unglazed and wood-fired; from Seto, with brown iron glazes; and from Shigaraki, with natural hues and a pebbly finish, are among the ceramic varieties thought to exemplify the wabi aesthetic.

Wabi tea is ideally conducted in a very small room in a teahouse that resembled a modest mountain hut. The doors are low, so that all guests must crouch and enter on hands and knees. In this way, all seated in the tearoom are symbolically of the same status, a feature very meaningful to the merchants who adopted this art form alongside their social betters. This style of tea is most often associated with the sixteenth-century tea master Sen no Rikyū (1522–91), who purportedly described the religious philosophies that inform wabi tea as follows:

> The tea ceremony of the small room is above all a matter of performing practice and attaining realization in accord with the Buddhist path. To delight in the refined splendor of a dwelling or the taste of delicacies belongs to worldly life. There is shelter enough when the roof does not leak, food enough when it staves off hunger. This is the Buddhist teaching and the fundamental meaning of the tea ceremony. We draw water, gather firewood, boil the water, and make tea. We then offer it to the Buddha, serve it to others and drink ourselves. We arrange flowers and burn incense. In all of this, we model ourselves after acts of the Buddha and past masters. Beyond this, you must come to your own understanding.[9]

Rikyū was born to a family of merchants in the port city of Sakai, which was governed by a council of wealthy merchants and was a peaceful and prosperous city where the arts flourished. He studied tea under Takeno Jōō, a merchant who earned his fortune producing military saddles and who was an early proponent of wabi-style tea. Jōō sought to conduct tea ceremonies that captured the rustic tranquility of a mountain hut, like the ten-foot-square hut of Kamo no Chōmei, in the midst of the city. His pupil Rikyū further developed the wabi tea aesthetic, as seen in the Tai-an tearoom he designed for Kyoto's Myōkian Temple, featuring rough earthen walls and exposed cedar beams. His wabi taste is further demonstrated in the assymetrical, matte-black tea bowls that he is said to have commissioned from a tile maker named Chōjirō for use by Hideyoshi. The pleased magnate presented the tile maker's family with a seal reading *raku* (enjoyment), and the family adopted this as a name, passing down its techniques through generations of what became a ceramic dynasty. True raku ware is still highly prized, but the term *raku* has been adopted more generally to denote low-fired pottery.

Rikyū eventually developed such renown in the tea world that he was employed as tea master by Oda Nobunaga, who used tea as a political tool to win influence among merchants trading in military goods. Nobunaga used his power to command prized tea utensils *(meibutsu)* from allies and enemies alike, sometimes awarding these to influential supporters or loyal vassals. Tea ceremony offered a source of refinement for the samurai class; for merchants, it became a vehicle for mingling with the ruling samurai class and provided an arena for demonstrating their wealth and taste. By Nobunaga's time, it was thought that men with sufficient wealth who did not practice tea were boorish, completely lacking in intellectual and aesthetic sophistication. Tea played several important political roles: tea masters acted as envoys between daimyo, tea gatherings provided a civilized meeting place for diplomatic negotiations, and valuable utensils acted as gifts to strengthen alliances.

After Nobunaga's death, Rikyū served as tea master for Hideyoshi, who inherited his predecessor's precious collection and demonstrated even more passion for the tea ceremony. The new ruler's enthusiasm for tea became the source of fortune and misfortune alike for Rikyū. Initially they got along very well; Rikyū became a close confidante of the ruler, whose sponsorship of chanoyu further propelled its popularity among both warriors and wealthy commoners. Hideyoshi once stated, "People must be moderate in their desires, but I willfully pay too much attention to chanoyu, as I do to hunting."[10] He sometimes favored a grand, ostentatious approach to tea that contrasted with Rikyū's more austere teachings, for example, by constructing a portable tearoom with walls, shelves, and utensils completely covered in gold—either gold leaf or gold-sprinkled lacquerwork. In 1587, Hideyoshi ordered that an enormous, unprecedented ten-day tea party be held on the grounds of the Kitano-tenmangu Shrine in Kyoto; he commanded tea masters and practitioners from around the realm to attend. The party was attended by as many as eight hundred masters, alongside tens of thousands of Kyoto-ites, including courtiers, samurai, and townspeople. Eventually, however, Hideyoshi and Rikyū had some sort of falling-out that led the short-tempered ruler to order that his tea master commit ritual suicide through disembowelment *(seppuku)*. Legend has it that Hideyoshi was insulted because he had to walk under a wooden statue of Rikyū installed above the gate of Daitokuji Temple in Kyoto. Another popular explanation is that Hideyoshi was jealous of a treasured tea bowl in Rikyū's possession. The tea master's fate may also have been due to the politics of the day. Because of Hideyoshi's planned invasions of Korea, the city of Sakai had been eclipsed by Hakata, a port city in Kyushu where the campaign would be launched. Hakata merchants and tea masters had risen in importance around Hideyoshi and may have exercised their new influence by denouncing Rikyū.

Following the invasion of Korea, many daimyo brought back Korean ceramics and even captive potters, seeking to circulate or produce new types of ceramic wares that might become popular in the lucrative tea-ceremony trade. Korean artisans introduced new technologies, like kilns capable of firing fine white porcelain. One result was the development of Imari ware, prized by European and American collectors, featuring a cobalt blue under-glaze, overglazes of red and gold, and intricate designs of flowers, plants, or scenery.

Not long after the deaths of Rikyū and Hideyoshi, the stricter class boundaries enacted by the Tokugawa Shogunate resulted in further separa-tions in the world of tea. The leading tea masters, including Furuta Oribe, Kobori Enshū, and Katagiri Sekishū, were themselves daimyo, whose fol-lowers were limited to the elite members of the ruling warrior class. Commoners flocked to the schools established by the descendants of Sen no Rikyū: Urasenke, Omotesenke, and Mushanokojisenke. Tea remained an essential element for demonstrating refinement among elite warriors and spread more widely among the townspeople as a discipline for learning proper etiquette and comportment.

Another quintessentially Japanese art, ikebana, was also formalized dur-ing the sixteenth century and served as a means to demonstrate one's taste and cultural capital. Like the tea ceremony in modern Japan, ikebana is often considered a feminine art, when in fact both were elite, masculine arts rarely open to women until the nineteenth century. Appreciation of flowers is well recorded in both literature and the visual arts since at least the Heian era, with writers celebrating the beauty of wisteria, irises, chrysanthemums, peonies, and other seasonal blossoms. Paintings of interiors often featured large arrangements of flowers in elegant containers. Flower-comparison *(hana-awase)* games among courtiers challenged competitors to match peerless blossoms with containers that would best highlight their beauty.

Some claim that ikebana's earliest roots lie in seventh-century floral offerings to Buddhist deities. According to one account, when court noble Ono no Imoko returned from his journey as envoy to the Sui court in China, he brought back instructions that floral offerings should not be hap-hazard but should represent a Buddhist trinity, with a long central stem flanked by two shorter stems. Imako became the abbot of Kyoto's Rokkakudo Temple, which eventually became the headquarters of Ikenobo, Japan's oldest and largest school of ikebana. A text compiled by Ikenobo monks, *Sendensho*, describes fifty-three types of arrangements befitting different ceremonial occasions, such as departure for battle, a boy's coming of age, and weddings. The shogun Ashikaga Yoshimasa (1436–90), a well-known patron of the arts, gathered leading ikebana designers at his Silver Pavilion estate and gave the Ikenobo school the title "master of the way of flowers." In the seventeenth century, Emperor Go-Mizunoo was also an avid patron of ikebana.

Like Rikyū's spiritualization of tea, Ikenobo attached Buddhist significance to the number and placement of stems, claiming that ikebana's main aim was religious and not merely decorative—to "search for and obtain the seed of enlightenment in the face of the wind that scatters flower petals and leaves, never seeking mere entertainment for a day."[11] As with Zen rock gardens, nature was the model for ikebana arrangements: they should create symbolic Buddhist landscapes, with a large evergreen stem symbolizing a sacred mountain, willow stems or vines acting as shade forest, white flowers serving as waterfalls, and stems from flowering shrubs as foothills. Ikenobo specialized in complex, towering arrangements of seven to eleven large branches, known as *rikka*, suitable for the mansions of the wealthy.

As we have seen with tea, Hideyoshi's tastes tended toward the grand and extravagant. One observer remarked, "The very privies are decorated with gold and silver, with paintings in fine colors. All of these precious things are used as if they were dirt."[12] The rooms of the ruler's palace were filled with gigantic rikka arrangements. His tea master, Rikyū, disdained such ostentatious compositions. Chanoyu also required ikebana in the tokonoma of the teahouse, but Rikyū believed that the best floral arrangements should be natural and unforced, made by simply tossing a few scant stems into a well-chosen container—a style of ikebana that became known as *nage-ire* (thrown in), which contrasts with the highly regulated composition of rikka. A legendary story about the two men portrays the tea master's attempt to demonstrate his simpler aesthetic sense to Hideyoshi. The ruler had heard that Rikyū's garden was filled with a spectacular blossoming of a rare variety of morning glory and asked to visit. When he arrived, he was surprised to see that all of the vines and flowers had been removed and the grounds of the garden covered with sand and pebbles. Angrily allowing himself to be led to the teahouse, he was greeted by Rikyū, who had placed a single, perfect morning-glory blossom on an ancient Chinese bronze vessel in the tokonoma.

As ikebana developed over the following centuries, it retained both highly formal, structured styles and more quick and casual styles. Degrees of formality in Japan's spatial arts—including architecture, garden design, ikebana, and calligraphy—are often expressed by three terms introduced in chapter 3: shin, gyō, and sō, just as the speed and rhythms of Nō drama and other temporal arts are expressed with jo, ha, and kyū (see chapter 4). Shin represents the most formal, associated with the slow, the symmetrical, and the imposing, and with human control or shaping. Sō is the most informal, associated with speed, assymetry, and a relaxed attitude—with things in their natural state. The gyō middle way represents a blending of shin and sō styles. These three styles are readily apparent in calligraphy, with shin characters evenly spaced and perfectly formed while sō features loose, flowing brushstrokes and letters of different sizes that run into one another.

THE ARRIVAL OF EUROPEANS—JAPAN'S CHRISTIAN CENTURY

Many historians have contemplated the possible connections between tea and Christianity, both of which thrived in Japan during the Sengoku era. The Jesuits, the first Catholic order to arrive in 1549, encountered chanoyu in their audiences with daimyo and recorded the ritual in detail. Some have theorized that Rikyū's wabi tea, emphasizing humility, modesty, and equality, was influenced by Christian teachings, or that cross-like designs on some tea wares symbolized Christian faith. While the evidence is far from conclusive, there is no doubt that several influential daimyo who were followers of Rikyū were also Catholic converts and that the arrival of the Portuguese and Spanish in the sixteenth century deeply affected political and cultural developments.

In 1506, a treaty sanctioned by a papal bull divided the newly discovered non-Christian world between then leading European powers, giving Spain dominion over lands to the south and west and Portugal rights to the east. The Portuguese established outposts in Goa in the south of India, Malacca on the Malay Peninsula, the Molucca Islands in Indonesia, and Macao in China. At that time Europeans knew of Japan as "Zipangu," a remote country revealed in the thirteenth-century travel accounts of Venetian explorer Marco Polo. Those stories had inspired Christopher Columbus to set sail for Asia in search of Zipangu, but he found the New World instead. The Portuguese were the first Europeans to arrive in Japan, by accident, in 1542 when a Chinese junk carrying three Portuguese merchants was shipwrecked on the island of Tanegashima, off Kyushu. The matchlock muskets the Japanese acquired from the merchants became known as *tanegashima*. Soon afterward, Portuguese ships traveling through Asia began to include stops in Japan.

The Portuguese arrived first as merchants carrying knowledge of Western civilization alongside their trading goods to the Japanese, who proved curious about the outside world and eager to experiment with new ideas, technologies, and fashions. They found the Europeans themselves rather barbaric—unable to use chopsticks and eating with their fingers instead, and incapable of understanding written characters. The Japanese called these new visitors *nanbanjin* (southern barbarians), because they

FIGURE 25. Kanō Sanraku, *nanban byōbu,* seventeenth century, Suntory Museum of Art, Tokyo. Source: Wikimedia Commons.

arrived from the south, where Portuguese holdings were located. Many forms of material culture brought by the Portuguese were captured in paintings on large folding screens, known as *nanban byōbu,* that depicted long-nosed merchants in hats and billowing pantaloons accompanied by dark-skinned servants, priests and monks of different Catholic orders, large Portuguese carrack ships with gleaming white sails, and churches constructed in southern Japan.

Portuguese merchants traded silk, medicines, and weapons for Japanese silver, which they carried to Ming China. Sengoku-era daimyo eagerly welcomed the ships to their ports for opportunities to trade. The firearms supplied by the Portuguese directly influenced the political balance of power during the age of civil war. The Japanese carefully studied the arquebus to learn how to manufacture their own and quickly established weapons factories. Cannons were acquired later and were used in Sengoku warfare for the first time in the 1580s. The Europeans also shared navigational and shipbuilding technology, enabling the Japanese to establish trading outposts throughout Southeast Asia. The introduction of glass lenses allowed the Japanese to explore both the heavens above and the microscopic world of the earth below. Other cultural imports, like playing cards, clothing, tobacco, and food, were also widely adopted by the Japanese populace. New foods, including spices like pepper, New World crops like sweet potatoes and pumpkins, sugar, deep-fried foods *(tempura),* and other delicacies like bread *(pan),* sponge cakes *(kasutera),* and candies *(konpeitō),* transformed the Japanese diet and remain popular today. Many Japanese admired the foreigners' fashions; Nobunaga, Hideyoshi, and other daimyo would sometimes amuse themselves by dressing in velvet pantaloons, adorning themselves with rosaries and jewelry bearing images of Christ or the Virgin Mary.

Indeed, Christianity was such a powerful agent of change that the era is sometimes known as Japan's "Christian century." Missionaries arrived soon after the merchants. In 1544 a man named Yajirō, wanted for manslaughter, escaped from Japan on a Portuguese ship headed for Goa in India. There, he was baptized as a Christian and studied at the Jesuit College with Francis Xavier (1506–52). Yajirō told Xavier that Japan was ripe for Christianity, and they soon set sail with two Spanish Jesuits, arriving at Satsuma in Kyushu in 1549. The Roman Catholic Church was seeking new converts to offset its losses to the Protestant Reformation in Europe. When the missionaries arrived during the Sengoku era, the domains were governed by autonomous daimyo, whom the missionaries referred to as "kings." The Japanese initially believed that the Jesuit missionaries were bringing new Buddhist teachings, since they had arrived from India. This mistake was due in part to Yajirō, who translated *Deus* as *Dainichi*, the cosmic Buddha of Shingon.

Missionary activity spread as the daimyo came to see the advantages of throwing in their lot with the Europeans. Along with religion came the possibility for lucrative trade with China and Southeast Asia via the impressive Portuguese ships. The Jesuits urged ship captains to dock only at ports where the daimyo was Christian or allowed churches to be built in his domain. Nagasaki became the main Portuguese trading depot, quickly transforming from a small fishing village into an international trading center. By the 1560s, a Christian community was also established in Kyoto, but Kyushu remained the center of Catholicism and the site of most Jesuit colleges and churches—especially after 1580, when daimyo Ōmura Sumitada, christened Dom Bartolomeu, gave Jesuits full control of the city of Nagasaki. The rate of Jesuit success in southern Japan was largely due to the conversion of Ōmura and two other powerful daimyo, whose subjects were subsequently ordered to also accept Christ en masse. These daimyo agreed to destroy the "idols" and shrines of the native faiths in their lands, and in return they received access to the weaponry, wealth via trade, and material assistance that helped them achieve victories in the wars of Sengoku. Mass conversions account for how a small band of missionaries could report such impressive numbers of converts. In 1553, five foreign missionaries reported four thousand converts; by 1579, fifty-five missionaries achieved one hundred thousand. By the end of the sixteenth century, nearly 2 percent of the Japanese population were considered Christian, more than double the percentage in Japan today.

The Jesuit strategy in Japan, as in China, was to target the elites with the hope that they might order such mass conversions in their territories. To help make converts, the missionaries composed dictionaries, printing these and other European works like *Aesop's Fables* with movable-type presses they introduced in 1590. Alexandro Valignano (1539–1606), supervisor of the Jesuit mission in Japan, believed that in order to win over the Japanese daimyo, Jesuits must not only learn the language but also abandon European dress and habits, learning to eat, drink, and behave like the Japanese themselves. He championed the training of native Japanese priests, over the doubts of his colleagues, who were not convinced of the sincerity of their Japanese acolytes. Their suspicions were confirmed by the case of Fabian Fucan, a Kyoto native raised in a Zen temple who entered the Jesuit seminary in 1586 and taught Japanese literary classics to other Jesuits at a missionary college in Amakusa in Kyushu. Resentful over the Jesuits' refusal to grant him a promotion to full priesthood, Fucan abandoned Catholicism. In 1620, as religious persecution grew under the subsequent Tokugawa regime, he published *Deus Destroyed*, a harsh critique of both Christianity and the Europeans who propagated it, which became the foundation of much anti-Christian polemic. Fucan charged that the "adherents of Deus" sought to "destroy the Law of the Buddhas and Way of the Gods." He wrote: "They have sent troops and taken over such countries as Luzon and Nova Hispania, lands of barbarians close to animals in nature. But our empire surpasses other lands by far in its fierce bravery. For that reason the ambition to usurp this country by diffusing their doctrine, even if it takes a thousand years, has penetrated the very marrow of their bones."[13]

The Christian mission had flourished under the favor of Oda Nobunaga, whose use of the arquebus gave him an advantage in the unification of war-torn provinces. Nobunaga's alliance with the Christians was partially due to the leverage it gave him against the powerful Buddhist sects. Hideyoshi also initially showed favor toward the Christians, but on a visit to Kyushu he was shocked to see the extent to which the religion had taken hold, since it remained small and unthreatening in the capital. He further turned against the Portuguese after learning of the extent of the slave trade, primarily Japanese girls sold into sexual slavery for service on ships or in Portugal and Macao. Hideyoshi wrote Gaspar Coelho, vice-provincial of the Jesuit mission in Japan, in July 1587 to demand an end to the purchase and enslavement of Japanese men and women and the return of Japanese slaves. Later that year he issued an edict banning Christian proselytization and ordering the expulsion of the foreign missionaries from Japan within twenty days. The ban was not strictly enforced, however, and the missionaries continued their activities, although a bit more discreetly.

Pope Gregory XIII had guaranteed the Jesuits an exclusive mission in Japan in 1585, but Franciscans, Dominicans, and Augustinians began to arrive in the 1590s nonetheless. Competition between sects resulted in aggressive rivalries and territorialism. In 1596, relations between Hideyoshi and the Jesuits and Franciscans were aggravated when a Spanish galleon en route from Manila to Acapulco was blown off course and its rich cargo was confiscated by local daimyo. This action sparked bitter protests by both the Franciscans and the Jesuits. In the controversy that resulted, Hideyoshi's suspicions about imperialist intentions on the part of the Spanish and Portuguese crowns were further intensified. He ordered the crucifixion of all Christians in Kyoto. While the original list contained hundreds of names, sympathetic officials reduced it to twenty-six, including a mixture of native Japanese Christians and priests, four Spaniards, one Mexican, and one Indian. They were marched south from Kyoto to Nagasaki for their crucifixion so that their execution might serve as a warning to the large Christian population there. The martyrs became known as the Twenty-Six Saints of Japan.

After being appointed shogun in 1603, Tokugawa Ieyasu initially opened all ports to foreign trade without restrictions, hoping to expand revenues through international commerce. He ignored Hideyoshi's anti-Christian edicts, tolerating the Catholic missionaries and priests. The Protestant rivals of the Spanish and Portuguese, the Dutch and British, soon began to arrive. The first Dutch ship landed in 1600, the only surviving vessel of a five-ship expedition dispatched in 1598. The second Dutch ship arrived in 1609, followed by the British in 1613, but the latter abandoned pursuit of trade with Japan in 1635, unhappy with the paltry profits. Trading companies, not national governments, operated the ships of both countries. Dutch and British traders warned Ieyasu about the tendency of their Catholic enemies to instigate social and political unrest and then take control of countries, as the Spanish had done in Central and South America and the Philippines, and as the Portuguese, on a smaller scale, had done in Macao and Goa. They assured the shogun that, as traders, they were more interested in profit than either conversion or conquest.

One of these European advisers, Will Adams (1564–1620), has been immortalized in James Clavell's best-selling novel *Shogun* (1975), later adapted into a popular TV miniseries with a relatively high degree of historical accuracy. Adams was an English navigator who reached Japan on the Dutch ship *Liefde* in 1600. He settled there and became a trusted advisor to

Ieyasu on issues of diplomacy and maritime trade. Forbidden to leave Japan by the shogun, Adams was granted samurai status—a rare occurrence for non-Japanese throughout history—and given a high-ranking position among Ieyasu's vassals. He was rechristened Miura Anjin, "the pilot of Miura," and given an estate in Uraga, next to the entrace of Edo Bay. Unable to return to his wife and children in England, he married the daughter of a local official and immersed himself in a Japanese lifestyle. He died in 1620, at age fifty-five. Adams's gravesite is adjacent to a memorial to Francis Xavier in Nagasaki.

When Adams and his nine surviving crewmates arrived on Japanese shores, they were met by local officials and Jesuit priests. Recognizing that the arrivals represented their national enemies, the Jesuits claimed that the *Liefde* was a pirate vessel and that its crew should be executed. Under Ieyasu's orders, the crew were imprisoned at Osaka Castle, where Adams was interrogated by the future shogun himself. In a letter to his British wife, he described the interview and Ieyasu's decision to spare the lives of his crew:

> Coming before the king, he viewed me well, and seemed to be wonderfully favourable. He made many signs unto me, some of which I understood, and some I did not. In the end, there came one that could speak Portuguese. By him, the king demanded of me of what land I was, and what moved us to come to his land, being so far off. I showed unto him the name of our country, and that our land had long sought out the East Indies, and desired friendship with all kings and potentates in way of merchandise, having in our land diverse commodities, which these lands had not. . . . Then he asked whether our country had wars? I answered him yea, with the Spaniards and Portugals, being in peace with all other nations. Further, he asked me, in what I did believe? I said, in God, that made heaven and earth. He asked me diverse other questions of things of religions, and many other things: As what way we came to the country. Having a chart of the whole world, I showed him, through the Strait of Magellan. At which he wondered, and thought me to lie. Thus, from one thing to another, I abode with him till mid-night.[14]

Ieyasu denied the Jesuits' request to execute the navigator and his crew. Adams's ability to gain the shogun's confidence was worrisome for the Jesuits, who first attempted to convert him, and, after failing, offered to sneak him out of Japan on a Portuguese ship in defiance of Ieyasu's will. Adams's astute counsel and the many disturbances among the Catholic sects were undoubtedly factors influencing Ieyasu's 1614 edict ordering expulsion of all Catholic priests and missionaries and ordering all Japanese to renounce Christianity and register their families' Buddhist affiliations at state-approved temples. Ieyasu died in 1616 and was replaced as shogun by his son Hidetada, who exerted stronger efforts to destroy Christianity and control the Europeans, restricting their merchants to ports at Nagasaki and nearby Hirado.

The third Tokugawa shogun, Iemitsu, who began his reign in 1623, further accelerated the process of stamping out Christianity. Since Ieyasu's days, various forms of torture were used to force believers to renounce their faith; common methods included mutilation, fire, waterboarding, and being hung headfirst over sewage pits. Christian daimyo recanted quickly rather than lose their domains under the new Tokugawa regime; samurai tended to disavow Catholicism more readily than ordinary commoners, who often held steadfast and were subsequently executed. From 1614 to 1640, five to six thousand believers were killed in this way. In the 1630s, Iemitsu forbade all Japanese ships from leaving the home islands, prohibited Japanese from going abroad, and prevented those who had been abroad from returning.

The Shimabara Rebellion of 1637–38 led to the final steps taken by the Tokugawa to remove the scourge of Catholic Christianity from Japan. Shimabara Peninsula and the nearby island of Amakusa, near Nagasaki, were Christian strongholds. When the new daimyo assigned by the Tokugawa to rule the area imposed onerous taxes, the peasants of Shimabara and Amakusa, along with many masterless samurai (rōnin), rose in protest. Their rebellion had Christian overtones, invoking Jesus and Maria (Mary). Nearly forty thousand rebels converged at the site of Hara Castle and survived a three-month siege by an army of one hundred thousand, composed of forces from the Tokugawa bakufu and neighboring domains. Cannons acquired from the Dutch finally helped defeat the rebels. Following the rebellion, Iemitsu issued the strictest edicts, which abolished all foreign commerce except for trade conducted with Koreans, Chinese, and the Dutch. The European traders, however, were restricted to living on a small man-made island known as Deshima in Nagasaki Bay. As the only non-Asians allowed in Japan, the Dutch became the chief source of Japanese knowledge of European civilization for the next two centuries.

The orders issued by the first three shoguns to limit and control foreign interaction are often referred to as "closed country" *(sakoku)* edicts, but this is a misnomer that ignores the fact that trade with China, Korea, and the Ryūkyū kingdom (now Okinawa) continued under less restrictive conditions.

In summary, endemic warfare consumed the capital and countryside from the mid-fifteenth to the mid-sixteenth century as local warriors sought to gain control over the lands they occupied, religious sects fought among themselves, and daimyo competed to expand their autonomous territories. Daimyo military and economic aims were furthered through trade and weaponry acquired through Portuguese and Spanish merchants, who arrived in Japan accompanied by Catholic missionaries. Daimyo also forged alliances and built networks of merchant and temple supporters by cultivating cultural pursuits such as the tea ceremony, which served as an important forum for political maneuvering. The duality of their military and cultural lives is symbolized in the castles of the era, imposing martial facilities that, nonetheless, contained finely wrought paintings, Nō theaters, and tearooms.

In the 1560s, the young daimyo Oda Nobunaga began the process of national reunification, which would be completed under his deputy Hideyoshi, followed by Tokugawa Ieyasu, who established Japan's third and final shogunate in 1603.

FURTHER READING

Berry, Mary Elizabeth. *The Culture of Civil War in Kyoto.* Berkeley: University of California Press, 1997.

———. *Hideyoshi.* Cambridge, MA: Harvard University Press, 1989.

Clulow, Adam. *The Company and the Shogun: The Dutch Encounter with Tokugawa Japan.* New York: Columbia University Press, 2016.

Elison, George, and Bardwell Smith, eds. *Warlords, Artists, and Commoners: Japan in the Sixteenth Century.* Honolulu: University of Hawaii Press, 1981.

Hall, John W., Nagahara Keiji, and Kozo Yamamura, eds. *Japan Before Tokugawa: Political Consolidation and Economic Growth, 1500–1650.* Princeton, NJ: Princeton University Press, 1981.

Mitchelhill, Jennifer, and David Green. *Castles of the Samurai: Power and Beauty.* New York: Oxford University Press, 2013.

Pitelka, Morgan. *Handmade Culture: Raku Potters, Patrons and Tea Practitioners in Japan.* Honolulu: University of Hawaii Press, 2005.

———, ed. *Japanese Tea Culture: Art, History, and Practice.* New York: Routledge, 2007.

Tsang, Carol R. *War and Faith: Ikkō Ikki in Late Muromachi Japan.* Cambridge, MA: Harvard, 2007.

Watsky, Andrew M. *Chikubushima: Deploying the Sacred Arts in Momoyama Japan.* Seattle: University of Washington Press, 2004.

RECOMMENDED FILMS

Heaven and Earth. 1990. Feature film directed by Kadokawa Haruki. Relates the historical rivalry between two Sengoku daimyo, Takeda Shingen and Uesugi Kenshin.

Rikyu. 1991. Feature film directed by Teshigahara Hiroshi. Fictionalized biography of the late stages of the tea master's life, depicting his relationship with Hideyoshi.

Seven Samurai. 1958. Feature film directed by Kurosawa Akira. Historical drama about a Sengoku-era village that hires seven masterless samurai to combat bandits who plan to steal their crops. Considered one of the best films of all time.

Silence. 2016. Feature film directed by Martin Scorsese. This adaptation of Endō Shusaku's novel of the same name follows two Jesuit priests who travel to Japan after the Shimabara rebellion.

Throne of Blood. 1957. Feature film directed by Kurosawa Akira. Adaptation of Shakespeare's *Macbeth* set in Japan during the Sengoku era.

6   Maintaining Control

Tokugawa Official Culture, 1603–1850s

The Tokugawa shogunate (1603–1868) was the last and longest lived of Japan's three warrior governments. Many of its key social, political, and administrative policies built upon the foundations laid by Nobunaga and Hideyoshi. The three centuries of Tokugawa rule were a time of peace and prosperity, when violence was largely outlawed. As the first stable national government after a century of fierce civil war, the bakufu integrated all of Japan's independent domains into a single, national polity. Many of the policies Ieyasu and his sons designed were intended to maintain this state by freezing the status quo, with the Tokugawa clan as hegemonic power. Thus, the bakufu controlled and regulated potential rivals among the court, the daimyo, and Buddhist institutions, and it created elaborate systems to regulate identity in the four-class system of samurai, peasants, artisans, and merchants. Over time, the bushi became bureaucratized, serving as official functionaries who received hereditary stipends, rather than as warriors.

Although the Tokugawa shoguns sought support from Buddhist sects and sponsored various temples, they largely turned from Buddhism to Confucianism as the main ideology to legitimize their rule, emphasizing Confucian teachings on maintaining social order and stability through moral governance. Teachings on Confucian morality spread widely throughout the populace in a variety of formats. A new intellectual movement known as Kokugaku (National Learning) emerged in the eighteenth century as a nativist backlash against China's hegemonic influence on Japan. Kokugaku initiated renewed interest in Japan's indigenous history and literary classics and was an important influence on later imperial activists in the Meiji Restoration. A third development in intellectual culture was the spread of Rangaku (Dutch Studies). The Dutch were the only Europeans allowed to trade and reside in Japan. Texts and objects they provided allowed the Japanese to remain abreast of many Western developments in science and industry. Finally, although Buddhism did not develop any major new teachings or sects during this period, new forms of popular religiosity, including pilgrimage, spread widely among the populace.

Because there were so many developments in society and culture during the Tokugawa era, this chapter will address political, social, intellectual, and religious change, while chapter 7 will focus on the emergence of new forms of popular culture.

POLITICAL AND SOCIAL DEVELOPMENTS

Tokugawa Ieyasu was named shogun in 1603. Adopting the tactics of Heian emperors, he retired from the position two years later, allowing his son Hidetada to assume the title, but continued to act as the main authority behind the office until his death in 1616. There would be fifteen successive Tokugawa shoguns before the fall of the regime in 1868, but following Hidetada's successor Iemitsu, few exerted real authority or true leadership; most led the luxurious lives of royalty and left matters of governance to others.

The governing structure established by Ieyasu is sometimes referred to as the *baku-han* (bakufu-domain) system, in which government functioned through two political mechanisms: the Tokugawa bakufu and daimyo-led domains *(han)*. The bakufu rarely interfered directly in the internal affairs of the domains, giving daimyo considerable autonomy, but strictly insisted that all daimyo swear their vassalage to each shogun, agreeing to follow certain basic policies, such as keeping order within their own domains, providing military support when requested by the bakufu, and contributing funds, manpower, and materials for the maintenance of shogunal castles, imperial palaces, and public works. If they failed to perform these duties to the shogun's satisfaction, they could be transferred to less desirable domains or simply have their domains confiscated altogether. As chief of Japan's warrior class, the shogun was expected to preserve law and order domestically and to control foreign trade and diplomacy. To achieve these ends, the bakufu created institutions and policies in three key areas: administration, foreign policy, and social management. In addition, they exerted controls over other potential centers of power that had threatened earlier regimes, such as the imperial court, Buddhist temples, and especially other daimyo clans, the largest threat because they still held military and economic power. The shogunate did not possess absolute military superiority—of the two hundred thousand samurai in Japan, Tokugawa forces numbered around

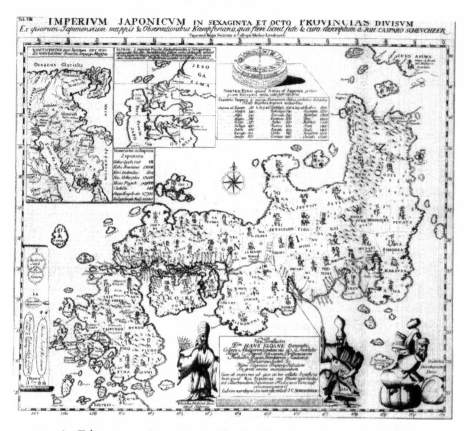

MAP 6.   Tokugawa-era Japan. Prepared by Englebert Kaempfer, employee of Dutch VOC, seventeenth century.

sixty thousand. Thus, Tokugawa rule depended on the support of the other daimyo to maintain their hegemony.

A senior council *(rōju)* of five or six daimyo considered to be close allies of the Tokugawa *(fudai daimyo)* oversaw national administration and affairs, including foreign relations, defense, and daimyo control. Each member served as head of the council for a month at a time, in order to prevent any single daimyo from taking control. Other important offices, like the commissioners of major cities, were also held by fudai daimyo. Daimyo whom the Tokugawa considered potential rivals for power (*tozama daimyo*, or outer lords) were kept at arm's length, prohibited from holding a seat on the senior council. Tozama daimyo held eleven of the sixteen largest and wealthiest domains, but these were located on the peripheries of the main islands. Fudai domains, by contrast, surrounded and protected Tokugawa-owned territories, which totaled around 25 percent of Japan's arable land and also included Japan's largest cities and its major gold and silver mines.

In order to avoid the intrigues, secret alliances, and rebellions of vassals against their lords that characterized the Sengoku era, the Tokugawa employed heavy surveillance, with networks of spies, inspectors, and censors at all levels of society. Known as *metsuke* (literally, to put one's eye upon), these spies scrutinized activities of daimyo, Tokugawa vassals, and bakufu officials. Each domain also had its own system of inspectors and spies for internal control. Villagers and townspeople were organized into groups of five or more households *(gonin gumi)*, who were held collectively responsible for the conduct of all members, creating a self-surveillance mechanism among the general commoner populace. In a sense, the metsuke inspectors were heirs to the much celebrated but historically rather insignificant "ninja" or *shinobi* tradition. Some ninja troupes existed during Sengoku; they clandestinely penetrated enemy territory to observe movements, obtain secret information, or engage in assassinations. In the Tokugawa period, however, their combat techniques were codified into martial arts and the business of spying became bureaucratic and systematized. This routinization of the skills of war, "the taming of the samurai," is an underlying theme of the period. Warrior skills, the prerogative of the samurai class, were unnecessary in a society where violence had been outlawed and where one's position depended on hereditary rank, so samurai largely became government functionaries. Their martial skills, the raison d'être for this privileged class, declined in importance over time.

To maintain its position as the hegemonic power in the new order, the Tokugawa shogunate limited the power of competing centers of authority, restricting the prerogatives of the imperial court, Buddhist temples, and other powerful daimyo. The court was a notorious source of intrigue that had threatened numerous past regimes. Control of the court was important because the shogun was officially only a delegate of the emperor, who, at least symbolically, possessed the ultimate authority of the land and could, theoretically, remove the Tokugawa from this position. In 1615, Ieyasu issued a seventeen-clause order prohibiting the imperial court from engaging in political activity and claiming veto power over the emperor's awards of court honors to military houses. Court nobility were physically confined to the palace enclosures in Kyoto and were closely monitored by the shogun's deputy, installed at the magnificent Nijō Castle, constructed using contributions ordered from western daimyo.

Buddhist temples and monasteries lost their military capabilities under Nobunaga but remained wealthy and influential. In order to ensure that they could not challenge Tokugawa rule, the bakufu required that they submit to state supervision in return for continued approval of their land rights, the source of the Buddhists' financial security. The sects that were firmly established by the seventeenth century became quasi-official organs of the state, responsible for maintaining population registers. All individuals required a certificate of affiliation with a Buddhist temple. Thus, at birth every person was enrolled in his family's temple, and registers of temple members were compiled and sent to the daimyo. The temple certificate was required for many important occasions, including marriage, travel, change of residence, or entry into certain occupations. Those suspected of Christian faith were sometimes ordered to trample on crucifixes or images of Jesus or Mary *(fumi-e)* in order to prove they were not Christian.

Control of the 250-odd daimyo, who autonomously ruled over four-fifths of the country, was critical. With the accession of every new shogun, each daimyo was required to re-swear a pledge of obedience; in return, he received certification of his right to the income earned in his domain. Misbehavior was punished by confiscating or reducing domains or transferring daimyo to new territories. In "Buke shohatto" (Laws for military houses), first issued in 1615, the shogunate issued orders that forbade daimyo from building new fortifications or large ships, from harboring fugitives, and from imposing tolls on domainal roads. Domains could not contract marriages that might lead to political alliances without shogunal approval.

One of the most remarkable methods of daimyo control was *sankin kōtai*, or alternate attendance. Under this policy, daimyo were required to reside in Edo every other year in attendance on the shogun and had to maintain residential estates there, where their wives and children were permanently held hostage. Requirements for sankin kōtai were specified in "Buke shohatto" and altered only once from 1635, when they were formally enacted, until 1862, when the practice ended. It was the bakufu's most effective form of control over the daimyo, inhibiting their ability to threaten the regime. Furthermore, sankin kōtai acted as an agent of major social transformation, stimulating economic growth and forging a sense of national culture.

In order to monitor the movement of daimyo armies to and from the capital, the bakufu created and administered a network of five central highways converging in Edo. This national transport system proved vital in integrating the new state through speedy and safe official communications, maintaining monopolies over military deployment, and controlling the circulation of both goods and individuals. The two major highways were the Tōkaidō, which ran along the coastline from the imperial capital at Kyoto to the shogun's capital at Edo; and the Nakasendō, which took a longer and

FIGURE 26. Andō Hiroshige, "Changing Porters and Horses" at Fujieda, 1830s, Tokyo Metropolitan Library. Source: Wikimedia Commons.

more mountainous inland route between the two cities. Travel along these roads was tightly regulated—officials checked identification at a number of barrier stations. Post station towns, spaced from three to ten miles apart along the route, provided services for travelers, such as fresh horses, porters, and lodging. There were fifty-three stations along the Tōkaidō and sixty-seven along the Nakasendō, immortalized in the woodblock prints of artist Andō Hiroshige (see chapter 7). The highways and post stations provided national integration in communications, the exchange of goods, and the circulation of people. Villages near these towns were assigned responsibility for providing men and horses and for bridge construction and road maintenance necessary to keep traffic moving.

The typical daimyo traveled to Edo in parade-like processions along the main highways with an entourage of one to six hundred vassals and servants, including pikemen, mounted and unmounted swordsmen, banner carriers, and other top domain officials with their own vassals and servants. The size of the retinue depended on the amount of rice income *(koku)* generated by the domain. Specialists that were needed to provide services for the daimyo during the journey included doctors, veterinarians, falconers, cooks, scribes, and sometimes poets. At the head of many processions,

FIGURE 27.   Detail from a scroll illustrating a nineteenth-century *sankin kōtai* procession, 1904, Nantan City Museum of Culture, Sonobe, Japan. Source: Wikimedia Commons.

porters carried an array of religious objects to bring the journey good fortune and guard against mishaps and evil. Carpenters who made repairs to their lords' palanquins and rooms at inns, and other artisans who mended curtains and flags, were also part of the entourage. In addition to weapons and possessions, they had to carry food, drinking water, sake, and soy sauce. They needed items like rain gear, portable chairs, and lanterns for the route. The daimyo required his own exclusive traveling toilet and bathtub. Everyday goods, and porters to carry them, were often procured en route, helping to support the economies of highway towns. The daimyo himself traveled in the center of the procession in a palanquin surrounded by personal attendants and extra palanquin carriers. As the daimyo passed, commoners were ordered to drop to their knees and kowtow. Travel to and from Edo and the construction and upkeep of the official daimyo compounds there, each housing thousands of men, consumed about 50–75 percent of domainal income, preventing daimyo from heavy investment in military expenditures that might threaten the Tokugawa regime.

Sankin kōtai processions were "theaters of power," symbolizing both the authority of the Tokugawa regime to unify and command the realm and the wealth and status of the traveling daimyo.[1] Watching the parades pass into and out of the capital was considered the most popular form of sightseeing in Edo. The colorful, coordinated uniforms of retainers, depicted in pictorial scrolls, provided a sense of order and discipline among the domain's ranks. The weapons carried demonstrated the daimyo's military power, the parade itself mimicking the form of an army setting out for battle. On the long stretches between towns, however, the participants did not march in forma-

tion. Only before arriving at a major town or checkpoint, where a large audience awaited, would all in the procession smarten up their appearances, synchronize their steps, and raise their weapons. Footmen known as *yakko*, carrying lances decorated with feathers and fringes, would begin to dance, tossing and swirling their lances like baton twirlers at the head of a parade. When returning home, daimyo often employed temporary laborers at the borders of their domain to create a grander show of arrival.

Overall, the system provided a major stimulus for economic growth throughout the country. The domainal samurai residing in Edo were accompanied by artisans, tradesmen, and merchants who flocked to the city to supply their needs, quickly swelling the population. By the mid-eighteenth century, Edo became the largest metropolis in the world, with over one million residents. Osaka grew into a financial and commercial center, as daimyo sold tax rice and other commercial goods—such as foodstuffs, paper, cloth, and iron—to the local merchants in order to obtain cash to fund their living expenses. Kyoto thrived as the center for fine textiles and elegant handicrafts needed for daimyo mansions. The domains themselves developed new industries and attempted to create new monopolies on commercial products in order to raise funds to meet the daimyo's expenses. Networks of inns and restaurants arose to meet the needs of the massive traveling entourages. Sankin kōtai also brought cultural transformation, disseminating the tastes and trends of the capital to the provinces when vassals traveled home while simultaneously drawing new fashions and ideas from around the nation into Edo. Furthermore, sankin kōtai effected political change within the domains; the regularly absent daimyo, who generally preferred Edo sophistication to the rustic, rural lifestyles at home, became figureheads in their own lands, further bureaucratizing the management of the domain's government affairs. Sankin kōtai is so symbolic of the Tokugawa era that its processions are reenacted for tourists in many cities and towns across Japan today.

STATUS SYSTEM

The bakufu's fundamental method of social control over the populace was a strict separation of classes, upheld by rules and regulations designed to maintain the status quo. The bakufu built upon the four-class system of samurai, peasants, artisans, and merchants initiated by Hideyoshi to ensure that everyone would know and keep their place in society. This four-class hierarchy was modeled on Confucian hierarchies of social utility and virtue. According to this ideology, those at the top served the public interest, while those at the bottom promoted their own self-interest. Confucian economic philosophy was traditionally agrarian, hostile to commerce and to putting profit before virtue. The samurai ruling class, roughly 10 percent of the total population, was deemed most important because they provided leadership, order, and moral guidance to society. The peasants, over 80 percent of the population, were second in social status because they produced necessary sustenance and provided for the economic needs of the ruling class. Artisans, in third place, created necessary goods, but merchants, at the bottom, produced nothing useful and only distributed goods made by others for their own profit. Artisans and merchants were often collectively referred to as townspeople *(chōnin)*.

Individuals were born into their respective classes and prohibited from changing occupation or marrying outside of their status. The four classes were separated not just by job function, but also by different legal codes and lifestyle prescriptions. They resided separately, samurai within the walls of castle towns or daimyo compounds, peasants in rural villages, and townspeople in certain urban districts. To protect the privileged position of samurai in society, the shogunate issued minutely detailed instructions on every aspect of life, specifying the housing, clothing, entertainment, food, and even hairstyles appropriate to each class and to different age groups and genders within classes.

These sumptuary laws and edicts attempted to regulate the personal appearance and expenditure of wealth appropriate to each class. Segregation of material culture was meant to impose physical distinctions that matched the differences in status; in other words, one should live and spend according to one's social position, which should be immediately recognizable through visual cues. Rulers recognized that elements of appearance, such as styles of clothing, hairstyles, and accessories, might be used to subvert status and occupational boundaries. Sumptuary laws thus helped identify threats to the status system. Classes were also restricted in terms of the amounts that might be spent on entertainment and ceremonies, such as weddings and funerals. Ostentatious behavior and display of wealth were proscribed for all classes, but the shogunate was especially concerned that merchants, who tended to have the most discretionary income despite their lowly social ranking, should not outshine their betters, as this might undermine samurai morale and discipline.

Examples of rules for the samurai included regulations dictating the length of swords and the requirement to wear a topknot hairstyle with a partially shaved head. They were forbidden from sporting heavy facial hair. Peasants were ordered to live frugally, to consume rough grains like barley and millet rather than tax rice, to abstain from tea and sake, and to wear only cotton. Townspeople were prohibited from using gold and silver decoration in their clothing, housing, and accessories. They were forbidden from wearing "luxurious clothes" or high rain clogs, possessing long swords, or walking alongside a samurai in the streets.[2] Samurai were entitled to strike down commoners for disrespectful behavior. Wealthy townspeople resentful of such restrictions sometimes engaged in illegal behaviors subversively, in ways invisible to official eyes, such as using luxurious, gold-embroidered silks as the lining for plain cotton kimonos.

The bakufu relied more on threats and exhortations than on consistent punishment to compel compliance with sumptuary laws, but flagrant violaters were sometimes harshly punished to set an example for others. One such case occurred in 1681 with the household of wealthy Edo merchant Ishikawa Rokubei. Rokubei's wife loved extravagant clothing and had worn her best finery to view the procession of the fifth shogun, Tokugawa Tsunayoshi (1646–1709), remembered as the "dog shogun" for his eccentric edicts protecting canines in Edo. The elegant Mrs. Ishikawa caught Tsunayoshi's eye and he inquired after her, assuming she was a member of a high-ranking family. When told she was only the wife of a lowly merchant, the shogun was infuriated and demanded punishment. The town magistrate confiscated all of the family's property and they were banished from Edo.[3] Tsunayoshi, known as a profligate spender himself, soon issued an unprecedented number of sumptuary regulations regarding merchant clothing. A later example of enforcement involved Kabuki actor Ichikawa Danjūrō VII (1791–1859), the biggest star of his time, in 1842. Danjūrō used genuine weapons and armor on stage, the gifts of wealthy admirers, rather than stage props. This clear violation of the exclusive samurai privilege to own and carry such weapons resulted in the actor's ten-year banishment from Edo. Since Osaka also possessed a popular Kabuki theater, the actor did not actually suffer much, but his fame ensured that the warning against violating status restrictions would spread widely among the populace.

The four-class system provided a normative, static model of society designed to maintain support for the Tokugawa social and political order, but it did not accurately describe lived reality, where identities were less fixed and more complex. Many individuals and professions, including Buddhist monks and nuns, members of the court, and doctors, did not belong to any of the categories. Outcaste classes were also absent from the idealized social model. This varied group included those whose hereditary occupations were considered polluting, such as butchers, tanners, and undertakers, known collectively as *eta* (considered a discriminatory term today); those who engaged in itinerant lifestyles, known as *hinin* (non-people), such as prostitutes, entertainers, beggars, and blind masseuses; and the indigenous peoples of Ezo (northern Honshu and Hokkaido), known as Ainu today. The eta caste, referred to today as *burakumin* (people of the hamlet), faced numerous forms of discrimination. Like other classes, they were restricted to living in certain villages and required to wear cotton clothing and straw slippers, rather than wooden geta clogs. They were prohibited from owning or cultivating rice fields and had to abide by special curfews.

TOKUGAWA INTELLECTUAL CULTURE

Confucianism

Rather than sponsoring new schools of Buddhism to add to the legitimacy of the new regime, as previous groups of rulers had done, the Tokugawa shogunate turned to Confucianism to help undergird their rule. Confucianism was primarily concerned with maintaining order, stability, and moral governance, in keeping with Tokugawa aims after a century of chaos and warfare. It emphasized the importance of propriety, ritual, and hierarchy in personal relationships. In an age when the Japanese could no longer visit the continent, Chinese philosophy, especially the Neo-Confucianism associated with the philosopher Zhu Xi (1130–1200), flourished as never before. Neo-Confucian philosophy was rationalistic and human-centered. Zhu Xi advocated an approach to knowledge based on observing and studying the laws of nature and human society. The rationalism of Neo-Confucianism contrasted with the nonrational approach of Zen or the medieval Buddhist belief in mappō that viewed the world in negative terms.

Some aspects of Confucianism didn't suit Japanese society as well as China. For example, as noted in chapter 2, the Confucian doctrine of the "Mandate of Heaven" held that if the ruler was incompetent or unjust, he could be overthrown and the mandate would be transferred to whoever would rule best. Japan's imperial house, however, claimed its mandate through direct descent from the Sun Goddess, Amaterasu, and thus could not be replaced by a competing dynasty. The position of shogun, too, was restricted to members of the Tokugawa family. Many leading Japanese Zhu Xi scholars, such as Yamazaki Ansai (1619–82), infused their works with Shinto-related concepts to adapt Confucianism to Japan's imperial situation. Another difference between the two countries lay in the identity of the ruling class. In China, ruling bureaucrats were scholar elites who earned official positions based on merit, whereas in Japan they were members of the samurai class who held inherited rank. Nevertheless, the Confucian concept of hierarchical relationships, with rigid distinctions between ruler and subject, father and son, and men and women, suited the needs of the Tokugawa bakufu. Whereas the Chinese emphasized filial piety and the parent-child relationship, the Japanese emphasized the tie between rulers and subjects, interpreting this as the commitment of absolute loyalty to one's lord.

Tokugawa Ieyasu appointed Neo-Confucianist Hayashi Razan (1583–1657) as one of his key advisors. Hayashi played a critical role in drafting the laws and edicts issued by Ieyasu and served as key advisor to the first three shoguns. His descendants continued to advise subsequent shoguns. The Kansei Edict of 1790 made Zhu Xi Neo-Confucianism the official, orthodox philosophy of Japan, banning other studies of Confucianism as heterodox. Nevertheless, alternative schools of Confucian thought persisted and found wide audiences among the samurai class. Because scholars followed the historical Chinese practice of writing commentaries to Confucian classics to adapt teachings to their present age, conflicting views and rival schools emerged. One such rival was the Wang Yang-Ming school, favored by many independent, reform-minded samurai scholars and the daimyo that employed them. This school of thought, known in Japanese as Ōyōmei, stressed intuition and moral sense over intellect; in short, one did not have to be a scholar but ought to be a good person. Another fundamental Ōyōmei tenet was "the unity of knowledge and action," the belief that deeds were as important as words and that one's principles should be carried out directly in action. It was not enough to merely read about or discuss filial piety; one must actively practice it. The founder of Ōyōmei in Japan, Nakae Tōju (1608–48), embodied this teaching. He resigned from an official post to return to his remote native village in order to care for his aging mother. Tōju established a school in his village that attracted many scholars and became highly influential. In the late Tokugawa period, his teachings inspired zealous reformers and patriots who helped overthrow the shogunate and restore the emperor.

Other highly influential Confucian thinkers rejected Zhu Xi orthodoxy and advocated a return to the study of original, ancient Confucian texts. Itō Jinsai (1627–1705), the son of a Kyoto townsman, founded a private school dedicated to teaching humanistic ideals that applied to all classes. His teachings centered on the Confucian *Analects* and the teachings of Mencius and stressed compassion and humaneness, expressed through loving relationships with other people and through actions benefiting humankind. He believed that Zhu Xi Confucianism was too introspective and that it called for too much seriousness and self-restraint. Itō remained an independent scholar who attracted large numbers of students but steadfastly refused numerous offers for prestigious posts by daimyo.

Ogyū Sorai (1668–1728), a Sinophile and philologist, served as an adviser to the shogunate. Sorai rejected the Zhu Xi Confucianism of Song China, using the ancient Confucian classics on government and social order to criticize the contemporary economic and political order. He is considered a key thinker in making a breakthrough toward modern political consciousness. His 1717 work *Distinguishing the Way (Bendō)* defined the foundations of political power and offered prescriptions for regimes facing crises. One of Hayashi Razan's own students, Yamaga Sokō (1622–85), also criticized Zhu Xi orthodoxy, charging that Chinese scholars from the second to fifteenth centuries had misinterpreted the Confucian classics.

Sokō focused on defining the functions of, and rationalizing the privileges given to, the ruling warrior class during a time of peace. Sokō upheld the idealization of bun and bu (see chapter 4): samurai were obligated to maintain their martial skills while cultivating civilian arts such as poetry and history. According to Sokō, they must demonstrate utmost loyalty to their lord and devote themselves to duty and morality over personal gain in order to serve as leaders for the common people. Proper samurai lived "a life of austerity, temperance, constant self-discipline, and readiness to meet death at any time."[4] Here is an excerpt from Sokō's writings on the "Way of the Samurai" (Shidō) that demonstrates his concern for justifying the stipends and privileges the samurai class earned simply by virtue of their birth:

For generation after generation men have taken their livelihood from tilling the soil, or devised and manufactured tools, or produced profit from mutual trade, so that peoples' needs were satisfied. . . . But the samurai eats food without growing it, uses utensils without manufacturing them, and profits without buying or selling. What is the justification for this? . . .

The business of the samurai is to reflect on his own station in life, to give loyal service to his master if he has one, to strengthen his fidelity in associations with friends, and, with due consideration of his own position, to devote himself to duty above all. . . .

[I]f there is someone in the three classes of the common people who violates moral principles, the samurai should punish him summarily and thus uphold the proper moral principles in the land. It would not do for the samurai to know martial and civil virtues without manifesting them. Since this is the case, outwardly he stands in physical readiness for any call to service, and inwardly he strives to fulfill the Way of the lord and subject. . . . Within his heart he keeps to the ways of peace, but without, he keeps his weapons ready for use. The three classes of the common people make him their teacher and respect him.[5]

Sokō's text provided a guide for the lives of samurai, whose social role had shifted from military to political and intellectual leadership. They could rationalize their stipend by serving as moral exemplars for commoners and maintaining their martial skills, should they be called upon to protect their lord and society. In the twentieth century, Sokō's works became the basis for the ideology of Bushidō (the Way of the Warrior), which exalted samurai honor and chivalry but avoided discussion of hereditary material reward.

The Forty-Seven Rōnin

Yamaga Sokō's influence would be seen in the Akō Vendetta of 1703, a well-known historical incident that has been transformed into numerous, beloved pieces of popular literature, art, drama, and film under the names *The Forty-Seven Rōnin* and *Chūshingura (The Treasury of Loyal Retainers)*. The story is thought to represent the ultimate in the samurai ideal of honor and loyalty to one's lord. The incident began when Asano Naganori, the daimyo of the Akō domain, was ordered to arrange a reception for imperial envoys at the shogun's palace during his period of sankin kōtai service. The young daimyo was to be instructed in court etiquette by Kira Yoshinaka, the shogun Tsunayoshi's master of rituals, but Kira humiliated Asano instead, treating him with contempt. The daimyo soon lost his temper and attacked Kira with a dagger, an act completely forbidden within Edo Castle. He was ordered to commit seppuku that day; the bakufu confiscated the domain from his family, leaving his samurai retainers masterless.

Of the three hundred Akō rōnin, forty-seven—led by Ōishi Yoshio (a pupil of Yamaga Sokō)—decided to avenge their lord, although they realized they would face severe punishment. Suspecting a plot for revenge, Kira ordered spies to surveil the rōnin. To offset suspicions, the forty-seven dispersed around the country, adopting identities as merchants and monks. Ōishi located himself in Kyoto and began to drink heavily, frequent brothels, and act foolishly in public to convince Kira and the authorities that he was no threat. Some of the rōnin avengers gained access to Kira's mansion in Edo as workmen or merchants and became familiar with its layout and operations. Other avengers obtained weapons and transported them to Edo, which were illegal acts. After a year and a half, Kira let down his guard and the rōnin sprang into action.

In the early hours of January 30, 1703, during a heavy snowstorm, the avengers posted archers outside Kira's mansion—to prevent the inhabitants from sending for help—and began the attack. Breaking into the back of the house, they fought off Kira's retainers but could not find their enemy, who had hidden himself in a secret room. When the attackers finally discovered the hiding place, the occupant refused to identify himself as Kira, but he bore a scar on his head consistent with Asano's attack. In consideration of Kira's high rank, Ōishi presented him with the opportunity to honorably commit seppuku using Asano's own dagger, but Kira refused to answer, so the rōnin cut off his head to offer to their master at his tomb at Sengaku-ji Temple. To reach the temple, they marched more than six miles across the center of Edo. Their procession attracted a great deal of attention, and the story of their successful campaign of revenge spread quickly. After the rōnin made their offering at their lord's gravesite, the group turned themselves in and awaited judgment.

Shogunal officials debated the particulars of the case and the meanings of righteousness it held. On one hand, the rōnin had broken the law by exacting revenge, but on the other, they were motivated by samurai ideals of loyalty to their lord. Officials received many petitions on behalf of the rōnin from admirers. In the end, they were ordered to commit seppuku, spared the indignity of criminal execution because of the honorable nature of their actions. The loyal rōnin were buried in front of their master's tomb at Sengaku-ji, and Asano's younger brother was restored to the position of daimyo, although the size of his domain was vastly reduced. The gravesites became a site of pilgrimage, where many have come over the centuries to

FIGURE 28. Utagawa Hiroshige, *Act XI Second Episode: Rōnin Breaking into the Inner Building of Moronao's Castle*, from *Chūshingura*, 1830s, Los Angeles County Museum of Art. Source: Wikimedia Commons.

pray and offer veneration; the clothing and weapons of the forty-seven rōnin are preserved in the temple to this day.

Popular Morality

Literacy was surprisingly widespread throughout Tokugawa society, allowing Confucian teachings, often blended with aspects of Buddhism and/or Shinto, to diffuse widely throughout the classes. The samurai class was nearly 100 percent literate, because all its ranks were entitled to attend domainal academies where they studied the Confucian classics, military arts, and calligraphy, among other subjects. Wealthy commoners often achieved degrees of literacy matching or surpassing their samurai betters, while moderately well-off commoners were also surprisingly literate. In rural areas, the latter attended schools that were held at temples or at teachers' homes *(terakoya)*; in cities, educated samurai, rōnin, and priests operated private academies open to townspeople. Such schools taught the basics of reading and writing, employing the Confucian *Classic of Filial Piety* and other canonical texts; taught arithmetic using an abacus; and steeped students in conventional wisdom that placed stress on hard work, respectfulness, morality, and frugality. One frequently employed terakoya text, the *Dōjikyō* (Precepts for the young), contained dozens of instructions and admonitions for students. The *Dōjikyō* still seems relevant for both teachers and students today, warning against truancy, littering, mischievous pranks, rude language, sumo wrestling, and graffiti. Children were urged to keep their clothing clean and their hair tidy. The opening verse emphasized the importance of education: "To be born human and not be able to write is to be less than human. Illiteracy is a form of blindness. It brings shame on your teacher, shame on your parents, and shame on yourself. The heart of a child of three stays with him until he is a hundred, as the proverb says. Determine to succeed, study with all your might, never forgetting the shame of failure."[6]

Kaibara Ekken (1630–1714) is among the best-known popularizers of simplified Confucian teachings. He employed vernacular language, rather than classical Chinese, to present the basics of Confucianism to a broad audience, providing easy-to-understand moral doctrines for governing people's everyday conduct, their relationships with others, their duties within their families and to their feudal lords, and other topics. In short, he did for Confucian ethics what Pure Land had done for Buddhism in medieval Japan: he brought it down from the level of difficult, elite doctrine to the level of common speech available to all. Kaibara is especially well known for treatises addressing women and children. A 1733 work entitled *Onna daigaku* (Greater learning for women) is often attributed to him, although its authorship is unclear. This treatise appears shockingly patriarchal and sexist to modern sensibilities, defying Confucianism's aim of self-cultivation by denying women's selfhood and fully subordinating them to their husbands and families. Two particularly misogynist passages, translated by Japanologist Basil Hall Chamberlain in 1890, are as follows:

> The five worst maladies that afflict the female mind are: indocility, discontent, slander, jealousy, and silliness. Without any doubt, these five maladies infest seven or eight out of every ten women, and it is from these that arises the inferiority of women to men. A woman should cure them by self-inspection and self-reproach. The worst of them all, and the parent of the other four, is silliness. . . .
>   Let her never even dream of jealousy. If her husband be dissolute, she must expostulate with him, but never either nurse or vent her anger. If her jealousy be extreme, it will render her countenance frightful and her accents repulsive, and can only result in completely alienat-

ing her husband from her, and making her intolerable in his eyes. Should her husband act ill and unreasonably, she must compose her countenance and soften her voice to remonstrate with him; and if he be angry and listen not to the remonstrance, she must wait over a season, and then expostulate with him again when his heart is softened. Never set thyself up against thy husband with harsh features and a boisterous voice![7]

Schools and teachings specific to different classes explained the duties and responsibilities for a given status group, as Yamaga Sokō had done for the samurai class. A religio-ethical school known as Shingaku, established by Ishida Baigan (1685–1744) in Kyoto, urged merchants to strive for morality in their business dealings, devote themselves to their enterprises, and practice frugality. If they fulfilled their merchantly duties, they were entitled to profits, just as samurai were entitled to stipends for fulfilling their moral duties. Baigan promoted zazen-like meditation as a method for followers to know their minds and understand their place in the social order. Shingaku lecturers traveled throughout Japan, using stories and humor to help deliver teachings. By the nineteenth century, there were 180 centers of Shingaku learning across the nation. An official Confucian academy for merchants, the Kaitokudō, established in Osaka in 1727, offered higher education for the business classes. It became an important think tank for merchants to help formulate policies that would support domainal and bakufu finances; many Kaitokudō graduates were hired as economic advisers by daimyo and the shogunate.

Ninomiya Sontoku (1787–1856), a self-educated farmer known as the "Peasant Sage of Japan," developed a set of teachings to help improve rural lives. He emphasized three main points: first, that manual farm labor represented the highest form of human activity, allowing humans to receive food as the gift of the gods; second, that the unpredictability of nature and weather dictated that farmers must plan and budget for bad harvest years; and third, that successful agrarian life required cooperative communal organization. A main theme in his work, which stretches to thirty-six volumes, is "repayment of virtue," or humankind's obligations to repay the debts accumulated through benefits received from nature, family, and society by offering such benefits to others. For example, one's wealth and status were built on the virtues of ancestors and must be protected for descendants; one's food, clothing, and shelter depend on both the natural products of farms and forests and the labor of other people, so one must work hard and be thrifty to help share and preserve these gifts. Sontoku claimed his teachings were a "pill of three religions," one-half Shinto and one-quarter each Buddhism and Confucianism. When a disciple drew a pie chart of this "pill," with half of the circle marked Shinto and the other quarter-segments marked appropriately, Sontoku replied, "You won't find medicine like that anywhere. In a real pill all the ingredients are thoroughly blended so as to be indistinguishable. Otherwise it would taste bad in the mouth and feel bad in the stomach."[8]

National Learning

The new intellectual movement known as Kokugaku (National Learning) advocated an ethnocentric Shintoist revival. It was founded in the eighteenth century by scholars who wished to de-emphasize China's historical influence on Japan and initiate a renewal of interest in native Japanese history, literary classics, and cultural traditions. During the centuries of Buddhist and Confucian philosophical dominance, Shinto, lacking its own sophisticated systems of thought and doctrine, was blended into—and itself drew upon—the better-articulated traditions. Many disparate sects of Shinto, sometimes aligned closely with a school of Buddhism or Confucianism, were created over the centuries, such as Yoshida Shinto, tied to Neo-Confucianism; Watarai Shinto, associated with Ise Grand Shrine; and Ryōbu Shinto, derived from Shingon. In the early Tokugawa era, many Zhu Xi Neo-Confucian scholars opposed Buddhism but saw in Shinto a traditional form of worship that did not directly challenge the hierarchical values of Confucianism. Yamazaki Ansai founded Suika Shinto to fuse Confucian ethics with Shinto mythology and rituals. Most Kokugaku proponents, however, wished to purge Shinto of foreign elements. In nearly every community, ritual life continued to center around local Shinto shrines and festivals, which provided important symbols of communal identification and pride. On a fundamental level, Shinto continued to be deeply felt in the lives of the people, but scholars realized that if it were to become a truly national religion, rather than a collection of local practices, it would require a set of basic texts and teachings.

The poet Kada no Azumamaro (1669–1736), influenced by Ogyū Sorai's call to reexamine the Chinese classics, hoped to do the same for early Japanese texts. He petitioned the bakufu to support his study of Japan's ancient literature, which he called Kokugaku. By the middle of the nineteenth century, Kokugaku was regarded as the true expression of Japanese national feelings, unpolluted by alien culture. As scripture, it claimed not only ancient Shinto hymns and prayers *(norito)* but also the *Man'yōshū*, Japan's earliest extant collection of poems; the earliest national historical chronicles, the *Kojiki* and the *Nihon shoki;* classical Japanese literature such as *The Tale of Genji;* and the Heian imperial poetry collection the *Kokinshū.*

Kamo no Mabuchi (1697–1769) was Kada's disciple and the first important scholar of the Kokugaku movement. Kamo insisted, albeit incorrectly, that the eighth-century *Man'yōshū* was free of foreign influence. Its poems represented a true expression of archaic Japanese sentiment: open, spontaneous, and devoid of guile. He started composing his own poems in the *Man'yōshū* style and invited others to follow him.

The *Kojiki* had long been neglected, because of its difficulty and the greater historical importance assigned to the more reliable *Nihon shoki.* Motoori Norinaga (1730–1801), the second great scholar of Kokugaku and one of the finest scholars in all of Japanese history, took more than thirty years to translate the *Kojiki* into the language used in his day. Norinaga believed that emotion and sentiment were more central to Japanese life than Chinese ethics or philosophy and identified *The Tale of Genji* as a classic expression of native Japanese aesthetic sentiment, popularizing the notion of *mono no aware,* meaning sensitivity to beauty or pathos in nature or in the conditions of human life. In reaction to the Confucian orthodoxy that refuted Shinto mythology on the grounds of reason, he argued that matters pertaining to the gods were beyond the realm of human understanding and that rationalism was thus inadequate and inappropriate for assessing founding myths. In a work addressing the "true tradition of the Sun Goddess," he stated that all of the lands and all of the gods and goddesses of the world were brought into being by Izanami and Izanagi, but that China did not know of this act of divine creation and, hence, explained the principles of heaven and earth through theories such as yin and yang instead.

Norinaga's Kokugaku thus constituted a form of religious fundamentalism, upholding national mythology as literal truth to assert Japan's special position as a divine country, the home of the Sun Goddess, who cast her light over all countries. The ethnocentrism he espoused was taken even further by the next great Kokugaku scholar, Hirata Atsutane (1776–1843), whose reformulations of native faith, sometimes called Revival Shinto, was an important influence among imperial activists for the Meiji Restoration.

Early European and American scholars sometimes dismissed Atsutane as a zealot or huckster for his eclectic blend of spiritual and national teachings. Atsutane claimed that he met Motoori Norinaga in a dream and was his legitimate intellectual heir. Nevertheless, he diverged from his master on many counts, such as the nature of the afterlife and the gods of creation. Norinaga accepted the *Kojiki's* accounts of a pair of creator gods and of *yomi,* the dark, spectral land of the dead. Atsutane drew from Christianity and folk religion, proposing a monotheistic god of creation and expanding notions of the afterlife by collecting accounts of an "other world," contiguous to our own, visited by those who encountered supernatural beings. Atsutane was worldlier than his predecessors, more knowledgeable about Western science, medicine, and religion. Deeply aware of the outer and inner threats faced by Japan in the early nineteenth century, from an encroaching Russia and rural unrest, he sought to strengthen the nation by creating a syncretic faith superior to Buddhism, Christianity, and Confucianism. Aiming to launch a grassroots nativist movement, Atsutane worked with authors of farm manuals, creating simple, illustrated pamphlets that taught improved rice-cultivation techniques while introducing Atsutane theology by linking humans with cosmology and agricultural fertility. Evangelists traveled throughout central Japan distributing masses of pamphlets and earning Atsutane a large following among the rural peasant class.

Atsutane represents a break with the purely scholarly, urban culture characteristic of his classical Kokugaku forebears. Like Kaibara Ekken, he used vernacular idioms to extend a populist message to larger audiences. While Atsutane is credited with reviving reverence for the emperor and influencing the samurai who brought about the Meiji Restoration (see chapter 8), his far-reaching influence extended beyond politics. Yanagita Kunio and Origuchi Shinobu, influential folklorists of the Meiji era, incorporated many of Atsutane's views on the supernatual and afterlife into their studies of folk worldviews. Large, new religious movements that flourished among rural populations in the late nineteenth century, such as Konkokyō and Tenrikyō, adopted his notion of a monotheistic creator kami and the prayers and rituals devotees should offer the kami daily.

Dutch Studies

As previously mentioned, the Dutch were the only Europeans legally tolerated in Japan by the Tokugawa regime. During the seventeenth and eighteenth centuries they represented one of the wealthiest and most scientifically advanced nations of the world, with a large trading empire centered in the Dutch East Indies. The Dutch kept the Japanese abreast of many aspects of the industrial and scientific revolution occurring in the West. Although largely confined to a tiny, man-made island known as Dejima, a small Dutch contingent including the factory chief, company secretary, and a physician was required to travel to Edo annually to provide the shogun with gifts and updates on world events. The ninety-day journey, hauling food, wine, tables, and chairs, mirrored the sankin kōtai of daimyo and was understood as giving the Dutch factory chief a similar status, but the

FIGURE 29.   Rin Shihei, depiction of a Dutch meal with Javanese servants, 1790s. Courtesy of Rijksmuseum.

Europeans remained in Edo for only two to three weeks. The gifts they presented, including telescopes and microscopes, maps and globes, clocks, oil paintings, spectacles, magic lanterns, and mechanized puppets *(karakuri ningyō)*, became popular among many other daimyo and high officials. The Dutch embassy was also called on to provide amusement for the shogun, ordered to sing and dance, while the ladies of the palace watched their antics from behind screens. Japanese fascination with Dutch culture is seen in woodblock prints that recorded their customs, fashions, and possessions.

In order to curb the subversive influence of Christianity, early shoguns strictly forbade access to foreign books and knowledge. In 1720 the eighth shogun, Tokugawa Yoshimune (1684–1751), began to allow translation of Dutch texts on natural sciences that might prove useful in Japan. Allowable works were largely in two categories: astronomy, which included calendrical sciences, cartography, and geography; and medicine, including chemistry, physics, botany, mineralogy, and zoology. Knowledge of Western sciences and arts became known as Rangaku (Dutch Studies) and was limited to a small group of specialized bakufu scholars. Rangaku physicians also acquired knowledge of Western medical techniques, through observing the "redhair-style surgery" of Dutch doctors on Dejima.

Japanese views on human anatomy at the time were based on speculative theories from Chinese traditional medicine, as both Confucianism and Buddhism condemned the practice of dissecting corpses. When European anatomical charts that conflicted with Chinese theories began to circulate, Sugita Genpaku (1722–1817), an officially appointed surgeon, arranged to attend the autopsy of the corpse of a criminal, a woman known as the Green Tea Hag (Aochababa). Sugita was surprised to see that the woman's anatomy and organs matched the European charts rather than the traditional Chinese descriptions. He worked with other Rangaku scholars to translate an important Dutch text on anatomy, producing the *Kaitai shinsho* (New treatise on dissection) in 1774, after years of painstaking work. This text proved to be one of the most influential works on medicine in Japanese history. Japanese doctors began to blend Chinese and Western approaches, for instance combining acupuncture with the scientific view of anatomy. The subsequent translation and publication of Western surgical textbooks in the early nineteenth century allowed information on operations, wounds, bandaging, fractures, and bloodletting to circulate widely throughout the nation.

Another brilliant but eccentric Rangaku scholar, Hiraga Gennai (1728–80), was a low-ranking samurai exposed to Dutch ideas when studying herbal medicine in Nagasaki. Later moving to Edo, he experimented with Western sciences and arts, inventing thermometers, a form of asbestos fabric, and an electrostatic generator. Hiraga studied European painting techniques that incorporated a more natural perspective; his student Shiba Kōkan (1747–1818) became one of the first Western-style *(yōga)* painters.

TOKUGAWA RELIGIOUS CULTURE

During the Tokugawa and subsequent Meiji periods, critics charged that Buddhism had become "degenerate," or full of corruption, with monks violating vows and engaging in lewd behavior. These charges were due, in part, to the shogunate's control and co-option of Buddhist institutions, which inhibited Buddhist development such that no major new doctrines, no large new sects, and few truly notable priests or leaders appeared during the Tokugawa period—especially when compared to the medieval era's remarkable innovations in Buddhist doctrine and practice, championed by charismatic religious leaders. Under the Tokugawa bakufu, Buddhism became a form of state religion; all Japanese were ordered to register at their family's local temple to attest that they were not Christian. It was during this era that these temples became primarily associated with funerary and memorial services and rituals, an expensive cycle of thirty-three years of death rites that provided an important means of temple financial support. The idea of "funerary Buddhism" continues to characterize many Japanese people's view of the religion today.

There were, nevertheless, a number of remarkable monks who sought to purify and revive their traditions. Hakuin Ekaku (1686–1768), a Rinzai Zen monk, worked to refocus his sect on rigorous training in meditation and kōan practice. Although he was an amateur artist, his paintings and calligraphic works are much admired for their strong, personal, and straightforward expression, which served as a model for later Zen monks. Hakuin began to study calligraphy in his teens, but at the age of twenty-two he saw firsthand the work of a true Zen master and realized that calligraphy was a statement not of skill, but of human character. Hakuin's artistic strengths emerged after he turned sixty. He depicted a wide variety of subjects, from gods of good fortune to severe faces of Zen patriarchs, creating a new visual language for Zen that was not limited to landscapes or famous Zen subjects but included folk legends, animals and birds, and everyday objects and scenes. Hakuin made thousands and thousands of paintings, which he gave away freely to all who asked.

Religious developments in the Tokugawa period thus occurred less in the arena of institutionalized Buddhism than in the explosion of new forms of popular religiosity. For one, syncretic new religious philosophies, such as those of Hirata Atsutane, Ishida Baigan, and Ninomiya Sontoku, spread widely among the populace. Itinerant religious practitioners, from exorcists to beggar monks *(hijiri)*, traveled to every remote corner of Japan, providing a variety of religious and secular services for contributions, like the storytelling nuns and monks of the medieval era. Some engaged in divination, some peddled religious goods, others entertained by dancing or playing music on bamboo *shakuhachi* flutes or other instruments. During this era, popular deities and sacred sites acquired or further developed reputations for providing certain "practical benefits," including healing, bringing wealth, and guarding against fire, thus becoming major centers of worship. Another form of religious practice, pilgrimage to a sacred site or to a circuit of sites, mushroomed in popularity, aided by the appearance of scores of travel guidebooks and diaries from the mid-seventeenth century onward. Pilgrimages and excursions to popular shrines and temples were not necessarily solely religious in character. Devotees participated in a "culture of prayer and play" that simultaneously provided religious benefit and amusement.

The center of "prayer and play" in the Edo capital was Sensōji Temple in the townspeople's district of Asakusa. According to legend, the temple was founded in the seventh century by two brothers who found a golden statue in their fishing nets. They enshrined it and gave it offerings; afterward, their nets were always full. The village head realized that the statue was an incarnation of Kannon, the bodhisattva of compassion, and converted his house into a Buddhist temple, the first Sensōji. As Edo grew and developed, people of all classes came to the capital to sightsee, seeking out the places depicted in travel guides and woodblock prints (see chapter 7). The Asakusa area was popular among tourists, and the Sensōji grounds contained a vast network of amusements and commercial enterprises. Its inner precincts housed hundreds of booths purveying a wide variety of food, goods, and entertainment: tea and dumpling houses; liquor, candy, tobacco, and paper-goods stores; archery booths; and dozens of toothpick shops, which often doubled as fronts for prostitution. In Sensōji's outer precincts, permanent stores lined both sides of the street, specializing in such goods as sandals, toys, umbrellas, and Asakusa food specialties like seaweed, sake, soba noodles, and *senbei* (rice crackers). Hawkers touting nearby entertainment spectacles competed to lure customers. There were human freaks like the crab girl with two fingers on each hand, said to embody lessons in Buddhist karmic principles, and unusual animals, such as a giant toad, a porcupine, and an elephant. Circus acts, often used as a lure to sell herbal medications, featured acrobats, jugglers, tightrope walkers, and magicians. Sumo wrestling, which evolved from a religious practice to pacify resentful spirits or foretell harvest, was also performed. Sensōji staged playful quasi-sumo shows, such as in 1796, when a half-naked woman wrestled eight blind masseurs.[9] Each day, more than ten thousand people visited the complex.

In addition to the secular attractions, an unrivaled array of divine beings, Buddhist and Shinto alike, filled Sensōji's halls. The primary deity enshrined in the main building, the Asakusa Kannon, was the center of a large cult of devotees, but additional halls featured statues of new, "fashionable" deities said to be particularly efficacious for health and good luck, such as a statue of an old woman missing two front teeth that was believed to lessen toothache, and one of the Buddha of medicine, Yakushi Nyorai, venerated for its ability to cure eye disease.

The Sensōji fusion of prayer and play was favored by high and low alike. Shoguns and their families made visits to conduct services dedicated to Asakusa Kannon, followed by a lengthy inspection of entertainments. The eighth shogun, Yoshimune, loved street storytellers; and the eleventh,

FIGURE 30.   Utagawa Hiroshige, *Asakusa, Edo,* 1853, Los Angeles County Museum of Art. Source: Wikimedia Commons.

Ienari, often played archery or blowgun games. Sensōji was a very wealthy institution. In addition to rents received from the many businesses housed there, it sold talismans and votive offerings to visitors who wanted objects containing the power of the Asakusa Kannon. Buying such talismans and charms remains a must-do activity today when visiting famous shrines and temples. Another source of funds and offerings was religious confraternities, organized groups of one to two hundred lay supporters located throughout Japan. While Sensōji was one of the largest and most popular religious complexes, temples and shrines in other regions, such as Shikoku's Konpira Shrine, engaged in a similar blend of prayer and play. This may be one reason critics charged that Tokugawa Buddhism was decadent and corrupt, but it might be viewed instead as flexible, able to accommodate prevailing political and cultural trends to ensure financial survival.

Visits to famous shrines and temples and to sacred mountains were a part of pilgrimage, which had been a popular religious activity among elites since at least the Nara period but boomed in the Edo period, in part because of the improved travel infrastructure of national highways and networks of inns. Pilgrims set out to seek cures for diseases, to expiate sins, to venerate deities and holy men, and to petition the latter for benefits and rewards in this life and the next. But, as noted in regard to Sensōji, many pilgrims also

FIGURE 31. Katsushika Hokusai, *A Group of Mountaineers,* from series *Thirty-Six Views of Mount Fuji,* 1830s. Source: Wikimedia Commons.

had touristic motives—the desire to escape from their everyday lives and experience new places and new horizons.

Mountains were and are considered mysterious and sacred spaces, the dwelling places of spirits of the dead, containing entrances to the "other" world. Holy men and religious practitioners traveled to the mountains to engage in rigorous ascetic training that they believed would give them special powers. Heian nobility made pilgrimages to sacred mountains, such as Kumano and Yoshino, to experience a foretaste of the Pure Land while on earth. These journeys were hardly ascetic—they were luxurious outings for hundreds of courtiers. For commoners in the Tokugawa era, mountain pilgrimage involved difficult climbing as part of physical and spiritual discipline. Mount Fuji, the highest, holiest, and most beautiful of Japan's mountains, was an especially popular destination. The climb and descent of Fuji represented travel from the world of the living to the world of the dead and back, through which pilgrims could wash away their accumulated sins and impurities.

Membership in pilgrimage groups was predominantly male; women were forbidden from climbing sacred mountains because of a belief in their inherent pollution. Men had to conform to strict rules of abstinence and purification if they wanted to enter the mountain. Trips to climb the mountain entailed considerable hardship and expense. In order to make access to

Fuji easier, mounds resembling the sacred mountain were constructed throughout Edo, and on the first day of the sixth month, many city dwellers headed for the miniature Fujis in their vicinity.

Other popular pilgrimage routes were based on faith in a particular deity. The best-known route is on the island of Shikoku and consists of eighty-eight temples associated with the Shingon founder Kūkai. Another, located in western Japan, traverses a circuit of thirty-three temples dedicated to Kannon, the Buddhist deity of compassion. Every sixty years or so during the Tokugawa era, major pilgrimages to the Ise Grand Shrine attracted millions of pilgrims. Some traveled in organized village groups, but many others, especially women and children ineligible for membership in those groups, simply ran away to join the fun, leaving their work and families behind. Pilgrims were supported by almsgivers, who contributed everything from money, food, and clothing to hot baths and haircuts. The Ise pilgrimages were chaotic and festive, often characterized by ecstatic dancing, so they tended to be viewed negatively by officials and many elites.

The bakufu and domains did not usually allow commoners to travel outside their own village or city, making exceptions only when they sought permission for such pilgrimages or for medical treatment. Nonetheless, by the late Tokugawa period, travel and pilgrimage were a cultural obsession, supported through pleasure tours, hostelry chains, and guidebooks. Like many aspects of urban culture in the Edo period (described in chapter 7), pilgrimage sites—including Zenkōji Temple in Nagano, Ise Grand Shrine, and Konpira Shrine in Shikoku—were often associated with prostitution. It was sometimes said that prostitutes represented incarnated deities, and sexual contact with them was dubbed a form of *omatsuri*, or religious festival.

In summary, the Tokugawa shogunate forged a national polity and created effective systems of administration that restrained competing centers of power, such as temples and daimyo, and exerted control over the populace through the separation of status groups. Fearing subversion of the social order, the bakufu issued detailed regulations dictating lifestyles appropriate to each class. Confucianism, with its emphasis on stable governance, morality, and maintenance of order, proved a useful philosophy for the regime; its simplified teachings were propagated among all classes. New schools of thought, such as Dutch Studies and National Learning, also emerged, representing a shift away from the hegemony of Chinese intellectual and scientific systems. Few, if any, revolutionary changes occurred in the realm of religion, but a more playful and commercial approach toward religion became apparent among many temples, shrines, and adherents. This development was related to the larger cultural context of the Tokugawa era, in which urban commoners created and indulged in new forms of art, literature, and theater and in "pleasure quarters," a district of brothels and teahouses—all to be explored in the next chapter.

FURTHER READING

Burns, Susan. *Before the Nation: Kokugaku and the Imagining of Community in Early Modern Japan.* Durham, NC: Duke University Press, 2003.

Hanley, Susan. *Everyday Things in Premodern Japan: The Hidden Legacy of Material Culture.* Berkeley: University of California Press, 1997.

Hellyer, Robert I. *Defining Engagement Japan and Global Contexts, 1640–1868.* Cambridge, MA: Harvard University Press, 2000.

Hur, Nam-lin. *Prayer and Play in Late Tokugawa Japan: Asakusa Sensōji and Edo Society.* Cambridge, MA: Harvard University Press, 2000.

Ikegami, Eiko. *The Taming of the Samurai: Honorific Individualism and the Making of Modern Japan.* Cambridge, MA: Harvard University Press, 1997.

McNally, Mark. *Proving the Way Conflict and Practice in the History of Japanese Nativism.* Cambridge, MA: Harvard University Press, 2005.

Pitelka, Morgan. *Spectacular Accumulation: Material Culture, Tokugawa Ieyasu, and Samurai Sociability.* Honolulu: University of Hawaii Press, 2015.

Roberts, Luke. *Mercantilism in a Japanese Domain: Merchant Origins of Economic Nationalism in Eighteenth-Century Tosa.* New York: Cambridge University Press, 2002.

Sawada, Janine T. *Practical Pursuits: Religion, Politics and Personal Cultivation in Nineteenth-Century Japan.* Honolulu: University of Hawaii Press, 2004.

Teeuwen, Mark, and Kate Wildman Nakai, eds. *Lust, Commerce, and Corruption: An Account of What I Have Seen and Heard, by an Edo Samurai.* New York: Columbia University Press, 2017.

Vaporis, Constantine N. *Tour of Duty: Samurai, Military Service in Edo, and the Culture of Early Modern Japan.* Honolulu: University of Hawaii Press, 2009.

Walker, Brett L. *The Conquest of Ainu Lands: Ecology and Culture in Japanese Expansion, 1590–1800.* Berkeley: University of California Press, 2006.

RECOMMENDED FILMS

Harakiri. 1962. Feature film directed by Kobayashi Masaki. Early seventeenth-century tale of revenge based on the practice of rōnin who threatened to disembowel themselves in the courtyards of daimyo palaces unless they were given alms.

Red Beard. 1965. Feature film directed by Kurosawa Akira. Nineteenth-century tale of a compassionate rural doctor and his arrogant young apprentice, who had trained in Dutch medicine at Nagasaki.

The Ballad of Narayama. 1993. Feature film directed by Imamura Shohei. The legendary practice of poor rural villages that abandoned their unproductive elderly in the mountains to starve is depicted in this winner of the Cannes Film Festival's Palme d'Or.

The Forty-Seven Ronin. 1941. Feature film directed by Mizoguchi Kenji. Adaptation of the famous tale by an iconic director.

The Lower Depths. 1957. Feature film directed by Kurosawa Akira. An adaptation of Maxim Gorky's play of the same name, this film portrays the daily struggles of poor commoners in Edo.

The Twilight Samurai. 2002. Feature film directed by Yamada Yōji. Set during the final decade of Tokugawa rule, this film tells the story of a poor, low-ranking samurai bureaucrat content with his simple existence but forced to risk his life by domainal politics.

7   Edo Popular Culture

The Floating World and Beyond:
Late 17th to Mid-19th Centuries

The Tokugawa shogunate instituted political, administrative, and social policies to help ensure that they retained power, but the rigidity of the status system they created could not flexibly accommodate ongoing, long-term changes in the economy and society. Urbanization and the growth of the commercial economy worked to redistribute wealth from the samurai to commoners, undermining the system. It also helped fuel the development of lively new forms of culture among urban commoners.

Courtier and samurai elites had long enjoyed elegant amusements such as poetry gatherings, tea ceremonies, and flower-arranging parties. During the Edo period, another name for the era of the Tokugawa shogunate (1600–1868), wealthy commoners increasingly began to enjoy such pursuits. Peace and prosperity enabled the blossoming of a popular culture, affordable by the less privileged, that included books, woodblock prints, the theater, and the "pleasure quarters," filled with brothels and teahouses. This culture is often associated with the term *ukiyo* (the floating world). During the medieval era, the term was linked to Buddhist notions of impermanence, part of the suffering of the human condition, but during the Edo period it represented a world of play, characterized by humor, eroticism, and self-indulgence. The spirit of ukiyo culture was titillating, irreverent, and bold, essentially mocking the solemnity of the samurai elite. Artistic, literary, and theatrical facets of ukiyo culture were deeply intertwined with one another because all developed in the same great cities and catered to the same expanding clientele: increasingly wealthy groups of commoners.

The Genroku era (technically 1688–1704, but more generally referring to 1680–1720) represented a high point in urban culture. Early Edo culture was risqué and sexually oriented, but as the era advanced, ukiyo culture gained greater sophistication. While ukiyo art, literature, and drama were focused largely on Kabuki actors and the courtesans of the pleasure quarters, they also began to reflect the triumphs and tragedies of daily life for urban commoners. By the late seventeenth century, licensed quarters for theaters and brothels had matured into highly structured systems, with hierarchies of authority and status, elaborate codes of etiquette, and a rich body of tradition. Actors and prostitutes, as members of the caste of "nonhuman" vagrants, were considered sources of social pollution by the Confucian-oriented bakufu. They were thus restricted to special areas, fenced off from "decent society." Nonetheless, Kabuki actors and the women of the pleasure quarters were subjects of endless popular fascination and thus remained central subjects for drama, prose, and art in this period.

URBANIZATION

The establishment of the shogun's capital at Edo, along with the sankin kōtai system that ordered all daimyo and their samurai retainers to reside alternately at Edo and in a single castle town within their domains, initiated an accelerated degree of urbanization throughout Japan, bringing unprecedented levels of commercial growth. Following Ieyasu's victory at Sekigahara, he ordered all daimyo to contribute materials and manpower to the gargantuan project of constructing a capital city: reclaiming lands from floodplains, building his massive castle (now the Imperial Palace), and engineering a network of waterways and bridges. Remnants of these original efforts can be seen in contemporary Tokyo and provide a sense of the scope of Ieyasu's project. The inner moat circumscribed central Edo and remains an important avenue of transportation today as the Yamanote train line, a 21.4-mile loop that is Tokyo's busiest and most important line, linking all major centers in the city. The mansions of the daimyo were all located within the loop, to the north and west, occupying 70 percent of the land, while quarters for the townspeople were crammed in the "low city" *(shitamachi)*, representing 15 percent of the inner loop. Temples and shrines occupied the remaining land. Along the city's waterways, areas for amusement developed, intended for townspeople but eagerly frequented by many samurai. Evening pleasure boats hosted lively parties for clients they ferried to the theater or pleasure quarters.

Edo did not immediately achieve national dominance as a center of culture. Kyoto and Osaka, sometimes jointly known as Kamigata, remained at the forefront of literature, arts, crafts, religion, and commerce throughout the seventeenth century. The samurai presence in these cities was minor; elite classes of courtiers, merchants, and samurai mingled freely, borrowing

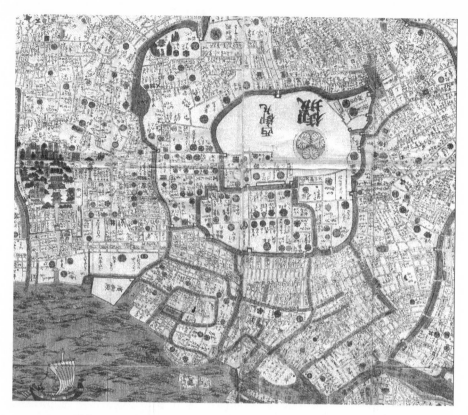

MAP 7. Edo, 1844. Courtesy of the University of Texas at Austin.

from one another in creating new cultural forms and forums. Kyoto painters and artists achieved elegant new heights, as illustrated in the work of
the Ogata brothers, Kōrin (1658–1716) and Kenzan (1663–1743), heirs to a
luxury textile business. The brothers engaged in all of the fashionable cultural pursuits of their day, such as tea, painting, and calligraphy. With the
death of their patroness in the late seventeenth century, their family fortunes declined and later collapsed, forcing the brothers to turn to careers as
artists. They brilliantly applied concepts associated with textile design to
painting and ceramics. Nevertheless, they too eventually left the declining
Kyoto for Edo, seeking wealthy patrons to support their work.

Kamigata elites valued elegance. They considered Edo-ites, with their
preferences for novelty and boldness over understatement, boorish and
rough. This lasting division between eastern and western styles is illustrated in regional preferences for Kabuki drama: the heroes of Edo Kabuki

FIGURE 32. Ogata Kōrin, *Red and White Plum Trees,* early eighteenth century. MOA Museum of Art, Atami, Japan. Source: Wikimedia Commons.

played warriors with exaggerated movements and bluster, a style called *aragoto* (rough business), while Kamigata Kabuki featured sophisticated, fashionable heroes, often known as great lovers, in *wagoto* (soft style) roles. From the eighteenth century onward, Edo gained the upper hand as the national center of cultural production. While it was less polished than the older cities, it was more dynamic. During the eighteenth and nineteenth centuries, commoner ukiyo culture originating in Edo spread throughout the other urban centers, while many courtly and samurai arts stagnated.

Edo and the domainal castle towns were military cities, constructed for the needs of the samurai class. The population of Edo was thus largely male, not only among the samurai but among the merchant classes, who staffed new establishments in the shogun's capital with male clerks and apprentices from their home domains, and among male laborers brought by the tens of thousands to work on construction projects. According to a census from the early eighteenth century, the population of Edo was approximately half samurai and half townspeople, with at least twice as many men as women. Such gender proportions account for the rough cultural preferences of early Edo and for the significant roles of prostitution and erotic art and literature in popular culture, as important forms of entertainment for a population of single men.

Concentrated urban populations spurred the growth of consumer culture, because residents were dependent on shops and markets to purchase food, clothing, and other desirables, available for budgets of all levels. The wealthy indulged in finely crafted fashions, ceramics, and lacquerwares; they ate delicacies like crane and carp at elegant restaurants, often near the theater or pleasure quarters, where they paid handsomely for entertainment. Poor laborers, on the other hand, could buy secondhand clothing and goods from street stalls, eat a variety of tasty street foods, drink cheap sake at bars, and entertain themselves at inexpensive storytelling houses or in the galley seats of Kabuki theater. Sushi, soba noodles, and grilled eel—iconic items of Japanese cuisine today—originated as cheap, fast food sold in street stalls to satisfy the appetites of Edo's labor force. In 1860, over 3,700 shops sold soba, meaning that a noodle shop could be found on every Edo block. Those with more middling incomes might shop at Edo's large, new dry-goods emporiums, such as Echigoya, opened in 1673. Traditionally, kimono vendors traveled to their customers' homes, making their wares to order and selling textiles by the bolt. Echigoya adopted a more consumer-friendly approach, opening large stores that sold premade clothing and accessories at fixed prices, eliminating the traditional haggling and making transactions more efficient. Allowing customers to buy cloth in small quantities rather than by the bolt resulted in a huge volume of sales, enabling Echigoya to open stores in other urban centers. Not until Le Bon Marché was opened in Paris in 1852 were such practices enacted in the Western world. Echigoya, eventually renamed Mitsukoshi, was forerunner of Tokyo's modern department stores.

Townsmen native to Edo, called Edokko, took pride in their identity, distinct from the parsimonious, moralizing samurai class and from rural yokels. By the middle of the Edo period, savvy Edokko were said to embody stylish chic (iki) and strength of character (hari). The spirit of iki was characterized by generosity with one's money; modesty and unostentatious behavior; and knowledgeability about art, fashion, and the rules and etiquettes of the pleasure quarters and theater. The most sophisticated townsmen, known as tsū (stylish connoisseurs), became role models for other men with cultural aspirations. Men who aspired to tsū status but made crude mistakes, such as wearing expensive but out-of-fashion clothing or behaving flamboyantly or arrogantly, were condemned as superficial phonies (hankatsū) or yokels (yabo). The quality of hari, in turn, was characterized by a straightforward nature, a spirit of resistance, and a refusal to pander. The sense of resistance grew from the dislike of oppressive samurai rule and its class-based restrictions. The courtesans and geisha of the pleasure quarters were also sometimes said to embody iki and hari, but the more prevalent ideal for women was coquetry (bitai), a charming and flirtatious allure that was erotic but never vulgar.

PRINT CULTURE

Qualities like iki, hari, and bitai were disseminated and popularized through the print industry, which experienced immense growth during the Edo period. They were illustrated in woodblock prints and explained via illustrated prose literature *(kana zōshi)*, written in vernacular language using kana characters so that large audiences with rudimentary literacy could enjoy them. As the publishing industry developed during the seventeenth century, printing techniques changed. Movable type—introduced by the Jesuits in the sixteenth century—gave way to the older form of woodblock printing, because type didn't allow for artistic integration of text and picture and discouraged calligraphic creativity. Block printing's capacity to combine text and picture enabled printers to reach a readership that ranged from the highly literate to the illiterate—crucial for creating a large consumer base.

In the early seventeenth century, the print industry helped define and legitimate the Tokugawa regime through the prolific production of maps of the nation, including maps of each of the provinces, major cities, the networks of highways, and popular travel routes. This was soon accompanied by an outpouring of commercial printing that included "atlases, encyclopedias, dictionaries, calendars, almanacs, rural gazetteers, urban directories, travel accounts, personnel rosters, biographical compendia, manuals of work, manuals of play, guides to shopping and local products, and school primers."[1] Mary Elizabeth Berry has identified the vast new range of data available to the commoner population as the "library of public information." Contemporary fiction was a highly popular genre among urban townspeople, who were its primary market. Best-selling novels often sold over ten thousand copies in a few months' time. Book lenders *(kashi honya)* enabled commoners who couldn't afford to purchase books to read widely. The lenders traveled to customers' homes with a large pile of books on their back or peddled their volumes on the streets, renting books for around one-sixth the price of purchase. There were around 650 such book lenders in Edo in 1808 and a similar number in Osaka. Some traveled to rural villages, thereby disseminating urban culture throughout the country.

During the seventeenth and early eighteenth centuries, the publishing world was centered in Kyoto and Osaka. Branches of Kyoto booksellers dominated the Edo market. The most popular and successful authors of the era, satirist Ihara Saikaku (1642–93) and dramatist Chikamatsu Monzaemon (1653–1725, discussed later in this chapter) resided in Osaka. By the mid-eighteenth century, however, entrepreneurial Edo publishers gained ground, producing new genres such as illustrated storybooks, including popular "pillow books" of erotica; and books of satiric verses and political lampoons, which often landed their authors in jail. Edo publishers produced numerous books on Dutch learning, including Sugita Genpaku's *Kaitai shinsho* (New treatise on dissection) and many other translations of Dutch works on medicine, physics, and other sciences. They ignored traditional copyrights, reprinting books popularized by their Kamigata rivals. They were especially successful in their sales of full-color woodblock prints *(nishiki-e)*. Edo bookstore chains such as Suwaraya and Tsutaya, which specialized in different types of texts and prints, eventually drove out their Kyoto-based competitors. In addition to books and artwork, the printing industry also produced the advertisements, handbills, guides, and rankings for the theater and pleasure districts. Librettos and commentaries for popular Kabuki and Bunraku (puppet theater) plays allowed enthusiasts to practice the roles themselves at home or among fan circles. The outpouring of print closely linked the producers of urban culture with its consumers.

Ihara Saikaku was a prolific poet and novelist, credited with popularizing the genre of *ukiyo zōshi* (tales of the floating world). Scion of a rich merchant family, he was well traveled and deeply engaged with the actors, courtesans, and wealthy connoisseurs at the forefront of his stories. His best-known works are hilarious parodies that explore the life of the townspeople, emphasizing themes like sex, money, and adventures in the pleasure quarters. His first novel, *The Life of an Amorous Man* (1683), is often viewed as a satire of the classic *Tale of Genji*. It chronicles the sex life of Yonosuke, an insatiable hedonist, from his first sexual venture at age seven to his departure for paradise, the fabled Island of Women, at age sixty, on a ship stocked with aphrodisiacs and sex toys. Yonosuke seduces both females and males; his diary records that he slept with 3,742 women and 735 boys.[2] Unlike the genteel Genji or his Heian courtier colleagues, Yonosuke is unmoved by beauty or the pathos of life; he is motivated only by lust and libido.

In one episode, Yonosuke meets one of the ladies-in-waiting who staff the females-only inner chambers of the shogun's castle. In popular culture, such ladies were often rumored to be starved for sex, trawling the theater districts on their days off. Yonosuke encounters the lady in question in that district, and she begs him to defend her from a mortal enemy. They retire to a nearby teahouse:

> "This will tell you all you need to know," she said demurely, nestling her face into the collar of her kimono, as she handed him a brocade bag. Yonosuke undid the scarlet thong and peered in—at an eight or nine inch long slender object which looked as if it had been worn down by years of hard use. "What's this?" he exclaimed, taken aback.
>
> "It's my mortal enemy. Every time I use this weapon I scream I'm dying! I want revenge on it!" And she threw herself against him.
>
> No sooner had he drawn his own weapon that he pinned her down and grappled fiercely with her, drenching several layers of mats beneath

them. But when they rose again to part, she dipped into her purse for a discreetly wrapped gold piece, slipped it into his hand, and said: "Don't forget, I have another holiday on the sixteenth."[3]

The Life of an Amorous Man was a best seller, and Saikaku followed it up with other, similarly themed works, such as *The Life of an Amorous Woman* (1685), which chronicles the descent of a lusty woman from a top young courtesan down through the seamier ranks of prostitution as she loses her beauty, ending up a common streetwalker. Another work, *The Great Mirror of Male Love* (1687), describes the homosexual love affairs of samurai, Kabuki actors, and Buddhist priests—a very common phenomenon among these populations, typified among samurai and priests by couplings of senior-ranking males with youthful boys and by prostitution plied by actors. Saikaku discusses the relative merits of loving men rather than women: "A woman can be likened to a plant which, for all its blossoms, has creeping tendrils that twist around you. A youth is aloof, but imbued with an indescribable fragrance, like the first plum blossoms. For this reason, if one discusses their relative merits one must end by discarding women in favor of men."[4]

Such works seem tinged with the misogyny of their time. Saikaku's *Five Women Who Loved Love* (1685) furthers the sense of gender inequity and sexual double standards for women and men. Its stories are based on actual scandals and, rather than featuring the usual courtesans, center on women of the merchant class, who were generally portrayed in popular culture as stoic and boring, faithful to their husbands, and devoted to the success of the family's enterprise. In Saikaku's work, however, they are strong, decisive women who pursue the men they desire but pay a heavy price. Four of the five suffer unhappy fates: executed for adultery or other crimes, driven to becoming nuns, or committing suicide. The following excerpt from one of the tales presents a comic example of a scene still familiar today—young men checking out and judging the appearances of women:

> There was in the capital a band of four inseparable young men
> who were known for their handsome appearance and riotous
> living. . . .
>   After the theater one evening they were lounging around a tea shop
> called Matsuya and one of them remarked, "I have never seen so many
> good-looking local girls as I did today. Do you suppose we could find
> others who would seem just as beautiful now?" They thought they
> might, and decided to watch for pretty girls among the people who had
> gone to see the wistaria blossoms and were now returning to their
> homes. After a worldly actor in the group had been chosen as chief
> judge, a "beauty contest" was conducted until the twilight hours,
> providing a new source of amusement for the jaded gentlemen.

At first they were disappointed to see some maids riding in a carriage which hid them from sight. Then a group of girls strolled by in a rollicking mood—"not bad, not bad at all"—but none of the girls quite satisfied their exacting standards. Paper and ink had been brought to record the entries, and it was agreed that only the best should be put on their list. . . .

Next they spied a lady of thirty-four or thirty-five with a graceful long neck and intelligent-looking eyes, above which could be seen a natural hairline of rare beauty. . . . Underneath she wore white satin, over that light blue satin, and outside—reddish-yellow satin. . . . Assuredly this was a woman of exquisite taste. . . . Around her head she had draped a veil like that worn by court ladies; she wore stockings of pale silk and sandals with triple braided straps. She walked noiselessly and gracefully, moving her hips with a natural rhythm. "What a prize for some lucky fellow!" a young buck exclaimed. But these words were hardly uttered when the lady, speaking to an attendant, opened her mouth and disclosed that one of her lower teeth was missing, to the complete disillusionment of her admirers.[5]

Playful comic fiction of the late eighteenth century and beyond is known as *gesaku*, and it comprises two main types. The first, *kibyōshi* (yellow cover), are often considered the first comic books for adults. They were typically printed in ten-page volumes; a single story spanned two or three volumes. Authors often drew the illustrations themselves, and blank spaces in the pictures were filled with dialogue, narrative, and labels identifying the characters portrayed. The second type, *sharebon* (books of wit and fashion), described the manners, language, and clothing styles of the pleasure quarters. Santō Kyōden (1761–1816), the son of an Edo pawnbroker, was a master of both forms. His kibyōshi masterpiece, *Edo umare uwaki no kabayaki* (Romantic embroilments born in Edo, 1785), is the tale of a very ugly young merchant, Enjirō, who desperately wishes to be seen as a great lover and tsū. He pays women to run after him in the streets of the pleasure quarters; begs his parents to disinherit him, as merchant families were likely to do with playboy sons; and stages a fake love-suicide with a courtesan. Characters include actual Kabuki actors, poets, and courtesans of the day.

In order to avoid violating censorship laws—which prohibited publishing books or prints that depicted current events, unorthodox theories, rumors, scandals, erotica, government officials, or anything directly related to the Tokugawa rulers or the imperial family—Kyōden gave his books superficial historical settings. Nevertheless, his sharp satires of social status and politics gained the attention of censors, and Kyōden was sentenced to fifty days in handcuffs, while his publisher Tsutaya Jūzaburō was fined half of his entire net worth.

Tōkaidōchū hizakurige (Shank's mare), written by Jippensha Ikku (1765–1831), was one of the best-selling comic novels of the early nineteenth century. It concerns the misadventures of Yaji and Kita, two buffoons on a pilgrimage to the Ise Grand Shrine, traveling along the Tōkaidō road between Edo and Kyoto, motivated mainly by their interests in eating, drinking, and sex. Since they are from Edo, they view themselves as superior to the provincials they meet, but their foolishness and stupidity are revealed through incidents that occur in the inns along the way. At one, they burn themselves trying to use the bathtub; at another, they question how to eat the hot stones they've been served, not realizing that the stones are for cooking and not to be consumed. Yaji and Kita frequently get into trouble trying to sneak into the beds of women travelers. *Tōkaidōchū hizakurige* served as a kind of guidebook to the fifty-three post stations of the Tōkaidō, supporting the travel and tourism boom of the Edo period.

Poetry

Haiku—brief poems of seventeen syllables in a 5-7-5 pattern that have become Japan's most characteristic form of poetry—emerged during the Edo period as an unpretentious form of verse that could be enjoyed and composed by commoners. Classical *waka* poetry had evolved into a stale, rule-bound form, judged mainly by its ability to allude to the famous poems of past imperial anthologies and limited to a handful of themes and images. During the Sengoku period, a poetic practice known as linked verse *(renga)*—in which groups of poets took turns composing stanzas linked to the preceding verse through wit, wordplay, or metaphor, according to a set of rules—gained popularity. There were two types of renga practiced by separate groups during Sengoku: serious *(ushin)*, composed in the high-minded classical tradition by the learned; and comic *(haikai no renga)*, which involved simple verses, often bawdy or celebrating crude behavior, composed by the commoners as a kind of game, resulting in works that were hundreds and sometimes thousands of lines long. The following example is a famous pair of comic links:

> Bitter, bitter it was
> And yet somehow funny.

> Even when
> My father lay dying
> I went on farting.[6]

Here, the first poet expresses a conflicted emotion, which the second illustrates by juxtaposing the sadness and solemnity of loss with the inability to control bodily functions. Scatological jokes were frequently found in Edo commoner verse and fiction alike.

The short opening verse of a comic renga developed into its own complete form, known as *senryū* if it was comic verse or as haiku if it was more serious. Senryū were frequently cynical or contained black humor, as in these three examples:

> 'She may have only one eye
> But it's a pretty one'
> Says the go-between.

> After he's scolded
> His wife too much,
> He cooks the rice.

> The laundryman—
> By his neighbors'
> Grubbiness he lives.[7]

Unquestionably, the master of the more serious haiku form is Matsuo Bashō (1644–94), who renounced his samurai status to become a master and teacher of linked verse to pupils from all walks of life. Bashō wrote the following haiku, among the most well known in the world:

> Ancient pond
> A frog jumps in
> Sound of water.

> Furu ike ya
> kawazu tobikomu
> mizu no oto.

Bashō dressed and lived like a monk, although he never took formal Buddhist vows. He believed that the true poets of the past rejected worldly ambition and embraced simple poverty, so he himself attempted to live this way, moving from the central Edo district of Ueno to a small cottage in the city's outskirts. Although he might have preferred a solitary life, like that of the medieval hermit Kamo no Chōmei, he was a master and teacher of linked verse, which required working closely with groups of poets. He adopted the name Bashō, a type of nonfruiting banana tree, after a disciple presented him with one as a gift.

The haiku master began embarking on a series of long journeys in 1684. These were difficult pilgrimages, often over remote roads that held many dangers. Many poets had died conducting such travels over the centuries.

Bashō's masterwork, *The Narrow Road to the Deep North*, combines verse and travelogue in a record of his 156-day, fifteen-hundred-mile journey into Japan's northern interior. Most of the trip was completed on foot, but horses and boats were used on occasion. He set off in early 1689 in homage to the late-Heian-era poet-monk Saigyō, to celebrate the five hundredth anniversary of his death. Bashō wished to visit all of the places Saigyō noted in his poetry, in order to reinvigorate his own work. *Narrow Road* opens with the following passage: "The moon and sun are eternal travelers. Even the years wander on. A lifetime adrift in a boat, or in old age leading a tired horse into the years, every day is a journey, and the journey itself is home. From the earliest times there have always been some who perished along the road. Still I have always been drawn by windblown clouds into dreams of a lifetime of wandering."[8]

During the journey, Bashō filled his notebooks with observations. It took him several years after returning to Edo to rework these into a slim volume, the masterpiece that emerged as *Narrow Road*. Each entry consists of lyrical observations about the place visited or events that happened there, followed by a haiku verse related to the emotions or ambience evoked by them. One celebrated section describes Hiraizumi, the home of a powerful branch of the Fujiwara family who, during the late Heian era, built a large capital, with a population of more than a hundred thousand, near the northern barrier of the realm. Hiraizumi (Izumi Castle in the excerpt below) was said to rival Kyoto in its size and splendor; its mountaintop temple complex, Chūsonji, was filled with golden treasure halls and elegant gardens. After the fall of the Fujiwara, the city fell into obscurity and its impressive buildings and sophisticated reputation rapidly decayed. The entry is suffused with a Buddhist sense of impermanence; it juxtaposes the transience of humans, their institutions, and their reputations with the raw, regenerative power of nature:

> Here three generations of the Fujiwara clan passed as though in a dream. The great outer gates lay in ruins. Where Hidehira's manor stood, rice fields grew. Only Mount Kinkei remained. I climbed the hill where Yoshitsune died; I saw the Kitakami, a broad stream flowing down through the Nambu Plain, the Koromo River circling Izumi Castle below the hill before joining the Kitakami. The ancient ruins of Yasuhira—from the end of the Golden Era—lie out beyond the Koromo Barrier, where they stood guard against the Ainu people. The faithful elite remained bound to the castle—for all their valor, reduced to ordinary grass. Tu Fu wrote:

> The whole country devastated
> only mountains and rivers remain.

In springtime, at the ruined castle,
The grass is always green.

We sat for a while, our hats for a seat, seeing it all through tears.

Summer grasses:
all that remains of great soldiers'
imperial dreams[9]

Bashō never wrote a theory of poetry, although many of his pupils later recollected his teachings in their own writings. He taught that the poetic spirit of good haiku must embody both change and permanence. It should transcend time and space in maintaining the artistic aims of the best poets of the past, but must always strive for freshness and novelty to prevent the ossification seen in classical waka verse. Along Bashō's immortalized route today, large stone monuments mark the sites of his observations, each inscribed with the poem he composed about that place.

Woodblock Prints

Pictures of the floating world, or *ukiyo-e*, were another important and popular aspect of Edo's print culture. Rather than religious art or the classical-style painting of the Kano and Tosa schools, which focused on birds and flowers, ukiyo-e focused on new subjects such as scenes from daily life and leisure, especially the courtesans of the pleasure quarters and popular Kabuki actors. With these prints, human figures became central, not incidental, to the picture.

In some ways, these prints were like the Internet of the Edo period, a new technology that provided ordinary people with a source of the latest news and gossip on popular culture—who was hot and who was not. Another similarity between ukiyo-e and the Internet is that both served as a primary mechanism for distributing pornography. Graphic depictions of sexual acts, known as *shunga* (spring pictures), were collected in "pillow books." Even the most renowned artists produced these popular erotic prints. Woodblock prints could be made cheaply, quickly, and in large production runs and thus were able to respond rapidly to emerging fashions. The large print runs made them affordable for many, unlike unique works of art. They were sold in publishers' shops and by street peddlers. Consumers used them for interior décor or collected them in albums or boxes.

Paintings that captured the interests of urban commoners were available in Kyoto in the late sixteenth century, followed by woodblock prints of these subjects. Early Genroku works were printed in black and white, then colored by hand. In the 1730s, print makers began using two colors, gener-

FIGURE 33. Hishikawa Moronobu, *Street Scene in Yoshiwara,* seventeenth century. Courtesy of The Metropolitan Museum of Art, New York.

ally rose and green. Edo printmakers gained their own recognizable identity in this medium in the 1760s when they mastered the techniques for full-color prints and began achieving predominance over Kyoto competitors. Edo prints depicted local tastes: Kabuki actors were depicted in the masculine aragoto roles favored by theatergoers, and the works contained more humor and satire than the softer products of Kyoto artists.

To make full-color prints, the engraver carved a block of wood for each color, sometimes using both sides to save on production costs. There were two crucial tasks: to carve the color blocks in exactly the correct place and to align each color block with the basic black-and-white print so that it received the added color precisely where intended. The printmaking process was a collaborative enterprise. Unlike our conception of a single artist-creator, a publisher initiated the design idea for a print and commissioned an artist to produce a rendition of the final work. Copyists, wood-carvers, and printers were then needed to reproduce that rendition in large runs, usually of two hundred in the eighteenth century, and of a thousand or more during the nineteenth. Prints came in two standard sizes, around fifteen by ten inches *(ōban)* or ten-and-a-half by eight inches *(chūban).* Over time, however, prints appeared in diverse sizes and shape for different functions such as fans, scrolls, triptychs, calendars, and New Year's cards.

Hishikawa Moronobu (1618–94), the son of an embroiderer, studied art in both the Kano and Tosa schools of painting. Considered the "father" of ukiyo-e, he was among the first to make prints outside of book illustrations and to sign his work. Moronobu's work ranged from complex compositions painted on byōbu screens—illustrating, for example, the workings of the Kabuki theater—to series of risqué black-and-white line drawings showing lovers in progressive states of undress. It was rare to see lovers completely naked in shunga, echoing the classical Heian notion that the unclothed human body was "without charm."

From early in the history of ukiyo-e, artists depicted Kabuki actors, in response to consumer interest. Actor prints were initially colored in orange and employed techniques called "gourd legs" and "earthworm lines" that allowed artists to exaggerate the muscles of the actors' legs in order to suggest strength. Torii Kiyonobu (1664–1729), one of Moronobu's students, developed a reputation for prints that were focused on a single famous actor in a masculine aragoto role. He also produced billboards and flyers for the Kabuki theater, and the school he founded continues to play this important promotional role.

The popularization of nishiki-e, or "brocade pictures"—prints using ten or more colors—is often associated with the artist Suzuki Harunobu (1725–70). Harunobu was the first to consistently use more than three colors in each print. He also used a thicker, more opaque application of paint and experimented with better woods for the woodblocks, using cherry instead of catalpa. Little is known of his life, but during its last five years he produced at least a thousand different works. His style and techniques were widely imitated by others after his death. Harunobu's prints were lyrical and romantic, with men and women both depicted androgynously as slender, fragile figures whose expressions suggested a kind of innocent elegance. His favorite subjects were not professional courtesans but other local beauties, who worked in teahouses or shops, often engaging in everyday activities. Like many of his contemporaries, Harunobu sometimes drew upon themes in classical art but changed the setting to contemporary Edo. For example, in a series of prints based on works by famous Heian poets, one print inscribes a well-known poem in the upper portion:

Gazing over the capital
Green willow threads entwine
Soft red cherry blossoms
As if the Heian capital
Had spread a spring brocade.

FIGURE 34. Suzuki Harunobu, *Night Rain at the Double-Shelf Stand*, 1766, The Metropolitan Museum of Art, New York. Source: Wikimedia Commons.

In Harunobu's illustration, two fashionably dressed young women reenact the poem in Edo, suggesting that this new world of urban culture had superseded the ancient capital as the center of style.

In the 1780s, Kitagawa Utamaro (1753–1806) became known for his daring new portraits of beautiful women. Kabuki actor prints frequently focused on just the head and upper half of their subject; Utamaro applied this style to women, enabling him to capture differences in the characters and temperaments of women of different social backgrounds and to lavish attention on their elaborate hairstyles and ornaments. Rather than using generic facial expressions, his individualized subjects could convey their emotional states, from passion to exhaustion. Utamaro included clever devices to allow glimpses of the faces of women, through transparent fabrics or, more famously, by using mirrors to reflect the expression of women with their backs turned to the viewer.

One of his contemporaries, Tōshūsai Sharaku (a pseudonym), was probably the source of Utamaro's inspiration for close-up portraits of women. Sharaku rose meteorically from obscurity in 1794 and abruptly disappeared ten months later. We know neither his true name nor the dates of his birth and death. In the short period he was active, he produced around 140 prints and became known for producing "big head" prints that captured an actor's facial expression during a climactic Kabuki scene. Rather than idealizing Kabuki performers, Sharaku depicted them truthfully, with their unflattering features, such as large noses or wrinkles, intact. Actors playing female roles (onnagata) were clearly revealed as men through their masculine features. The Edo public disliked Sharaku's realism, which may account for his sudden disappearance, but later audiences appreciated the dynamism and energy in his work.

Later ukiyo-e reflects the social currents of the closing years of the shogun's rule. Many artists began to incorporate European pictorial techniques and perspectives explained and depicted in Dutch texts. From around the beginning of the nineteenth century, there was an expansion of the audience for prints and a rapid increase in both the number of prints created and the quantity of copies printed. New genres, depicting landscapes and famous landmarks in Edo and beyond, accompanied the national passion for pilgrimage and tourism. Visitors to the capital eagerly purchased such prints as souvenirs. Katsushika Hokusai (1760–1849), known best for his landscapes, enjoyed a career that spanned more than seventy years and numerous styles. He painted actors and graceful women, famous historical scenes, and traditional birds and flowers. In 1812, he produced a sketchbook intended to teach students simple drawing techniques through whimsical drawings of scenes

FIGURE 35. Kitagawa Utamaro, *Naniwa Okita Admiring Herself in a Mirror,* 1790s, The Metropolitan Museum of Art, New York. Source: Wikimedia Commons.

FIGURE 36.   Tōshūsai Sharaku, print of actor Osagawa Tsuneyo, 1794. Courtesy
of Rijksmuseum.

FIGURE 37. Katsushika Hokusai, *The Great Wave off Kanagawa,* from the series *Thirty-Six Views of Mount Fuji,* 1830s. Source: Wikimedia Commons.

from everyday life. It became a best seller, and Hokusai produced fourteen additional volumes, known as *Hokusai manga,* on themes such as ghosts, animals, and Mount Fuji. His subsequent ukiyo-e series, *Thirty-Six Views of Mount Fuji,* brought him even greater renown. The first and most famous print of the series is *The Great Wave off Kanagawa,* with foamy ocean waves framing a snow-capped Mount Fuji in the background. The series featured dramatic views of the mountain alone, in different conditions of light and weather, along with distant views of the peak foregrounded by other famous sites or by individuals engaging in a variety of activities.

Utagawa Hiroshige, also known as Andō Hiroshige (1797–1858), rivals Hokusai as one of the greatest masters of ukiyo-e. Hiroshige came from a low-ranking samurai family that served in the Edo fire brigade. He studied painting with the Kano school and created many bird and flower prints. But like Hokusai, he is best known for his landscape prints. In 1832, Hiroshige participated in a daimyo's sankin kōtai procession from Edo to Kyoto. The journey served as inspiration for his most famous work, *The Fifty-Three Stations of the Tōkaidō,* issued the following year, with one illustration for each post station town. The serene, rural landscapes he depicted were highly popular; they became the best-selling ukiyo-e prints in history. Hiroshige followed up with *The Sixty-Nine Stages of the Kisokaidō,* depicting the stops on the more mountainous inland highway between the two capitals. Between 1856 and 1859, he issued the remarkable *One Hundred Famous Views of Edo*, depicting famous shrines, temples, gardens, and shops.

Ukiyo-e prints and other aspects of Japanese art and design began to influence European and American artists when Japan opened to trade with other nations in the 1850s (see chapter 8). Japanese textiles, ceramics, cloisonné enamels, and bronzes were immediately popular with collectors abroad. Ukiyo-e, considered a cheap, lowly art of commoners, was not initially exported, but was "discovered" when a French artist found that his shipment of Japanese porcelain was wrapped in a copy of *Hokusai manga*. Parisian shops that sold Japanese goods began carrying ukiyo-e prints, and renowned artists were among their most avid fans and collectors. Ukiyo-e's strong colors and compositional freedom inspired Impressionist masters such as Claude Monet, Édouard Manet, and Edgar Degas. Vincent Van Gogh owned a large collection of prints and imitated their vibrant tones, unusual perspectives, and motifs. His painting *Japonaiserie: Flowering Plum Tree* is a copy of Hiroshige's *Plum Park in Kameido*; his *Le Père Tanguy* depicts the proprietor of an art supply shop against a background of six ukiyo-e prints. American painter James McNeill Whistler also collected ukiyo-e and frequently incorporated kimonos, folding screens, fans, and other Japanese items into his works. Beyond painting, famous architects, including Frank Lloyd Wright and Charles Rennie Mackintosh, examined prints for the structures depicted and emulated their restrained use of natural materials, texture, and light and shadow, and their avoidance of excessive ornamentation.

THEATER CULTURE

A second major arena of urban culture, supported and promoted by the development of print, is the theater. There are three extant forms of traditional Japanese drama: Nō (see chapter 4), Kabuki, and Bunraku. Nō became popular among medieval warrior and courtier elites and continued to be appreciated by refined clientele during the Edo period. Bunraku and Kabuki, however, held the most appeal for urban townsfolk. The theatrical district and the pleasure quarters were the two areas designated by the bakufu for the amusement of lowly commoners, but over time they came to represent the quintessence of Japanese traditional culture.

Bunraku

The earliest references to puppetry in Japan date from the eleventh century, discussing itinerant bands of entertainers who performed plays with small hand puppets and engaged in prostitution. During the fifteenth and six-teenth centuries, chanted narratives from *The Tale of the Heike*, performed by blind bards who accompanied themselves on the lute, became popular. A new style of chanting emerged with the importation of the *shamisen*, a three-stringed, banjo-like instrument, from Okinawa. The arts of puppetry and stylized chanting *(jōruri)* to shamisen accompaniment were merged in Bunraku. The puppet theater reached its heyday in the late seventeenth century in Kyoto and Osaka, under the auspices of great chanters such as Takemoto Gidayū (1651–1714), who founded his own theater in Osaka, and the most talented dramatist of his day, Chikamatsu Monzaemon.

Bunraku performance is a composite of three elements. First are the puppets and their operators. Puppets acquired new technical features begin-ning in 1727, such as prehensile hands and movable eyelids and mouths. They later developed movable eyeballs and eyebrows, allowing a much wider range of expression. The two-thirds life-size puppets operated by three men were introduced in 1734. The puppets are not manipulated with strings; the main operator *(omozukai)* works the facial features and the right arm while two assistants manipulate the left arm and the legs, respec-tively. Female puppets have no legs because a kimono conceals the lower body; movement is simulated by manipulating the costume. Assistant pup-peteers usually wear a hooded black uniform to become "invisible" to the audience, but the omozukai wears ceremonial dress and remains unmasked, because he is the master practitioner. The second element of Bunraku is the chanter. A single chanter speaks for all the puppet characters on the stage—men, women, and children—so his voice must cover a broad range, from a high falsetto to a gruff bass. Finally, there is the musical accompaniment provided by the shamisen player, who dictates the pace of the narrative; both the chanter and puppet operators must synchronize with his rhythms.

Bunraku transformed into truly artistic theater when its plays acquired dramatic sophistication. Chikamatsu, who came from a family of rōnin and turned to writing drama because he had few financial prospects, lifted Bunraku to new heights. He drew upon classical tales, poetry, and story lines from Nō drama, using their imagery and literary techniques to write plays about both historical subjects *(jidaimono)* and contemporary society *(sewamono)*. His best-known historical play, *The Battles of Coxinga*, staged in 1715, is based loosely on the life of a young pirate with a Chinese father and Japanese mother who battles to help the Ming dynasty repel Manchurian invaders. It was so popular that it ran for seventeen months, rather than the usual month. Contemporary domestic dramas tended to emphasize the struggle between townspeoples' duties and obligations *(giri)*

FIGURE 38. Bunraku performance. Courtesy of JNTO.

and their human emotions and passions *(ninjō)*. Two of Chikamatsu's most popular plays, described below, deal with "love suicides" *(shinjū)* in which a pair of lovers, unable to resolve the conflict between their social duties and their romantic attachment to one another, agree to end their lives together. Such double suicides were a new phenomenon that acquired social notoriety in the late seventeenth century. Although the bakufu outlawed this behavior and prohibited its discussion in books and plays, townspeople clamored for the stories. Chikamatsu took advantage of this interest, staging fictionalized accounts of incidents just months after their occurrence. His two sewamono masterpieces, *The Love Suicides at Sonezaki* (1703) and *The Love Suicides at Amijima* (1721), both involve relationships between merchants and women of the pleasure quarters.

In the first of these plays, Ohatsu, a courtesan from Osaka, has fallen in love with Tokubei, a soy sauce salesman who had earlier agreed to marry the daughter of his employer and accepted an advance from the cash dowry. Tokubei, a kind but rather foolish character, loaned the money to his villanous friend Kuheiji, a rival for the courtesan's affections. Because of his romance with Ohatsu, Tokubei is no longer willing to wed his betrothed and asks Kuheiji to repay the sum so that he can return it to his boss, but the villain denies receiving any money and further accuses Tokubei of forging his seal on the debt document. Ohatsu fears that Kuheiji will use the loan to buy out her contract and claim her. Neither of the lovers can face the future—Ohatsu despondent over a future with Kuheiji, and Tokubei unable to live up to his obligations to his employer. In a famous scene at the tea-house where Ohatsu works, Tokubei hides from Kuheiji under her kimono robes. He signals his willingness to die together by secretly taking Ohatsu's foot and drawing it across his neck. The lovers decide to end their lives that evening, in the woods near Sonezaki Shrine, where a pine tree and palm tree grow from a single trunk. Gazing at the heavens, they vow to be husband and wife for eternity before Tokubei cuts their throats with a razor.

The plot of *The Love Suicides at Amijima* is somewhat more complex. Jihei, a paper merchant, is in love with the courtesan Koharu, but he cannot afford to buy her release from a brothel. To resolve their dilemma, the lovers vow to die together before a wealthy, obnoxious merchant named Tahei can claim her. One night Koharu reveals her pact with Jihei to a samurai customer and begs him to redeem her before the fated suicide. Jihei, eavesdropping outside, becomes furious that she plans to betray him and plunges a dagger through the paper door, trying to kill his lover, but he is seized by the samurai, who then reveals himself to be Jihei's brother Magoemon in disguise. Magoemon has staged this charade to prove Koharu's fickleness and bring Jihei to his senses, urging him to attend to his family and business.

The second act opens in Jihei's paper shop, where his wife, Osan, announces that Magoemon and his aunt (who is her mother) are planning to visit, concerned over gossip that a merchant was going to redeem Koharu. Jihei swears a sacred oath that he has forsaken Koharu, and his relatives depart, but Jihei weeps bitterly over the loss of his lover to the loathsome Tahei. Worried that Koharu will now kill herself to avoid an abhorrent fate, Osan pawns her own kimono to raise funds to rescue Koharu, but when this plan is thwarted, Jihei and Koharu escape together, beginning their journey toward death. As the lovers cross the two bridges across the stage, the chorus chants:

> Poor creatures, though they would discover today their destiny in the Sutra of Cause and Effect, tomorrow the gossip of the world will scatter like blossoms the scandal of Kamiya Jihei's love suicide, and carved in cherrywood, his story to the last detail will be printed in illustrated sheets. Jihei, led on by the spirit of death . . . is resigned to this punishment for neglect of his trade. But at times—who could blame him?—his heart is drawn to those he has left behind, and it is hard to keep walking on. Even in the full moon's light . . . he cannot see his way ahead—a sign perhaps of the darkness in his heart? The frost now falling will melt by dawn, but even more quickly than this symbol of human frailty, the lovers themselves will melt away. . . .[10]

Finally the lovers stop at a temple in Amijima, where they decide to commit their double suicide. During the final scenes, they each cut off their hair, claiming to become a Buddhist monk and nun who have no remaining obligations to society. Jihei stabs his lover and hangs himself in a nearby tree.

The plays of Chikamatsu represent the zenith of Bunraku; after the mid-eighteenth century, it was gradually overshadowed by Kabuki and went into decline. Today it survives largely through national government support. Few young artists are willing to endure the long apprentice period, which requires ten years of training each on the legs and arms of the puppet before one is allowed to become the main operator.

Kabuki

Kabuki, the theater of human actors rather than puppets, shared much in common with its dramatic predecessors, Nō and Bunraku: all three drew upon classics such as *The Tale of Genji* and *The Tale of the Heike* for their plotlines; all involved elaborate costumes; and each was considered a spectacle, more from the realm of fantasy than reality. As in Nō, dance played a central part in most Kabuki plays. It is perhaps closer to Bunraku, however, because both developed within the same urban milieu for the same commoner audiences. Like Bunraku, Kabuki staged both jidaimono and sewamono productions: the former allowed swashbuckling aragoto performances and the latter concerned the contemporary lives of shopkeepers, prostitutes, and other ordinary people, allowing urban audiences to view their own lived experiences on stage. Kabuki contained the same tensions between duty and desire featured in the plays of the puppet theater.

Kabuki was also deeply intertwined with the pleasure quarters. The denizens of both quarters—actors, prostitutes, musicians, and other entertainers—were official outcastes, whom the bakufu believed had to be confined and controlled. Nevertheless, the stars of the two quarters, top Kabuki actors and reigning courtesans, were the toast of urban society, models of fashion and style, and objects of titillating gossip. The intensity of fan culture surrounding both actors and courtesans helps account for Kabuki's ascendance over Bunraku; few fans could develop erotic or sentimental attachments to the inanimate puppets, who never behaved scandalously off stage. Authorities designated officially licensed areas of major cities to contain these two populations and their fans. In Kyoto, theaters for Kabuki, Bunraku, and storytelling were centered around the Shijō area. Other amusements were clustered nearby, including the same kinds of sideshows and spectacles found at Edo's Sensōji Temple. In Edo, the first theater was licensed in 1624, but the designated area for theaters was moved to different locations on the periphery of commoners' quarters.

Kabuki is said to have originated in the early seventeenth century when an itinerant female dancer called Okuni performed burlesque dances and skits at a riverbed in Kyoto. The term is derived from the verb *kabuku* (to tilt, behave oddly, or dress strangely). Okuni daringly performed dressed as a man and wore foreign styles like brocade trousers, animal-skin jackets, and even a large Christian cross. Other times, she danced in a gorgeous, feminine kimono with a male partner. Her success was imitated by troupes of prostitutes, including many men, and soon Kabuki performances were inseparable from the practice of prostitution. In 1629 the authorities banned women from the stage; they were replaced with attractive young men who played women's roles (forerunners of the onnagata discussed below) and continued to sideline as prostitutes. To dampen the rise of homosexual prostitution, authorities closed Kabuki theaters in 1652. Facing ruin, theater owners agreed to strict control over the behavior of their actors, whereupon the authorities allowed the theaters to reopen and present *yarō* (young fellows') Kabuki. Officials required that the young male actors shave their foreheads in the mature masculine fashion, rather than keeping the long bangs that were considered erotic. The actors responded by covering their bald pates with kerchiefs of dark purple silk to simulate lustrous hair.

By the eighteenth century, the kerchiefs were replaced with elaborate wigs, and those actors specializing in female roles evolved the art of the onnagata, creating a stylized repertoire of gestures and speech believed to represent an idealized femininity. They aimed not for transgender realism but for an exaggerated, fantasy portrayal of feminine grace, beauty, and mannerisms to parallel the exaggerated macho style and bombast of the aragoto roles. Onnagata actors of the time usually led female lives off stage, dressing in fashionable kimonos, coiffing themselves with female hairstyles, and even using the women's side of public bathhouses. Many Edo-period onnagata continued to have paid sexual relations, with male and female patrons alike. Note, however, that the majority of onnagata actors today do not lead transgender lives and often have heteronormative relationships and families.

The aragoto actors of male roles were generally the biggest stars of Kabuki and developed reputations for their romantic exploits, especially among the courtesans of the pleasure quarters. Their clothing, accessories, mannerisms, and speech were widely copied by their fans. The biggest stars earned fortunes from acting fees and from sales of products they endorsed, such as cosmetics, fans, and textiles. One, Ichikawa Yaozō II, noted for his portrayal of Sukeroku (described below), earned money selling water—in a climactic scene, his character hides in a water barrel to escape. Yaozō's female fans bought and sometimes consumed the barrel water, bottled after the show. Despite their outcaste status, leading actors and onnagata lived as luxuriously as daimyo, in mansions with legions of attendants. They made extravagant demands, like some top movie stars today who insist that their dressing rooms contain expensive delicacies or designer waters. Actor Sakata Tōjūrō refused to wear clothing once it had been washed and insisted that each grain of rice he ate was individually inspected before cooking, so that there were no small pebbles that could damage his teeth. Fans idolized and indulged their heroes.

Theater architectural features enhanced the sense of intimacy between the actors and their audiences. In its earliest days, the theater was a small, covered stage surrounded by a simple enclosure, which paying customers entered. By the late seventeenth century, the largest Kabuki theaters, like Edo's Nakamura-za, seated over a thousand, squeezing box seats and galleries into every inch of a relatively small space so that, for many spectators, actors were literally within reach. A stage feature called the *hanamichi*, a runway extending from the stage to the rear of the audience, allowed featured actors to move through the audience for dramatic entrances and exits. Audiences participated in the performances by shouting appreciation for a skillfully delivered line or pose, or by heckling poor actors as "daikon"— stiff, tasteless radishes. Fan clubs, often formed from members of a given trade, sat together in the theater in identical outfits, cheering on their favorites with clapping routines and songs. These groups often adopted the responsibility for supplying the theater or actors with designated gifts, from stage curtains to key props.

Most fans were familiar with their favorite actors' stock roles. Leading actors often selected a collection of canonic plays as their standard repertoire. The best known of these collections is Ichikawa Danjūrō VII's (1791–1859), known as the *Eighteen Best Kabuki Plays (Jūhachiban)*. The Ichikawa acting lineage owns the rights to perform these plays to this day. One of these, *Kanjinchō*, is a masterpiece of the historical genre, based on the Nō play *Ataka*, about the great warrior Minamoto no Yoshitsune's attempt to escape from his brother Yoritomo, founder of the Kamakura bakufu, who had ordered his death. Kurosawa Akira's film *The Men Who Tread on the Tiger's Tail* (1945) is partly based on this Kabuki play.

In *Kanjinchō*, Yoshitsune, his follower Benkei, and a small party have donned the distinctive costume of mountain ascetics associated with esoteric

FIGURE 39. Tsukioka Yoshitoshi, *Ichikawa Danjūrō IX as Masashibō Benkei in Kanjinchō*, nineteenth century, Los Angeles County Museum of Art. Source: Wikimedia Commons.

Buddhism *(yamabushi)* and pretend to be traveling in order to raise funds for repairs to Tōdaiji Temple in Nara. Warned to watch for Yoshitsune in disguise, the warrior Togashi Saemon stops the party at a barrier gate. Benkei instructs his master to pretend to be a porter while he takes charge of the interaction. The suspicious Togashi tests Benkei to see if he is a genuine priest, asking him to explain Buddhist scriptures and questioning him about symbolic aspects of his yamabushi costume. A former yamabushi himself, Benkei answers with ease, but when Togashi demands that he produce a *kanjinchō*, a subscription scroll listing the names of donors to the Tōdaiji campaign, he must improvise. In a famous moment in Kabuki, Benkei pulls out a blank scroll and begins reading from it as if it were a real list. Togashi catches a glimpse of the blank paper but is impressed by Benkei's courage and decides to let the party pass. Yoshitsune is on the verge of escape, but one of Togashi's guards spies him and calls out. To deflect suspicion, Benkei begins beating and berating the disguised Yoshitsune for bringing their party such troubles; he tells Togashi that he will kill the porter on the spot. Such behavior by a retainer toward his master is unimaginable, but Togashi sees through the ruse. He decides to allow them to pass, moved by Benkei's unthinkable actions out of devotion to Yoshitsune. Once past the barrier, Benkei breaks into tears, apologizing to Yoshitsune for his behavior. In the final scene, Benkei exits, performing a famous dance along the hanamichi.

FIGURE 40.   Toyohara Kunichika, *Nakamura Shikan as Hige no Ikyu, Ichikawa Danjuro IX as Hanakawado Sukeroku and Nakamura Fukusuke as Miuraya no Agemaki in the play Edo zakura,* nineteenth century. Courtesy of Rhode Island School of Design.

A second masterpiece from the classic repertoire is *Sukeroku*, a story that takes place in Edo's Yoshiwara pleasure quarters and illustrates the latter's rich culture of courtesans and the male connoisseurs known as tsū. Sukeroku is a gallant but street-tough samurai, the preferred companion of the stunning Agemaki, top courtesan of the Miura-ya teahouse, whose elaborate wig and hair ornaments are unparalleled. He is a charming and fashionable rake, known for his expensive purple headband and for picking fights with others. In truth, Sukeroku is the samurai Soga no Gorō, who seeks to avenge the death of his father. By provoking others into drawing their weapons, he will be able to identify the villain, who has stolen his family's heirloom sword. Another samurai, Ikyū, a wealthy but nasty elderly man with a long white beard, worships Agemaki and is one of her best clients. During one of their visits, he condemns Sukeroku as a thief, and Agemaki responds by refusing to see him again.

When Sukeroku enters the quarter, jauntily twirling his trademark bullseye-patterned parasol, he is surrounded by women who admire him and offer him gifts. He makes a famous speech about being the best fighter and lover alive. When Ikyū's retainers attack Sukeroku, he easily bests them, then challenges Ikyū to draw his own sword, but the old man refuses, saying it is too precious to be spoiled by the blood of a thief. He actually knows Sukeroku's true identity and later calls him out, condemning him for playing the man-about-town when his duty was to avenge his father. During this speech, Ikyū draws his sword to make a point but soon realizes his mistake. The sword identifies him as the murderer and he quickly departs. The play ends with Sukeroku's resolve to attack Ikyū and retrieve the sword.

THE PLEASURE QUARTERS

As we've seen, the pleasure quarters were in many ways the heart of ukiyo culture and the main subject of its novels, plays, and woodblock prints. The shogunate, always trying to restrain wasteful recreational excess, enacted measures to control the businesses of commercial sex and erotica. Brothel activity was confined to licensed quarters, surrounded by walls, with a single gateway to control passage. The quarters also contained teahouses and parlors for drinking and dining, where musicians, dancers, and jesters could be summoned for entertainment and where assignations between courtesans and their clients occurred. Courtesans and prostitutes were indentured to houses, where they lived, and were forbidden to exit the gates of the quarter unless redeemed by a wealthy patron. In Edo the pleasure quarters were established in 1617 and known as Yoshiwara, home to as many as six thousand female sex workers. In Osaka the pleasure quarters were called Shinmachi (founded in 1624), and in Kyoto they were known as Shimabara (founded in 1640). In these areas, wealthy spendthrifts held lavish parties day and night in the company of elaborately adorned courtesans and troupes of entertainers and attendants. Prostitution was never fully contained within the licensed quarters; large numbers of male and female sex workers plied their trade wherever possible—in bathhouses, on the streets, and in unregulated areas.

The pleasure quarters were not bound by the same class conventions and restrictions as normal Edo society. Samurai had to surrender their swords on entering the quarter. Here, money was the great equalizer and the sole criterion for receiving favored treatment. Merchants could dare to compete with daimyo for the favors of the highest-ranking courtesans. Indeed, wealthy merchants were usually more popular, because of their lavish spending in comparison to upper-class samurai who were constrained by the Confucian ethic of frugality and moderation. Samurai were discouraged, and daimyo officially barred, from visiting the quarter, but many could not resist. They disguised themselves, hiding under wide-brimmed hats that concealed their faces.

In addition to their renowned beauty, the upper ranks of courtesans usually possessed a high level of cultivation, needed to attract and retain the interest of the wealthy sophisticates who were their customers. They were adept at poetry, painting, and a host of other genteel arts. Like their Kabuki-actor counterparts, these women were trendsetters, their styles of clothing and accessories dictating new fashions and cultural trends. The highest courtesan rank was *tayū*. An association of the quarter's experienced residents, teahouse and brothel proprietors, and official supervisors determined who was promoted to this rank. Beauty, intelligence, cultural refinement, deportment, and earning power were the main criteria for tayū status. According to one document, the criteria for tayū rank were as follows: "Her eyes should be a little large, with dominant black pupils. Eyebrows should be close together, on the smoky side. The face should have the shape of a melon seed. . . . Fingers and toes should have delicate nails, fingers tapered and supple and double jointed hands are good. . . . The top of the head should be flat and not pointed."[11] Unacceptable features included a low bottom, droopy eyes, buckteeth, kinky hair, and bowed legs.

The most important possessions of the tayū and other courtesans were their ornate kimonos, made of fine silks embroidered with intricate patterns, brilliant brocades, and textured satins, and their elaborate hair ornaments. Tayū advertised themselves via processions, elaborate parades to the teahouse where they would rendezvous with their clients. In these processions, courtesans wore their finest apparel, usually of original design, and walked very slowly, accompanied by girl attendants in matching dress. A top-ranking courtesan stepped in a distinctive figure-eight pattern, arranging her clothing so that her red undergarment would flip open to reveal a flash of white ankle or calf. It was rumored that when men witnessed this sight, they went insane and spent all their money in attempts to meet with her. Over time, the processions became more ostentatious, with increasingly ornate headwear, higher footwear, and a larger number of attendants who carried long-handled parasols, lanterns, and the tayū's smoking set.

Tayū had stringent standards of behavior, including not touching money, not eating in front of clients, and never speaking vulgarly. In turn, they were protected by an elaborate protocol that did not permit a client to achieve his desire until his third appointment. Unlike common prostitutes, tayū had the power to reject new or unattractive clients. If a regular client two-timed her with another courtesan, he could be captured and punished, commonly by cutting off his topknot, a shameful condition that required a visit to a toupee specialist before appearing in public.

The cost of a tayū for one visit was around $600 by today's standards, but clients were also expected to pay for entertainers, food, and drink and to tip lavishly, so that the overall cost ran to several thousand dollars. Well-mannered Edokko who tipped nine times the cost of the visit knew to place the tip in an inconspicuous place, rather than drawing attention to their own generosity. Only the wealthiest merchants and samurai could afford such extravagance. Many men were ruined through debt incurred to finance such visits. Tayū were sometimes called "castle topplers" *(keisei)* for their ability to impoverish their daimyo admirers. On the other hand, courtesans faced heavy financial pressures to maintain their glamour and their entourage and were always hopelessly in debt to their houses. Each had a daily quota to meet, which she would have to pay herself if she missed a day's work for any reason, even illness or a death in the family.

The male counterpart to the tayū in the pleasure quarters was the tsū, discussed earlier—a man-about-town, of elegant sophistication and savoir faire, who embodied the spirits of iki and hari. His ideal characteristics were generosity, courtesy, consideration, intelligence, wit, candor, refinement, and urbanity. He dabbled in painting, poetry, song, tea ceremony, flower arrangement, and calligraphy. Negative appraisals of tsū condemned them as dandies and dilettantes, yet all men who frequented the pleasure quarters, samurai and commoner alike, aspired to this status. In the eighteenth century, sharebon books instructing readers on how to become tsū were especially popular. The Kabuki hero Sukeroku's sophisticated appearance, behavior, and impeccable tastes represent the ideal aesthetic consciousness of Edokko men.

Female geisha, professional entertainers who danced and played the three-stringed shamisen, began to appear in the quarters during the 1770s. Until that time, all musicians in the quarter were male. The female geisha's hairstyle was less elaborate than that of courtesans; her kimono was less ornate, a plain monochrome with crests and a white collar. Geisha prided themselves on their simple beauty and the artistry of their music and dance, the source of their livelihood. This did not mean that they did not engage in paid sex, which remained a common practice among entertainers of all kinds, but this was not integral to their occupation. Over time, geisha began to eclipse the courtesans themselves.

Reflecting on women's lives in the quarters, there are generally two different interpretations. Some observers see women who led miserable lives, sold into indentured sex work by their fathers or husbands, heavily guarded and unable to escape. Courtesans and prostitutes suffered frequently from venereal and other diseases, and most died in their twenties. Others, however, celebrate the women of the quarter as among the most free and powerful women in urban society—trendsetters able to earn their own disposable income who evaded the heavy burdens of raising families and managing households. In any case, it is important to realize that the sex trade varied widely by location and changed significantly throughout the course of the Edo period.

THE RURAL PERIPHERY

Rural inhabitants were able to gain glimpses of Edo's rich urban culture through traveling Kabuki and geisha troupes or through their own pilgrimages to the capital. Nevertheless, the lives of the peasantry remained more insular and static than those of their urban counterparts. The traditional Tokugawa village community was relatively autonomous. As long as taxes were paid and order maintained, the authorities left the elders and village headmen to run things their way. In many ways, rural peasant women were freer than their urban sisters. They were considered important working members of the family, not only contributing labor in the fields alongside male relatives but managing the household. Peasant women also had greater autonomy in their personal relationships: virginity at marriage was not expected, as it was among the samurai class, and they could more easily obtain divorces and return to their natal families than the "borrowed womb" brides of samurai.

Most rural protests were brought on by the authorities' efforts to squeeze more money from the peasantry through higher taxes on land or local products. Protests might also be sparked by excessive demands for free labor on construction projects or as porters along the major highways. The majority of Tokugawa-era peasant protests were nonviolent and had little "revolutionary" content—that is, they were not designed to secure basic changes in governance or social structure, but instead sought *jinsei* (benevolence) from samurai rulers, such as reduction of taxes in times of famine or drought. The sacrificial figures who petitioned the authorities were known as *gimin* (virtuous men), and the tales of their heroism would be celebrated in stories and songs for generations. The quintessential gimin was Sakura Sōgorō (1605–53). As a village headman, he petitioned the daimyo of his domain to reduce the heavy tax load that brought suffering to his neighbors. Unsuccessful in his plea, he went to Edo and presented a direct appeal to the shogun, an action punishable by death. His petition was granted, but he and his family were executed.

In the eighteenth century, however, there was a change in the nature and composition of peasant protest. No longer simple appeals to the authorities by village headmen, they grew larger and more violent, involving thousands of peasants across several domains. Such protests spiked in periods of natural disaster, crop failure, and famine, and huge waves of protests occurred in the 1780s, 1830s, and 1860s. In addition, protests were increasingly aimed not only at government authorities, but at merchants and wealthy members of rural communities for excessive rents, loan-sharking, and other exploitative practices.

In 1867, as opposition to the shogunate swelled, a yearlong wave of carnivalesque riots swept villages over a wide swath of central and western Japan, the densely populated heartland from Hiroshima to Yokohama. They were kicked off by the seemingly miraculous descent of paper talismans *(ofudafuri)* of shrines and temples from the sky. Food riots, rent riots, and farm uprisings also peaked in 1867, after several years of bad harvests. In the face of this chaos, the people believed that the falling talismans were signals of the start of *yonaoshi,* a kind of millennial world renewal, and celebrated by dancing and singing in the streets, dressing up in absurd costumes, cross-dressing, or just plain running around naked. Dancers in huge crowds barged into houses and businesses demanding that the occupants join them. They coerced the wealthy in their communities to supply food, drink, and entertainment. Their songs had the refrain *ee ja nai ka,* or "What the hell! It's all OK!" In total the phenomenon involved hundreds of thousands of ordinary people over a nine-month period. Movements would emerge in one area, then evaporate several days later, only to emerge in another village. While this may seem an unconventional form of protest, the dancing and singing masses aimed to achieve world renewal, a cleansing away of evil and an ushering-in of utopia—semireligious ideas with political implications. Their activities clogged the main highways, paralyzed commercial neighborhoods and city centers, interrupted farming, and obstructed official business and traffic at a crucial moment in history, contributing to the chaos that surrounded the fall of the Tokugawa shogunate.

In summary, many cultural developments of the Edo period reflected the interests of urban commoners, rather than their samurai or courtier superiors. Townspeople eagerly consumed the affordable products of a rapidly developing print industry, including a wide array of book types, from satirical novels to reference works to travel guides, alongside mass-produced woodblock prints depicting their favorite actors or courtesans or famous landscapes. They attended Kabuki and Bunraku plays that retold beloved tales of the past or reflected their own everyday struggles. Despite the strict class divisions, men of all ranks began to admire male gender ideals depicted in popular culture—including generosity, stylish refinement, and a spirit of resistance that sometimes clashed with official ideology. During the ensuing Meiji period, many class restrictions would be legally abolished, but many gaps in lifestyle and opportunity—between classes, between genders, and especially between urban and rural residents—would persist.

FURTHER READING

Berry, Mary E. *Japan in Print: Information and Nation in the Early Modern Period*. Berkeley: University of California Press, 2006.

Gundry, David J. *Parody, Irony and Ideology in the Fiction of Ihara Saikaku*. Leiden, The Netherlands: Brill, 2017.

Guth, Christine. *Art of Edo Japan: The Artist and the City, 1615–1868*. New Haven, CT: Yale University Press, 2010.

Ikegami, Eiko. *Bonds of Civility: Aesthetic Networks and the Political Origins of Japanese Culture*. New York: Cambridge University Press, 2005.

Matsunosuke, Nishiyama. *Edo Culture: Daily Life and Diversions in Urban Japan, 1600–1868*. Honolulu: University of Hawaii, 1997.

Pflugfelder, Gregory M. *Cartographies of Desire: Male-Male Sexuality in Japanese Discourse, 1600–1950*. Berkeley: University of California Press, 2007.

Screech, Timon. *Sex and the Floating World: Erotic Images in Japan 1700–1820*, 2nd ed. London: Reaktion Books, 2009.

Seigle, Cecilia S. *Yoshiwara: The Glittering World of the Japanese Courtesan*. Honolulu: University of Hawaii, 1993.

Shimazaki, Satoko. *Edo Kabuki in Transition: From the Worlds of the Samurai to the Vengeful Female Ghost*. New York: Columbia University Press, 2016.

Stanley, Amy. *Selling Women: Prostitution, Markets, and the Household in Early Modern Japan*. Berkeley: University of California Press, 2012.

Walthall, Anne. *Peasant Uprisings in Japan: A Critical Anthology of Peasant Histories*. Chicago, IL: University of Chicago Press, 1991.

Yonemoto, Marcia. *Mapping Early Modern Japan Space, Place, and Culture in the Tokugawa Period, 1603–1868*. Berkeley: University of California Press, 2003.

RECOMMENDED FILMS

An Actor's Revenge. 1963. Feature film directed by Ichikawa Kon. Tale of an onnagata actor who takes revenge against those responsible for the deaths of his parents.

Double Suicide. 1969. Feature film directed by Masahiro Shinoda. Adaptation of Chikamatsu's *The Love Suicides at Amijima* that blends Bunraku theater traditions with live action.

Eijanaika. 1981. Feature film directed by Imamura Shōhei. Fictional story of the turmoil and revelry among urban commoners on the eve of the Meiji Restoration.

Miss Hokusai. 2015. Animated film directed by Hara Keiichi. Fictionalized account of the daughter of Katsushika Hokusai, herself a gifted artist, based on a popular manga series.

The Life of Oharu. 1952. Feature film directed by Mizoguchi Kenji. Adaptation of Saikaku's novel *The Life of an Amorous Woman*.

Utamaro and His Five Women. 1946. Feature film directed by Mizoguchi Kenji. Fictionalized account of the life of artist Utamaro by an iconic director.

8   Facing and Embracing the West

1850s–1900s

By the mid-nineteenth century, the systems of control established by the Tokugawa shogunate were under severe strain. A Confucian belief stated that dynasties fell when they faced "troubles within and threats without" *(naiyū gaikan)*. Growing social unrest among the peasantry and the samurai class alike suggested the bakufu's troubles within; threats from without came from Western imperialist nations, clamoring for Japan to open for trade. The arrival of American gunboats under the command of Commodore Matthew C. Perry in 1853 put an end to centuries of enforced isolation.

Many were angered by the bakufu's inability to protect Japan from the encroaching barbarians. Some samurai supported overthrowing the bakufu and restoring the emperor to rulership. The result, the Meiji Restoration of 1868, allowed Japan to centralize authority and resources so that it could quickly modernize its political institutions and begin to industrialize its economy. The Meiji Restoration is often described as having a dual nature. On one hand, it signaled a return to imperial sovereignty, an ancient form of rule. On the other, it provided an opportunity to enact revolutionary, progressive changes to Japanese society and culture.

Two slogans characterized the monumental changes to Japanese society, economy, politics, and culture during the Meiji period (1868–1912). The first, "Civilization and Enlightenment" *(Bunmei kaika)*, called for the country to embrace the political and cultural values of Western civilization by promoting science and a spirit of independence and free inquiry and by adopting Western-style political institutions. In the popular mind, "civilization and enlightenment" was associated with the adoption of Western material culture, such as fashions, foods, and architecture. The second slogan, "Rich Country, Strong Army" *(Fukoku kyōhei)*, urged the development of the national economy and military so that Japan could remain an independent nation, unlike the majority of non-European nations that had been colonized. To achieve this goal, Japan would have to build railroads and shipyards, schools and science. The textile industry and the construction of a network of railroads played key roles in generating both wealth and power for the fledgling nation. A third slogan applied to individuals free to pursue their destiny without regard to status restrictions—"Rise in the World!" *(Risshin shusse)*. This call encouraged Japanese youths to educate themselves, persevere, and achieve success and a name for themselves in the new world.

POLITICAL AND SOCIAL DEVELOPMENTS

In terms of "troubles within," in the mid-1800s the bakufu faced growing discontent not only among oppressed commoners, but also among the ruling samurai class itself. The fundamental cause of the trouble was the commercialization and growth of the economy. In rural areas, diversification of production brought new sources of income to peasants. The expansion of markets for products such as indigo, oils, sesame, cotton, tobacco, textiles, and handicrafts allowed farm families to accumulate profits. Widespread literacy among peasants allowed them to consult farm manuals describing improvements in seeds, fertilizers, and systems of irrigation for better harvests. New rural income, however, flowed primarily to the wealthiest farmers, creating greater economic disparities in the villages, which fomented social unrest.

Peasants were not the only class discontented with the Tokugawa status quo. Many samurai were suffering economically. The majority of low-ranking samurai, who lived on fixed stipends, were unable to meet daily living expenses. Many went into debt to merchants or had to stoop to doing menial work or force their families to produce handicrafts to make ends meet. Although samurai held the highest social and moral position in society, they were poorer than many commoners, which they resented. The desire to hide the incongruence between their social and economic status was captured in the proverb "Even a destitute samurai holds his toothpick high" *(Samurai wa kuwanedo takayōji)*, meaning that a samurai would swagger around with a toothpick in his mouth, as if he'd eaten a sumptuous meal, even if he were actually starving, owing to his pride of status. There was discontent among the daimyo as well, because their official rankings did not always accurately reflect their wealth. A daimyo's rank was based on the assessment of rice produced by his domain; it determined the size and location of his mansions in Edo, his seat during shogunal audiences, the size of his sankin kōtai retinue, and his ceremonial obligations. For many domains, the official assessment made in the seventeenth century no longer matched the daimyo's actual wealth. Some had difficulty paying for the trappings of their rank, while others resented being unable to demonstrate their wealth and improve their status.

Beginning in the second half of the eighteenth century, the bakufu also faced new threats from abroad. Russians had increasingly encroached on Japan's northern borders. Technological progress in weapons and transportation generated a new phase of expansionism among imperialist nations. In 1842, the Japanese watched warily as the British forced China's Qing empire to accept unequal trade treaties during the Opium War. The acquisition of a Pacific seaboard by the United States brought opportunities for direct trade between California and China, and Japan would serve as a useful supply depot en route. Commodore Perry (1794–1858) embarked on a mission to seek a treaty with Japan, reaching Edo Bay in July 1853 with a small squadron of ships, threatening to return with a larger force if his demands weren't met. Bakufu officials faced the difficult task of avoiding hostilities while refusing to fully open their country, which would overturn centuries of seclusionist foreign policy. Perry eventually earned an agreement to open two ports, Shimoda and Hakodate, for refueling; to provide better treatment for shipwrecked sailors; and to appoint a U.S. consul. It was a beginning, but far from a full-fledged commercial treaty.

The only European language that officials knew when Perry arrived was Dutch, and the Americans had to rely on shipwrecked Japanese fishermen who had been rescued by American whaling boats as interpreters. Nakahama Manjirō (1827–98), a fisherman from Tosa province, was one such individual, shipwrecked in 1841 and saved by an American whaler, whose captain sent him to school in Massachusetts. Manjirō returned to Japan in 1851 and was employed by the daimyo of Tosa as an advisor. When Perry arrived, Manjirō acted as an interpreter on the Japanese side and later published the first English-language phrasebook. For the first Perry Expedition, there were no Americans who spoke Japanese aboard. Perry brought along a rescued Japanese fisherman, known as "Sam Patch," who refused to speak to Japanese officials for fear of punishment by the samurai. Stephen Sondheim's Broadway musical *Pacific Overtures* (1976, revived 2004) is based on the life of Manjirō.

While the promise of commerce drove U.S. demands, within Japan it did not produce pressures to overthrow the policy of national isolation just for the sake of trade, officially denigrated as the occupation of lowly merchants. In fact, the opposite was true—Perry's arrival strengthened antiforeign feeling among many samurai and commoners alike. Xenophobia rallied around the slogan "Revere the Emperor, Expel the Barbarian" (*Sonnō jōi*).

This antiforeign movement aimed to preserve national unity and tradition in the face of bakufu impotence. It spread widely among both samurai activists and at the grass roots among the peasantry, primed by the evangelism of Hirata Atsutane. Activists believed that foreigners would colonize Japan and drain the nation of its resources. In conjunction with the teachings of Kokugaku and the Mito school of history, they advocated the view that Japan consisted of a unified national body (kokutai) with the emperor, direct descendant of the Sun Goddess, Amaterasu, at its peak. These ideas influenced the Meiji Restoration in 1868.

Townsend Harris, a New York merchant, was appointed the first U.S. consul general in Japan, arriving in 1856 with instructions to secure a full commercial treaty. The bakufu had been unable to obtain approval for any kind of treaty from the imperial court, so in 1858 the powerful bakufu regent, Ii Naosuke (1815–60), arranged to sign the treaty without imperial sanction; this disrespect toward the emperor intensified agitation against the shogunate. The 1858 Harris Treaty set the pattern for Japan's commercial agreements with European nations, beginning with the Dutch, Russians, British, and French. The treaties stipulated the exchange of diplomatic consuls; the opening of five Japanese treaty ports; the right of foreign citizens to reside in those ports, trade without interference, and enjoy extraterritoriality, meaning that they were exempt from local laws; the opening of Edo and Osaka for foreign trade; and the setting of import and export tariffs disadvantageous to Japan. In 1860, the Harris Treaty was ratified in Washington, D.C., where a large entourage of Japan's first ambassadors traveled—the first such official trip abroad after two centuries of relative seclusion. The eighty-one-man embassy to the United States was the first of six missions to the West dispatched before the Meiji Restoration in 1868, sent to negotiate problems connected with the treaties or obtain technical knowledge. These missions opened up perspectives for low-ranking bakufu delegates, who began questioning the wisdom of the traditional social and political order, looking toward the West for new models.

Treaty Port Life

After the treaties were ratified, one of the first orders of business was to set up the treaty ports for the entry of foreigners. After two-and-a-half centuries of isolation, the adjustments required to turn Japanese towns into international trading posts were difficult and painful. Bakufu authorities wished to place the foreigners at a distance from local populations. Before Yokohama was opened to trade, it was a small fishing village lying across the bay from the thriving post town of Kanagawa on the Tōkaidō road. Geographically,

FIGURE 41. Utagawa Hiroshige III, *View of the Seafront in Yokohama*, 1870, The Metropolitan Museum of Art, New York. Source: Wikimedia Commons.

Yokohama was a narrow strip of land bounded by water to the east, west, and south and was thus a location that was easy to monitor and control. The U.S., British, French, and Dutch consuls established offices in bustling Kanagawa. To create inducements for the newcomers to settle in Yokohama instead, authorities busily erected Western-style buildings for use as residences, shops, and warehouses. As merchants, shopkeepers, and tradesmen steadily arrived, they were glad to take advantage of the new facilities available at Yokohama.

Nagasaki, the center of Japan's foreign trade for centuries, also became an official treaty port. In 1860, a year after the port was opened, the population of Nagasaki was estimated at sixty-five thousand, with one hundred Europeans and over four hundred Chinese; by 1864, there were as many as seven thousand foreigners in residence. Because the new treaties specified that only nationals whose governments had signed treaties with Japan could land at the new ports, Chinese traders faced a problem in establishing legal residence. They found a canny solution, posing as servants of other foreigners who were legally allowed to enter Japan. Thus protected, some Chinese engaged in clandestine businesses such as gambling and smuggling. Treaty-port officials found it difficult to determine who were genuine servants and who were poseurs.

A key institution for all treaty ports was the Customs House, which not only regulated customs but also served as a place to exchange currency and bullion, an employment office, and a liaison office for all matters where the activities of foreigners intruded on the lives of the native population.

Customs officials even undertook the duty of finding mistresses for foreigners—and checking potential candidates for venereal disease.

While diplomatic and treaty negotiations were carried out by statesmen in an orderly manner, they were acted upon by a motley group of foreigners and Japanese who did not necessarily care about the same matters as their governments. To the dismay of local consuls, the first groups of traders to arrive in the new treaty ports were often unsavory or less-than-desirable types seeking profit and adventure. A Catholic bishop in Nagasaki observed that the new arrivals to the city consisted of "disorderly elements of California adventurers, Portuguese desperadoes, runaway sailors, piratical outlaws, and the moral refuse of European nations."[1] When foreign ships were in port, saloons and brothels did a brisk business. Authorities established their own brothel for foreigners, the Gankiro teahouse in Yokohama. Diplomats from the treaty nations were under constant pressure to rescue their nationals from the Japanese police and to account for the bad behavior of drunken sailors and ne'er-do-wells.

Foreigners were restricted from traveling beyond a radius of twenty miles from the treaty port, which made sightseeing difficult if not impossible. Residence beyond this area was permitted only for reasons of health or for those employed by Japanese. Bored European and American troops and traders attempted to entertain themselves by establishing clubs and engaging in horse races. In 1864, English troops imported dogs and established the famous Yokohama Hunt Club, whose moonlight events became a highlight of community life. The hunt was followed by an elaborate dinner party, with music supplied by the regimental band. Foreign hunters shot large numbers of pheasant, wild geese, ducks, wild boar, and deer, offending local sensibilities and Buddhist beliefs, which prohibited such indiscriminate slaughter.

Life within the settlements was dangerous. Antiforeign activists continued their activities through the 1860s, attacking and assassinating foreigners and domestic collaborators. In response, foreign consuls brought in their own guards and troops; at one point, there were over a thousand English and three hundred French troops garrisoned in Yokohama.

Meiji Restoration

Tensions between the shogunate and activists aiming to topple the Tokugawa and restore the emperor to rule continued to grow during the 1860s. Two outer *(tozama)* domains, Satsuma and Chōshū, excluded from positions of power within the bakufu, emerged as leading anti-bakufu forces. They drew the support of young sonnō jōi activists who engaged in campaigns of domestic terror, even assassinating Townsend Harris's Dutch secretary, Henry Heuskin. The bakufu enlisted the aid of the French to help build Tokugawa military power to punish dissident domains. In 1866, factions from Satsuma and Chōshū made a secret pact pledging mutual support if the shogunate attacked either domain. Satsuma had developed a substantial arms trade with Britain, which wanted to counter French influence in Japan. Chōshū had created a peasant conscript army in 1865 but lacked access to modern weapons. Sakamoto Ryōma (1836–67), a swashbuckling activist from Tosa, brokered the secret pact. When the bakufu called for a punitive expedition against Chōshū in the summer of 1866, Satsuma refused to supply troops and several other daimyo followed its lead. Chōshū's armies easily turned aside the bakufu's undermanned battalions. The following year, the newly installed shogun, Tokugawa Yoshinobu (1837–1913), announced plans to further increase bakufu military power, intent on wiping out dissenting domains. The Satsuma-Chōshū (Sat-Chō) alliance, along with leaders from neighboring domains and supporters within the imperial court, began their own plans to overthrow the bakufu. In late 1867, armed rebels moved toward Kyoto's Imperial Palace, closely guarded by the Shinsengumi—bakufu forces composed of roguish rōnin swordsmen installed to prevent contact between the court and their imperialist activist supporters.

On January 3, 1868, pro-imperial forces stormed into the palace, where they were welcomed by a group of courtiers. The fifteen-year-old Crown Prince Mutsuhito had been elevated to the throne the previous year as Emperor Meiji, meaning "enlightened rule." He issued a proclamation that abolished the office of shogun, restored power to the emperor, and created new government offices to be staffed by court nobles, daimyo, and other "men of talent." The third and final shogunate had officially ended. Nevertheless, for over a year, forces loyal to the Tokugawa and those of Sat-Chō's imperial faction fought battles in Edo and provinces in northern Honshu and Hokkaido, where the last remnants of Tokugawa support fled. Collectively, these conflicts are known as the Boshin War (1868–69). The total number of casualties, around 3,500, is relatively low in comparison to great revolutionary wars fought in other nations. This fact led earlier historians of Japan to praise the Meiji Restoration as a "bloodless revolution" or "revolution from above." After Edo was captured by imperial forces, it was renamed Tokyo, or "eastern capital," and the young emperor was transferred from Kyoto to the former palace of the shogun.

In March 1868, Emperor Meiji summoned nearly four hundred officials to the Imperial Palace, where they were read a statement of the

FIGURE 42. Uchida Kuichi, *Portrait of the Emperor Meiji*, 1873. Source: Wikimedia Commons.

new national policy, known as the Charter Oath, which contained five directives:

1. Deliberative assemblies shall be widely established and all matters shall be decided by public discussion.

2. All classes, high and low, shall unite in vigorously carrying out administration of affairs of state.

3. The common people, no less than civil and military officials, shall each be allowed to pursue his own calling, so that there may be no discontent.

4. Evil customs of the past shall be broken off and everything based upon the just laws of Nature.

5. Knowledge shall be sought throughout the world, so as to strengthen the foundations of imperial rule.[2]

The articles of the Charter Oath served as framing principles for the sweeping changes that would take place in governance and society. The first clause made an appeal for national unity by suggesting, disingenuously, that the small clique of Sat-Chō revolutionaries and their allies would not monopolize decision making but would include other influential persons in making policy. The next two clauses expanded on this idea by offering people of all status the opportunity for mobility and participation in national development. The final two articles addressed the concerns of foreign powers, assuring them that Japan intended to become a stable and respected member of the international community, under the tutelage of the "civilized" Western nations.

Meiji leaders launched a revolutionary program of reforms in order to ensure national independence and build the promise of future greatness. Before they could negotiate revisions to the humiliating, unequal treaties that had placed Japan in a semicolonial status, they would first have to foster national unity and build strength and wealth. In just three short decades, Meiji leaders would reorganize the social structure, create a constitutional polity and national assembly, and foster capitalism through rapid industrialization. From early on, they adopted the imperialist outlook of the Western powers, first "colonizing" the Ainus of Hokkaido and the Ryūkyūans of Okinawa, then forcibly opening Korea to trade in 1876 by using their own gunboat diplomacy. The First Sino-Japanese War (1894–95; see chapter 10) allowed Japan to demonstrate the effectiveness of its modernized military, quickly earning a victory that surprised and impressed other nations and gained Japan control over its own colonial territories in Taiwan, the Pescadore Islands, and the Liaodong Peninsula.

"CIVILIZATION AND ENLIGHTENMENT"

Political Reforms

The most pressing matter for leaders was to create a centralized political structure that would permit them to exercise authority throughout the nation. A Grand Council of State, made up of Sat-Chō leaders and their allies, was established to act as the chief policy-making organ. Men like Okubo Toshimichi (1830–78) and Saigō Takamori (1828–77) from Satsuma, Itō Hirobumi (1841–1909) and Yamagata Aritomo (1838–1922) from Chōshū, and Prince Iwakura Tomomi (1825–83) monopolized control of state policy for decades. Although the new state ostensibly returned rule to the emperor, it was this group of men, in fact, who guided the nation while the young emperor served only as its symbolic head. The Grand Council persuaded daimyo to give up their traditional autonomy through generous financial settlements and titles of nobility. In 1871, Emperor Meiji announced that the domains had been eliminated and 302 prefectures established under new imperial governors appointed by the council. The number of prefectures was reduced to seventy-two later that year and finally to the current forty-seven in 1888.

In 1869, the Grand Council eliminated the Tokugawa four-category status system, lifting restrictions on occupational and social mobility. Commoners found changes such as the right to take surnames and to marry and adopt between the former classes liberating, but many ex-samurai were disgruntled. Not only did they lose their monopoly on surnames; they were deprived of their right to carry swords, and, most seriously of all, the state eventually stripped them of their hereditary stipends, forcing the samurai to accept fixed-term interest-bearing bonds instead, which bore just half the annual cost for the national treasury. Another measure that upset many former samurai was the formation of a conscript army. Initially, Meiji leaders envisioned turning ex-samurai into a professional army. The Conscription Law of 1873, however, was based on the practices of Europe's modern armies, requiring that all males serve for three years after reaching twenty years of age and spend an additional four years in the reserves. Meiji leaders hoped the law would forge ties of loyalty between commoner men and the new state. Nevertheless, large protests soon erupted in rural areas over compulsory military service, known as the "blood tax," which would deprive farms of necessary labor. Rumors circulated that this term was literal—that blood would be drained from conscripts and used for a variety of purposes, including dyeing blankets and being rubbed on telegraph wires.

Many ex-samurai, bitter about their loss of privileges, also engaged in uprisings during the 1870s. The largest protest was led by Saigō Takamori, a military hero of the Restoration and a member of the Grand Council. Upset by the loss of morale among ex-samurai, Saigō proposed invading Korea as an outlet for their frustrations but was rebuffed by other members of the council. Saigō then resigned from politics and returned home to Kagoshima in Kyushu, where he established private academies for several thousand young ex-samurai to study military tactics and Confucian classics. In 1877, he and forty thousand followers mounted a rebellion against the central government, but this was quashed in a few months' time by the national army, a mixed force of three hundred thousand conscripts and ex-samurai. The so-called Satsuma Rebellion represented the last hurrah of the samurai class. After 1878, Meiji leaders were free to pursue their agenda without the threat of violent resistance from reactionaries attempting to overturn the new government.

Hollywood borrowed from Saigō's story in *The Last Samurai* (2003), but the movie is highly misleading. While the real Saigō was, indeed, fighting to protect the "samurai way," he was more concerned with their loss of social status and hereditary stipends than with a vague sense of "honor" or preserving traditional ways of life. Saigō's forces used modern guns and cannons and wore Western-style military uniforms, resorting to swords only after running out of ammunition.

Saigō most likely committed suicide at the end of the battle, and his body was retrieved, but multiple rumors circulated about the popular leader, beloved by many as a paragon of samurai virtue. Some claimed that he went abroad to fight the imperialist powers in India and China, or that he would return with the Russian tsar to overthrow the Meiji regime. One story even claimed that Saigō's image had appeared in a comet. The Grand Council granted their former colleague a posthumous pardon in 1889, perhaps out of respect, but in effect echoing the pacification of angry spirits such as Sugawara no Michizane in past centuries.

Learning from the West: Hired Foreigners and the Iwakura Mission

Another aspect of Meiji reforms was the rapid westernization of institutions. In 1868, the floodgates to Western knowledge opened wide, and within a decade several hundred Japanese were studying in the United States and Europe. An even greater number of foreigners came to Japan, employed by national and prefectural governments to instruct the Japanese in Western politics, medical practices, legal philosophies, technology, and education.

The "hired foreigners" *(oyatoi gaikokujin)* who advised Meiji leaders provided specialized knowledge to assist in the modernization of Japanese institutions through technology transfer and counsel. The government hired over three thousand such experts over three decades, and many more were employed privately. The oyatoi were highly compensated; in 1874, the salaries for 520 foreigners consumed over a third of the new nation's annual budget. They were typically offered nonrenewable three-year contracts and were expected to train Japanese replacements before returning to their home countries. Several, however, became enamored with Japan and decided to settle there. The official system was ended in 1899.

Among the most influential of these oyatoi were Josiah Conder (1852–1920), Basil Hall Chamberlain (1850–1935), Lafcadio Hearn (1850–1904), and Ernest Fenollosa (1853–1908). These men developed expertise in native arts and literature, which greatly influenced both Japanese and Western views of Japanese culture. Conder arrived from Britain in 1877 as the first professor of architecture at Tokyo Imperial University. He trained Japan's first generation of modern architects and was hired to design and build iconic projects such as the Rokumeikan Pavilion and the Marunouchi area of Tokyo, which was to resemble a London business district. Conder developed a deep interest in Japanese arts, especially ikebana and landscape gardening, writing several popular books that introduced Western audiences to these subjects. He remained in Japan for the remainder of his life. Chamberlain taught at the Imperial Japanese Naval Academy but gained his reputation for his translations of Japanese literature into English, including many haiku and the *Kojiki* (1882). His most popular work, *Things Japanese* (1890), was a compendium of miscellaneous Japan-related topics, from samurai to superstitions, pilgrimage to pottery, for the edification of European and American travelers. Hearn, a journalist and professor of English at Tokyo Imperial University, became a naturalized citizen, married a Japanese woman, and adopted the name Koizumi Yakumo. He is best known for his many books on Japanese legends and ghost stories, such as *Glimpses of Unfamiliar Japan* (1894) and *Kwaidan: Stories and Studies of Strange Things* (1904). The American Fenollosa was hired to teach philosophy at the Imperial University and developed a deep interest in Japanese art and Buddhism. During the early Meiji period, in the heady rush toward westernization, many traditional arts were neglected, insofar as art studies taught by the oyatoi focused on Western forms such as oil paintings. Fenollosa advised Meiji leaders to preserve and protect their traditional arts. With his disciple Okakura Kakuzō (1863–1913), he inventoried national art treasures for the government. He and his wealthy friend William Bigelow amassed large collections of art and ancient Buddhist treasures, which they bequeathed to the Museum of Fine Arts in Boston and the Smithsonian's Freer Gallery of Art in Washington, D.C. Fenollosa also helped establish both the Tokyo School of Fine Arts and the Tokyo Imperial Museum.

Fenollosa and Okakura were also highly influential in the establishment and promotion of *nihonga*, or Japanese-style paintings—a new, syncretic style that combined traditional artistic conventions and materials with

Western painting techniques, such as perspective, shading, and realism. The style was termed *nihonga* to distinguish these works from purely Western-style oil paintings known as *yōga*. Nihonga were painted on washi paper or silk using brushes. They were either monochrome, using ink, or polychrome, using pigments made from natural ingredients such as minerals and semiprecious stones. Nihonga were originally displayed as hanging scrolls or on folding byōbu screens and sliding fusuma doors, but over time, they generally shifted to Western framing styles.

As foreign advisers were helping to shape Japan's future, the Meiji leaders wanted to see conditions in the world for themselves. In 1871, Prince Iwakura Tomomi led a delegation of forty-nine government officials on an extended trip to the United States and Europe. The Iwakura Mission had three primary objectives: to make goodwill visits to the heads of fifteen countries that had official diplomatic relations with Japan; to inquire about renegotiating the unequal treaties; and to learn the secrets of Western progress by studying institutions, society, and culture. The embassy quickly learned that these countries refused to consider treaty revision until Japan had proved itself a true international citizen by reforming domestic laws and institutions so that they more closely resembled those of their treaty partners. The disappointed ambassadors redoubled their efforts to study the secrets of Western civilization. They divided into subgroups assigned to study different topics: one addressed constitutions and political systems; another handled trade and economics, including industry, banking, taxation, and currency; a third group examined educational systems and philosophies. All visited a wide variety of institutions: prisons and police offices, schools and museums, mints and chambers of commerce, shipyards, textile mills, and sugar refineries. The pace was unrelenting.

The mission convinced its members of the gaping economic and social gap between Japan and the "civilized nations." Many came to believe that this gap was attributable not only to superior science and technology, but also to the progressive cultural and social values of Western nations. The mission also began to understand the competition between nations in terms of "social Darwinism"—ways of thinking that sought to apply Charles Darwin's theories of evolution and natural selection to human societies. They came to believe that, in a world in which only the fittest of nations would survive, those that supported modern technology, "civilized" institutions, and Western liberal values were destined to dominate the international environment. Nations that failed to adopt these stances faced colonization or even extinction. Japan would have to be relentless in its efforts to achieve international respect and avoid the fate of weaker nations.

Meiji Constitution

After the Iwakura Mission's return, Japan's leaders realized they would not be able to renegotiate the unequal treaties until they had established elected assemblies and a constitution, idealized attributes of Western political culture. As they began planning for these new institutions, their primary goals included clarifying the sovereignty of the emperor and continuing the concentration of power in the hands of the ruling clique, with minimal real power delegated to popular assemblies. According to these principles, the emperor would reign but not rule—just as in past centuries.

As the oligarchs deliberated, ex-samurai, intellectuals, and wealthy villagers began to demand greater political rights. By the end of the 1870s, the Freedom and Popular Rights (Jiyū minken) movement would include more than a thousand organizations, with over a quarter of a million members, who demanded that the new political institutions be broadly inclusive and representative. Groups circulated mass petitions; some even drafted their own constitutions, advocating a more liberal sharing of power than the oligarchs had in mind. Meiji leaders attempted to quell the movement by combining repressive laws with a few strategic concessions. In 1875, they enacted strict laws governing the press and rights of assembly in order to limit the Popular Rights movement's ability to organize. The Press Ordinance suspended any newspaper deemed threatening to the public order. Police presence was required for all public political assemblies, and discussion was limited to preapproved topics. Furthermore, soldiers, police, teachers, students, and women were forbidden to attend political meetings. To mollify the activists, the leadership agreed in 1878 to establish prefectural and city assemblies; in 1881, they promised to open a national assembly by 1890.

The Meiji constitution was promulgated on February 11, 1889. Early that morning, the emperor, dressed in ancient court garments, informed his ancestors of the new fundamental law of the state in a Shinto ritual before a shrine deep in the imperial compound. He then changed into formal Western attire and appeared on a red-carpeted dais in a lavish European-style reception hall as a benevolent modern sovereign, bestowing a constitution upon the nation. The juxtaposition of such different ceremonies underscores the dual nature of the Meiji Restoration as both a return to ancient forms of rule and a springboard for radical changes to Japanese society and culture.

Nevertheless, during the early Meiji period, the emperor remained a remote, invisible figure to the masses. In order to increase popular support for a constitutional monarchy, Meiji leaders sent the young emperor off to

FIGURE 43.   Adachi Ginkō, *View of the Issuance of the State Constitution in the State Chamber of the New Imperial Palace,* 1889. Source: Wikimedia Commons.

visit every corner of Japan. During the two-and-a-half centuries of Tokugawa rule, emperors had ventured outside of Kyoto just three times; but during the forty-five years of his reign, the Meiji emperor made over a hundred excursions, including six so-called Great Circuits in the 1870s and '80s. Thus, during the critical first decades of the new nation, its sovereign was absent from the halls of power as he covered thousands of miles, visited every major island, accepted the well-wishes of farmers, and stayed with local notables who installed specially constructed toilets for imperial use only. In order to further foster a sense of emperor-centered nationalism, Meiji leaders invented forms of imperial pageantry modeled on impressive ceremonies conducted for European monarchies on the occasions of weddings, funerals, and commemorations of war victories.

MEIJI MATERIAL CULTURE

The Charter Oath had also declared the need to abandon the "evil" customs of the past, and both the state and intellectuals attempted to reform aspects of traditional material culture. In 1872, officials were ordered to adopt Western-style clothes and hairstyles. The solar calendar was adopted, replacing the traditional lunar cycle that had governed the conduct of rituals and the lives of farmers. The government issued fiats at local and national levels to try to eliminate practices that visiting foreigners would consider unseemly, antiquated, or superstitious. Day laborers were prohibited from removing their loincloth *(fundoshi)* when urinating in the streets, and women were prohibited from appearing bare-breasted in public. In attempting to promote Western medicine, many traditional cures offered by exorcists and shamanistic religious figures were outlawed. The goal here was to prove to the foreign powers that Japan was a civilized nation, so that the unequal treaties might be overturned. But official pronouncements were often met with indifference as the people continued to engage in their normal daily lifestyles.

Among the populace in the cities and areas around treaty ports, however, novel elements of Western material culture became fashionable. Short haircuts and beards become common among men. Suits with trousers and leather shoes replaced kimonos as chic male attire; tailors and shoemakers were among the most prosperous businessmen in Tokyo. Efforts to Westernize one's personal appearance often resulted in a mixture of native and foreign styles; it was common to see Meiji-era gentlemen in kimonos and bowler hats. Umbrellas, gold watches, and diamond rings became conspicuous signs of one's enlightened attitude—and wealth. Westernizing one's appearance was generally limited to men in early Meiji, even within the imperial family; the emperor generally appeared in Western formal or military dress, but the empress typically wore traditional court clothing.

Another example is the change in diet. Bread, cakes, and ice cream spread outward from treaty-port areas to the larger population. Beef and beer were enthusiastically embraced as fashionable items of consumption. Buddhism traditionally proscribed the eating of beef; the limited livestock held by farmers were reserved for pulling plows. Nevertheless, in 1872 Emperor Meiji encouraged Japanese to begin consuming beef and mutton to build strong national physiques. Beef stews and other adaptations of Western cuisine were incorporated into the diet of the Imperial Japanese Army. Beef shops where townspeople could sample the new culinary fashion proliferated; eating beef became emblematic of civilization itself. "Aguranabe" (Sitting around the beef stew pot), an 1871 short story by Kanagaki Robun, satirized townsmen who blithely adapted foreign fashions and trends. The brief tale describes a pompous "man about thirty-five" who uses new imports like eau de cologne, carries a Western-style umbrella, and ostentatiously consults his cheap watch. While dining at one of the new beef restaurants, he strikes up a conversation with a fellow diner, first rapturously praising how "even people like ourselves can now eat beef, thanks to the fact that Japan is steadily becoming a truly civilized country."[3] He goes on to profess the marvels of Western inventions like the telegraph and steam engine, but his misinformed explanations betray his true ignorance.

During the Edo period, the Dutch partook of imported beer; during the early Meiji period, foreigners in treaty ports continued to import the beverage. In 1869, American brewmaster William Copeland established a company in Yokohama that would eventually become the Kirin Brewery Company, one of Japan's three largest beer producers today. In 1876, the government established Sapporo, another of the three largest breweries, to spur development in Hokkaido; the third, Asahi, was launched in Osaka in 1889. All made a German-style lager that was far too expensive for the average worker but that became fashionable among wealthy urbanites. The opening of affordable beer gardens and German-style beer halls that served tankards of relatively cheap beer began around 1900, expanding markets to less wealthy domestic consumers. By the 1920s, it was common for groups of male workers to socialize at beer halls after work.

Turning to architecture, as new buildings designed by Western architects and their Japanese students proliferated, the physical face of Japan's cities changed. After the Ginza area of central Tokyo—which had been a neighborhood of humble artisan shops—was consumed by fire in 1872, it was reconstructed as a showplace of westernized civilization, with brick buildings and wide streets illuminated by gaslights. Ginza became the material embodiment of "Civilization and Enlightenment," with Western-style pharmacies, fancy cafés, and the Seiko watch company (established in 1881). The government hired Josiah Conder to build the Rokumeikan Pavilion, a two-story brick structure in an ornate French style, with grand dining rooms, ballrooms, and even a billiard hall, near Ginza. The Rokumeikan symbolized the state's determination to appear equal to the "civilized" imperial powers, in order to speed renegotiation of unequal treaties. It provided the main site for elite Japanese men and women, dressed in imported tuxedos and evening gowns, to dance and mingle with their foreign counterparts, partake of French cuisine, drink American cocktails, and smoke British cigarettes. Many Japanese conservatives were appalled by the expense and scandalous behaviors that reportedly occurred there. Some foreign visitors were ungenerous in their appraisals. French naval officer and novelist Pierre Loti dismissed the European-style balls as "monkey shows," while his countryman Georges Ferdinand Bigot published a cartoon likening the elite Japanese habitués to apes, who unattractively mimicked their betters. Some Japanese writers and cartoonists, repulsed by the exaggerated passions for all things Western, also satirized the wholesale adoption of Western culture.

"RICH COUNTRY, STRONG ARMY":
TRAINS AND TEXTILES

In the early Meiji period, Japan's economic prospects looked gloomy as Western products flooded the treaty ports. Machine-made cotton cloth from abroad was stronger and cheaper than domestic hand-loomed cotton. Imported wools were valued for their warmth and reasonable price. Traditional lamp oils pressed from seeds could not compete with less costly and more effective imported kerosene. From 1868 to 1881, imports exceeded exports by a large margin. In order to balance its foreign trade accounts, Japan would have to build its economy, manufacture import substitutes, and develop desirable export products.

Transportation

Meiji leaders recognized the need to develop an industrial infrastructure that included a network of railroads, a new postal system, and a rationalized banking system. The railroads were vital to the overall development of industry and were strategically necessary for Japan's defense. For the nineteenth-century Japanese, just as for their contemporaries in the American West, the steam locomotive was the quintessential symbol of progress and civilization, the epitome of modern industrial power. The railroad had an enormous impact on Japanese society, revolutionizing the overland transport of people and goods and helping engineer a sense of nationhood. The railroad also had a transformative effect on Japanese culture, altering public consciousness of time, space, speed, and leisure travel.

In 1854, Commodore Perry had presented his Japanese hosts with gifts that represented the mechanical wonders of the industrial revolution, including a quarter-sized model railroad complete with a tiny locomotive, cars, and several miles of track. Less than twenty years later, in 1872, Emperor Meiji officially inaugurated Japan's first daily train services, between Tokyo and Yokohama. In the early Meiji period, reporters were most taken with the advent of speed; trains were spoken of as "putting wings on the people." In a different kind of comparison, one reporter exclaimed that you could travel from Shimbashi Station in Tokyo to Yokohoma "faster than it takes a hemorrhoid sufferer to empty his bowels."[4] Early passengers were disoriented by the speed of railroads. When one of the first trains to leave Shimbashi Station in Tokyo arrived at Yokohama, passengers reportedly refused to get off because they did not believe they could have reached their destination so quickly.

FIGURE 44. Utagawa Kuniteru, *Illustration of a Steam Locomotive Passing Shiodome in Tokyo,* 1872. Source: Wikimedia Commons.

In its first year of operation, nearly half a million passengers—mostly bureaucrats, businessmen, and foreigners—rode the Tokyo-Yokohama line, but train fares were initially exorbitant for ordinary Japanese. Larger numbers of people began to take the train as new routes were added, fares reduced, and services improved. From 1890 to 1900, the number of rail passengers leaped from 23 million to 114 million.

By the mid-1890s, the railways were a frequent theme and setting for literary works. Artists inundated the public with colorful woodblock prints of trains—even if trains were not the main subject of a print, they were often depicted in the background. The Tōkaidō line, paralleling the old post-station route from Tokyo to Kobe, accounted for over a third of train riders in the Meiji period. This trip had traditionally taken twelve to fourteen days on foot or by palanquin; the recently introduced steamship made the trip in a few days. But the train could cover the distance in just twenty hours. Passengers saved not only time but fees for hotels and meals along the way. The result of this new economy of time and space was a change in people's conception of time and distance.

Railroads altered the conception of time because they emphasized timetables and precision, promoting the habit of punctuality and strengthening their riders' appreciation of the economic value of time. During the Tokugawa era, there had been a relaxed, nonchalant attitude about travel time: river ferries had no fixed timetables, simply waiting until enough customers arrived. Trains, however, operated on schedules and did not wait

for passengers. Railway authorities realized the need to stress the importance of punctuality and to inform the public accurately of time. Trains left
the terminals conveniently on the hour, but at intermediate stations they
came and went at fractions of the hour. This introduced a radically new
conception of time, calibrated by the minute. Taking the train required the
use of clocks and watches, which barely existed in Japan at the beginning of
the Meiji period but soon became ubiquitous.

Railroads also altered popular conceptions of travel and recreation. In
the Edo period, leisure travel revolved around pilgrimages to famous
shrines and temples. Several private rail companies capitalized on this tradition and were founded with the goal of transporting worshippers to popular
pilgrimage sites. The idea of getaway weekend travel emerged by the late
1890s as wealthy Tokyoites took trains to nearby pleasure resorts such as
Kamakura, Enoshima, and Hakone. By the 1900s, with special group rates,
recreational train travel was within reach of ordinary people, and the railways ran special excursion trains to popular destinations and scenic spots.
In 1909, factories with fifty or more employees were offered discounts of
40–60 percent for group travel. Using such discounts, many who otherwise
would have little chance to travel went on excursions to shrines, temples,
and scenic spots with neighbors, schoolmates, or fellow workers. Thus,
while the railroad institutionalized social divisions with different classes of
service, they also had a leveling effect by enabling more people to travel and
share experiences that factored into the emergence of a national identity.

Another mode of Meiji transport was the *jinrikisha* (person-powered
car, aka rickshaw). Wheeled vehicles had been prohibited within the city of
Edo; elites traveled in sedan chairs or palanquins carried by two people. The
rickshaw, a light cart mounted on springs and two wheels pulled by one
runner, was far smoother and more comfortable. Over forty thousand were
in service by 1872, providing employment for many urban laborers.
European and American tourists and residents were especially enamored
with the rickshaw as a quaint and exotic form of transport. Japanese manufacturers were soon exporting rickshaws to China and colonized Asian territories. Runners averaged five miles per hour and could cover twenty to
thirty miles in a day. They were initially much less costly than the train,
considerably less than second-class train fare. But as train ridership grew
and fares dropped, rickshaw men found it difficult to compete with the
faster, more comfortable ride trains offered. By the 1930s, with widespread
forms of automated transport, rickshaws had nearly disappeared. After
World War II, when gasoline was scarce, they made a temporary comeback

but became something of an embarrassment, in Japan and elsewhere, as a symbol of racial and class differences.

Textiles

The silk and cotton textile industries provided the backbone of Japan's modernization efforts, earning necessary foreign currency to help build military and industrial strength. Machine silk reeling was the first industry to develop extensive factories. Its workforce, heavily female and very young, formed a large proportion of Japan's labor force during the first decades of industrialization. These women made a double contribution to Japan's modernization: the profitability of textile factories paid for Meiji modernization and, at the same time, wages they remitted to their families allowed the rural poor to pay rents to landlords, who invested the funds in other industries and in national modernization efforts. Silk production provided work at many different sites beyond the factory. Rural households engaged in sericulture—planting mulberry trees, raising cocoons, and producing homespun thread. Raising silk worms was an important by-employment for many farm families but required strenuous effort to feed the demanding larvae, which consumed thirty thousand times their body weight in mulberry leaves. Some households sold their cocoons to wealthy neighbors who opened small local businesses employing ten or more women to hand-reel silk thread. Others sold their cocoons to silk merchants, who distributed them to rural women for hand-reeling at home.

During the first year of the Meiji period, European silkworms suffered a severe blight, providing an excellent opportunity for Japan to earn much-needed foreign currency by meeting the foreign demand for silk. The Meiji government took the initiative in supporting industrial development, providing direct and indirect financial assistance as well as technical aid, in order to produce a high-quality thread for export markets. Modern silk reeling began with the establishment of government mills in the 1870s, model plants that employed Italian and French silk reelers to teach techniques to Japanese workers. The most ambitious was the large mill built in 1872 at Tomioka, designed to train groups of four hundred women in modern machine-reeled silk production. The government recruited young women from respectable ex-samurai or prosperous farm families to volunteer, offering the chance to train in a new industry. Tomioka recruits were treated generously: they were given new clothes, regular rest periods, and plentiful food. They lived in a spacious dormitory, and the factory facilities included a modern hospital and beautiful gardens. After finishing their

FIGURE 45. Utagawa Yoshitora, *Imported Silk Reeling Machine at Tsukiji in Tokyo,* 1872. Source: Wikimedia Commons.

training, students often set up factories in their own prefectures, financed by local authorities or private entrepreneurs.

Such positive factory conditions, however, deteriorated sharply in the 1880s with the revival of European competition and severe state deflationary policies. Japanese silk quality was still not up to par with Europe; their advantage was in low labor costs, with minimal wages paid to young female workers. State-owned mills like Tomioka were sold to private industry, which reduced rations, benefits, and time off. In order to remain competitive, the private silk mills instituted longer work hours, introducing gas and then electric lighting so that workers could begin at 4:30 A.M. and stay until after sunset, with just a brief break for a noontime meal. Companies built prison-like dormitories surrounded by tall fences, topped with broken glass or barbed wire, to prevent workers from running away. Dorm conditions were cramped and unsanitary: toilet and washing facilities were limited and could be used only at stipulated times; communicable diseases, especially tuberculosis, killed textile workers at much higher rates than among the population at large. The rapid expansion of the industry soon outstripped the pool of available workers. With worsening labor conditions, respectable families no longer sent their daughters to the mills; poor peasant families were subjected to deceptive, high-pressure tactics by recruiters to turn their daughters over to the factories, providing critical funds for many tenant-farmer families facing pressing debts. In 1886, an alliance of silk manufacturers and merchants unilaterally set wages and developed a system of heavy fines for infractions of discipline or poor work quality.

To combat poor morale due to the horrible working conditions, companies made special efforts to raise workers' spirits through patriotic songs praising the silk workers' contributions toward building the nation, for example:

Raw silk,
Reel, reel the thread.
Thread is the treasure of the empire!
More than a hundred million yen worth of exports
. . .

Put all your strength into your work.
It's for yourself
It's for your family,
It's for the country of Japan.[5]

Companies also distributed moralistic textbooks with lessons stressing duty to the nation and self-sacrifice. Such books praised female workers as soldiers of peace, producing textiles that enabled Japan to accumulate money through exports. These textbooks urged absolute obedience to factory rules and supervisors; punctuality; moderation in eating, drinking, and speech; and patience, forbearance, honesty, and frugality. Factory girls were warned that if they failed to work their hardest, "the country of Japan will become poorer and poorer."[6]

Despite such high moral tones, few workers showed much enthusiasm for serving the nation or the abusive mills. Some were resigned to their fates; others were defiant. Their own songs, such as the following, made their feelings about their employment conditions clear.

THE PRISON LAMENT

Factory work is prison work
All it lacks are iron chains

More than a caged bird, more than a prison,
Dormitory life is hateful

Like the money in my employment contract
I remain sealed away

If a male worker makes eyes at you
You end up losing your shirt

How I wish the dormitory would be washed away
The factory burn down,
And the gatekeeper die of cholera![7]

The cotton industry was more complicated and expensive to modernize than silk, requiring mastery of other technologies. While international demand for silk was stimulated by the blight in Europe, the cotton industry initially fared less well. Domestic cotton was forced to compete with cheap, superior foreign cloth that flooded into Japan under the unfair treaties. By 1878, Meiji leaders decided that foreign cotton posed a threat and resolved to open government mills and to subsidize private ventures. They ordered equipment for ten factories from England, intending to employ poor ex-samurai. By 1886, state efforts had resulted in a modern cotton-spinning industry, although most factories were small. The opening of the Osaka Cotton Spinning Mill in 1882 marked a new age in cotton production. This mill was the creation of Shibusawa Eiichi (1840–1931), one of the Meiji period's most successful entrepreneurs. The Osaka mill operated 10,500 spindles, five times as many as the next largest company. Rather than hiring ex-samurai and providing housing, the mill hired poor urban commuters from Osaka. To increase profitability, the mill operated twenty-four hours a day and paid lower wages than other mills. Nighttime accidents and fires were regular occurrences. One large fire at the plant in 1892 killed ninety-five workers and seriously maimed twenty-two others.

CHANGING GENDER NORMS

Alarmed by what they saw as excessive individualism in the cities, Meiji leaders sought ways to re-inculcate an ideology of conformity and obedience. Conservative bureaucrats were apprehensive over how the individual was beginning to take the place of the family as the unit of society. These conservatives wanted to reinstate the strong patriarchal authority that had prevailed in samurai households. They issued a Civil Code in 1898 that made the extended household *(ie)* a legally binding corporate entity.

All decision-making power was vested in the male head of household, who chose the place of residence, managed all household property and business affairs, and had the authority to approve or disallow marriages of his children—up to age twenty-five for daughters and thirty for sons. Women were completely subordinated to the patriarch—their primary obligation was to provide a male heir and household labor. Once wed, women could not testify in courts of law, bring legal action, transact business without their husband's consent, or initiate divorce except in cases of extreme cruelty. A wife's adultery, but not her husband's, was grounds for divorce and criminal prosecution. The model woman was to be a "good wife, wise mother" *(ryōsai kenbo)* who would dedicate herself to raising educated, modern children and creating a sanctuary for her husband to relax, away from the challenges of his career. This notion essentially targeted middle- and upper-class women, who didn't have to perform wage-earning labor. Many working-class women were cynical about the new models of Victorian femininity advocated by the state and mainstream society.

The state mandated compulsory elementary education in 1872, extending its duration to six years in 1907. Initially, girls' education lagged behind that of boys in both quality and attendance levels. The 1889 Girl's Higher Education Law required each prefecture to establish at least one public, four-year middle school for girls who had completed four years of primary education. These public schools, however, failed to provide the same quality of education found in boys' schools, focusing more on preparing girls for future roles as "good wives and wise mothers" through teaching morality, etiquette, and home economics. In the 1910s, schools began including tea ceremony and ikebana as part of their curriculum, previously male-dominated arts now considered necessary skills for refined Japanese women.

Some were opposed to this approach to women's education. One such individual, Tsuda Umeko (1864–1929), had traveled to the United States at the age of six as the youngest member of the Iwakura Mission and remained there for twelve years. By the time she returned to Japan in 1882, she had almost forgotten her native language. Tsuda was vexed by the inferior position of women in Japanese society. In 1885, she began to work in a school for the daughters of nobility but was dissatisfied with its orientation as a mere "finishing school." She returned to the United States and attended Bryn Mawr College in Philadelphia. After passage of the Girl's Higher Education Law, Tsuda founded the Women's Institute for English Studies in Tokyo, which aimed to provide women the opportunity for a liberal arts education, regardless of their status.

Meanwhile, in the eyes of the foreign community, Japan (like other Asian societies) was commonly viewed as a weak, feminine nation, associated with arts and culture, rather than one associated with masculine military and economic strengths. Such views were reflected in Western popular culture. For example, Giacomo Puccini's nineteenth-century opera *Madama Butterfly* depicted a Japanese woman victimized and abandoned by her American lover, and Gilbert and Sullivan's 1885 comic opera *The Mikado* portrayed the Japanese as backward and uncivilized. Meiji leaders advocated wholesale adoption of Western civilizational norms and material culture to combat such views. Ideas about masculinity began to shift accordingly during the Meiji era. The archetypical samurai—educated, moral, frugal, valuing loyalty and honor over personal gain—embodied the main traditional masculine ideal.

With Meiji mandates for officials to update their appearance and adopt Western values, such as independence and self-advancement, representations of ideal masculinity became bifurcated. Men who adopted the demeanor of fashionable, modern gentlemen—with top hats, frock coats, gold spectacles, and walking sticks—were labeled "high collar" (*haikara*) for the starched white collars they wore. State officials dressed in this manner and participated in lavish Western-style parties at the Rokumeikan. Itō Hirobumi, one of the most powerful of the Meiji oligarchs, was especially associated with performing this foreign identity, and his administration was derisively dubbed "the dancing cabinet." Critics who opposed the clique government dominated by Sat-Chō leaders caricatured the oligarchs in their finery as decadent, corrupt, inauthentic, and effeminate. An alternative masculine style, known as *bankara* (rough and uncouth), arose to contest this image. Bankara men were proudly unfashionable, wearing wooden clogs and frayed kimonos, with sleeves characteristically tucked up to expose muscular arms. They were associated with political activism and fighting for national advancement, in contrast with haikara men pursuing individual financial success. As men increasingly adopted Western dress in the early twentieth century, these contrasts lessened but never fully disappeared. By the end of Meiji, the term *haikara* had broadened to indicate all that was stylish and novel. Schoolgirls who tied their hair with ribbons and rode bicycles to school were thus deemed haikara.

MEIJI INTELLECTUAL LIFE, LITERATURE, AND RELIGION

While the Meiji leadership was pressing for westernization, other intellectuals echoed their message. Works by Western political theorists such as John Stuart Mill and Alexis de Tocqueville were translated and circulated widely, encouraging the Japanese to develop an independent and vigorous spirit and stressing the importance of expressing one's own political opinions. Popular translations included Daniel Defoe's *Robinson Crusoe*, the quintessential tale of the independent, self-reliant man; works by Benjamin Franklin; and Samuel Smiles's 1845 best seller *Self-Help*, which urged the enlightenment and education of the working classes so that all could cultivate civility and accomplish great feats. Jules Verne's *Around the World in Eighty Days* and *A Journey to the Moon* met the era's spirit for new vistas and scientific progress.

The most influential propagator of Western knowledge in the 1870s was Fukuzawa Yukichi (1835–1901), whose image appears on Japan's 10,000-yen note. Fukuzawa was born into a low-ranking samurai family. He studied Dutch and English and served as a translator for the 1860 embassy to ratify the Harris Treaty. Two years later, he traveled with another bakufu mission to England, France, Holland, Portugal, and Russia, where he absorbed all he could of Western civilization. Fukuzawa concluded that Japan was weak and backward because traditional culture did not promote scientific curiosity, self-reliance, and an ethos of individual achievement. To help inculcate these values into his countrymen, he became an educator and writer, establishing a school in 1868 that later became Keio University, founding the influential newspaper *Jiji shimpō*, and authoring over a hundred books. In his often-reprinted work *The Autobiography of Fukuzawa Yukichi*, written shortly before his death in 1901, Fukuzawa declared that his life's ambitions had been fulfilled by the abolition of feudal privileges and institutions and by Japan's victory in the First Sino-Japanese War of 1894–95.

In *An Outline of a Theory of Civilization* (1875), Fukuzawa held that all civilizations must pass through three stages: "primitive," characterized by temporary communities dependent on nature for food and daily needs; "semi-developed," with permanent communities in which daily needs are met and there are basic structures of governance, while people remain tied to tradition and are incapable of original production; and "civilized," in which people pursue knowledge, act independently, and plan for the future. Fukuzawa asserted that Western nations were the most highly civilized, that Asian countries such as China, Japan, and Turkey were semi-developed, and that Africa and Australia were "still primitive lands." He believed that a nation's level of development could not be judged by its leadership alone, for "civilization is not a matter of the knowledge or ignorance of individuals but the spirit of entire nations."[8] As illustrated in the following excerpt, Fukuzawa called on all educated persons to advocate adopting Western norms and values, which he found indisputably superior to native achievements:

> If we compare the levels of intelligence of Japanese and Westerners, in literature, the arts, commerce, or industry, from the biggest things to the least, in a thousand cases or in one, there is not a single area in which the other side is not superior to us. . . . Only the most ignorant thinks that Japan's learning, arts, commerce, or industry is on a par with that of the West. Who would compare a man-drawn cart with a steam engine or a Japanese sword with a rifle? . . . While we regard Japan as the sacrosanct islands of the gods, they have raced around the world, discovering new lands and founding new nations.[9]

The introduction of Western literature inspired young Japanese writers to adopt and adapt Western up-to-date literary conventions and techniques.

They faced a significant challenge because their traditional literature was written in a classical style that did not resemble vernacular speech. In addition, many new words adopted from foreign terms had entered the language. Reform movements advocating a standardized writing style *(genbun-itchi)*, launched in the 1880s, slowly infiltrated Japanese writing. In 1900, the Ministry of Education announced reforms aimed at improving writing and reading by standardizing the kana syllabary, limiting the number of Chinese characters *(kanji)* taught in school, and standardizing the pronunciation of kanji.

In his groundbreaking work *The Essence of the Novel* (1885), Tsubouchi Shōyō was the first to call for a modern Japanese literature that would discard the "frivolous" writings of late-Edo period and early-Meiji gesaku fiction. He advocated the view that the novel was a serious genre that should strive for realism and focus on expressing human emotion and modern selfhood. Futabatei Shimei's *Floating Clouds* (1887) is usually considered Japan's first successful modern novel. Its protagonist, Utsumi Bunzō, is an unsuccessful intellectual who tries to win the love of his cousin, but she prefers his friend Noboru, an ambitious young man with the tools to succeed in the achievement-oriented Meiji era. The novel plumbs the depths of Bunzō's mental sufferings and is written in the modern genbun-itchi style.

Two writers who provided meaningful commentary on Meiji modernization are Mori Ōgai (1862–1922) and Natsume Sōseki (1867–1916). Both had studied abroad, Ōgai in Germany, as an Imperial Army officer studying medicine, and Sōseki in Great Britain, as a literary scholar. Their shared experiences abroad and extensive readings of foreign literature influenced their lives and works. Ōgai was a prolific writer of fiction, essays, and biography alike. His 1890 novella *The Dancing Girl* was written in an autobiographical, confessional style that became popular as the "I-novel" *(watakushi shōsetsu)*. In the story a young man named Ōta, living in Berlin, has an affair with a German girl, but when called to return home to accept a government position he abandons her, leaving her pregnant and suffering from a nervous breakdown. In Ōgai's serialized novel *The Wild Geese* (1911–13), a young woman decides to provide for her aging father by becoming the mistress of a sleazy moneylender. As she becomes disillusioned with her luxurious new life, she becomes infatuated with a young medical student, Okada, who passes under her balcony, but Okada leaves Japan to pursue medical studies in Germany.

Sōseki is among Japan's most revered novelists, as demonstrated by his portrait on Japan's 1,000-yen note. He was sickly, suffering from ulcers and mental afflictions. After graduate studies in English literature at Tokyo

Imperial University, followed by a professorship in English at that prestigious institution, he achieved acclaim with two humorous novels in 1906: *I Am a Cat*, in which a cat who speaks in a posh, upper-class manner comments on the foolishness of his middle-class "master" and his friends; and *Botchan*, about a rowdy Tokyo boy who becomes a teacher in Shikoku. One of Sōseki's best-known works is *Kokoro* (1914), a novel composed of two distinct parts. In the first half, a young male student narrates how he has developed a relationship with a reserved older man he calls Sensei—a term of respect used for teachers and elders—whom he met at the seashore. Back in Tokyo, he visits Sensei and his wife Shizu and tries unsuccessfully to learn why his older friend is so deeply unhappy. Called back to the countryside to attend to his dying father, the young man receives a lengthy letter from Sensei. The second half of the novel consists of the letter itself, a suicide note. In it, Sensei explains that when he was a young man he and his best friend K had both fallen in love with Shizu. When Sensei obtained permission to marry the girl from her mother, K felt betrayed and committed suicide. Sensei had been tormented by guilt ever since, but Shizu never learned the reason for K's death and thus could not understand her husband's melancholy. He explains why he has decided to confide in his young friend, but implores him to never reveal the truth to Shizu:

> You asked me to spread out my past like a picture scroll before your eyes. Then for the first time I respected you. I was moved by your decision to grasp something that was alive within my soul. You wished to cut open my heart and see the blood flow. I was then still alive. I did not want to die. That is why I refused you and postponed the granting of your wish to another day. Now I myself am about to cut open my own heart and drench your face with my blood. And I shall be satisfied if, when my heart stops beating, a new life lodges in your breast.[10]

Sensei explains that he has been moved to commit suicide by the actions of Russo-Japanese War hero General Nogi Maresuke, who committed *junshi* (ritual suicide following the death of one's lord) on the night of Emperor Meiji's funeral in 1912. Nogi's suicide touched off emotional debates in Meiji society about traditional codes of honor and samurai virtue in the modern age. After the funeral procession left the palace, Nogi committed *seppuku* (ritual disembowelment) and his wife took her own life in the manner prescribed for a dutiful samurai wife—by severing her jugular vein *(jigai)*. Social commentators debated the meaning of the deaths. Some condemned the act as a barbaric remnant of outmoded feudal codes. Others claimed that it reflected Nogi's disgust with the decline in moral values. The suicide note itself claimed that it was an act of atonement for the many deaths he felt responsible for during his military career. Nogi became a symbol of loyalty and self-sacrifice invoked by many social commentators over the following years.

MEIJI RELIGION

The Meiji Restoration brought a radical change in Japan's religious climate. Under the Tokugawa regime, Buddhist sects had served as a semiofficial branch of the government, enforcing anti-Christian laws. Most large religious complexes contained both Buddhist and Shinto elements. The early Meiji government, however, aimed to use the emperor as a sacred foundation for the new state and elevated Shinto into an official state religion, adopting a strongly anti-Buddhist attitude. The critics of Buddhism charged that it was an imported, foreign religion that was superstitious and irrational and, furthermore, not engaged in social and charitable activity like the Christianity of the Western imperialist nations. In critics' eyes, Buddhism could no longer be associated with Shinto, which would officially represent the "pure" Japanese spirit that now faced the challenge of modernization. State officials adopted policies to forcibly separate Buddhism from Shinto, resulting in the large-scale destruction of Buddhist temples, images, and texts throughout Japan during the first decade of Meiji. Between 1868 and 1874, over a thousand Buddhist temples disappeared. Shinto shrines that previously identified native kami with Buddhist deities were purged of all traces of Buddhist imagery and ritual.

Temple lands were seized and Buddhist monks were forced to become Shinto priests or to laicize. In 1872, the Meiji government changed the laws regarding Buddhist priests, decriminalizing meat eating, marrying, growing out their hair, wearing ordinary clothing, and other practices that were previously punishable for clergy. The pivotal changes in religious policy created Japanese Buddhism as we know it today, anomalous in the world for the fact that almost all male Buddhist priests are married and pass management of their temples to their sons. Despite their brief persecution, Buddhist sects remained wealthy and popular and soon began to regain their power and standing.

One faction of Buddhists, led by educator Inoue Enryō (1858–1919), attempted to align Buddhism with Western thinking concerning social evolution, to present Japanese Buddhism as progressive and rational. They differentiated Japanese Buddhism from the Theravadan traditions prevalent in Southeast Asia and Sri Lanka. European Orientalist scholars of Theravadan schools had professed that Buddhism was atheistic and idolatrous, and that the passivity it fostered was responsible for Asia's relative lack of development. Japanese Buddhists fought this characterization by asserting that their form of Buddhism was an ethical faith in tune with Enlightenment ideals, in contrast to Christianity, which relied on myths. Leaders of this "new Buddhism" made their case at the World's Parliament of Religions in Chicago in 1893, attempting to convince Judeo-Christian religious leaders of the "civilized" nature of Japanese religion, which could provide answers for Christians struggling to reconcile their faith with science.

After the Meiji Restoration, Shinto was reconceived as a means to bind the nation together under the emperor, with a mix of devotion to kami, ancestor-worship, and group loyalty to family and nation. The emperor, as divine descendant of the Sun Goddess, was not only head of state but also the high priest of Shinto, responsible for conducting rituals to ensure the well-being of the nation. Shinto priests were ordered to undergo standardized training, but many disagreed with the official pantheon, which prioritized Amaterasu over the kami Ōkuninushi of Izumo, seen by many as equal or superior to the Sun Goddess. Since this view posed a threat to the legitimacy of the Meiji state, officials decided to create a separation between Shinto rites, performed by the state agents and considered part of civic responsibility for all Japanese, and Shinto doctrine, which was a matter of individual religious belief.

In order to propagate correct understanding of Shinto as the foundation of the nation and fight against the possibility of widespread Christian conversions, officials initiated a campaign known as the Great Promulgation Movement from 1869 to 1885. Officials in charge of the campaign were disciples of Hirata Atsutane. They appointed a cadre of National Evangelists that included both Shinto and Buddhist priests, who were trained at institutes in Tokyo and in each prefecture to lecture local people on the new national creed, which combined elements from Shinto mythology and Confucian morality with indoctrination in the need for patriotism and gratitude to the emperor. To educate commoners about "civilization and enlightenment," lectures also included topics like taxation, the military, and foreign relations. The evangelists were prohibited from "preaching" or engaging in "religious" activity such as presiding over funerals or faith healing. As one might surmise, the movement was unpopular among people who had heretofore gathered at local shrines for communal celebrations, rather than dull sermons, but it lingered until 1885, after which elementary schools took on the task of Shinto education.

Article 28 of the Meiji constitution, which granted the Japanese freedom of religious belief "within limits not prejudicial to peace and order and not antagonistic to their duties as subjects," was carefully worded to protect the primacy of the new, state-oriented Shinto while guaranteeing religious choice—an important matter for other imperialist nations that firmly desired the ability to proselytize Christianity in Japan.[11] Under the constitution, performance of Shinto rites and Shinto education were deemed part of national ethics, required of all subjects, and not "religion" as such.

Shintoist groups that maintained religious teachings and practices and could not easily fit into the new national conception of Shinto as civic duty were placed into a separate category—Sect Shinto. There were thirteen officially approved Shinto sects that varied widely in belief and practice: some were based on mountain-worship; others focused on purification, ascetic practices, or faith healing; and some combined Confucian and Shinto teachings. Approved sects also included monotheistic new religions, such as Kurozumikyō, Konkokyō, and Tenrikyō, which were formed in the nineteenth century in rural areas. Some of these new religions rejected the legitimacy and authority of the Meiji state, denounced the growing cult of the emperor, and envisioned an egalitarian sociocultural order. The charismatic founders of these salvationistic groups often gained their reputations as faith healers or by claiming that they were divinely possessed.

Nakayama Miki (1798–1887), the female founder of Tenrikyō, became famous for her abilities to cure smallpox and ease the pain of childbirth. As the vessel and mouthpiece of God the Parent (Oyagamisama), she wrote prophecies, developed spiritual practices involving music and dance, and encouraged charity, while she herself led a life of poverty. Tenrikyō often opposed or violated state laws, and Miki was imprisoned on multiple occasions. As the group grew to massive proportions, it was condemned as irrational and heterodox by the mainstream media. After Miki's death, her son reformed her teachings to conform with state policy and gained approval of Tenrikyō as the thirteenth and final sect of Shinto. Thereafter, any popular new groups advocating Shinto beliefs or practices would be considered heterodox and subject to suppression by the state.

One such heterodox group was Oomoto, founded in 1892 by Deguchi Nao (1836–1918), an uneducated peasant woman. Nao expressed her dissatisfaction with the changes in Meiji society by describing her earthly paradise as a place where people would grow their own food and rely on natural products for all necessities such as clothing and housing. There would be no money. No one would eat meat. There would be no silk, tobacco, or Western-style clothes, no fancy sweets or cakes, and no gambling. There would be no need for education, because everything would be clear and easily understood by all. Laws and policemen would be unnecessary because all would be honest, sincere, and pure in spirit. This utopian vision overtly rejected the westernized, urban-centered capitalist model promoted by the Meiji state. The group reached national proportions in the 1920s under the leadership of Nao's charismatic son-in-law, Deguchi Onisaburō (1871–1948), a gifted spiritualist who created rituals and practices modeled on "Ancient Shinto."

Another religious development during Meiji was the growth of Protestantism among the Japanese, many of whom considered it a factor in the success of Western nations. Protestant missionaries became active in the treaty ports in the late 1850s. Numerous members of the ex-samurai class who had been aligned with the Tokugawa and were thus alienated from Meiji leaders believed that Christianity might provide a path to help them revitalize their status and build a future for the nation. Some became educators, opening private colleges. Prominent Christians included Niijima Jō, also known as Joseph Hardy Neesima (1843–90), who studied in the United States and later established Doshisha University in Kyoto. Niijima believed that Christianity, westernization, and civilization were an inseparable trinity needed for national progress. Nitobe Inazō (1862–1933) became a convert under the influence of William S. Clark, an oyatoi and lay missionary appointed to establish Sapporo Agricultural College. While studying in the United States, Nitobe adopted the Quaker faith and married an American Quaker woman. Returning to Japan, he served in top government and teaching positions and cofounded Tokyo Woman's Christian University. He is perhaps best known for his work *Bushido: The Soul of Japan* (1899), written in English in an attempt to explain Japan's traditional ethos to Western audiences, identifying "the Way of the Warrior" as the source for national values including honor, loyalty, sincerity, and self-control.

Finally, Uchimura Kanzō (1861–1930), another Clark convert, gained notoriety when, as a teacher, he refused to bow before a copy of the Imperial Rescript on Education in 1891 and was forced to resign on account of this gesture of disrepect. He later became disillusioned with the racism he perceived among Western Christians and founded the Nonchurch (Mukyōkai) movement, an indigenous sect that eschewed professional clergy and sacraments, in search of an authentic Christian life. In his well-known essay "Two J's" (1925), Uchimura declared:

> I love two J's and no third; one is Jesus, and the other Japan.
> I do not know which I love more, Jesus or Japan.
> I am hated by my countrymen for Jesus' sake as a yaso [Jesus, hence Christian] and I am disliked by foreign missionaries for Japan's sake as national and narrow. . . .

> I know that one strengthens the other; Jesus strengthens and purifies
> my love for Japan; and Japan clarifies and objectivises [sic] my love for
> Jesus. Were it not for the two, I would become a mere dreamer, a fanatic,
> an amorphous universal man.[12]

Despite such noteworthy individuals, Christianity was never able to obtain
a large Japanese following, claiming less than 1 percent of the population
during the Meiji period and ever after.

In summary, two centuries of economic growth threatened the highly ordered
society envisioned by the shogunate. In 1853, when the United States
demanded that Japan open to trade and accept highly disadvantageous trade
treaties with imperialist nations, faith in the bakufu was further undermined,
eventually leading to the restoration of imperial governance. A small group of
oligarchs monopolized power in the new Meiji government and enacted
sweeping reforms to the society and economy that would allow Japan to meet
the threat of further encroachment and the challenges of building a modern,
industrialized society. Many of their initiatives, from the hiring of oyatoi to
the establishment of a constitution and elected assembly, were designed to
prove that Japan was a "civilized" nation according to Western norms. In
urban areas, many embraced aspects of Western material culture such as
foods, fashions, and architectural styles; intellectuals and writers urged their
countrymen to adopt Western values as well. Meiji leaders, however, wished
to foster a strongly patriarchal society of patriotic citizens and enacted laws
and measures to limit individual rights, especially those of women.

Early state modernization efforts were driven by a sense of threat and
inferiority, undergirded by nineteenth-century social theories about racial
and civilizational hierarchies. In the decades that followed, economic development and education helped reduce the perceived gap between Japan and
the imperialist powers. By the 1920s, Tokyo and Japan's other major cities
were fully modern metropolises, equal in stature to those of other industrialized nations and facing the same global trends, such as the expansion of
mass consumerism and mass media and the emergence of political philosophies, such as socialism and communism, that threatened the authorities.

FURTHER READING

Cwiertka, Katarzyna J. *Modern Japanese Cuisine: Food, Power, and National
Identity.* London: Reaktion Books, 2006.
Fujitani, Takashi. *Splendid Monarchy: Power and Pageantry in Modern Japan.*
Berkeley: University of California Press, 1998.

Gluck, Carol. *Japan's Modern Myths: Ideology in the Late Meiji Period.* Princeton, NJ: Princeton University Press, 1987.

Howell, David L. *Geographies of Identity in Nineteenth-Century Japan.* Berkeley: University of California Press, 2005.

Jansen, Marius B. *The Emergence of Meiji Japan.* New York: Cambridge University Press, 1995.

Karlin, Jason. *Gender and Nation in Meiji Japan: Modernity, Loss and the Doing of History.* Honolulu: University of Hawaii Press, 2014.

Keene, Donald. *Emperor of Japan: Meiji and His World, 1852–1912.* New York: Columbia University Press, 2005.

Ketelaar, James E. *Of Heretics and Martyrs in Meiji Japan: Buddhism and Its Persecution.* Princeton, NJ: Princeton University Press, 1993.

Miller, Ian J. *The Nature of the Beasts: Empire and Exhibition at the Tokyo Imperial Zoo.* Berkeley: University of California Press, 2013.

Phipps, Catherine L. *Empires on the Waterfront: Japan's Ports and Power, 1858–1899.* Cambridge, MA: Harvard University Press, 2015.

Stalker, Nancy K. *Prophet Motive: Deguchi Onisaburō, Oomoto, and the Rise of New Religions in Imperial Japan.* Honolulu: University of Hawaii Press, 2007.

RECOMMENDED FILMS

Nomugi Pass. 1979. Feature film directed by Yamamoto Satsuo. Historical drama of the travails faced by young females employed in the silk-spinning industry in the early 1900s.

Rurouni Kenshin. 2012. Feature film directed by Ōtomo Keishi. Tale of a former assasin who wanders the country in the Meiji period offering aid to others, based on a popular manga and anime series.

Taboo. 1999. Feature film directed by Ōshima Nagisa. Highlights homosexual relationships among the Shinsengumi at the end of the Tokugawa era.

The Rickshaw Man. 1958. Feature film directed by Inagaki Hiroshi. Tale of a poor rickshaw driver who becomes a surrogate father to a middle-class boy at the turn of the twentieth century.

The Story of the Last Chrysanthemum. 1939. Feature film directed by Mizoguchi Kenji. Melodramatic story of a family of kabuki actors in Tokyo and Osaka circa 1885.

9   Modernity and Its Discontents

1900s–1930s

Although the Taishō period formally lasted from 1912 to 1926, some historians identify 1900 to 1930 as the "Greater Taishō" era, a time of cosmopolitanism and optimism, marked by increased participation in politics and society, empowered through compulsory education and mass literacy. Furthermore, this era witnessed the rapid growth of mass consumerism, the development of sophisticated mass media, and the flowering of new forms of mass culture, primarily in urban areas. Many of these changes were associated with the term *modanizumu* (modernism), visible in striking shifts in urban lifestyles and dramatic new movements in the arts and popular culture. Tokyo was the undisputed center of Japanese modernism, Japan's first modern metropolis. It contained the majority of the nation's government facilities and a high concentration of its cultural institutions.

Mass literacy allowed urban and rural consumers alike to encounter images and descriptions of fashionable trends and new ways of thinking, stimulating desires for both material goods and alternative lifestyles. Two terms are often employed to describe these emerging tastes: *bunka seikatsu* (the cultured life), associated with material aspirations of middle-class consumers, especially in terms of household architecture and décor that promoted hygiene and convenience; and *ero guro nansensu* (erotic-grotesque nonsense), associated with literature, art, and amusements that were decadent, deviant, bizarre, or absurd. The eroticism, playfulness, and taste for novelty prevalent in Edo urban culture—but less visible in the serious-minded Meiji period—thus resurfaced in the 1920s and '30s as urban commoners once again indulged proclivities for the sexy, comical, and twisted in novels, theater, and art. Many conservatives were appalled by these trends and sought a "return" to native Japanese values and norms. As the nation achieved parity with Western powers, some began to reject Western modernity as a role model and advanced the idea that Japan would lead the world in a synthesis between East and West, an attitude sometimes known as Japanism.

As these developments occurred domestically, Japan was emerging abroad as a major military and economic power, in possession of several of its own colonies, a topic that will be explored in chapter 10.

POLITICAL AND SOCIAL DEVELOPMENTS

Emperor Meiji died on July 30, 1912. His life had symbolized the changes of his period so perfectly that at his death there was a clear sense that an era had come to an end. The reign of Emperor Taishō ("great righteousness") began in 1912 and ended in 1926. Because of Taishō's poor mental and physical health, his son, Crown Prince Hirohito (1901–89), took over official duties as prince regent in 1921. Hirohito reigned as Emperor Shōwa from 1926 until his death at age eighty-seven, witnessing Japan's rise and fall as a great power, along with its postwar resurrection.

Political accomplishments of the era include the advent of powerful political parties, the emergence of labor and women's movements, and the proliferation of democratic political ideologies. When Japan went to the polls for the first time in July 1890 to elect three hundred members to the House of Representatives in the Imperial Diet, the bicameral legislative body established in the Meiji constitution, popular political parties captured a majority of 171 seats. These new Diet members denounced the "clique" government of the Meiji oligarchs, but their only real weapon was their right to deliberate on the state's annual budget. Nevertheless, over the course of thirty years, political parties patiently wrestled the reins of state from the hands of the oligarchs, inaugurating an era of party government, under which the heads of major political parties routinely served as prime ministers and named their own cabinets. As political party members continued to be the majority elected to the lower house, the old generation of leaders had to rethink their negative attitudes toward party government. In 1896, Prime Minister Itō Hirobumi named Itagaki Taisuke, former leader of the Freedom and Popular Rights movement, to be his home minister. Two years later, Ōkuma Shigenobu (1838–1922), president of the Kenseitō political party, became prime minister, the first leader of a political party to serve in that office.

Itō even formed his own political party, a pro-government, national unity party that merged with the Kenseitō in 1900, forming the Seiyūkai party, which held an absolute majority in the Diet from 1908 to 1915. In

1918, Seiyūkai leader Hara Takashi (1856–1921), "the great commoner," became the first elected member of the Diet to become prime minister. Hara won voters for the party through classic pork-barrel politics, promising schools, roads, and railroads to districts electing Seiyūkai candidates. The party was also criticized for stuffing ballot boxes and falsifying election returns. Katsura Tarō (1848–1913), a protégé of Yamagata Aritomo (another member of the ruling Sat-Chō clique), organized a counterattack against the Seiyūkai by forming his own party in 1913, called the Rikken Dōshikai. Katsura's party was joined by several minority parties frustrated by Seiyūkai success, forming the Kenseikai party in 1916.

One major catalyst for the shift to party-dominated cabinets was the outbreak of rice riots throughout the country in 1918. Between 1914 and 1918, inflation related to World War I severely drove up the prices of consumer goods, with rice prices leaping by 60 percent in 1918. Irate consumers took action. The unrest began in July in a small fishing village, where a group of women mounted a protest against the cost of local rice, then spread like wildfire to Osaka, Kobe, Nagoya, and other industrial centers in western Japan. Angry citizens forced rice dealers to sell their stock at discounted prices and clashed with the police and army in street battles throughout the summer. Collectively, the riots constituted the largest mass demonstration in modern Japanese history, as a million or more people took to the streets. The state mobilized a hundred thousand troops to suppress riots in over a hundred locations. Protesters were arrested en masse, and more than five thousand were given stiff sentences for relatively minor offenses. Nevertheless, officials were afraid of further popular unrest and granted many of the rioters' demands, increasing imports of cheap rice from Japan's colonies in Korea and Taiwan (see chapter 10), enacting laws to reduce the possibility of inflationary price bubbles, and accepting the appointment of Hara Takashi (1856–1921) to the post of prime minister. Handing the reins of state to the president of a political party, alongside the emergence of two strong mainstream parties, marked the advent of democratic, party-based government.

Factory laborers remained a small proportion of Japan's total work force during the early Meiji era; nearly two-thirds of all employed persons still worked in agriculture. In the 1870s, there were only a few thousand factory workers, primarily working in textile mills. This number rose dramatically, however, reaching more than four hundred thousand in the 1890s, although men still constituted less than half of factory workers and were usually engaged in skilled industries such as metalworking, shipbuilding, machine tools, munitions, and chemicals. As skilled workers they received much higher wages and enjoyed a higher social status than female textile workers. During World War I, there was a dramatic increase in heavy industry; market opportunities resulted as allied countries placed orders in Japan, and the economy expanded on all fronts, but particularly in iron and steel, shipbuilding, and heavy machinery. From 1914 to 1918, the number of factory workers in Japan increased by 63 percent; the majority of these were male career workers in heavy industry.

Propelled by the World War I boom, Japan passed several major economic milestones in the 1920s. Manufacturing's proportion of the gross domestic product surpassed that of the agricultural sector. Japan's manufacturing sector was characterized by a dual structure: the top tier consisted of profitable heavy industries, conglomerates *(zaibatsu)*, and other large textile, cosmetic, and pharmaceutical firms; the bottom half contained small- and medium-scale workshops that made consumer goods, and small subcontractors that supplied parts to top-tier firms. In the 1930s, at least 70 percent of retail shops were small, family businesses that usually produced and/or sold a single product such as tofu or tatami mats. Life was hard for the owners and workers of the modest enterprises in the lower tier. Wage cuts, layoffs, and bankruptcies were common when the economy hit a periodic downturn.

Following World War I, however, the Western nations once again competed with Japan for trade in Asia, resulting in an economic recession. Inflation rose faster than wages, and factory workers became increasingly involved in labor-union movements, engaging in strikes and confrontations with management and calling for higher wages and improved work environments. Many blue-collar workers also resented the perks that were given to management employees, such as company housing, profit sharing, and health benefits. They further resented society's view that urban laborers were social undesirables. In a letter to a newspaper in 1913, one worker complained about the lack of respect uniformed laborers received from mainstream society, explaining that many factory workers left home in disguise, dressed as businessmen or students to commute to the plant, in order to avoid the contempt of the public. The writer claimed that if workers wore their uniforms in public, "people would be astonished not only by our numbers but also by our good behavior."[1]

Management employees were part of the city's new middle class—in contrast with the older middle class, which consisted of merchant or artisan business owners. Most earned their positions on the basis of educational qualifications earned at public and private universities established during Meiji. Male white-collar workers, known as *sarariman* (salarymen), numbered about 1.5 million in 1920. They enjoyed status and standards of living that set them apart from their blue-collar colleagues. In the first three decades of the twentieth century, popular "how-to" books advised how one could enter the desirable ranks of the middle-class sarariman. They described how to behave in the large new corporate environments, focusing less on intellectual competence and more on the ability to conform. Qualities for success included being temperate, orderly, and harmonious. One shouldn't be peculiar or radical. Such advice marked a return to emphasizing obedience and conformity—a moving away from early-Meiji exhortations to be individualistic and self-reliant. The emerging middle class also included government officials, doctors, teachers, policemen, military officers, and bankers in large cities like Tokyo, Osaka, and Nagoya. During and after World War I, women also gained new opportunities to work in white-collar professions as nurses, teachers, salesclerks, switchboard operators, bus conductors, office clerks, and receptionists. Status for most middle-class women, however, was still best attained through making a good marriage match.

A 1924 version of the board game Sugoroku visually depicted the routes to success (or failure) in life by gender. The goal at the center of the board is a beautiful nude dancer, reached on the right-hand, male side through success in business or politics. On the female side, one can attain the goal only through marriage to a successful man—and it's unclear how reaching the dancer constitutes a reward for women.

Labor movements were supported by the wide emergence of liberal thought and radicalism among intellectuals, including currents such as democratism, socialism, and anarchism. Many intellectuals had lost faith in the capitalist system, which exploited the underprivileged. Several powerful professors on the faculty of law at Tokyo Imperial University popularized liberal and democratic ideas. These academics were highly influential: their students manned the most important state agencies, and they were often consulted by officials or asked to serve on government commissions. Many identified with the Left, believing strongly in freedom of expression and equality of the sexes, alongside greater popular participation in politics. Professor Yoshino Sakuzō (1878–1933) promoted the idea of democracy based on the people *(minponshugi),* campaigning for universal male suffrage. Under the Meiji constitution, only male property holders over age twenty-five who paid at a certain tax threshold were eligible to vote. In 1890, this comprised just 1 percent of the populace. Extension of the vote to all male citizens over age twenty-five was achieved in 1925. Minobe Tatsukichi (1873–1948), a scholar of constitutional law, popularized an

FIGURE 46. Takabatake Kashō, *Greater Success Amidst Life's Ups and Downs Sugoroku*, 1924. Insert in *Kōdan kurabu* magazine.

"organ theory of government" that bolstered political parties' authority. Minobe argued that the state was a legal person composed of separate institutions, or organs, such as emperor, cabinet, Diet, and bureaucracy. Each organ had to function properly to keep the national body healthy. Each organ was separate, however, and the Diet, which expressed the highest will of the people, did not depend on the emperor for its power.

Marxist philosophy attracted many intellectuals, professors, and students because it provided a systematic methodology for analyzing how all nations might undergo the transition from feudalism to capitalism and from capitalism to socialism. Marxism held out an integrated view of the problems in society, offering an attractive alternative to what many saw as corrupt capitalism and repressive government. Socialists and communists both drew from Marxist ideas. A short-lived Socialist Party was first formed in 1901, espousing pacifism, reduction of armaments, and universal suffrage. A more robust version, focused more squarely on economic issues and working-class concerns, was established in 1926 and won four Diet seats in the 1928 elections. Its platform condemned the capitalist system and called for nationalization of basic industries, the redistribution of land to tenant families, welfare legislation, and women's suffrage. The Japanese Communist Party was founded in secret in July 1922 by a small group of journalists and political activists. Outlawed by the state and hampered by factional disputes, it largely acted as an underground party engaged in propagandistic and educational activities until after World War II, when it became a legal political party.

The most radical political actors were the anarcho-syndicalists, who believed in instigating "direct action" to topple the state. Journalists Kōtoku Shūsui (1871–1911) and his partner Kanno Suga (1881–1911) were leaders of a movement that believed in replacing the government, by allotting all political power to the people, and in abolishing the private ownership of land and capital. In 1905, Kōtoku visited American anarchists in San Francisco and returned to Japan convinced that only direct action—a massive general strike by workers—would overthrow the state and put economic and political power in the hands of the working class. Kanno began living with Kōtoku in 1909. They were arrested, along with many other political dissidents, following the 1910 High Treason Incident, a bungled plot to assassinate Emperor Meiji with a bomb. Twenty-four anarchists were sentenced to death; twelve, including Kōtoku and Kanno, were actually executed. The incident led to increased repression of ideological movements thought to be subversive. Another influential anarchist, Ōsugi Sakae, had been in prison during the incident and was spared the noose. The police later arrested Ōsugi and his lover Itō Noe, editor of the feminist journal *Seitō*, in the chaotic aftermath of the 1923 Great Kanto Earthquake. The couple, along with Ōsugi's six-year-old nephew, were beaten to death and their bodies were thrown into wells. Ōsugi famously advocated free love, engaging in multiple affairs with women. His relationship with Itō drove another jealous lover, the writer Kamichika Ichiko, to stab the anarchist in 1916, leading to a public scandal that inspired the 1969 film *Eros Plus Massacre.*

The earthquake occurred in Tokyo on September 1, 1923, killing over 120,000 and leaving over two million homeless. The massive destruction made large swaths of Tokyo available for reconstruction. Old wooden buildings were replaced with impersonal concrete structures. Major new avenues were cut through the rubble of small streets. Moats dating from Edo, which had provided city transport and evening entertainment, were paved over to support more roads, railways, and subways. Displaced middle-class families moved to Tokyo's suburbs in increasing numbers. Pre-earthquake Tokyo still contained green expanses from the gardens of former daimyo estates, but redevelopment radically reduced the city's green space; it would disappear almost entirely following the city's destruction by fire-bombing in 1945.

Film director Kurosawa Akira devotes a portion of his memoirs to the earthquake, which had a profound effect on him as a young boy. Kurosawa had started the day at Japan's largest foreign bookstore, Maruzen. A few hours later the store would be in ruins. He remembers how he heard a rumbling sound from the earth and saw the wall of a nearby storehouse crumble: "Then before our eyes, the two storehouses belonging to the pawnshop started shedding their skins. They shuddered and shook off their roof tiles and then let go of their thick walls. In an instant they were skeletons of wooden frame."[2] Kurosawa recounts how fires erupted everywhere and darkness swallowed the city, creating an atmosphere of fear and suspicion, because electricity was completely cut off. A tragic consequence of the earthquake was the massacre of Korean residents by gangs of vigilantes who claimed that the Koreans were poisoning water wells. Kurosawa recalls being told to avoid drinking from a well with strange notations written in white chalk, supposedly Korean code to indicate it had been poisoned. Because he had scribbled the lines himself, he realized that the rationale for lynching Koreans was dubious. Kurosawa's elder brother dragged him to see the aftermath of the fires in order to conquer the fear of death. Mountains of ghastly corpses, charred black, were piled up on bridges and in gutters while others floated in rivers of brownish red.

THE NEW METROPOLIS

With the end of sankin kōtai and the loss of samurai stipends that supported many Edo-era merchants and artisans, the population of Tokyo dropped steeply in the early Meiji period, falling below six hundred thousand by 1873. Nevertheless, as Tokyo was reestablished as the national center of industry, commerce, entertainment, and consumption, its population swelled once again, reaching 1.4 million by 1898 and over two million by 1908. Like early seventeenth-century Edo, Tokyo and other Japanese cities witnessed an accelerated process of urbanization in the 1890s as people from rural areas increasingly moved to the city to work in the new factories, shipyards, and other industries fostered by state industrial policies. Cities that acted as centers of foreign trade and were connected by the national transport system, including Osaka, Nagoya, Kobe, and Yokohama, grew fastest. From the 1890s to the 1920s, new patterns of urban life that supported the growing populations emerged, including advanced transportation, mass-consumer-oriented businesses, and modern forms of popular recreation. New city dwellers who had moved from the countryside were no longer able to lead the self-sufficient lifestyles of farmers; they needed to purchase food, clothing, and daily goods. They also needed affordable distractions to provide relief from the rigors and boredom of factory and office labor. Mass culture and mass consumption advanced with the prosperity of the war years and accelerated after the 1923 earthquake opened large areas of Tokyo for redevelopment.

Japanese modernism, like varieties of modernism emerging in other leading nations, was characterized by "new technologies of speed, sound, and light—the motorcar, airplane, telephone, radio, rotary press, and moving pictures."[3] These technologies enabled the mass marketing of products and services to urban consumers. Modernist tastes, however, did not fully replace traditional preferences; most urban residents freely consumed both trendy fashions and older styles of apparel, traditional foods and new imports, time-honored amusements and the talkies.

Modern businesses and institutions clustered in different areas of the city. Ginza reinforced its early-Meiji reputation as a retailing and banking center. Its streets were lined with department stores, fashionable boutiques, and cafés. The popular practice of window-shopping there even generated its own word—*ginbura*, or strolling leisurely in Ginza. Other emerging centers of entertainment and consumption included Shinjuku and Shibuya. Asakusa, the center of popular amusements during the Edo period, retained this niche by updating its offerings with cinema, burlesque, and other attractions. The Kasumigaseki section of Tokyo acted as the center of government, with brick structures housing the Supreme Court, the metropolitan police department, and most national ministries. Leading corporations and big businesses began to cluster their headquarters in Marunouchi during the 1920s.

As private green spaces disappeared, parks were set aside for public use for the first time. In 1873, Ueno Park in northeast Tokyo—site of a Buddhist temple where Tokugawa defenders made their last stand—became the first public park. Facilities constructed in Ueno Park included a zoo and several art and science museums, all on scenically beautiful grounds where the public could enjoy recreation and relaxation. Hibiya Park, near Ginza, formerly the site of a military parade ground, opened in 1903 as Tokyo's first "Western-style" park. There, visitors could admire some of the oldest trees in the city and glimpse a portion of the moat from the old Edo Castle. Rather than traditional gardens, Hibiya featured large expanses of lawn and seasonal flower beds. Many came to sample the novel facilities, such as an

FIGURE 47. Photograph of a subway entrance in Tokyo, 1929. Source: Wikimedia Commons.

area dedicated to the new bicycling craze, a monumental fountain with a huge water-spewing crane, a modern bandstand where orchestras performed on Sundays and holidays, and a restaurant serving Western-style foods. Professional baseball parks began to appear in cities in the 1920s, when Japan's first professional teams were formed, accompanied by other types of public facilities for spectating or engaging in sports.

All of the new workplaces, shopping areas, and entertainment quarters were tied together via growing networks of streetcars, railroad lines, and subways. Horse-drawn streetcars were commonly used in early Meiji but were phased out with the introduction of electrified streetcars in 1903. Private railroad companies, serving outlying and suburban areas, constructed many intra-Tokyo rail lines. These companies also constructed houses in residential suburbs, allowing occupants to live in more spacious and fashionable housing while commuting farther to employment and shopping in the metropolis. Private rail lines terminated at convenient stops along the Yamanote line encircling central Tokyo. At the terminal station, the private rail companies—such as Tokyu and Seibu in Tokyo, and Hankyu and Hanshin in Osaka—opened large department stores, allowing commuters to pick up food or sundries before returning home. The first subway, billed as "the first underground railway in the Orient," was built in 1927 between Asakusa and Ueno, a distance of just over a mile. New segments were added almost annually until, by 1940, the lines stretched from east to west across the entire city, from Asakusa to Shibuya, allowing Tokyoites to travel speedily by avoiding street traffic.

Desirable urban housing was scarce for the aspirational middle class. Local and national authorities constructed modern public utilities for city dwellers, such as improved water supplies, sewer facilities, gas, and electricity, but many older houses still lacked indoor toilets or bathing facilities. The working class continued to live in cramped, tenement row houses without kitchens, toilets, or baths, relying on cheap food stalls and public bathhouses for everyday needs. After World War I, newly constructed suburban housing offered the ideal of "cultured lifestyles" *(bunka seikatsu)* centered on the family, with private bedrooms for couples, floored kitchens, and bathrooms. These bourgeois domestic spaces were hybrids of Western and traditional styles that allowed families to blend fashion, habit, and convenience. Parlors for entertaining guests were typically furnished with Western-style chairs, sofas, and tables, often constructed of lightweight bamboo or rattan so that they might be placed on rugs without damaging tatami mats underneath. Parlors were decorated with framed paintings and chandeliers and usually included a phonograph and radio. Other areas of the home retained Japanese features. Most occupants continued to sleep on portable futon mattresses on tatami, putting their bedding away during the day. Entrance halls *(genkan)*, where shoes were removed, remained ubiquitous. For dining, individual trays were exchanged for round, short-legged tables *(chabudai)*. Family members sat around the tables on floor cushions *(zabuton)* rather than on chairs.

Department stores were the urban temples to mass consumption. In the early Meiji period, large stores followed the Edo tradition of specializing in dry goods but gradually increased the variety of their offerings. Edo's Echigoya, renamed Mitsukoshi, capitalized on the desire for Western-style fashions, bringing in a French designer to develop a new apparel department and stocking foreign-made goods. In the early 1900s, Mitsukoshi pioneered innovative advertising, with life-size poster displays of new fashions at railway stations. They also offered a catalog sales department and home delivery services. In 1904, Shirokiya (forerunner of today's Tokyu chain) began to carry jewelry, luggage, and food and to offer other services, including a photography studio. Their newspaper advertisements emphasized the convenience of one-stop shopping for an enormous variety of merchandise. In 1911, Shirokiya erected a four-story building featuring Japan's first elevator. Three years later, Mitsukoshi countered with its new flagship, a five-story, Renaissance-style structure—reportedly the largest building east of

FIGURE 48. Painting depicting interior décor of a "culture home": Wada Seika, *Mrs. T,* 1932, Honolulu Museum of Art. Source: Wikimedia Commons.

Suez—that featured central heating, Japan's first escalator, banks of elevators, and row after row of glass display cases. Salesclerks were all identically attired young women, originally in kimonos but, after World War I, increasingly in Western-style women's suits, complete with hats and gloves.

At these vast emporiums, consumers could learn about, examine, and purchase the latest domestic and imported products and fashions, advertised in rapidly expanding varieties of print media. Clothing and accessories occupied significant floor space, accompanied by cosmetics, fountain pens, tableware, furnishings, and small electrical goods such as fans, heaters, and sewing machines. Other floors housed groceries, prepared foods, and gift-oriented foods, from fancy imported chocolates and caramels to exquisite, seasonally themed tea sweets from famous traditional makers. The stores purveyed culture as well as merchandise, featuring art and exhibition galleries and multiple restaurants, usually occupying the top floors. Even the rooftops offered entertainment, with game rooms, amusement parks, and

FIGURE 49. Shiro Kazama, Advertising poster for Isetan department store in Tokyo's Shinjuku district, 1936. Source: Wikimedia Commons.

small zoos for children. In short, a major department store held something of interest for everyone, and a Sunday outing to the store was an eagerly anticipated event for all members of the family. Before the 1923 earthquake, customers were usually required to exchange their street shoes for store slippers at the entrance, but afterward, marble and wood were used to replace tatami flooring, allowing consumers to enter and leave quickly.

The most sought-after goods were not necessarily new fashions or confectionaries from Paris or America. Traditional goods and foods also evolved with new methods of production and advertising. The Dentsu advertising agency, founded in 1907, was a pioneer in designing colorful, graphic images for labels, ads, and posters for new and older products alike. Brand-name varieties of sake, miso, rice crackers, pickles, and other traditional foods gained popularity. Kimono styles changed rapidly, and the development of inexpensive silks *(meisen)* and silk cottons allowed women to purchase larger numbers of kimonos for different seasons and moods. They could be accessorized by a dizzying array of shawls, handbags, and removable collars, some made with fur or embellished with gold or precious stones.

Despite the iconic status of department stores, consumers generally preferred to buy daily provisions in their neighborhoods. Most urban neighborhoods then, as today, had their own purveyors of vegetables, tofu, tea, rice, fish, and other daily foods. Most also contained drugstores that stocked both traditional herbal remedies and modern pharmaceuticals; office supply shops that carried ink, brushes, and handmade paper alongside fountain pens and utilitarian notebooks; hardware stores; and ceramics sellers. For most people, everyday consumer life was a seamless fusion of traditional and modern elements. Furthermore, while modern tastes were often influenced by Western fashions, products were often significantly adapted to suit Japanese preferences and needs.

Food choices continued to broaden during this era. Foreign foods introduced during Meiji now reached larger audiences, often modified to accommodate local ingredients and tastes. The meatier, oilier fare of Western and Chinese cuisine was believed to provide higher levels of nutrition, along with a chance for culinary adventure; foreign dishes were consumed in greater quantities both at home and in restaurants. Chinese noodles, different in taste and texture from traditional udon and buckwheat soba, first gained popularity in Nagasaki as *champon* (slang for "mix"), a cheap and savory combination of leftover meats, soup, and noodles. Following the First Sino-Japanese War (1894–95), over a hundred thousand Chinese entered Japan as students or workers, clustering in Yokohama, Kobe, Sapporo, and parts of Tokyo, which resulted in a proliferation of cheap eateries serving Chinese foods. Some began to adapt their fare to Japanese tastes, introducing dishes such as ramen, which used Chinese noodles cooked in a Japanese manner. Housewives began to incorporate popular Chinese and Western recipes into their repertoires to increase the variety of home-cooked meals. Instructions for preparation, written in easy-to-follow language for beginning cooks, were readily available in women's magazines and cookbooks, which underwent a publishing boom in the early twentieth century. Many urbanites also swapped traditional breakfasts of rice and tea for the simpler-to-prepare bread and coffee.

By 1923, there were around five thousand Western-style restaurants in Tokyo. Department stores dedicated one or two floors to these eateries, providing an array of culinary styles. Chinese and Western restaurants were often more convenient and comfortable than Japanese establishments, where one generally had to remove one's shoes and sit on the floor. Furthermore, most women felt uncomfortable entering male-dominated traditional eateries, so department stores offered welcome options for females who wished to dine out. At high-end Western-style restaurants, customers sat on wooden chairs at tables with white tablecloths and dined on beefsteak and imported wine. More affordable eateries adapted Western dishes to suit Japanese tastes, usually serving entrées with white rice. The most popular dishes were breaded pork cutlets *(tonkatsu)*, rice with curry sauce, and deep-fried potato and meat croquettes *(korokke)*. One popular hybrid dish, omelet rice *(omuraisu)*, consisting of an egg omelet stuffed with fried rice and topped with ketchup, was invented in 1902 at a restaurant called Rengatei in Ginza and is still operating today. All of the dishes used relatively small amounts of meat and were thus affordable for many.

Tokyo's large population of working-class consumers also frequented new establishments offering cheap, quick, Japanese-style dishes. Yoshinoya, a purveyor of stewed, soy-sauce-flavored beef over rice *(gyūdon)*, became the world's first fast-food franchise, opening at the Nihonbashi fish market in 1899 and spreading quickly through Tokyo and other cities (the first such franchises in America were A&W in 1916, followed by White Castle in 1921). Sushi grew in popularity, and shops instituted home delivery by bicycle. *Terry's Japanese Empire*, a 1914 English travel guide, was perhaps the first to describe the dish for non-Japanese audiences, identifying "small silvery trout seasoned with vinegar, cooked with rice, and called sushi." It noted that sushi, "though unsavory and unpalatable to foreigners, is much liked by the Japanese."[4]

Another type of influential new eating and drinking space in urban society was the café, which appeared in Tokyo in the early 1910s. Cafés were fashionable hangouts for artists, intellectuals, and chic young people, who gathered to engage in free-wheeling conversations while imbibing coffee, black tea, cocktails, or newly invented soft drinks like Ramune, a carbonated lemonade. Cafés symbolized the modern liberated spirit but simultaneously had a reputation for decadence. Popular authors frequently used them as settings for their stories.

CHANGING GENDER NORMS

Waitresses were the heart of café life, their "flower and spirit." Different areas of Tokyo were known for the distinctive styles of their waitresses: in Ginza they were refined, elegant, and often dressed in kimonos; in Shinjuku they wore Western fashions and were more boldly flirtatious and better educated than their Ginza counterparts. Waitresses did not earn wages and worked solely for tips. They had to repay café owners for meals and buy their own kimonos or uniforms.

After the 1923 earthquake, larger, more elaborate cafés sprang up throughout urban entertainment districts. While older cafés were modeled on small European bistros and salons, the new establishments were multistory buildings with colorful neon signage and luxurious furnishings. They played jazz and served a larger clientele of male white-collar workers attracted by the prospect of engaging in fashionable modern life and mingling with young female waitresses in a relatively cheap and direct manner, in contrast with the expensive and time-consuming rituals of teahouses and geisha. Prostitution was not technically part of the waitress's job, but like Edo-period geisha and bathhouse attendants, many provided erotic services to clients in order to earn extra income. In the 1920s and '30s, such services became more apparent as café owners urged waitresses to attract clientele by offering amenities like "subway service," allowing the customer to slip his hand through a slit in the waitress's skirt, or "organ service," in which a waitress lay across the laps of a few customers and they played her body like a keyboard.

Beginning in 1929, ordinances in various cities attempted to restrict the location of the increasingly immoral cafés, but that didn't stop their proliferation; the number of cafés and bars in Japan grew rapidly in the late 1920s and early '30s, reaching a peak of over thirty-seven thousand in 1934. They ranged from small, cheap backstreet establishments to the ornate extravaganzas of Ginza. Even the poorest young male student could enjoy a night in a café that suited his budget. The popularity of cafés offering erotic adventure represents another parallel with Edo-period tastes, replicating the pleasure quarters for modern audiences. Café waitresses, along with other new female urban occupations such as dance-hall girls, modern actresses, and cabaret performers, faced social disapproval. Their labor did not correspond to either traditional work for women, in the home, the farm, the family business, or the brothel; or to modern work considered suitable and respectable, at the factory, the hospital, the office, the department store, or the school.

Author Tanizaki Jun'ichirō commented on the "sordid, craven" nature of cafés that "appear to be places for eating and drinking, whereas in reality eating and drinking are secondary to having a good time with women."[5] His first important novel, *Naomi* (1924–25), relates the story of a fifteen-year-old café waitress who becomes an object of obsession for Jōji, a wealthy young engineer. In an echo of Genji's adoption of Murasaki in *The Tale of Genji*, Jōji decides he will raise Naomi to become his perfect mate, a glamorous, westernized woman. He funds English, music, and dancing lessons and excursions to the movies and theater. The manipulative Naomi eventually gains complete control over Jōji, forcing him to make more extravagant purchases and to endure her relationships with other men. Naomi is often identified as the quintessential example of a *moga* (modern girl), characterized by the mass media as selfishly obsessed with the latest fashions and sexually promiscuous.

Moga were identifiable through their shockingly short skirts that revealed bare legs and short, bobbed hairstyles. Their counterpart was the modern boy, or *mobo*, who favored a slicked-back hairstyle and horn-rimmed spectacles called "roido" glasses because they were popularized by silent-film star Harold Lloyd. Moga and mobo frequented the beer halls, cabarets, and jazz clubs in entertainment enclaves like Ginza, Shinjuku, and Asakusa. They knew all the latest movies, dance steps, and fashions, spending hours window-shopping at Ginza's famed department stores.

During the 1920s, only a very small percentage of Japanese women actually wore Western dress on the streets, but the new presence of the moga in urban society was magnified by the mass media. Her face and figure dominated advertising posters for products such as beer and perfume. Newspapers and magazines published racy stories, real and imagined, about the adventures and affairs of moga. The short, waved bob hairstyle of the moga was thought to signal eroticism, but many women who cut their hair were not advertising their wantonness. Rather, they opted for an easy-care style that suited their busy lives, liberating them from time-consuming traditional coiffures.

The moga challenged official gender ideology, which urged women to become "good wives and wise mothers," and served as a symbol of women's increasing agency. By playing freely in the streets and openly flaunting

FIGURE 50. *Moga* on a poster advertising Sapporo beer, ca. 1920s–1930s. Source: Wikimedia Commons.

sexuality, moga demonstrated they would not be enslaved by old-fashioned gender norms. For mainstream society, they represented both threat and titillation. The public's continued fear of such modern women as dangerous—along with its appetite for the erotic and grotesque *(ero guro)*—was demonstrated in the media and popular obsession with the 1936 case of Abe Sada, a waitress who strangled her married lover, then cut off his genitals and carried them in her purse as a symbol of their undying love. The passionate tale was translated to film in a 1976 Franco-Japanese production, *In the Realm of the Senses*.

Feminist publications began addressing women's changing circumstances in the 1910s. Japan's first such journal, *Seitō* (Bluestocking, a term describing intellectual European women), was dedicated to improving women's status and welfare and began publication in 1911, spearheaded by novelist Hiratsuka Raichō (1886–1971). The graphic, art deco cover of its first issue pictured a Grecian-looking female figure standing in front of a kimono. The issue opened, famously, with Hiratsuka's words, "In the beginning, woman was the sun." Members of *Seitō* and their readers often referred to themselves as "New Women," who wore Western dress, had educated opinions, and insisted on selecting their own romantic partners. The pages of the journal provided an array of lively views on women's issues, such as premarital sex, legalized prostitution, abortion, and women's suffrage.

Movements for women's suffrage began in 1918, before universal male suffrage was passed in 1925 and while just four nations had given women the right to vote. In 1922, legal prohibitions against women's participation in politics and attendance at political meetings were repealed. Journalist Ichikawa Fusae (1893–1981), a *Seitō* cofounder, emerged as a tireless activist for women's political rights and for fighting corruption in government. After the postwar constitution allowed women to be elected to the Diet, she gained a seat in 1953 and remained in office through the early 1980s. Another postwar female Diet member, Katō Shidzue (1897–2001), was a strong advocate of birth control during the 1920s and cofounded the Japanese branch of Planned Parenthood in 1948. Katō brought activist and sex educator Margaret Sanger to Japan six times to raise awareness of reproductive rights.

The role of full-time housewife also expanded and professionalized during these years. During the Meiji period, most middle- and upper-class households had employed maids to clean and cook, but these responsibilities shifted to the modern housewife. The tasks she was now expected to manage included keeping household account records, planning and executing nutritious and enticing menus, and maintaining proper household hygiene. She replaced her husband as the primary decision maker for home-based consumption, making choices about furnishings and interior décor that had been left to men in previous eras. Bridal encyclopedias *(hanayome bunko)* became popular aids for young homemakers expected to master the myriad domestic tasks associated with modern, cultured lifestyles. They contained as many as twenty volumes, each dedicated to a single topic such as sewing Japanese clothing, sewing Western clothing and items like curtains, cooking traditional side dishes, cooking Western and Chinese dishes, household economics, etiquette and beauty, ikebana and chanoyu for the home, knitting and crocheting, cleaning and laundry techniques, and home medicine. Housewives even adopted a kind of uniform—the *kappōgi*—a pristine, white apron-smock that protected their kimonos and kept the long sleeves from obstructing chores.

MASS MEDIA AND MASS CULTURE

During the Taishō era, new forms of mass media proliferated, resulting in the wide dissemination of information and images about modern urban life. Newspapers and magazines evolved to become major commercial concerns, targeted toward demographically distinct audiences. Products of technology such as photography, recordings, radio, and movies became accessible in everyday life and began to shape and influence the lives of ordinary people.

After decades of compulsory education—by 1930, nearly 90 percent of adult Japanese had at least six years of elementary education—Japan's masses were remarkably literate. An immense outpouring of print supported their reading interests. By 1920, there were over a thousand different newspapers published for an audience of six million subscribers. The largest, *Osaka mainichi,* climbed from a circulation of 260,000 in 1912 to 670,000 in 1921 and reached 1.5 million in 1930. Newspapers had changed in character, from the Meiji-era small enterprises espousing particular political causes to complex big businesses with platoons of college-graduate reporters. With large sums of capital at stake, major newspapers adopted a conservative outlook on national affairs in order to avoid trouble with official censors, who could suspend issues or shut down production.

Readers could browse through books and magazines at one of the nation's ten thousand retail bookstores. Thousands of magazine titles were created to cater to specific audiences of different genders, ages, and interests. Serious readers found discussion of contemporary policy and serialized literary novels in the intellectually minded *Chūō kōron* (Central review) and the bolder and more critical *Kaizō* (Reconstruction). *Taiyō* (Sun), established in 1894, was the first national journal specifically targeting the middle class. *Kingu* (King), an entertainment-oriented serial, became Japan's first million-seller in 1927. Women's magazines, such as *Fujin kōron* (Women's review) and *Shufu no tomo* (Housewife's friend), were especially numerous, as they targeted the main consumer for a household. They generally offered articles supporting the official ideology of "good wife, wise mother," encouraging efforts to improve marriage, family life, and domestic management. Other articles, however, urged women to tap their human potential, to dare to pursue professional or artistic careers. Children too

FIGURE 51. *Fujin Gahō* (Lady's graphic) magazine, January 1908. Courtesy of
Rijksmuseum.

enjoyed their own publications, such as *Shōnen kurabu* (Boy's club) and *Akai tori* (Redbird). All magazines provided key forums for advertising targeted toward a certain demographic, further encouraging consumerism as a form of status among all segments of society.

Record companies produced music for all tastes, from patriotic marches to jazz, to be played on the radio and on phonographs. Radio stations began operations in Tokyo, Osaka, and Nagoya in 1925. The first broadcast programs included classical music and radio plays. The following year, three independent broadcasting companies merged into the state-sponsored NHK—modeled after the British Broadcasting Company—which remained the country's sole broadcaster for two decades. Radio was largely an urban medium; 95 percent of households owning receivers lived in cities. As part of their "cultured lifestyle," middle-class families gathered in sitting rooms to enjoy Beethoven or plays by famous writers especially commissioned for radio. In 1928, NHK initiated brief morning calisthenics programs, which they continue to air daily on national TV.

The first permanent cinema opened in Asakusa in 1903. The Electric Palace (Denkikan) was originally a showplace for scientific oddities, including experiments in electricity, photography, and x-ray technology. Reborn as a movie house, its façade was decorated with banners and murals featuring scenes from popular films. The public quickly embraced the movies, and theaters proliferated throughout major cities. Japanese fans followed stars such as Charlie Chaplin, Rudolph Valentino, and Harold Lloyd as eagerly as their American counterparts. A special class of entertainers called *benshi* narrated the silent films in Japanese. These individuals followed in the tradition of jōruri narration from Bunraku, dramatically reading the on-screen scripts in different characters' voices and explaining the narrative or social context, especially for unfamiliar foreign settings or situations.

The Japanese began to make their own films in 1899, just two years after first importing movie projectors, and began producing their own cameras the following year. Early films often starred Kabuki actors in both male and female roles or featured demonstrations of martial arts and swordsmanship. By the mid-1910s, there were more than a dozen studios making over a hundred films a year. The most popular genres were samurai epics *(chambara)*, like the ever-popular story of *The Forty-Seven Rōnin*, and light, flirtatious comedies. In the 1920s, studios began to produce realistic contemporary dramas with improved scripts; in the 1930s, they introduced talkies. By 1940, there were 2,363 movie houses in Japan and per capita consumption averaged six films per year. Most cinemas were located in cities, but they could also be found in provincial towns such as Saga, a relatively remote, small city in Kyushu that boasted four movie theaters in the 1920s. Over time, Japan's well-honed studio system would produce numerous masterpieces by renowned directors such as Ozu Yasujiro (1903–1963) and Kurosawa Akira (1910–98). Ozu's *Tokyo Story* (1953) and *Late Spring* (1949) and Kurosawa's *Seven Samurai* (1954) and *Rashomon* (1950) are usually considered among the fifty best films ever made. Japan ranks third among all countries (following France and Italy) in the number of Academy Awards won for Best Foreign Film.

Film was not simply a medium for entertainment. Documentary films or newsreels shown before features helped generate patriotism and support for nationalist projects, such as the Russo-Japanese War, Emperor Meiji's funeral, and Japan's colonizations of Taiwan and Korea (see chapter 10). The new religious group Oomoto employed a traveling crew to attract potential adherents in remote rural areas by showing movies. Film was also an important medium for avant-garde art. Kinugasa Teinosuke's 1926 silent work, *A Page of Madness (Kurutta ippeiji)*, set in a lunatic asylum, used experimental film techniques, such as double exposure and superimposition, to represent blurred visions of insanity and reality.

Live theater also thrived in both traditional and new forms. Storytellers and Kabuki continued to attract large popular audiences. During Edo, Kabuki had been seen as a disreputable art for the townsfolk; fans from the samurai class would have disguised themselves for a visit. As Western enthusiasm for exotic Japanese traditions climbed higher in the twentieth century, Kabuki, like ukiyo-e, came to be canonized as a unique cultural treasure, representative of Japanese aesthetic identity. New forms of dramatic theater that contrasted with the stylized dance-dramas of Kabuki and Nō also emerged. "New drama" *(shingeki)* adopted naturalistic acting styles, contemporary themes, and the use of actresses in female roles. Urban audiences welcomed productions of classical and modern foreign plays such as Greek tragedies, works by Shakespeare, and more recent works by Henrik Ibsen and Anton Chekhov. Audiences also loved vaudeville and burlesque revues, such as the Casino Folies, established in Asakusa in 1929, which played to tastes for ero guro nansensu, characterized by sexiness and absurdity. Another new form of theater, the Takarazuka Revue, an all-female theater group, was founded in 1913 by Kobayashi Ichizō, the president of Hankyū Railways, at a hot-spring resort town that served as terminus for a rail line from Osaka. The "Takarasiennes" performed spectacularly staged musicals and revues featuring several hundred girls, resembling Hollywood extravaganzas. Stars were billed as "beauties in male dress," a twist on Kabuki's onnagata, and were idolized by young women who developed crushes on the "actors." A second Takarazuka theater was soon opened in Tokyo.

Asakusa, the center of Edo commoner amusements, successfully blended old and new attractions. Acrobats, performing monkeys, and archery stalls manned by seductive young women still captivated many, but they were accompanied by modern diversions such as merry-go-rounds, aquariums, burlesque revues, and jazz clubs, not to mention fourteen movie houses. Kawabata Yasunari's modernist novel *The Scarlet Gang of Asakusa* (1929– 30) describes how "in Asakusa, everything is flung out in the raw. Desires dance naked. All races, all classes, all jumbled together forming a bottomless, endless current, flowing day and night, no beginning, no end. Asakusa is alive. . . . The masses converge on it constantly. Their Asakusa is a foundry in which all the old models are regularly melted down to be cast into new ones."[6] The novel claimed that a hundred million people a year frequented Asakusa's many attractions.[7]

MODERNISM IN LITERATURE AND ART

By the 1920s, writers like Kawabata were deeply steeped in all manner of Western literature, philosophy, and art. With cheap translations available for nearly every notable foreign publication, modern intellectuals read novels by Proust, Kafka, and Joyce, dramas by Strindberg and Brecht, and poetry by Rilke and Eliot. They were keenly aware of European literary trends, such as tendencies toward irony and detachment and the disruption of seamless chronological narratives. Japanese literary modernists, including Kawabata, Tanizaki Jun'ichirō, Okamoto Kanoko, and detective-fiction pioneer Edogawa Ranpo, whose pen name was created to evoke Edgar Allen Poe, rejected the naturalist trends of Meiji literature, characterized by the flat, confessional style of the "I-novel" that strove to transparently represent reality without stylization. They also rejected direct imitation of Western styles, seeking their own authentic, modern voices. Their works were action-driven and highly stylized; characterized by cosmopolitanism, often featuring foreign characters and settings; and conveyed a sharply visual sense of spectacle that reflected the popularity of the movies.

Kawabata was one of Japan's first modern writers to be translated into English and the first to receive the Nobel Prize for Literature, in 1968. Although he is best known for the novel *Snow Country*, another novel, *Scarlet Gang of Asakusa*, better represents the spirit of Japanese literary modernism, with its pastiche of snatches of conversation, song lyrics, and lists. The narrator is a flaneur, a denizen of Asakusa who befriends a gang of delinquents with names like Boat Runt and Left-handed Hiko. Rapidly shifting scenes featuring punchy slang underline the importance of chic fashionability and knowledge of the latest trends among urban cognoscenti; the parallels between Edo's pleasure quarter and modern Asakusa are unspoken but apparent. Translator Alisa Freedman notes the novel's theme of "simultaneous lament for a fading way of life and celebration of the new sites and entertainments that have replaced lost landmarks and pastimes."[8]

In art, the modernist group MAVO presented groundbreaking conceptual work that presaged better-known, post–World War II avant-garde groups like Gutai and Hi-Red Center (see chapter 11). MAVO was a short-lived art-activist commune of around fifteen members who wished to fuse modernist aesthetics with radical politics. It was founded in 1923 and led by Murayama Tomoyoshi, who had been impressed by the social potential of movements such as Dadaism and Constructivism when he studied in Weimar Germany. The group opposed state authoritarianism, bourgeois norms, commodity culture, and the official art establishment. Their first group act was to shatter the glass roof of an exhibition hall housing the annual exhibition of the Nika Art Association, an elitist group established in 1914 to promote "fine" contemporary art. MAVO identified politically with anarchists and Marxist revolutionaries, championing the proletariat. They considered themselves cultural anarchists and declared, "Lazily, like pigs, like weeds, like the trembling emotions of sexual desire, we are the last bombs that rain down on all the intellectual criminals."[9] Members engaged in painting, architecture, performance art, and illustration. Two of their primary art forms, collage and assemblage, incorporated mundane items such as shoes or machine fragments to more closely tie art to daily proletarian life. MAVO also staged street parades and avant-garde performances of dance and theater. Like modernist writers and the larger cultural trend of ero guro, their work was sensational and sometimes commercial; they produced advertisements, product designs, and manga comics alongside more politically charged works.

REVOLT AGAINST THE WEST

Another new philosophical turn that became apparent during the Greater Taishō era was increased criticism of the West—which, after World War I, many began to imagine as a collective threat to Japan's national independence and sense of cultural autonomy. Following Japan's rise to "great power" status and its position as the strongest nation in Asia, some writers and intellectuals imagined a Japanese destiny surpassing Western accomplishments, leading the world to a higher level of civilization that would fuse Western and Asian elements. In order to achieve this, some advocated protecting Japan's pure, indigenous culture from further adulteration by Western pollutants such as science and technology. This culturalism, or Japanism, emphasized stronger ties to Asian nations, grounded in their common struggle to combat Western racism and exploitation of colonial peoples. The resurgence of cultural nationalism reflected Japan's centuries-old pattern of embracing and then rejecting foreign influences: from Nara mass importation of Chinese civilization to Heian indigenization of arts, from Tokugawa isolationism and nativism to Meiji enthusiasm for Western institutions and culture. In contrast with Fukuzawa Yukichi's earlier assertion that Japan must "leave Asia" and become a Western-style civilization, cultural nationalists now urged leadership over Asia, conservation of traditional culture, and abandonment of Western norms and values. This stance assumed that Japan, as the strongest Asian nation, would take responsibility for "civilizing" underdeveloped Asian nations by removing the influence of Western imperial powers. Culturalists also assumed that it was somehow possible to disentangle "pure" native culture from modernity.

Art historian Okakura Kakuzō, a disciple of Ernest Fenollosa, was among the first to articulate pan-Asian views. His works, written in English during his tenure as curator at the Boston Museum of Fine Arts, aimed to educate American audiences about Japanese cultural superiority over Western nations. In *The Ideals of the East* (1903), Okakura declared that "Asia is one. The Himalayas divide, only to accentuate, two mighty civilizations, the Chinese with its communism of Confucius and the Indian with its individualism of the Vedas."[10] This claim suggested that all Asians shared a spiritual, aesthetic worldview, but Okakura also pointed out that Japan alone had successfully assimilated both Asian ideals and the competitive, scientific spirit of Europe and America. In his view, it was Japan's mission to lead the world to a higher synthesis of East and West.

Okakura's *The Book of Tea* (1906), still much admired, proposed that the tea ceremony acted as a microcosm of Japanese philosophy and aesthetics and as evidence of its cultural superiority over the West. The book explained how tea, originally a product of China, was a globally valuable commodity, a staple of English life, but only Japan had developed sophisticated arts around tea appreciation. China was a defeated nation that could not protect Asian heritage, while the United States and Europe were too crassly commercial and materialistic to cultivate elevated levels of aesthetic appreciation. Western Orientalists eagerly received Okakura's florid praise of Japan, seemingly failing to notice the sharp rebukes of European and American practices contained in the work. In describing the carefully orchestrated décor of the Japanese tearoom, he contrasts this with the methods of "the Occident":

> In Western houses we are often confronted with what appears to us useless reiteration. We find it trying to talk to a man while his full-length portrait stares at us from behind his back. We wonder which is real, he of the picture or he who talks, and feel a curious conviction that one of them must be fraud. Many a time have we sat at a festive board contemplating, with a secret shock to our digestion, the representation of abundance on the dining-room walls. Why these pictured victims of chase and sport, the elaborate carvings of fishes and fruit? Why the display of family plates, reminding us of those who have dined and are dead?[11]

Okakura claims Japan's superior respect for nature, in contrast with Western disregard and abuse of the environment, in this passage about ikebana:

> The wanton waste of flowers among Western communities is even more appalling than the way they are treated by Eastern Flower Masters. The number of flowers cut daily to adorn the ballrooms and banquet-tables of Europe and America, to be thrown away on the morrow, must be something enormous; if strung together they might garland a continent. Beside this utter carelessness of life, the guilt of the Flower-Master becomes insignificant. He, at least, respects the economy of nature, selects his victims with careful foresight, and after death does honor to their remains. In the West the display of flowers seems to be a part of the pageantry of wealth, the fancy of a moment. Whither do they all go, these flowers, when the revelry is over? Nothing is more pitiful than to see a faded flower remorselessly flung upon a dung heap. . . . Anyone acquainted with the ways of our tea- and flower-masters must have noticed the religious veneration with which they regard flowers. They do not cull at random, but carefully select each branch or spray with an eye to the artistic composition they have in mind. They would be ashamed should they chance to cut more than were absolutely necessary. It may be remarked in this connection that they always associate the leaves, if there be any, with the flower, for the object is to present the whole beauty of plant life. In this respect, as in many others, their method differs from that pursued in Western countries. Here we are apt to see only the flower stems, heads as it were, without body, stuck promiscuously into a vase.[12]

Anti-Western feelings increased in 1919, when the Paris Peace Conference refused to approve a Japan-sponsored racial-equality clause in the Treaty of Versailles. After the war, many Japanese feared that the newly established League of Nations, predecessor to the United Nations, would perpetuate white privilege. Japanese delegates to the League of Nations drafted a clause for the Treaty of Versailles requiring that member nations not discriminate against one another on the basis of race or nationality and that they try to grant equality to foreign subjects living in their territory. Adoption of the clause would have challenged established norms of imperialism, including the colonial subjugation of nonwhite peoples. The other member nations refused to endorse the proposal, and this rejection led to public anger in Japan—particularly against the United States, since the chairman of the League of Nations was President Woodrow Wilson.

The 1924 U.S. Immigration Exclusion Act, intended to preserve the ideal of white American homogeneity, also fanned anti-Americanism in Japan. The act favored Northern Europeans, providing large quotas to "Nordics," with smaller allowances for Eastern and Southern Europeans. Immigration from Asia was prohibited entirely, and this applied pointedly to the Japanese, given that the Chinese had been legally excluded since 1882. Many Japanese viewed the new law as a deep racial insult, amounting to a declaration of war between the "yellow" and "white" races. A high-profile suicide expressing opposition to the U.S. law galvanized popular protest in different forms. Massive anti-American rallies were organized, and boycotts of American goods and movies became widespread throughout the summer of 1924, agitated by extensive media coverage of American racism.

Another strain of the new anti-Western sentiment included the condemnation of mass consumerism and the elevation of native rural life as an antidote to decadent, foreign ways. Conservative officials and intellectuals viewed consumption as wasteful, immoral luxury and urged citizens to save and to exercise self-control. They idealized rural thrift and reliance on traditional goods and warned that city life brought moral corruption and decadence. The new urban world of mass consumption and entertainment still represented only 20 percent of the nation's population in the 1920s and '30s. Sparkling representations of wealthy, exciting urban life caused resentment among rural populations. The countryside still lacked many basic amenities, from modern medical treatment to hygienic water and sewage systems. Farmers could not taste exotic new foods; their diets were bland and monotonous, and many suffered from malnutrition. During Meiji, most had continued to mix their rice with cheaper grains like barley or millet; but by the 1920s, even poor tenant families—who spent half or more of their income on food—practiced the formula "white rice plus three side dishes" *(ichiju sansai)* as the standard for civilized meals. Their side dishes, however, were often tofu dregs or pickles made from radish leaves or weeds. Common staples such as soy sauce, miso, and sugar were luxuries used sparingly by the rural poor. Commonplace urban foods like meat cutlets, bread, or ice cream could not even be dreamt of. The growing divide between urban and rural lifestyles created a major source of discontent among the 80 percent of the populace who still resided in the countryside. This resentment spawned support for military factions in the 1930s that advocated expansionism on the continent as a means to improve rural standards of living.

As rural life came to be portrayed by ideologues as a pure reservoir of national values, movements nostalgically promoting folkways arose in the 1910s and '20s. The folk craft *(mingei),* movement spearheaded by Yanagi Sōetsu (1889–1961) and the folklore movement, associated with Yanagita Kunio (1875–1962), were both attempts to locate the native spirit of Japan in the everyday lives of common rural people, rather than in elite traditions of art and literature. Both men were products of Tokyo Imperial University, deeply educated in Western literature, art, and philosophy—and thus, ironically, their quests for a unique Japanese identity were heavily influenced by Western models. Yanagi drew from the English craft movement, championed by William Morris as part of a reaction against the Industrial Revolution. Under the guidance of English artist Bernard Leach, Yanagi and potters Hamada Shōji and Kawai Kanjirō started a movement to reappraise the country craft of the people, including handwoven textiles, utilitarian pottery, basketry, and simple furnishings. They valued irregularities and imperfections in works, just as the tea masters of earlier centuries valued wabi aesthetics. In his book *The Unknown Craftsman,* Yanagi criticized industrial goods, describing the value of handmade crafts: "On reflection, one must conclude that in bringing cheap and useful goods to the average household, industrialism has been of service to mankind—but at the cost of the heart, of warmth, friendliness and beauty. By contrast, articles well made by hand, though expensive, can be enjoyed in homes for generations. . . . Machine-made things are children of the brain; they are not very human. The more they spread, the less the human being is needed."[13]

Yanagita, revered as the father of Japanese folklore and rural anthropology, was influenced by the nineteenth-century European boom in folk and fairy tales, associated with authors like Hans Christian Andersen and the Brothers Grimm. During Meiji, foreign advisors like Lafcadio Hearn and Basil Hall Chamberlain gathered and translated miscellaneous Japanese folklore and myths. Yanagita hoped to systematize collection of such tales from remote rural regions. Initially a bureaucrat who served in a variety of prestigious posts, Yanagita gained greater renown for his vast surveys of village life in the 1920s and '30s. In 1910, he published his first book of folklore, *The Legends of Tono,* an assortment of ghost stories and explanations of local customs from a remote area in northern Japan that he dedicated to "people living in foreign countries." Yanagita heard the tales from local storyteller Sasaki Kizen but felt a responsibility to polish the rough anecdotes, crafting the stories in the literary style of European folklorists. Sasaki found them unrecognizable and published his own collection in 1935, which included this story to explain local taboos:

> If you go into the mountains, at times you will find trees that have two separate trunks growing out of a common base. Only some of the trees are growing with the two trunks twisted around each other. Those twisted together are that way because on the twelfth day of the twelfth month, the mountain deity counts the trees in his territory. To mark the total of how many thousands or tens of thousands of trees he has, he twists the two trunks of the last tree together. For this reason, only on the twelfth day of the twelfth month, people in the nearby community are prohibited from climbing the mountain. It would be terrible if by mistake someone went to the mountain and was counted as a tree.[14]

Yanagita often romanticized rural life in his works, yet in reality he had little regard for farmers and country ways. He criticized the rural mentality for its servile, submissive attitude toward superiors, its ignorance, and its fear of strangers. He applied double standards to rural and urban lifestyles, believing that farmers should not be allowed to squander their resources on consumption of modern or luxury goods, unnecessary for country life but desirable for urban elites like himself.

Both Yanagi and Yanagita created significant new fields of Japanese studies in their respective efforts to construct a modern Japanese identity grounded in traditional rural values and practices. Their momentous achievements nevertheless demonstrate how deep the divide between the urban and rural had grown. Urban intellectuals, far removed from the primitive beliefs and daily misery that typically characterized agrarian life, could nostalgically romanticize the rural while ignoring real farmers' impoverishment and their demands for more equitable standards of living.

Another aspect of the revolt against the West occurred among iconic writers like Kawabata Yasunari and Tanizaki Jun'ichirō (1886–1965), who had both championed literary modernism. As they grew older, they reverted to more traditional narratives that celebrated native aesthetics. Tanizaki's novel *Some Prefer Nettles* (1929) pits the westernized "cultured life" of an unhappy couple, Kaname and Misako, against that of Misako's traditionalist father, who lives happily like an Edo-era merchant, dressing in antique kimonos, collecting Bunraku puppets, and keeping a young mistress with blackened teeth. The novel seems to critique the state of Japan's cultural hybridity, represented by the tawdry Eurasian prostitute Louise whom Kaname frequents. Over the course of the plot, Kaname turns away from his preference for American culture, English literature, and foreign prostitutes, embracing the arts and aesthetics of Japan's past. Tanizaki's later essay *In Praise of Shadows* (1933) eloquently laments how the necessities of modern life, such as heating and lighting, mar the aesthetics of traditional Japanese architecture. He includes a paean to old-fashioned Japanese toilets. Although cold and dark, their wooden construction offered the "inexplicable power to calm and sooth [*sic*]. The ultimate, of course, is a wooden 'morning glory' urinal filled with boughs of cedar; this is a delight to look at and allows not the slightest sound."[15] By contrast, he finds Western toilet facilities with gleaming white tile and porcelain "very crude and tasteless," exposing unmentionable bodily functions to "excessive illumination."

In summary, Tokyo and other Japanese cities experienced accelerated urbanization during the Taishō era, spurring the rapid expansion of mass transit, consumerism, and mass media. The face of the capital changed following the devastation wrought by the 1923 earthquake, allowing for extensive development of modern facilities, such as broader streets and enormous department stores. The literate public increasingly advocated for their own interests, participating in a wide variety of political, labor, and feminist movements. In material culture, middle-class preferences in food, housing, clothing, and décor frequently blended imports with Japanese tastes and sensibilities. New technologies such as the radio, phonograph, and especially movies offered modern amusements but did not displace older forms of entertainment like Kabuki or erotic teahouse culture, now transplanted to the café. National economic development and military success abroad spurred confidence in native cultural identity, expressed in both anti-Western sentiment and nostalgic celebration of rural life. Nationalistic claims of cultural exceptionalism and racial uniqueness would help undergird state efforts to rationalize expansion and control of neighboring East Asian countries, as explored in the next chapter.

FURTHER READING

Gardner, William O. *Advertising Tower: Japanese Modernism and Modernity in the 1920s.* Cambridge, MA: Harvard University Press, 2006.
Gerow, Aaron. *Visions of Japanese Modernity: Articulations of Cinema, Nation, and Spectatorship, 1895–1925.* Berkeley: University of California Press, 2010.

Harootunian, Harry D. *Overcome by Modernity: History, Culture, and Community in Interwar Japan.* Princeton, NJ: Princeton University Press, 1987.

Minichiello, Sharon, ed. *Japan's Competing Modernities: Issues in Culture and Democracy 1900–1930.* Honolulu: University of Hawaii Press, 1998.

Sand, Jordan. *House and Home in Modern Japan: Architecture, Domestic Space, and Bourgeois Culture, 1880–1930.* Cambridge, MA: Harvard University Press, 2003.

Sato, Barbara. *The New Japanese Woman: Modernity, Media and Women in Interwar Japan.* Durham, NC: Duke University Press, 2003.

Schencking, J. Charles. *The Great Kantō Earthquake and the Chimera of National Reconstruction in Japan.* New York: Columbia University Press, 2013.

Silberman, Bernard S., and H.T. Harootunian, eds. *Japan in Crisis: Essays on Taishō Democracy.* Ann Arbor: University of Michigan Press, 1999.

Silverberg, Miriam. *Erotic Grotesque Nonsense: The Mass Culture of Modern Times.* Berkeley: University of California Press, 2006.

Young, Louise. *Beyond the Metropolis: Second Cities and Modern Life in Interwar Japan.* Berkeley: University of California Press, 2013.

RECOMMENDED FILMS

A Page of Madness. 1926. Feature film directed by Kinugasa Teinosuke. Silent avant-garde film depicting life in an asylum.

Eros Plus Massacre. 1969. Feature film directed by Yoshida Yoshishige. Fictionalized biography of anarchist Ōsugi Sakae, considered one of the most representative films of the Japanese New Wave movement.

I Was Born But. 1932. Feature film directed by Ōzu Yasujiro. Silent film about two young brothers who are disillusioned by their father's workplace servility.

In the Realm of the Senses. 1977. Feature film directed by Oshima Nagisa. Explicit treatment of the relationship between the notorious Abe Sada and her lover.

Kagero-za. 1981. Feature film directed by Suzuki Seijun. Tale of a playwright in the 1920s who meets a beautiful woman whom he believes is the ghost of his wife.

Kanikōsen. 2009. Feature film directed by Sabu. Adaptation of well-known short story from the proletarian literature movement, depicting the mutiny of workers, who have been subjected to harsh working conditions, on a crab cannery boat.

10　Cultures of Empire and War

1900s–1940s

The reign of Emperor Hirohito (1926–89), known as the Shōwa era, witnessed the dramatic rise and fall of Japanese military power. The nation achieved success in joining the ranks of the great powers as a colonizing nation just as the territorial grabs of nineteenth-century imperialism were coming to an end. In pursuing expansion, Japan entered a collision course with the other powers. Like earlier imperialists, Japan administered its colonies in a manner that left a mixed legacy of development and repression, uplift and brutality.

Imperialism deeply shaped not just the occupied territories but the metropole itself; the colonizer was as affected by the experience as the colonized. The territories of the empire transformed the Japanese economy and quickly became an important part of Japan's national pride and imagination of self. The empire animated popular culture, with depictions of life and adventure in the colonies in film, literature, and media that prompted tourism in Japanese-held territories. Control of new lands also enabled mass migration, with Japanese agents traveling to labor in all corners of the empire, while subject populations moved to fulfill the home country's labor needs under both voluntary and coercive conditions.

POLITICAL AND SOCIAL DEVELOPMENTS

The European and American imperial powers lauded Japan's unexpected victory in the First Sino-Japanese War (1894–95), which catapulted Japan from semicolonial status to an imperialist nation with its first major colony, Taiwan. The war was fought in Korea. Japanese leaders had long been concerned over the fate of Korea; they called it "a dagger pointing at the heart of Japan," because its proximity to Kyushu meant that if Russia or another power gained control of Korea, it was then but a small step to attack Japan. Hoping to spur its East Asian neighbor to undertake its own path of strengthening and modernization, Japan borrowed from the playbook of Commodore Perry. In 1876, it used "gunboat diplomacy" to force Korea to open to commercial trade under unequal conditions. In 1894, a large religious uprising, the Tonghak Rebellion, threatened Korea's Joseon dynasty. Both China, its traditional protector, and Japan intervened to help quell the violence, coming into conflict themselves. The world expected that the great Qing empire would defeat the upstart nation, but Japan prevailed in less than a year, owing to its heavy investment in modern military training and equipment. The victors imposed a harsh treaty on the Qing, including a massive cash indemnity and cession of Taiwan, the Pescadore Islands, and the Liaodong Peninsula.

Japan's leaders, mass media, and citizenry alike were jubilant over the outcome. They would have to swallow their pride, however, when other nations intervened to reinforce Japan's unequal status with the other great powers. Because the Liaodong Peninsula was prized as a militarily strategic promontory, France, Germany, and Russia forced Japan to return the peninsula to Chinese control in an event known as the Triple Intervention.

Nevertheless, given Japan's new status as an imperialist nation and a modern military power, its leaders were finally able to begin renegotiating the old, unequal treaties, achieving an end to extraterritoriality in 1899, with the promise of regaining full tariff autonomy by 1911. In 1900, when foreign legations were under attack in Beijing during the Boxer Rebellion, a popular religious rebellion that opposed foreign incursions into China, Japan was a major participant in internationally coordinated efforts to defeat the Boxers. Its efforts earned new respect from Great Britain, resulting in the Anglo-Japanese Alliance of 1902, a guarantee that the British Royal Navy would come to Japan's assistance in the event of conflict with a third country. Both viewed Russia as their most likely foe. Following the Triple Intervention, Russia had taken control of the Liaodong Peninsula, and after the Boxer Rebellion, it refused to withdraw a large army from Manchuria, threatening Korean independence. War fever mounted in Japan, with a jingoistic press clamoring to chastise the Russian bear.

With its back covered by the Anglo-Japanese Alliance, Japan attacked Russian ships at Port Arthur in February 1904 and declared war. Battles were brutal, with massive losses on both sides. In the Manchurian city of Mukden, corpses of Russian and Japanese soldiers littered the streets. By spring 1905, nearly fifty thousand Japanese soldiers were dead. A great naval victory turned the situation to favor the Japanese. Admiral Tōgō Heihachirō (1848–

FIGURE 52. Watanabe Nobukazu, print depicting battle at Port Arthur, 1904. Courtesy of Rijksmuseum.

1934) gathered ships in the Tsushima Straits between Korea and Japan to await the Russian fleet, which he successfully annihilated, sinking all battleships and most cruisers while losing just three torpedo boats.

The Battle of Tsushima altered the course of world history. The defeat was a severe blow to the ruling Romanov dynasty and contributed to the mass political and social unrest surrounding the Russian Revolution of 1905. Russia's defeat seriously destabilized the European balance of power, contributing to the onset of World War I. Furthermore, the weakening of the tsar aided the cause of the 1917 revolution that resulted in the creation of the Soviet Union. In the eyes of the world, Japan's victory over Russia heralded its arrival as a major world power. The victory especially attracted attention among nationalists in territories colonized by other nations. Arab, Indian, and Asian nationalist leaders—including Sun Yat-Sen (1866–1925), father of the Republic of China, established in 1911, and Ho Chi Minh (1890–1969), leader of Vietnam's independence movement—found inspiration in Japan's achievement. Colonized peoples everywhere celebrated the first modern Asian victory over a Western power as a strike against white supremacy. It gave nationalists hope that they too might be able to overthrow their colonial overlords.

In August 1905, President Theodore Roosevelt brokered a peace settlement between the exhausted combatants at Portsmouth, New Hampshire, later receiving the Nobel Peace Prize for his efforts. Negotiations were difficult. In the end, Japan compromised in order to avoid more war, some-

MAP 8. Battlefields of the Russo-Japanese War. Published by P.F. Collier & Son, 1904–5.

thing neither country could afford. The Portsmouth treaty gave Japan the Russian leasehold at Port Arthur on the Liaodong Peninsula, the tsar's railroad and mining rights in Manchuria, and sovereignty over the southern half of Sakhalin, an island north of Hokkaido that the Japanese called Karafuto. The Japanese had hoped for a large war indemnity, such as the one received from the Qing, because the conflict had severely sapped national wealth.

Among the ordinary Japanese masses, the Portsmouth settlement was seen as inadequate. The jingoistic press had trumpeted reports about Japan's stunning victories but had not reported the full stories of losses. An outpouring of visual propaganda, including woodblock prints and, increasingly, photography, had kept the public abreast of war events and helped mobilize support. Photographic images of the conflict were widely reproduced in magazines and newspapers and as part of movie newsreels. Tens of millions of war-related postcards were purchased by patriotic countrymen. Wartime imagery was not limited to print but was reproduced on fans, cakes, lanterns, fabrics, toys, and other products. Writer Lafcadio Hearn was surprised that even silk dresses for baby girls might feature scenes of naval battles, burning warships, and torpedo boats.

The people had enthusiastically supported the war: sacrificing their sons, converting their savings to war bonds, and folding good-luck origami for the troops. They felt a personal connection to the war and expected a large indemnity or the cession of a major territory, such as Siberia. The treaty was popularly judged a disgrace, and large crowds gathered in Tokyo's Hibiya Park on the day it was to be signed. Rioting soon broke out and spread throughout Tokyo and other cities, lasting several days. Martial law was declared to restore order, but crowds had already destroyed 250 buildings in Tokyo alone, including the residences of ministers, pro-government newspapers, and police stations. The Hibiya Riots provided indisputable evidence of popular support for Japanese expansionism.

Following the victory, Japan sought to formalize its authority over Korea, forcing representatives to sign a treaty that made the nation a protectorate of Japan, turning over its sovereignty in international diplomacy, police affairs, and the legal system. In 1910, Japan fully annexed Korea as a colony, launching broad transformations to its political, educational, and social structures, mirroring the rapid changes undertaken in Japan during the early Meiji period. Colonial administrators built railways, roads, harbors, a telegraph system, and a modern postal system to support economic development that benefited the homeland. They constructed modern hospitals and a modern education system to replace traditional schools focused on Confucian classics. In theory the Koreans, as subjects of the Japanese emperor, enjoyed the same status as the Japanese; but in fact they were treated as a conquered, inferior people, deprived of freedoms of assembly, speech, and press.

After Germany's defeat in World War I, Japan acquired some of its territories and colonies, including the leasehold on China's Shandong province and the Marshall, Caroline, and Mariana islands in the South Pacific, holdings that the Japanese collectively called Nan'yō (South Seas). In the late 1910s, political liberalization in Japan under Taishō democratic movements began to influence policies and attitudes toward the colonies. Political parties pushed for both more democratic domestic policies and better treatment of colonial populations. Japan's brutal suppression of nonviolent demonstrations in Korea in 1919 brought criticism from around the world. In response, Prime Minister Hara Takashi began to reform colonial administration, emphasizing assimilation of Koreans as fully Japanese. Assimilation policies took several different forms, from teaching the Japanese language in schools to forced attendance at Shinto shrines and pressure to abandon Korean names for Japanese ones. Change was slow, and often deeply resented for its intent to destroy traditional culture.

In the early 1930s, Japan felt a sense of crisis that raised new doubts about capitalism and about the ability of political parties and party-based cabinets to address entrenched social and economic problems. The sense of national emergency was based on two developments: the Great Depression and the Manchurian Incident of 1931, described below, when Japan's Kwantung Army, headquartered at Port Arthur, occupied Chinese territory without approval from their commanders in Tokyo. The renegade soldiers instigated several more incidents in the early '30s that placed Japan firmly on an expansionist path in China, eventually leading the two countries to another war. The fighting in Manchuria erupted when Japan was experiencing the worldwide effects of the depression. Between 1929 and 1931, Japan's exports fell in half and investment in plants and equipment dropped by a third. In the cities, more than a million men and women lost their jobs as big businesses scaled back and medium-sized and small firms collapsed in bankruptcy. Many returned to their home villages but found that rural communities were faring even worse. In the '30s, the perception of national emergency was accompanied by increasingly authoritarian and militarist state policies.

Farms and villages, hard-hit by several years of famine, were seen as the worst victims of the depression. Mass emigration programs seemed to offer a potential solution to the rural economic crisis; Japan had earlier sponsored such programs in Hokkaido and Korea. Many young army officers in the Kwantung Army came from rural families and saw expansion on the continent as a solution for rural distress. Control of Manchuria's rich natural resources would further offer a "lifeline" for Japan.

Kwantung Army officers had presented Tokyo with a plan for expansion in Manchuria, but when told to wait for provocation by the Chinese, they decided to stage their own pretext, dynamiting a section of the South

Manchurian Railway near the city of Mukden on September 18, 1931. They blamed the action on the Chinese, using the ploy to militarily occupy Manchuria. The incident shocked the cabinet in Tokyo. The army minister telegraphed orders to refrain from further hostile acts, but the Kwantung Army continued to expand territorial control, justifying their actions by claiming field command. The public and mass media applauded the army's bold actions and did not question the claims of Chinese instigation. When censured by the League of Nations for its invasion of Manchuria, Japan withdrew from the league and began to abandon treaties and agreements it had signed with other powers. In 1932, a pro-Japanese puppet state called Manchukuo was created to include the captured territories, with Pu Yi (1906–67), the Qing monarch deposed by China's 1911 Republican Revolution, installed as its emperor. By 1945, nearly three hundred thousand Japanese immigrants resided in Manchukuo.

In the early 1930s, thousands of small radical groups proliferated, made up of students, activists, and military officers who condemned the selfishness of party politicians and big business. They envisioned a Shōwa Restoration to push aside a corrupt, incompetent regime, in the spirit of the Meiji Restoration. Societies such as the Cherry Blossom Society (Sakurakai) and the Blood Brotherhood (Ketsudankai) plotted domestic revolution and assassination of political and business leaders who had enriched themselves at the expense of farmers and poor workers. In the May 15th Incident of 1932, eleven young naval officers stormed into Prime Minister Inukai Tsuyoshi's residence and shot him to death. The original plan included killing film star Charlie Chaplin, visiting Japan at the time, but Inukai's son had taken Chaplin to a sumo wrestling match, saving both their lives. The most dramatic event by activists was the February 26th Incident of 1936, an attempted coup d'état in which twenty-one junior officers led over fourteen hundred soldiers in a mission to overthrow the government. Assassination squads shot several important officials; Prime Minister Okada Keisuke barely escaped death, fleeing his house disguised as a woman. Soldiers seized the center of Tokyo and demanded the installation of a cabinet more sympathetic to their aims. The emperor, angry over the murder of high officials, ordered the military to squash the mutiny, and the rebellion was quickly ended. The incident sobered the nation, and after 1936 there were no more large, violent challenges to state authority.

Mishima Yukio (1925–70) authored a short story entitled "Patriotism" (1960) that centers on this incident. The protagonist, a young lieutenant, has been ordered to attack the mutineers, his longtime colleagues, and is torn between loyalty to the emperor and to his friends. He chooses to commit seppuku, asking his wife to serve as his witness, but she vows to die with him. In 1966, Mishima released a highly stylized film of the story. An ardent nationalist who had created his own right-wing militia, Mishima himself committed seppuku in 1970 after a failed attempt at coup d'état.

Newspaper and radio accounts of the period itself, however, created an image of a country united behind its government. A few dissidents expressed opposition to overseas aggression, but they found it increasingly difficult to speak out because of censorship and peer pressure. The mainstream mass media encouraged people to unite behind war and expansion efforts. Majority opinion increasingly called for the preservation of the *kokutai*, or the unique national essence, a vague term that referred to the family-like ties uniting the divine emperor with his loyal subjects. In 1937, the Ministry of Education issued *Kokutai no hongi* (Cardinal principles of the national essence), an official booklet intended to further indoctrinate the Japanese in patriotic values and quell social unrest. Conservatives became increasingly intolerant of anyone who failed to conform to their ideology. This included the scholar Minobe Tatsukichi, whose Taishō-era "organ theory" stated that the emperor was but one organ within the larger body of state. Although this idea had been widely accepted by politicians a decade earlier, in 1935 Minobe was accused of lèse-majesté and his theories were officially condemned by the Diet.

The Home Ministry's Special Higher Police (Tokkō) significantly increased its surveillance and suppression of political and religious groups on both the right and the left, as the government lost tolerance for dissidents of any persuasion who challenged its authority. Communists, socialists, and radical right-wing groups alike were arrested and pressured to publicly renounce their views. Writers associated with the Proletarian Literature Movement, suspected of supporting communism, were arrested and tortured. The 1933 "conversion" *(tenkō)* of jailed Communist Party leader Sano Manabu, who renounced allegiance to the Comintern and pledged his loyalty to the emperor, led to a wave of other defections. The government also cracked down on nonofficial religious groups, arresting leaders of some of the most popular movements. The new religion Oomoto, which claimed eight million supporters, had established its own patriotic society; its membership included Diet members and top military officials. The police feared Oomoto's potential to unite the fragmentary right wing. In December 1935, they launched a massive campaign against the group, arresting over five hundred members and demolishing millions of dollars' worth of property. The Diet then passed a Religious Organizations Law that allowed authorities to dissolve any group judged incompatible with the kokutai. Two other large, nonofficial religions were crushed under the law in 1938 and 1939.

In the summer of 1937, Japan's military expansion in China escalated into all-out war. It began with a skirmish at the Marco Polo Bridge near Beijing in July. When Tokyo was informed, army leaders ordered local commanders to work out a settlement. They believed that war in China would become a quagmire, sucking up manpower and resources and leaving the nation vulnerable to threats from other imperial powers. Chiang Kai-shek (1887–1975), leader of China's Nationalist Party, rejected negotiations. Chiang faced pressure from Mao Zedong's Communist Party, which called for Chiang to join them in a "united front" against Japanese aggression. Ten days after the incident, Chiang delivered a stirring address that concluded, "If we allow one more inch of our territory to be lost, we shall be guilty of an unpardonable crime against our race." In this way, the Bridge Incident was magnified into one that demanded settlement by national governments. Japan responded with a show of force, hoping this might persuade Chiang to back down, but violent clashes broke out between the two sides. By August, the Japanese army occupied Beijing. In Shanghai, Chinese nationalists bombed Japanese settlements and naval installations; the Japanese responded by dispatching additional troops to the continent, leading to a full-fledged war, which continued for eight years, until Japan's defeat by the Allied Powers. By the end of 1938, the Japanese found themselves stalemated. As the situation shifted into a bitter war of attrition, casualties mounted. By 1941, nearly three hundred thousand Japanese and one million Chinese were dead; the war had indeed turned into a quagmire. The Second Sino-Japanese War was the largest Asian war of the twentieth century, resulting in more than 50 percent of the casualties in World War II's Asian theater.

Chiang was strongly backed by the United States. His wife, Soong Mei-Ling, daughter of a wealthy missionary, had attended Wellesley College, where she made many influential friends. Madame Chiang made several U.S. tours to generate support for the Chinese nationalist cause against Japan. In 1943, she addressed both houses of Congress, becoming the first Chinese person and the second woman ever to do so. Her friend Henry Luce, the publishing magnate, whose parents had been missionaries in China, supported her efforts through a torrent of anti-Japanese, pro-Chinese pieces in *Time* and *Life* magazines.

In Japan the hawkish media heralded victories, but the public remained ignorant of atrocities committed by the army in China. The Rape of Nanking—a six-week orgy of arson, brutality, rape, and murder—began in December 1937 after the Japanese captured the nationalists' capital at

Nanking, although Chiang had already escaped, eventually setting up new headquarters in Chongqing. Eyewitness and photographic accounts—from foreign residents, Chinese survivors, and journalists—documented troops engaged in rampant acts of violence against civilians. The extent of the death and destruction remains a sensitive subject and a stumbling block in Sino-Japanese relations today. Foreign observers estimated forty thousand deaths, later histories up to three hundred thousand. A small but vocal group of nationalistic historical revisionists in Japan even denies the massacre altogether, insisting that the Chinese killed in Nanking were all military operatives.

Nanking was not unique, however. Throughout China, Japanese soldiers were ordered to plunder, rape, and murder. In the north, where villagers were suspected of communist sympathies, soldiers tortured peasants, set them on fire, bayoneted pregnant women, and forced children to walk in suspected minefields. Other atrocities occurred at the notorious Unit 731 in the city of Harbin, where biological-warfare tests and chemical experiments were conducted on live human subjects. Test subjects included not only captured soldiers and criminals, but also infants, the elderly, and pregnant women. After infecting them with diseases like plague, cholera, smallpox, syphilis, and botulism, scientists performed vivisections on live victims, amputating limbs and removing organs to study the effects of diseases. Between ten thousand and forty thousand victims died on site; another two to six hundred thousand died as a result of field experiments. Despite the horrendous nature of these war crimes, General Douglas MacArthur (1880–1964), during the postwar occupation of Japan, exempted those who had directed Unit 731 from prosecution so that they could contribute to U.S. intelligence.

In 1940, Japanese officials announced the creation of the Greater East Asia Co-Prosperity Sphere, a zone centered on Japan, Manchukuo, and China but also including French Indochina and the Dutch East Indies. Japan desired access to the resources of these colonies in the Pacific and Southeast Asia because it still depended heavily on the United States, China's ally, for imports of raw materials, machine tools, and especially oil. In 1940, Japan got nearly 80 percent of its fuel from the United States. Southeast Asia offered a treasure trove of raw materials that could free Japan from dependence on increasingly hostile Americans. In September of that year, Japan signed the Tripartite Pact, allying itself with the Axis Powers, Germany and Italy, and its military forces commenced occupation of northern Indochina. The United States countered these actions with economic sanctions that would be lifted only if Japan withdrew from all of China. This was unacceptable for the Japanese, as it would roll back fifty years of hard-won gains. The United

States, followed by several other nations, then issued a total embargo on oil exports to Japan, which meant strangulation of Japan's war in China unless it could gain fuller access to Southeast Asian resources. Japanese leaders began accepting the inevitability of war with the United States, believing that if Japan retreated fully from China, the latter would fall into communist hands, endangering Korea, Manchukuo, and then Japan itself. Furthermore, they imagined that Americans would not have the fortitude to fight a two-front war in Europe and in the Pacific. If Japan could quickly strike the U.S. fleet in Hawaii and gain access to Southeast Asian oil and resources, they could wage a defensive war and eventually negotiate for peace.

After the United States rejected Japan's final efforts for a peaceful resolution, which proposed withdrawal from Indochina and all but a few northern territories in China, the Japanese ratified the call for war and sent their fleet toward Hawaii with orders to strike Pearl Harbor at dawn on December 8, 1941. Japanese pilots were surprisingly successful in their nimble Zero fighter planes. They sank or damaged eight battleships, destroyed nearly two hundred planes, and inflicted nearly four thousand casualties, while losing just a few dozen aircraft and sixty-four men. Just hours after Pearl Harbor, Japanese airplanes destroyed most American aircraft in the Philippines. Two days later, bombers sank British battleships off the Malay Peninsula. Troops occupied Hong Kong on Christmas day and marched into Manila on January 2, where they accepted the surrender of American and Filipino forces. For several months Japan's military seemed invincible; in February they captured Singapore, Britain's "impregnable fortress." They seized control of Sumatra's oil fields and occupied the Dutch capital at Batavia (now Jakarta) and the British capital at Rangoon in Burma. By the end of 1942, however, the American counterattack shifted into high gear.

The vision of a Greater East Asia Co-Prosperity Sphere expressed Japan's opposition to Anglo-American hegemony and contained a pan-Asian racial idealism advocating that Asian nations unite and benefit their own peoples, rather than white imperialists. This idea was welcomed by many colonized Asian nations. Nationalist activists in Burma, Indochina, and Indonesia initially welcomed the Japanese as a means of removing the yoke of their overlords. The Japanese played on these hopes, granting "independence" to territories they occupied, such as Burma and the Philippines. Many nationalist leaders soon found out, however, that the Japanese were as exploitative and brutal as their former colonizers, especially under the harsh conditions of war. The military controlled local economies to prioritize production of energy and war-related materials. Oil from the Dutch East Indies ended Japan's petroleum shortage. The Philippines and Burma supplied metals and minerals.

Rubber and tin came from Thailand and Indonesia. Acquisition policies were carried out only with the needs of the home islands and military in mind, and many early supporters of the Japanese became disillusioned.

Local women, especially, suffered under the so-called "comfort woman" system, the Japanese name for officially condoned military prostitution, instituted to provide for soldiers' "recreation" while monitoring venereal disease. Japanese prostitutes were initially recruited, but too few were available to meet military needs. Recruiters deceived and coerced young women from throughout the occupied territories, enlisting them to work in overseas factories but sending them to primitive brothels instead, where the women were forced to service as many as fifty soldiers per day. Korean women made up the majority of comfort women, but Chinese, Filipina, Malaysian, and Dutch women were also forced into this degrading practice. In all, as many as 250,000 women were brutalized by the system. The autobiography of Maria Rosa Henson, a Filipina, testifies to the tragic conditions of sexual slavery faced by young comfort women:

> Twelve soldiers raped me in quick succession, after which I was given half an hour rest. Then twelve more soldiers followed. . . . I bled so much and was in such pain, I could not even stand up. . . . I could not resist the soldiers because they might kill me. . . . At the end of the day, I just closed my eyes and cried. My torn dress would be brittle from the crust that had formed from the soldiers' dried semen. I washed myself with hot water and a piece of cloth so I would be clean. I pressed the cloth to my vagina like a compress to relieve that pain and the swelling.[1]

Wartime Japanese occupation brought immense carnage and suffering. The Philippines suffered 125,000 civilian and combat-related deaths. Famine under Japanese rule killed hundreds of thousands of Indochinese. A United Nations report estimated that four million Indonesians were either killed by the Japanese or died from hunger, disease, and lack of medical care under Japanese occupation. The number of Chinese soldiers and civilians killed is estimated at a nearly unfathomable nine to twelve million. This was the brutal reality of Japan's ideal of pan-Asian brotherhood; wartime savagery against and mistreatment of civilians remain major reasons why tensions linger between Japan and its Asian neighbors, especially Korea and China, today.

JAPANESE COLONIALISM

During the Meiji period, authorities had extended control over the populations of indigenous Ainu in Hokkaido and the Ryūkyūan islanders of

Okinawa, engaging in a form of domestic colonialism. The Hokkaido Colonization Office opened in 1869 to encourage migration to the northern island and to try to assimilate the native Ainu population. It encouraged ex-samurai families to populate the northern frontier so the outside world would recognize Hokkaido as an indivisible part of Japan, offering loans to buy land and providing settler families with a house, utensils, farm equipment, and a three-year supply of food. Nearly eight thousand ex-samurai settled there. In the 1890s, the office broadened its bid to all classes, offering rent-free homesteads for ten years; the number of new settlers rose substantially.

The Japanese tried to assimilate the native Ainu population by ordering them to stop wearing earrings and tattooing themselves, pressuring them to adopt Japanese clothing and hairstyles instead. Ainu were compelled to assume Japanese names, speak the Japanese language, and worship at Shinto shrines. The state tried to eradicate their hunting-and-gathering lifestyle by teaching them to farm and giving them small plots of land, but Japanese settlers often swindled the Ainu out of their holdings. Many ended up working in fisheries and living in city slums. By the end of the Meiji period, Hokkaido was indisputably Japanese. In 1908, the Ainu constituted only 1.25 percent of the island's population of 1.5 million. Yet while official policy dictated assimilation, mainstream Japanese continued to view Ainu as exotic tourist attractions, and Ainu villages were often part of official anthropological exhibitions intended to contrast Japanese civility with barbarian ways of life.

The Ryūkyū Islands to the south were an independent kingdom and a Chinese tributary state. Satsuma had exercised dominance over the islands during the Tokugawa era, profiting from Ryūkyūan trade with China and Southeast Asia. Ryūkyūan sovereignty was nominally maintained to avoid conflict with China, but in 1871, when the domains were abolished, the Meiji government claimed the islands. In 1879, the last king was forced to abdicate and the Ryūkyūs were formally incorporated into Japan as Okinawa prefecture. As with the Ainu and later colonies, native language, culture, and religion were suppressed as Okinawans were forced to assimilate but never really treated as equals with the mainlanders.

As Japan acquired its first territories overseas, it modeled its colonial policies and actions after Western examples. Nevertheless, the Japanese empire differed from its competitors in several important ways. First, it was a late imperial power and had itself been subject to semicolonial subjugation under unequal treaties. Japan's overriding concern was strategic national security. Aware of its weakness vis-à-vis the other imperialist powers, Japan justified

FIGURE 53.   Postcard depicting Ainu bear festival, 1902–18. Courtesy of Special Collections and College Archives, Skillman Library, Lafayette College, and the East Asia Image Collection.

acquisition of empire as a measure for preserving national independence in a turbulent geopolitical environment. Leaders wanted "buffer zones" to protect the homelands and the new colonies. By contrast, other imperialist nations had predominantly economic motivations, concerned with opening new markets and new investment opportunities on foreign shores. European colonies were often established to protect thriving economic interests, as in British India and the Dutch East Indies. Japan began imperial expansion, by contrast, with a shortage rather than an excess of capital. A second, related difference was the compact size of Japan's empire, especially in comparison to the globe-spanning colonies of Great Britain, France, and the Netherlands. The Japanese empire centered on East Asian neighboring areas to maximize their more limited economic and military resources. A final key difference was the sense of cultural affinity with its subject peoples, particularly in Taiwan and Korea—the idea that Japanese were of the same racial stock and shared cultural and religious beliefs, values, and practices with the peoples of their colonies. This situation, unique among the imperial powers, deeply shaped Japanese attitudes toward colonial governance.

Colonial life is often described through simple binaries of collaboration and resistance, but these do not accurately reflect the reality for many colonized peoples, who usually cooperated with pressures to assimilate, in order to survive or gain advantages, even if they felt sorrow or resentment at loss of local sovereignty. All successful colonial enterprises require a degree of cooperation and support among the colonized. Many of the elite and wealthy among them—who had the most to lose or sensed opportunities for advancement or profit—worked cooperatively with Japanese officials. Most did not then believe they were betraying their nation, but the perception of collaboration with foreign rulers usually became a highly sensitive issue in the years following independence.

The Japanese leadership considered acquisition of overseas colonies as proof of its level of civilization. Like other late empires, including Germany and the United States, Meiji leaders initially studied and often mimicked European colonial practices. They described their colonial holdings in the same derogatory terms—as dirty, noisy, barbaric, and uncivilized. Like their predecessors, they used international law to justify Japanese rule over other peoples, adopting the "civilizing mission" of extending the benefits of civilization to benighted and backward nations. Japanese colonialism, however, was distinct from its Western competitors in a significant manner. Namely, while the European and American colonialists drew a clear line between themselves and those they ruled, emphasizing the "otherness" of colonized peoples, Japanese colonial policy and propaganda emphasized the "sameness" between themselves and their subjects, at least in rhetoric, if not in popular consciousness or popular culture. As the Japanese colonized their East Asian neighbors and the islands of the South Seas, they presented themselves as brothers-in-arms with shared racial and cultural roots who had also suffered from Western imperialism.

Emerging academic disciplines like ethnography and anthropology also helped rationalize the expansion of the empire. Japanese scholars and intellectuals began to conceive of their home islands not as an isolated archipelago but as part of a continuum that included the Asian continent and the Pacific islands. Shared heritage with the peoples of occupied territories was more obviously applicable in East Asia than in the South Seas. Intellectuals began to theorize that the Pacific islands were the birthplace of the Japanese people—in prehistoric times, islanders had traveled across the ocean and became the homeland's original residents. Thus, the Japanese were said to also share roots with their subjects in Nan'yō, who needed their help to civilize and develop, providing a rationale for the expansion of empire.

Taiwan

When Taiwan was ceded to Japan following the First Sino-Japanese War, the Meiji government had no experience as a colonizer and no real long-term objectives for the island. Chinese officials did not seem to consider the island a major loss. Statesman Li Hongzhang reportedly dismissed its cession to Japan by remarking to the Qing empress dowager, Cixi, that "birds do not sing and flowers are not fragrant on the island of Taiwan. The men and women are inofficious and are not passionate either."

Japanese authorities planned to redevelop Taiwan, especially the capital city Taihoku (known today as Taipei), into a model colony to improve Japan's standing among the imperialist powers, in hopes of negotiating revision of unfair treaties. Officials extensively researched European colonial policies and implemented a massive modernization program that established school systems, hospitals, and transportation and communications infrastructures, transforming a backward territory into a modern colonial possession. Taihoku featured tree-lined boulevards, parks, and fountains. The colony was an expensive burden for the fledgling colonial power, however, and had to be made economically self-sufficient as quickly as possible. State monopolies in sugar, camphor, and other agricultural products helped achieve this goal.

The Japanese attempted to win over local leaders by sponsoring tours of the home islands, allowing colonial representatives to witness Japanese modernity in person. Nevertheless, from 1895 to 1915, popular resistance to Japanese rule was high, and the world questioned whether a non-Western nation such as Japan could effectively govern its own colony. In 1897, the Japanese Diet debated whether to sell Taiwan to France. Han Chinese immigrants in Taiwan first resisted the Japanese, engaging in guerrilla tactics to combat colonial rule. After they were suppressed, the colonial regime turned to subduing aborigines in the mountainous interior. In 1909, they launched a genocidal five-year campaign against aboriginal groups. In the 1915 Tapani Incident, Han Chinese and aborigines, united by popular religious beliefs that they were invulnerable to modern weaponry, launched an attack on Japanese police stations. As a result, colonial authorities took steps to ameliorate their rule, but aboriginal tribes continued their resistance nonetheless. In the Musha Incident of 1930, six villages protested forced labor policies by attacking a school athletic event and killing 134 Japanese. Educated, urban Taiwanese also initiated movements for home rule and equal rights, but these were nonviolent and never seriously challenged the colonial order.

There were two distinct views on how Japan should approach ruling Taiwan. The first, supported by the head of civilian affairs, Gotō Shinpei (1858–1929), held that the Chinese and indigenous inhabitants of Taiwan could never be completely assimilated and that the island could not be

FIGURE 54. Mori Ushinosuke, postcard depicting Formosan (Taiwanese) "savages," 1902–18. Courtesy of Special Collections and College Archives, Skillman Library, Lafayette College, and the East Asia Image Collection.

governed like the homeland. The opposing viewpoint, that assimilation and equality were possible, was represented by political party leaders Hara Takashi and Itagaki Taisuke. They believed that the Taiwanese (and later Koreans) were similar enough to the Japanese that the same legal and governmental approaches used domestically should be adopted in the colonies, and that colonial populations should share the same privileges and duties as Japanese citizens.

Gotō, a medical doctor by training, served in a remarkable range of official positions, including as first director of the South Manchuria Railway, seventh mayor of Tokyo, first director of NHK (the state broadcasting company), home minister, foreign minister, and chief scout for the Boy Scouts of Japan. He believed that Taiwanese habits and customs called for distinct policies. Opium addiction was a significant problem, but rather than prohibiting the drug, Gotō designated a licensing system for official suppliers, earning major revenues for the colonial government. Taiwanese elites who cooperated with the regime were granted opium licenses as a reward for loyalty. Colonial policy mainly followed Gotō's approach between 1898 and 1918. Japanese authorities passed special laws and wielded complete executive, legislative, and military power. Japanese colonists, enjoying high levels of expatriate privilege, heavily opposed any attempts to grant the Taiwanese equal rights. Following World War I, however, the perception of colonialism was changing dramatically around the world, with support for national self-determination gaining ground and independence movements among colonies growing across the globe. Most colonial powers began making greater concessions to subject populations.

When Hara Takashi became prime minister in 1918, he appointed Taiwan's first civilian, rather than military, governor-general and advocated pursuit of assimilation *(dōka)*, under which Taiwan would be viewed as an extension of the home islands, and Taiwanese would be educated to understand their role and responsibilities as Japanese subjects. Over the next twenty years, colonial authorities instituted local governance, gave Taiwan seats in the Diet's Upper House, and forbade caning or corporal punishment of islanders by Japanese settlers. Previous administrations had been concerned with demonstrating Japan's civilizational influence by providing railways and sewage systems. They were unconcerned that the Taiwanese were second-class citizens in their own land, abused by Japanese settlers. Dōka initiatives aimed to reduce inequalities. A new public school system for the benefit of Taiwanese was established, encouraging and rewarding the use of the Japanese language. Fifty-seven percent of the population had become literate in Japanese by 1941. With the outbreak of the Second Sino-Japanese War in 1937, efforts to more fully "Japanize" the Taiwanese intensified. Locals were pressured to convert to Shintoism, adopt Japanese names, and volunteer for the Imperial Japanese Army and Navy.

Korea

Meiji-era oligarch Itō Hirobumi was appointed as the first resident-general of the Korean protectorate in 1905. It was the final appointment of the Chōshū statesman's long career, and he hoped to replicate in Korea the achievements he and his fellow oligarchs had engineered in Japan following the Meiji Restoration. With the help of several thousand Japanese officials, he began to forcefully modernize Korea, but the Korean court resented his presence and resisted his efforts. King Gojong sought international support to regain control of Korea, sending representatives to the 1907 Hague Peace Convention to plea for help from foreign governments. Itō ordered Gojong's abdication in favor of his young, weak-minded son, Sunjong (1874–1926). Japan's efforts to build Korean wealth and strength could hardly evoke the same support they received at home during the Meiji period, when they were designed to seek national independence rather than benefit an occupying nation.

Japanese actions in Korea neither surprised nor upset other imperial powers. On the contrary, the disparity between Korean and Japanese power made it seem inevitable. Under the 1905 Taft-Katsura agreement, the United States traded Japan's recognition of American control of the Philippines for American recognition of Japan's superintendence of Korea. As in Taiwan, colonial administrators initiated broad and rapid transformations of Korea's political, educational, and social structures: constructing railways, harbor facilities, roads, and modern telegraph and postal systems to aid in economic development; introducing modern medicine and facilities for improved public hygiene; and replacing traditional schools centered on Confucian classics with a modern educational system. Primary-school enrollments rose from 1 percent in 1910 to 47 percent by 1943. Development benefited Japanese settlers and Korean residents unevenly. By 1940, for example, all Japanese households in the colony had electrical service, compared with only one in ten Korean households.

In addition to the strategic advantages that Japan gained through control of Korea, there were several economic advantages. Fishing, timber, and mining rights were distributed to Japanese firms to facilitate imports of food and raw materials to the home islands. The products of Japan's light industry, such as cotton cloth, watches, buttons, eyeglasses, matches, and kerosene lamps, were exported to a captive Korean market. In addition, the colony provided new job opportunities for the Japanese; by 1908, over 125,000 had taken up residence there. Beyond the bureaucrats and military men, Japanese workers occupied a wide range of positions: laborers sought temporary work in construction or as porters for the army; small merchants peddled Japanese goods at military camps, in village markets, or door to door. Some Japanese settled more permanently, opening small factories to produce leather goods and ceramics. Land confiscated from Korean elites was taken over by Japanese farmers, reducing many Korean peasants to tenancy or forcing them to migrate to Japan or Manchuria for work as laborers. In the cities, Japanese immigrants opened restaurants, teahouses, and brothels catering to the expat community. Economic development brought little benefit to Koreans, as virtually all industries and businesses were owned by Japanese corporations or individuals.

Unlike many Western colonies, in which powerful states exerted control over diverse tribal or ethnically heterogeneous groups in Africa, India, Southeast Asia, and South America, Korea had been a unified country for at least as long as Japan. Furthermore, it shared cultural, religious, and linguistic roots deriving from China with its colonial master. While some elite Koreans welcomed modernization projects and cooperated enthusiastically with the Japanese, others fiercely resisted what they saw as an illegitimate takeover of their homeland. Opposition took different forms. Some high officials committed suicide when Korea became a protectorate. Many former members of the Korean military forces, disbanded by Itō in 1907, turned to guerrilla resistance activity, forming "righteous armies" that fought skirmishes against Japanese police, armies, and armed settlers. Such struggles claimed eighteen thousand Korean and seven thousand Japanese lives. In 1909, a young Korean patriot gunned down Resident-General Itō at a railroad station in Manchuria. His assassination made it clear to Tokyo that Koreans would not cooperate with Japanese control unless more stringent measures were taken. One result was full annexation in 1910 and the appointment of the iron-fisted army general Terauchi Masatake (1852–1919) as Korea's first governor-general.

Following World War I, U.S. president Woodrow Wilson's declaration on the right to national "self-determination" motivated popular protest. On March 1, 1919, a massive assembly gathered in Seoul's Pagoda Park to hear a Proclamation of Independence. The statement included a list of complaints about discrimination against Koreans, including unequal opportunity in education and careers, mistreatment by settlers and officials, and suppression of Korean heritage and language. The crowds erupted, setting off street riots and demonstrations throughout the country, involving an estimated two million Koreans. The Japanese military police could not contain the riots and called in the army and navy to help quell them, resulting in a violent suppression that claimed thousands of Korean lives.

U.S. and European leaders were horrified by the brutality of the campaign and expressed strong critiques of Japan's colonial administration. In response, the governor-general instituted a series of reforms known as "cultural rule" that prioritized assimilation over coercion. Cultural rule permitted limited press freedoms and the formation of labor and political movements while promising better educational and employment opportunities for Koreans. A civilian police force replaced the brutal military police. As in Taiwan, measures to ameliorate colonial life were strongly opposed by Japanese settlers who wished to preserve their own privileges.

By the end of the 1920s, protests declined as the elite and middle classes, educated in Japanese and accustomed to Japanese-controlled mass media, began to identify with the culture of colonial modernity, enjoying the same types of urban entertainment found in the metropole, such as radio and cinema. In the 1930s and '40s, as in Taiwan, the war in China resulted in tighter control and heightened development of heavy industry. Assimilation policy was more rigidly enforced: the Korean language was banned in schools and public offices, and subjects were ordered to take Japanese names and worship at Shinto shrines. Over four million Koreans were drafted,

FIGURE 55. Postcard depicting "Civilized Korea" that combines traditional customs with Japanese modernity, 1907–18. Courtesy of Special Collections and College Archives, Skillman Library, Lafayette College, and the East Asia Image Collection.

coerced, or kidnapped to work in mines and factories in Japan and Manchuria, or as comfort women to serve the Japanese military.

Enforcement of assimilation was accompanied by increased rhetoric on the "sameness" between Koreans and Japanese, who shared common ancestry and linguistic roots, expressed in the official slogan "Japan and Korea as One Body" *(Naisen ittai)*. Koreans were said to be indistinguishable from Japanese in cranial and body measurements. Thus, scholars argued that both Japanese and Koreans were part of a single racial and cultural grouping that encompassed most of North Asia and had originated in archaic times in the Pacific.

Nan'yō

During World War I, Japan seized several groups of Pacific islands—including the Marianas, Carolines, Marshalls, and Palau—that had been ruled by Germany since the late nineteenth century and were highly desirable for their strategic locations. These islands were collectively known as the Nan'yō. The relatively docile populations offered little real resistance to the Japanese naval forces that took control. The islands were poor in natural resources, and any significant economic development was considered infeasible because of their distance from the homeland.

Civilian government of the islands was far less authoritarian than the administration of Taiwan and Korea. Japanese educational and language programs were instituted and were well received by many islanders, but the dispersed nature of territories meant a wide variety in islanders' attitudes toward the Japanese. In Saipan and Palau, deep resentment grew over time. In Saipan, the Japanese developed a plantation economy in sugar and a fishing industry that required large labor forces, but they did not employ indigenous people, considered undesirable workers, instead importing laborers from Okinawa and Korea. Over three decades of rule, the settler population eventually outnumbered indigenous Saipanese by ten to one. Palau, as the seat of colonial government, also experienced a sharp influx in the population of Japanese, causing local frictions. In 1943, when the war reached the Pacific islands, the military population swelled further and made increasingly harsh demands of the islands' inhabitants.

Manchukuo

Unlike the examples above, Manchukuo was never a formal colony of the Japanese; the fiction of the puppet state was created to mask Japanese control of northeastern Chinese provinces. To create an air of legitimacy, the last Qing emperor, Pu Yi, deposed by China's 1911 revolution, acted as the head of state over the historical homeland of the Manchus, founders of the Qing dynasty. Nevertheless, Manchus formed a minority in Manchukuo; the largest ethnic group was Han Chinese. Other large minorities included Koreans, Japanese, Mongols, and Russians.

The Japan-Manchukuo Protocol of 1932 confirmed recognition of Manchukuo as a state and defined a mutual defense agreement, allowing Japanese troops to be stationed there indefinitely. Japanese firms invested heavily in extracting Manchukuo's rich natural resources, and the area soon became an industrial powerhouse, the "lifeline" that could save Japan from its economic woes. Manchukuo's Legislative Council was largely a ceremonial body, created to rubber-stamp decisions issued by the Kwantung Army. The commanding officer of the army served as Japanese "ambassador" to Manchukuo and possessed the power to veto decisions by Pu Yi or his cabinet. The façade of independence was constructed for the sake of international opinion in an era when direct annexation was no longer condoned. Japan wished to misleadingly assure other imperialist powers that it was not pursuing expansion in China, but rather following the demands of local residents in Japanese-occupied territories, who favored partition from China and the return of Emperor Pu Yi.

Pu Yi is one of the most tragic figures of modern Chinese history. Named emperor at the age of three, he was deposed just a few years later by China's Republican Revolution but was initially allowed to keep living within the Forbidden City while receiving a stipend. This arrangement was canceled in 1924 and he was expelled from the palace. In 1931, Pu Yi sent a letter to the Japanese minister of war, expressing his desire to be restored to the throne in a Manchurian state. His wish was granted, but his activities were closely controlled by the Kwantung Army. In 1946, during the Tokyo War Crimes Tribunal, Pu Yi testified against the Japanese, denying all collaboration, claiming that the letter was fake and that he had been kidnapped. In a later autobiography, he admitted that he had falsified his testimony to protect himself. When the Chinese Communist Party came to power in 1949, Pu Yi spent ten years in a prison reeducation camp. After he was declared reformed, he spent the remainder of his life in a modest editorial position. Bernardo Bertolucci's 1987 film *The Last Emperor* beautifully captures the tragedies and ironies of the life of the last ruler of China's final dynasty.

The establishment of Manchukuo as Japan's "lifeline" had far-reaching effects for Japanese society, providing significant new economic and career opportunities during the depression. Hundreds of Marxist and liberal intellectuals, unwelcome in Japan, took bureaucratic or commercial positions that allowed them to pursue progressive social agendas in Manchukuo. The

FIGURE 56. Postcard commemorating Pu Yi's 1935 visit to Tokyo. Courtesy of Special Collections and College Archives, Skillman Library, Lafayette College, and the East Asia Image Collection.

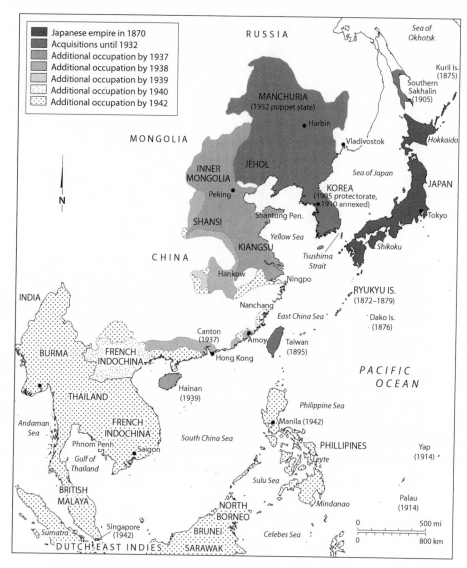

MAP 9. Japanese empire, with dates of expansion.

largest number of emigrants came from the poor tenant-farmer class. An official colonization program envisioned resettling five million impoverished farmers—that goal was never reached, but over three hundred thousand farmers, mostly from hard-hit northeastern provinces, emigrated. The South Manchurian Railway Company, known as Mantetsu, a semi-private organization involved in most aspects of Japanese economic development and control of Manchuria, produced a pamphlet that glorified settler heroism in facing bandits and hardships for the sake of expanding the sacred Japanese empire. It victoriously declared: "We are the apostles who descended to Manchuria from the holy land of Japan. Just as in the ancient age of the gods the children of heaven descended to the home of the gods, now we will build a new home of the gods in a corner of North Manchuria."[2] Such pronouncements confirmed that, despite propagandistic official rhetoric extolling racial equality and opportunity for all Asians, many Japanese believed that a hierarchy of civilizations indeed existed. Their superiority over other Asian nations provided the rationale for aggressive expansion.

COLONIAL CULTURES

Japanese journalists, novelists, and bureaucrats mimicked Western writers and officials in their imagination and representation of savage populations among the colonies they ruled. Their stories emphasized exotic locales and promiscuous local women. Like author Robert Louis Stevenson and artist Paul Gauguin, travelers to Nan'yō fancied themselves romantics fleeing modern civilization for a primitive tropical paradise. Exoticized portrayals of the colonies tended to dominate popular culture about Nan'yō and Taiwan, where aborigines represented only 2 percent of the population but were portrayed disproportionately in literature and media. The image of "the savage" offered writers and artists a romanticized alter ego, a glimpse into their primordial self. The spectrum of colonial barbarity represented ranged from the frightening cannibals among Taiwanese aboriginals to the happy, childlike peoples of Nan'yō. While colonial policy and propaganda claimed racial affinities between the Japanese and their subject populations, depictions of colonial savagery allowed them to imagine that Japan occupied a different temporal space than their backward relations, whose archaic lifestyles were part of Japan's deep past. Thus, some writers argued that Taiwanese headhunters were noble savages, with courage and military skill that recalled the samurai of Japan's bygone days.

Literature

Japanese writers in Taiwan often conveyed romanticized views of the colony and its natives and/or highlighted the primitivism, violence, and superstitions of aboriginal hill tribes for home audiences. Satō Haruo's 1923 tale "The Devilbird" was based on the indigenous legend of a white bird with red claws trained to kill by hereditary lineages of shamanic masters. In reality, those suspected of being bird masters were often persecuted and murdered. Satō recorded a tale he had heard about the victimization of one such family. In their brutal pacification campaigns, the Japanese army would gather all the adult males of a village into a single hut and burn it down. As the army approached one village, its residents blamed the fate they faced on the actions of a family suspected of shamanism. Villagers trapped the family in a hut and set it on fire, but the teenage daughter and son escaped and lived in the forest. The day the daughter died, a rainbow appeared, reportedly to provide her with a bridge to her bird-master ancestors. Nakamura Chihei's 1939 short story "The Mist-Enshrouded Barbarian Village" fictionalized the 1930 Musha Incident, framing the rebellion as the dying gasp of a "pure, simpleminded people." Nakamura used familiar tropes to describe the motivation for Musha: "These barbarians were driven by their evanescent, lingering savageness. They tried one last fight, however ineffectual, against civilization, against a lifestyle that did not suit them."[3]

After several decades of colonial education policy, native Taiwanese writers began emerging as a modern class of intellectuals, educated in Japanese but maintaining cultural ties to China. They wrote literature that explored their hybrid identities, publishing their works alongside Japanese writers in local journals such as *Bungei Taiwan* (Literary Taiwan). Two different strands were apparent in the local literary scene. One group of writers, active especially in the 1920s and '30s, maintained ties to their Chinese roots and were critical of colonial policies, although heavy censorship dictated that their critiques be indirect. Another group, ascendant in the '40s, advocated embracing assimilation and becoming true imperial subjects.

Among the first group, the works of Yang Kui highlighted the social and economic inequities of the colony and expressed anti-imperialist views. His short story "Water Buffalo" describes the colonial government's program of confiscating domesticated buffalo from Taiwanese peasants in order to send them to Nan'yō to aid in plantation development. The narrator is a student who has returned to his home village for the summer and strikes up a friendship with a young girl who used to care for her family's now seized livestock. With the loss of the family's livelihood, the girl's father plans to sell his daughter to the polygamous father of the narrator. Lu Heruo's 1935 story "The Oxcart" similarly describes how an oxcart driver has been driven out of business by Japanese cars and trucks. In order to earn funds and buy a plot of land to farm, his wife must become a prostitute. The story concludes with the driver being fined for using his old cart on modern roads. In these stories, local characters are trapped by both oppressive colonial economic policies and patriarchal Chinese social practices. Japanese-educated elite Taiwanese who observed these conditions expressed frustration over both colonial inequities and the rigidity of tradition.

In the early 1940s, some Taiwanese writers turned to the question of how to become better imperial subjects. Writers whose entire education had been in Japanese, many of whom had also lived in Japan, believed in the benevolence of their colonial masters and sought their approval—which would earn them scorn as collaborators in the postcolonial era. "Volunteer Soldier," an award-winning story by Zhou Jinpo, epitomizes the "imperial subject" movement in literature. Zhou spent his childhood in Japan but returned to the colony after the Great Kanto Earthquake of 1923. The protagonist of the story has returned to Taiwan after studying in Japan and feels uncomfortable with the cultural backwardness of his home. He debates the most effective means for truly Japanizing Taiwan with a childhood friend. The narrator believes it best to raise the level of local culture, while his friend advocates joining the Patriotic Youth Brigade and achieving spiritual union with Japanese deities through worship at Shinto shrines. Shortly after their conversation, the friend volunteers for the Japanese army, earning the deep respect of the narrator. The story reflects Taiwan's military recruitment system, initially fully voluntary but more coercive over time. In wartime, those who failed to volunteer were expelled from school and forced into war-related factory labor.

Like their Taiwanese colleagues, many Korean colonial authors held complex attitudes about their cultural hybridity and many received their higher education at elite Japanese institutions, where they were immersed in both Western literary theories and Japanese modernist writing. They endeavored to develop a unique Korean literary voice that articulated their own anxieties as ethnically and racially separate from the Japanese and thus subject to discrimination, yet culturally and intellectually the peers of their masters. The sad saga of author Yi Kwangsu (1892–1950) demonstrates the complexity and instability of colonial intellectual identity. Yi was a leader of the 1919 movement, had studied at prestigious Waseda University in Tokyo, and seemed destined to become a nationalist leader. But in the 1920s, he suddenly returned from Japan and withdrew from the independence movement. After an arrest for nationalist activity in 1937, Yi transformed into an enthusiastic proponent of Japanese rule, becoming one of the first to change his name, urging Koreans to volunteer for the Imperial Japanese Army and celebrating the sacrifices of Japan's kamikaze pilots. After Korea gained independence, he was ostracized as a collaborator. During the Korean War (1950–53), when North Koreans briefly occupied Seoul, they rounded up collaborators, including Yi, and sent them north to be imprisoned. He died in a prison in Pyongyang in 1950.

Yi's 1917 work *Mujong (The Heartless)* is often considered the first modern Korean novel. It was serialized in the colony's sole Korean-language newspaper and became an immediate sensation. The plot centers on a love triangle. A shy, chaste young man teaching English at a middle school is torn between two women, the traditionally raised daughter of his mentor, who was forced through family misfortune to become a *kisaeng* entertainer (like geisha, kisaeng sang, danced, and played music for patrons), and a modern young woman from a Christian family who planned to study in the United States. When the kisaeng is raped, she decides to commit suicide, as she is no longer pure enough to marry the teacher, but is saved by a chance encounter on a train when a modern young woman urges her to reconsider. Like Yi's other early works, *Mujong* addresses conflicts between traditional ideals and colonial modernity. The narrative is highly critical of the custom of arranged marriage, which resulted in husbands who kept concubines and frequented kisaengs, while their oppressed wives contemplated suicide.

Writer Yom Sang-sop was also educated in Tokyo. His 1924 short story "On the Eve of the Uprising" expresses the anxiety and melancholy of cosmopolitan Koreans forced to return to colonial existence. The protagonist, a student in Tokyo, receives a telegram that his wife is dying and that he must return home. Before departing, he dawdles in the city, visiting his favorite café waitress and shopping for gifts at department stores. During the journey from Tokyo to Shimonoseki to Pusan, he must confront ethnic discrimination and his hybrid identity. On the train from Tokyo, he can pass unnoticed as a Japanese, but on the ferry from Shimonoseki, where people of different classes and ethnicities intermingle, he overhears anti-Korean slurs—yet feels himself superior to money-grubbing Japanese hoping to earn profits by exploiting Korean resources and labor. At a train stop in Korea, he observes a group of mournful Korean criminals in the custody of Japanese police, including a woman with a baby on her back, prompting the narrator to exclaim that his homeland is a graveyard: "A graveyard swarming with maggots! . . . all will be decomposed by the maggots and become particles and soil, and it will enter my mouth and your nose. . . . Be gone! Be removed; not even a sprout left! Collapse! Be ruined! When it all ends there might emerge someone who will make a little better of a man."[4] The impending death of the narrator's wife and legal troubles he faces over his family's burial site under colonial law support the theme of his homeland as a graveyard, where colonial rule is decomposing and degrading the Korean nation.

From the early twentieth century, Japanese traveled to Nan'yō in search of adventure or riches, their imaginations fired by depictions in Japanese popular culture of a primitive tropical paradise. Meiji educator Nitobe Inazō

FIGURE 57.   Shimada Keizō, illustration from *Bōken Dankichi*, 1934. Dankichi is depicted leading a native to a Shinto shrine.

saw Japan's role in the South Seas as a form of manifest destiny. He used the famous folktale of Momotaro the Peach Boy as a metaphor for Japanese expansion. In the original story, a boy born from a peach is adopted by a childless old woman. He eventually leaves home to travel to Ogre Island, planning to capture riches held there. Nitobe interpreted Ogre Island as Japan's constantly receding frontier and portrayed Momotaro's journey there as a "homecoming," in which he encounters "proto-Japanese" people.

Daring Dankichi (Bōken Dankichi), a popular 1930s boys' manga comic and animated film series, depicted Japan's role in Nan'yō. Dankichi is an ordinary boy who falls asleep while fishing with his friend Kariko the rat. They awake after drifting far away to a Nan'yō island inhabited by dark-skinned primitives. Dankichi discards his schoolboy uniform for a grass skirt but keeps his shoes and wristwatch, emblems of his more advanced civilization. He proceeds to dazzle the natives with his intelligence and ingenuity and they make him their king, but he cannot distinguish between his dark subjects, who have names like Pineapple and Banana. His solution is to use the sap of a rubber tree to paint white numbers on their chests. For audiences, *Dankichi* represented the desire to bring civilization to ignorant peoples by demonstrating Japanese superiority. Critics have noted how stories like *Dankichi* freely jumbled the floras, faunas, and populations of a diverse range of cultures from Africa, India, and South America, along with the South Pacific, creating wildly inaccurate stereotypes of the actual colonial territories in Nan'yō.

Film

Film is widely recognized as an especially powerful medium for propaganda. The government used film and other media to mold domestic popular consensus behind the war effort and to justify its actions to the peoples of Asia. Two primary messages were stressed in propaganda films: that Japan had a sacred mission to wage war against the West in order to liberate the people of Asia and enable all nations to be at peace; and that the West was immoral, racist, culturally imperialistic, and ambitious to dominate the East. To ensure that people understood these messages correctly, officials increased their control of the mass media, censoring stories that suggested popular discontent or pessimism. Propaganda via print, radio, film, and even children's literature was a powerful weapon that targeted human emotions, encouraging Japanese subjects to think and behave in a manner supporting the state's wartime goals.

Beginning around the 1910s, the major Japanese film studios established movie theaters in Taiwan and Korea. By the end of 1945, there were sixteen theaters in Taipei alone. Studios were even more active in Korea. The largest—Nikkatsu, Shochiku, and Tekine—established branch offices in Seoul for distribution and production. Colonial officials believed that films provided an effective tool for both indoctrinating colonial subjects and managing the colony's image internationally. Unlike literature or theater, the mass colonial populace could grasp films without knowing the Japanese language. They could actually see how modern life in Japan appeared, thus learning to appreciate the superiority of their colonial masters while envisioning their own future potential. Authorities sponsored film screenings that usually combined educational and feature films. Educational films might explain colonial structures, presenting figures like the police or teachers as helpful, enlightened forces for civilizing the colony. The Korean

Colonial Cinema unit produced around two films per month that were intended to "spread a correct understanding" of Korea to Japan while making the "mother country familiar to Koreans by introducing them to Japanese scenery."[5]

Feature films about Taiwan and Korea, however, were not very popular with Japanese audiences. By contrast, movies about Manchuria, which were shot on location and typically told a "wild west" story about frontiers inhabited by bandits and treacherous Chinese, had been popular since the 1920s. The semiofficial Manchurian Motion Picture Corporation, known as Man'ei, was established in 1937 and quickly became the most extensive film facility in Asia, with a stable of well-established stars and its own studio film magazine. Man'ei successfully competed with Japanese, Chinese, and European films in its home markets because it made films by and for Manchurians, intended to entertain rather than propagandize.

Around 1941, the Japanese film industry announced the Greater East Asia Film Sphere, which would produce films that represented the pure "Oriental spirit" and protect Asian film markets against the decadent products of Hollywood. As with the Co-Prosperity Sphere, Japanese leadership of this sphere was assumed. Films were often set in China, with Japanese protagonists constructing modern roads and canals to help backward people in underdeveloped areas lead better lives. A classic example of the genre is 1940's *Vow in the Desert*. Its hero, Sugiyama, is a Japanese engineer sent to build a road from Beijing to Xian. As he and his Chinese colleague Yang stand on the Great Wall, watching camels cross the sands below, Yang calls the wall "a useless colossus" because "you can't drive a truck over it." Sugiyama responds, "Why don't we build a Great Wall that you *could* drive a truck on. A modern Great Wall that could stand up to this one." The gist is clearly that Japanese technological and engineering accomplishments have superseded China's ancient glories and hold the key to China's future well-being.

This film and others set in China and Manchuria made a star of actress Yamaguchi Yoshiko (1920–2014), better known as Ri Kōran, a Japanese national born and raised in Manchuria. A bilingual beauty with a strong singing voice, she could change costumes or languages to play characters that were Chinese, Manchurian, Korean, and even Russian, and she soon became a popular star throughout Asia. Her Japanese identity was hidden by Man'ei to heighten her appeal to Chinese and Manchurian audiences. Yamaguchi often starred in interracial love melodramas that formulaically featured a strong Japanese male who captures the heart of a beautiful, feisty local woman, metaphorically representing Japan's hopes in Asia. In 1940's

China Nights (Shina no yoru) she plays Keiran, an upper-class Chinese woman who has lost her parents and home to Japanese bombs and has resorted to begging on Shanghai streets. She despises Japan and initially cannot see the good intentions of the Japanese boat captain Hase, yet after he slaps her face to bring her to her senses, she falls in love with him. The film was released in different national versions: in China, the couple lives happily ever after, while in the Japanese version Keiran commits suicide.

The Film Law of 1939 abolished films considered sexual, frivolous, or as commenting on sensitive issues. Instead, films were to elevate patriotism and present the wartime situation appropriately. Propaganda films for the home front were often sentimental and melodramatic, depicting hardships and suffering associated with war to elicit empathy from the audience. Unlike U.S. propaganda films that tended to portray the American military as invincible, Japanese films often portrayed their own military as the underdog. A common storyline depicted how families coped when a son or father went off to war or died honorably for his country. One classic, 1940's *Chocolate and Soldiers*, depicts a father-son relationship during the war in China. While fighting at the front, the father takes the time to regularly send chocolate to his son, who reciprocates this paternal concern by mapping the movements of his father's platoon. The depiction of their mutual devotion and sacrifice touched audiences' heartstrings and was designed to inspire support for the troops. Another frequent theme of wartime films was self-sacrifice, giving up individual desires for the greater good. Kurosawa Akira's propagandistic work *The Most Beautiful* (1944), which opens with a screen reading "Attack and Destroy the Enemy," depicts the lives of teenage girls living in a dormitory while working at a factory producing optical equipment for weapons. The film portrays their patriotic fervor in refusing to miss work, even when ill or when a family member dies at home. Every morning the girls recite a pledge, "Today we will do our best to help destroy America and Britain." Other films attempted to generate sympathy for soldiers on the front; 1939's *Fighting Soldiers* and *Mud and Soldiers*, for example, both display the endless tedium and emotional exhaustion that characterized soldiers' lives in China.

Animated features were also used as vehicles to glorify Japan's civilizing mission and war against the immoral West. The epic *Momotaro: Divine Soldiers of the Sea (Momotaro umi no shinpei*, 1945) employs animal characters, including dogs, rabbits, bears, and monkeys, to represent members of Japan's military forces. After completing their training at home, the forces are stationed on a Pacific island, where they construct an airbase with the help of the locals, portrayed as jungle animals such as elephants, cheetahs, and crocodiles. The simplistic natives are eager to share their food and resources with the glamorous new arrivals. A key sequence depicts a soldier attempting to teach the savage animals the Japanese syllabary, resulting in chaos. When he sets his lesson to music, however, the natives finally begin to understand and begin to sing along while cooperating with the military: doing their laundry and cooking, and engaging in other forms of heavy or menial labor for the benefit of the clearly superior Japanese. When the Japanese general, Momotaro, leads an attack on an Allied fort, cowardly British soldiers panic and quickly surrender to Japanese rule.

Museums

Museums were deployed throughout the empire to celebrate Japanese achievements and demonstrate their stewardship of the arts and resources of their colonial possessions. Exhibits worked to position Japan as an advanced and civilized metropole, placing Korea, Taiwan, and other colonies hierarchically beneath the homelands as regions with an inferior status. The first museum opened in Taiwan in 1908, with the aim of educating the public on the island's natural resources and promise for industrial development. Exhibits emphasized natural sciences, such as geology, botany, zoology, and maritime resources; they minimized historical ties between Taiwan and China. Museum contents were, however, at odds with those of Taiwan pavilions at Japanese expositions, which highlighted primitive or exotic aspects of island life, from opium smoking to aboriginal head hunting. In 1915, the museum began to include more anthropological materials on indigenous groups and their "ancient customs," which were being eradicated through Japan's civilizational influence. During the 1920s and '30s, colonial authorities constructed a network of prefectural and municipal museums throughout the colony that collectively presented an imperial version of Taiwanese history and heritage. These museums identified Taiwan with nature and the primitive, in contrast with the culture and modernity of the homeland.

In Korea, three museums were established on palace grounds in Seoul, displacing the royal family and opening previously exclusive spaces to the general public. Museum exhibits tended to emphasize the ties between Japan and Korea in ancient history and suggest the colony's more recent decline. The Yi Royal Family Museum, opened in 1909, exhibited ancient arts, including calligraphy, Buddhist imagery, and especially pottery. Celadons from the Goryeo dynasty (918–1392) dominated pottery collections and were deemed the "quintessence of Korean art," suggesting that the current Yi dynasty was responsible for Korea's artistic deterioration.[6]

The Government-General Museum of Korea opened in 1915 to celebrate the fifth anniversary of annexation. It featured archaeological treasures that revealed ties between ancient Japan and the Korean Peninsula. A 1938 official report on the museum, in English, stated:

> Tyosen [Korea], one of the oldest countries of the Orient, was once a highly advanced nation from which Japan learned many arts and crafts. . . . Though Japan was always ready to lend a helping hand to Tyosen in the maintenance of her independence and in the promotion of her welfare, Tyosen was utterly unable to stand on her feet owing to long years of misgovernment, official corruption, and popular degeneration. . . . [I]n view of the situation Japan came to the conclusion that the best way to save Tysosen was by making her a Japanese protectorate.[7]

The Yi Royal Museum of Fine Arts opened in Deoksu Palace, a former residence of the king, in 1933. It showcased modern paintings, sculptures, and fine craftwork, all created by Japanese artists. It purported to guide and educate aspiring Korean artists, but it served to emphasize the difference in status and perceived levels of accomplishment.

By 1932, museums in colonial Karafuto and Japanese-controlled territories in Guangdong China joined Taiwan's four and Korea's six museums. These featured confiscated artifacts from nobility, temples, and aboriginal peoples and engaged in research that justified Japanese expansionism.

Tourism and Consumption

Tourism and consumption provided other avenues for the Japanese and their colonial subjects to expand their relationship with the empire. Department stores in both Japan and the colonies regularly featured exhibitions on occupied territories. A 1939 exhibition on Karafuto at Tokyo's Isetan contained a life-sized diorama of a traditional village; department stores in Taipei and Manchukuo featured exhibitions on Korea. Nearby tourism desks could assist spectators with planning travel to visit these places themselves. Japanese imperial consumers developed passions for Korean folk arts and folk music, such as the hit song "Arirang." Fondness for Korean folk culture reflected a nostalgic view that Korea still maintained the "beautiful customs of the past," lost in Japanese modernity.

Popular enthusiasm for visiting imperial heritage sites in the homelands and colonies was stimulated through the booming travel industries, which produced a flood of tourist publications and promotional films. Domestically, prefectures competed among themselves to earn official recognition of (often mythological) imperial sites, such as the starting point of legendary

Emperor Jimmu's campaign to unify Japan. Intra-empire tourism was aided by developments in transportation, including commercial flights that allowed well-heeled Japanese travelers to reach Korea in six hours and Manchukuo in nine. Passenger steamships and a comprehensive system of railway networks offered more affordable travel alternatives.

Colonial authorities promoted tours as a way for imperial subjects to experience exotic cultures in safe, Japanese-controlled spaces with familiar amenities, such as Japanese restaurants, hot-spring resorts, and department stores. Korean itineraries featured visits to experience unspoiled nature in the Diamond Mountains (Kongōsan). Tours of Seoul were conducted by female bus guides in traditional costume who pointed out ancient sites, like the city's South Gate (Namdaemun) and Pagoda Park, along with markers of Japanese domination, such as the Chōsen and Keijō Shinto shrines and the museums and gardens built on sites confiscated from the royal family. Tourist tastes for exoticism were fulfilled through visits to the pleasure quarters, where kisaeng performed traditional songs and dances; by eating Korean specialties like grilled meat *(yakiniku)* and barbecued beef ribs *(kalbi);* and by buying local handicrafts. Another popular tourist activity was taking commemorative photos dressed in local costumes. The consumerist taste for experiencing cultural difference existed in tension with official assimilationist rhetoric emphasizing sameness.

Tours to Manchuria became popular in the early twentieth century and focused on sites from the First Sino-Japanese War and the Russo-Japanese War. The most important was Port Arthur, the location of gripping war campaigns that sealed Japan's destiny as an imperialist power. Battlefield monuments in major cities were considered sacred sites that validated Japanese control of Manchuria by reminding visitors of the sacrifices made. Mantetsu railway funded trips throughout Northeast Asia for famous writers, such as Natsume Sōseki, Akutagawa Ryūnosoke, Yosano Akiko, and Tanizaki Jun'ichirō, who published travelogues or articles about their journeys through Manchuria and Mongolia. After 1931's Manchurian Incident and subsequent Japanese occupation, many more facilities were constructed for tourist comfort. In Manchukuo's modern new capital, Shinkyō (Xinjing in Chinese, known as Changchun today), visitors could choose among hotels and restaurants in Japanese, Chinese, Korean, and Western styles. Many visitors played golf or attended horse races. For exotica and souvenirs, tourists favored the cities of Mukden, where they could view the mausoleums of Manchu Qing emperors; and Dairen, where they could shop at chaotic traditional street bazaars.

OTHER ASPECTS OF CULTURE ON THE HOME FRONT

On the Japanese home front, the state organized labor to support war-related industries, taking control of wages to channel workers into strategically important economic sectors. The military's manpower needs, however, were paramount. By August 1945, 7.2 million men had been drafted for military service. As factories lost workers, coercive methods were needed to obtain factory labor. A National Mobilization Law authorized the state to register males aged sixteen to fifty-nine and unmarried females from twelve to thirty-nine as potential conscripts for factory work. Women were never actually drafted, but they were intensely pressured into "volunteering" for war-related work and entered heavy industries in higher numbers than ever before. As labor shortages mounted, the state turned to schools, drafting millions of middle and high school students for labor at munitions factories. Prisoners of war and forced labor from Korea and other colonies filled the shoes of drafted workers in dangerous, arduous jobs such as coal mining.

To build popular support for the war, state agencies began to create mass organizations. Sanpō, an organization for industrial laborers, made certain that workers understood production targets, ran consumer cooperatives, and dispensed extra rations of sake and rice to diligent employees. Membership climbed from 3.5 million in 1940 to nearly 6.5 million by the end of the war. Following Sanpō's success, patriotic associations were created for nearly every occupational, age, and gender group in the country. Farmers, writers, and ikebana teachers alike were herded into their own associations. The Greater Japan Young Adults Corps, composed of fourteen million males from ten to twenty-five years of age, was charged with cleaning parks and repairing roads and schools. The Greater Japan Women's Society mandated membership for single women over age twenty and all married women. It had nearly nineteen million members, responsible for arranging send-offs, assembling care packages for soldiers at the front, and engaging in national defense activities. Members vowed to forgo extravagance and promote frugality by, for instance, renouncing permanent hairstyles that wasted precious chemicals or preparing Rising Sun *bento* lunches—consisting simply of white rice with a red pickled plum in the center to resemble the Japanese flag—for their families. A postcard promoting women's defense activities reads, in part, "C'mon enemy aircraft, we're ready for you! We can rely on the brave, firefighting girls in *monpe* pants. With them protecting our skies, we are safe."

Buddhist institutions also mobilized for war. Their involvement in war may shock those who expect Buddhists to universally advocate peace and

FIGURE 58.   Nitta Yoshiko, postcard depicting firefighting activities of Neighborhood Home Defense Brigade, 1940s. Courtesy of Special Collections and College Archives, Skillman Library, Lafayette College, and the East Asia Image Collection.

FIGURE 59.   Propaganda poster labeled "Sacrifice and Gratitude on the Home Front," depicting the Rising Sun *bento,* 1937. Courtesy of Special Collections and College Archives, Skillman Library, Lafayette College, and the East Asia Image Collection.

nonviolence, but it is not fundamentally different from Christian churches' support of American military ventures during and after World War II. It is important to recall that Japan's Buddhist institutions had been closely tied to the state for over a millennium. After the suppression of Buddhism during early Meiji, most Buddhist leaders expressed strong support of imperialist expansion. Japanese Buddhist philosophers contorted doctrines on self-lessness into teachings that advocated unquestioning obedience to the state, encouraging soldiers to give their lives without hesitation or regret—or face religious punishments.

Propaganda directed toward children included textbooks, manga comic magazines, and *kamishibai* ("paper theater"), a form of storytelling. Itinerant kamishibai practitioners set up easels on street corners and used a sequence of illustrated boards to help explain their stories. They earned a living by selling candy to children in the audience. Cheaper than movies and more accessible than radio, kamishibai was an excellent tool for indoctrination. In 1933, there were reportedly 2,500 such storytellers, who performed up to ten times a day in Tokyo alone. They helped persuade millions of children that the war was glorious through tales of heroic soldiers who sacrificed their lives on battlefields, becoming "gods of war" who made their families proud. More practical stories instructed children on how to respond to air-raid warnings or urged them to save money, obey their parents, and keep physically fit to maintain their "fighting spirit." Kamishibai were also specifically produced for children in colonial territories, where stories centered on praise for the "paradises" achieved under Japanese rule.

In summary, the acquisition of colonies through war and other means helped lift Japan's economy and international status to that of the major imperialist powers. Governance of Japan's colonies resembled that of territories held by other nations, exploiting native labor and resources while building up facilities to benefit the homeland and Japanese residents. Unlike the other powers, however, Japan also promoted the ideal of full assimilation, deemed a possibility because of purported racial and cultural similarities between colonizer and colonized. In the 1930s, as the Great Depression and rural crisis spurred cries for greater expansion on the continent, Japanese forces seized several provinces in northern China, creating a puppet state that provided invaluable natural resources to Japan. Conflict with China erupted into a brutal, all-out war in 1937, followed by the onset of the Pacific War with the United States and its allies, which opposed Japan's expansionist policies. To support war efforts, increasingly harsh

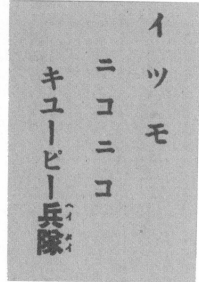

FIGURE 60.   Children's alphabet card for the letter "I" that reads "The Kewpie Soldier is always smiling brightly," 1935. Courtesy of Special Collections and College Archives, Skillman Library, Lafayette College, and the East Asia Image Collection.

demands were made of colonies and newly occupied territories in Southeast Asia.

Japanese of all classes and ages embraced their nation's role as a world power, destined to dominate Asia. Conditioned by both the state and mass media, they believed in the righteousness of Japan's cause and did their part to assist with war efforts. Peer pressure and official intimidation made it difficult to dissent, but most Japanese had no wish to do so; they were patriotic supporters of their nation. Most never imagined, however, the scale of destruction that would accompany their defeat.

FURTHER READING

Aso, Noriko. *Public Properties: Museums in Imperial Japan*. Durham, NC: Duke University Press, 2014.

Baskett, Michael. *Attractive Empire: Transnational Film Culture in Imperial Japan*. Honolulu: University of Hawaii Press, 2008.

Ching, Leo T.S. *Becoming "Japanese": Colonial Taiwan and the Politics of Identity Formation*. Berkeley: University of California Press, 2001.

Duus, Peter. *The Abacus and the Sword: The Japanese Penetration of Korea, 1895–1901*. Berkeley: University of California Press, 1998.

Fujitani, Takashi. *Race for Empire: Koreans as Japanese and Japanese as Americans during World War II*. Berkeley: University of California Press, 2013.

Henry, Todd A. *Assimilating Seoul: Japanese Rule and the Politics of Public Space in Colonial Korea, 1910–1945*. Berkeley: University of California Press, 2014.

Kleeman, Faye Yuan. *Under an Imperial Sun: Japanese Colonial Literature of Taiwan and the South*. Honolulu: University of Hawaii Press, 2003.

Soh, C. Sarah. *The Comfort Women: Sexual Violence and Postcolonial Memory in Korea and Japan*. Chicago, IL: University of Chicago Press, 2009.

Tansman, Alan. *The Aesthetics of Japanese Fascism*. Berkeley: University of California Press, 2009.

Tierney, Robert. *Tropics of Savagery: The Culture of Japanese Empire in Comparative Frame*. Berkeley: University of California Press, 2010.

Uchida, Jun. *Brokers of Empire: Japanese Settler Colonialism in Korea, 1876–1945*. Cambridge, MA: Harvard University Press, 2014.

Young, Louise. *Total Empire: Manchuria and the Culture of Wartime Imperialism*. Berkeley: University of California Press, 1999.

RECOMMENDED FILMS

Japanese Devils. 2001. Documentary film directed by Matsui Minoru. Interviews with former Japanese soldiers who committed war crimes in China.

Millennium Actress. 2001. Animated feature film directed by Kon Satoshi. Tale of an actress, loosely based on the life of Setsuko Hara, who moves to Manchukuo in the 1930s.

Nanking. 2007. Documentary film directed by Bill Guttentag. Combines actors reading from the diaries and letters of Western missionaries and business-men during the Rape of Nanking with archival footage and interviews with survivors.

Senso Daughters. 1989. Documentary film directed by Sekiguchi Noriko. Investigates the exploitation of local comfort women in Papua New Guinea.

The Human Condition. 1959–61. Feature film directed by Kobayashi Masaki. Epic film trilogy based on a series of novels by Gomakawa Junpei on the travails of a pacifist who moves to Manchuria and is drafted by the Kwantung Army.

The Last Emperor. 1987. Feature film directed by Bernardo Bertolucci. Lavish film based on the autobiography of Pu Yi, from childhood to life under the Japanese regime to rehabilitation by China's Communist Party.

11 Defeat and Reconstruction

1945–1970s

World War II ended in tragedy and devastating loss for the Japanese. Their country's infrastructure and economy were largely demolished and they faced military occupation by their former enemies. In the sweep of Japanese history, the occupation years (1945–52) stand with the national reunification under the Tokugawa and the Meiji Restoration as one of the country's great turning points. During those seven years, Japan experienced changes as profound and rapid as those found in any revolutionary period in modern world history: people's rights became constitutionally guaranteed, the military was limited to national self-defense, and massive land and labor reforms improved the prospects of the working classes. The occupation, nevertheless, also represents years of hardship and deprivation for many Japanese. The legacy of being made second-class citizens in their own nation left long-lasting scars.

In 1956, the Japanese government famously declared that the postwar period was "over." Indeed, beginning in the late 1950s, there was noticeable improvement in the lifestyles of ordinary Japanese as economic growth began to benefit the masses. Consumption of appliances, fashionable clothes, and varied diets containing more meat, dairy, and processed foods represented a "bright new life" *(akarui seikatsu)* based on the American lifestyles made visible through imported movies and TV programs. The notion (or myth) that Japan was composed of middle-class consumers leading homogeneous lifestyles—possessing the same consumer goods and engaging in the same leisure activities—became prevalent. This "middle mass" society was celebrated as a demonstration of Japanese achievements in creating a democratic, equality-oriented society. This image, however, ignored both the continuity of conservative gender norms, based in prewar ideals, and the voices of the disaffected, which erupted in major protests on several occasions through the decades.

318

POLITICAL AND SOCIAL DEVELOPMENTS

The Battle of Midway, in June 1942, cost the Imperial Japanese Navy four irreplaceable aircraft carriers; afterward, Japan's shipbuilding and pilot-training programs could not keep pace with military losses. More significantly, American industry had responded very positively to the challenge of war. American war-related manufacturing churned out ten times as many weapons as Japan.

Its resources depleted, the Japanese military turned to desperate tactics, sacrificing its soldiers in a heroic but tragic attempt to slow the enemy's advance. In autumn 1944, special attack squads *(tokkōtai)*, popularly known as kamikaze, were created as a national strategy for a final defense of the homeland. The term *kamikaze*, or "divine wind," referred to the storms caused by Japanese deities to drive off Mongol attacks in the thirteenth century. Twenty-three volunteers took off on the first mission to crash-dive their bomb-laden Zero fighters into American battleships. They succeeded in sinking one carrier and damaging several others. More squadrons were then quickly recruited, and new vehicles of attack, including mini-submarines and motorboats, were equipped with bombs, but very few managed to inflict any damage. The kamikaze became the principal means of self-defense in the final years of the war, but their sacrifices did little to slow the Americans. By the end of the war, nearly five thousand young men had died on their missions.

When the Americans were within striking distance of Japan's home islands, they directed a ferocious attack on the Japanese people. High-altitude B-29 bombers designed for industrial targets would instead fly low over major cities, dropping incendiary bombs on civilian populations. Japan's residential districts were highly flammable and tightly packed, so the damage was immense. Americans hoped their new strategy, raining death and destruction on the innocent, would break Japanese morale. The first raid in February 1945 destroyed around one square mile of Tokyo. On March 9 and 10, over three hundred B-29s converged on Tokyo's densely populated Asakusa district and dropped nearly four million pounds of incendiary bombs, completely obliterating around sixteen square miles of the city. In a single night, a fifth of Tokyo's industry disappeared and over a million people were left homeless. The heat from incendiary bombs was so intense that rivers bubbled and steel beams melted. General Curtis LeMay later described how firebombing victims were "scorched and boiled and baked to death."

The B-29s then took their campaign to Osaka, Kobe, and Nagoya. The Japanese had few defenses remaining to stop the attacks. Throughout the summer of 1945, sixty-six cities were firebombed; many were effectively leveled. In total, a quarter of the nation's housing burned. Nearly 250,000 Japanese died, and 300,000 more were maimed or injured in the firebombings. Officials urged people not needed in war-related factory production to evacuate the major cities; children were relocated to vacant inns and temples in rural areas, separated from their families and forced to help out on nearby farms.

In April 1945, American forces reached Okinawa, the jump-off point for the invasion of the mainland. The Battle of Okinawa involved some of the fiercest fighting of the war, lasting eighty-two days and resulting in 49,000 American casualties, the most ever experienced in U.S. military history. Japanese losses were higher still; over 120,000 Okinawans died and 11,000 were taken prisoner. Hundreds, perhaps thousands, committed suicide rather than face the anticipated horrors the Americans would bring. Most of the main island became a scorched wasteland; important cultural artifacts and buildings, including the ancient Shuri Castle, were destroyed.

The Japanese cabinet decided to approach the Soviet Union to broker a settlement with the United States, but Soviet leader Joseph Stalin was already meeting with British prime minister Winston Churchill and U.S. president Harry Truman to discuss Japan's surrender. On July 26, the allies issued the Potsdam Declaration, demanding that Japan surrender unconditionally or face utter destruction; the fate of the emperor was not mentioned. Although the Japanese hoped to end the war, they could not accept such an open-ended surrender, allowing a foreign army to occupy Japan, dismantling the imperial system, and possibly indicting their divine monarch as a common criminal. When they did not respond to the allies' demands, President Truman authorized use of America's expensive new weapon, the atomic bomb.

At 8:15 A.M. on August 6, the Enola Gay, a B-29 named after the pilot's mother, dropped a ten-foot-long bomb nicknamed "Little Boy" on Hiroshima. The bomb generated energy equivalent to 15,000–20,000 tons of dynamite. The temperature at its epicenter reached more than 7,000 degrees, incinerating everything and everyone within a mile-and-a-quarter radius. A wall of shock waves spread from the epicenter at the speed of sound, obliterating concrete buildings; the wind velocity at ground zero was five times stronger than winds generated by the severest hurricanes. There are no accurate figures for the number of deaths caused by the bomb, but estimates range between 140,000 and 200,000. Two days later, the Soviet Union announced its intent to declare war on Japan and to invade Manchuria and Korea. To help contain the Soviet advance into Asia, the United States responded by dropping a second atomic bomb, called "Fatman," on Nagasaki, killing another 74,000 individuals. The decision to use a nuclear weapon on a second Japanese city represents one of the first salvos of the Cold War between the United States and the Soviet Union. In all, nearly 500,000 Japanese civilians were killed in U.S. bombings of Japanese cities. It is worth noting that nuclear weapons today are over a thousand times more powerful than the bombs dropped in 1945.

Survivors in the vicinity of the bombings began to suffer from acute radiation poisoning. Symptoms began with vomiting, followed by hair loss, reduction of blood cells, and temporary sterility. Victims who received high doses of radiation died of bone marrow disorder two or more months after exposure. Many first responders and others who entered the cities well after the bombings also suffered and succumbed to the sickness.

While most of the cabinet wished to surrender, military leaders refused, as they still had millions of soldiers successfully waging war in China. The emperor finally broke the deadlock, demanding that the military accept surrender. He recorded a message to the nation to be broadcast the following day—the first time that an emperor spoke directly to his subjects. As the nation gathered around their radios, static crackled around the emperor's words; his voice was high-pitched, and he spoke in a formal, classical style that many did not fully understand. Their neighbors translated the bad news—Japan had lost the war. Hirohito never spoke explicitly of either surrender or defeat but presented Japan's capitulation as an act that might save humanity: "The enemy has begun to employ a new and most cruel bomb, the power of which to do damage is, indeed, incalculable, taking the toll of many innocent lives. Should we continue to fight it would not only result in an ultimate collapse and obliteration of the Japanese nation, but also it would lead to the total extinction of human civilization."[1] The emperor called on his subjects to "endure the unendurable and bear the unbearable," meaning military occupation by a foreign power.

The Allied occupation forces arrived two weeks after the broadcast, led by U.S. general Douglas MacArthur, designated the supreme commander for the Allied Powers in Japan (or SCAP, an acronym that represented all occupation authority in Japan). MacArthur, sometimes called the "Blue-eyed Shogun," held unprecedented powers, including authority to dissolve the Diet, censor the press, disband political parties, and issue laws by fiat. Five thousand Americans worked under his command at SCAP; more than 350,000 U.S. military personnel were stationed throughout Japan. U.S. forces immediately assumed control of central Tokyo, taking over nearly all the buildings still standing.

FIGURE 61.   Douglas MacArthur and Emperor Hirohito. U.S. Army photo by Lt. Gaetano Faillace, 1945. Source: Wikimedia Commons.

Allied leaders wanted to prevent the reemergence of militarism and resist communist influence in Japan; since the United States dominated the occupation, MacArthur's agenda of democratization was based on an American model. American mass media during (and after) the occupation often portrayed the U.S.-Japan relationship in terms of gender or maturity: Japan was immature and childish, in need of America's paternal guidance so that it could grow up into a "real," modern, capitalist democracy. Alternatively, Japan was conceived of as an exotic "geisha" subservient to U.S. masculine desires. The new power structure in Japan was visually captured in a photo of the first meeting between MacArthur and Emperor Hirohito. The monarch, dressed in formal attire for the momentous occasion, appears stiff and diminutive next to the general, who gazes sternly into the camera while adopting a casual pose. Dressed in khakis, MacArthur apparently did not consider the meeting important enough to don a full-dress uniform.

During the first phase of the occupation, between 1945 and 1947, sweeping policies were enacted, focused on the "Three D's": demilitarization, democratization, and decentralization of wealth and power. MacArthur began by dismantling Japan's colonial empire and destroying its potential to wage war. SCAP stripped Japan of all territorial holdings outside the four main islands. It abolished the army and navy and began the huge task of demobilizing more than five million troops, nearly half of whom were still overseas.

Loss of the colonies also required the repatriation of three million civilians, who had migrated throughout the empire as administrators, entrepreneurs, farmers, and workers. In 1945, nearly 9 percent of the home islands' total population resided in imperial outposts. In turn, several million former colonial subjects who resided in Japan were deported back to their countries of origin. One result of SCAP's repatriation and deportation programs was the recreation of more ethnically homogeneous East Asian nations. Japan was no longer the center of a multiethnic empire in East Asia; it became instead a monoethnic nation on the far edge of America's sphere of influence.

Demilitarization also entailed a purge to remove personnel associated with militant nationalism from public office. More than two hundred thousand police officers, newspaper publishers and reporters, and political figures were forced out of work. SCAP placed around six thousand individuals on trial as war criminals for atrocities committed in battle and executed more than nine hundred throughout the former empire. The Tokyo War Crimes Tribunal, convened in May 1946, prosecuted twenty-eight high-ranking government and military officials, including members of the cabinet. After two years of deliberations, the tribunal sent seven men to the gallows, including the wartime prime minister, Tōjō Hideki (1884–1948). Some critics charged that the Tokyo trials were nothing but a forum for "victor's justice" (i.e., vengeance, vindication, and propaganda) because, from the perspective of international law, it was not technically a war crime to participate in a nation's decision to wage war. Judge Radhabinod Pal of India agreed, dissenting from all guilty verdicts and dismissing the legitimacy of the tribunal altogether. Judge Pal believed that the indiscriminate destruction of civilian life and property through the U.S. firebombing and atomic bombs constituted more heinous war crimes. Emperor Hirohito and all members of the imperial family were exonerated from any charges because MacArthur hoped the imperial family would help provide postwar stability and encourage people to cooperate with SCAP directives.

The second "D" of early occupation policies was democratization. U.S. leaders decided that the Meiji constitution required revision in order to guarantee civil liberties. MacArthur appointed two dozen Americans— military officers, lawyers, professors, journalists, and businessmen—to a committee tasked with preparing a model constitution. The document that resulted from the unprecedented task of rewriting the national charter of a defeated enemy shocked the Japanese leadership. The constitution's first article deprived the emperor of sovereignty, converting the monarch into a powerless "symbol of the State and of the unity of the people," with duties limited to ceremonial functions. Article 9, the famous peace clause, renounced war and the threat or use of force as means of settling international disputes. No other state in modern history had renounced its right to wage war. Other articles strengthened civil rights, providing for universal adult suffrage, freedom of assembly, and freedom of the press.

The third "D" was decentralization of wealth and power, which included breaking up the *zaibatsu* (multi-conglomerate industries that had worked with the military to enlarge the empire), fostering labor unions, and carrying out land reform. The zaibatsu dominated three-quarters of Japan's wartime industrial and commercial activities. SCAP dismantled giant firms like Mitsubishi and Mitsui, which were later reconstituted in modified form. MacArthur envisioned a strong labor-union movement as an essential step toward creating a stable middle class supportive of SCAP reforms. New labor laws set minimum wages and maximum work hours, provided for paid holidays, and mandated plant safety and training. Japanese workers responded by organizing on a massive scale. By 1948, nearly half the workforce—6.7 million—belonged to over thirty-three thousand different unions. Land reform deeply transformed the lives of rural residents, who still made up nearly half the populace. Tenant farmers cultivated over two-thirds of farmland, paying around half of their harvest to a landlord. SCAP confiscated fields from absentee landlords and sold them at low prices to the tenants. Resident landlords were allowed to keep only as much land as they could farm themselves, plus five acres to rent. By 1950, three million poor tenant farmers had acquired their own land, helping to dismantle rural power structures dominated by wealthy landlords.

Despite the explicit promise of freedom of speech and freedom of the press, censorship was extensive in occupied Japan. SCAP's Civil Censorship Detachment employed over six thousand individuals to monitor newspapers, radio scripts, magazines, and other media. The lists of taboo topics included any criticism of SCAP, the United States, or other allies; mentions of crimes committed by Allied military forces; reports on the atomic bombs;

and discussion of the black market, starvation, or fraternization between Allied personnel and Japanese women. Media could not refer to the huge cost of the occupation for Japan or the contradictions between the American rhetoric of freedom and democracy and actual conditions on the ground, where Americans lived luxurious lives while the Japanese experienced hunger, deprivation, and discrimination. Finally and ironically, the mention of censorship itself was forbidden.

By the late 1940s, the specter of communism had grown with Mao Zedong's victory in China, the creation of Soviet satellites in Eastern Europe, and bitter hostility between the two Koreas. U.S. leaders began reconsidering SCAP's priorities. If they looked to Japan to be a staunch ally against communism in East Asia, it would require political stability and economic revival, best cultivated with different approaches. The reorientation in U.S. policy was so distinct that some historians have called it the "Reverse Course." Under the new strategy, the "Three D's" of 1945–47 gave way to the "Four R's" of 1948–52: reconstructing the economy, restraining labor, rehabilitating purged individuals, and rearming the military.

The new agenda suited conservative Japanese leaders, including Yoshida Shigeru (1878–1967), the curmudgeonly former British ambassador who served as prime minister from 1946 to 1947 and from 1948 to 1954. Yoshida believed that the occupation should enact only slight reforms focused on economic rehabilitation and restoration of Japanese status within the international community. Early on, he quipped that GHQ, the acronym for SCAP's general headquarters, stood for "Go Home Quickly." As prime minister he emphasized economic recovery and reliance on U.S. military protection, even at the expense of independence in foreign affairs—positions known as the Yoshida Doctrine, which strongly shaped Japanese foreign policy during the Cold War era and beyond. Under Yoshida's leadership, earlier SCAP laws favorable to labor were scrapped in favor of statutes restoring power to management and giving the state more power over unions.

The occupation drew to a close with the signing of a pair of treaties on September 8, 1951. The Peace Treaty provided for withdrawal of occupation personnel, restored sovereignty, and spelled out Japan's right to self-defense, placing no limits on its future economic development. The second, the U.S.-Japan Security Treaty, known in Japan as ANPO, permitted the United States to station troops in Japan indefinitely and to veto military privileges for any third nation. Most Japanese supported the Peace Treaty but objected to ANPO, fearing that it subordinated national defense needs to U.S. policy and compromised Japan's rights as a sovereign nation. Critics charged that Yoshida had condemned Japan to "subordinate independence," and the public agreed; a 1952 poll revealed that only 18 percent of Japanese considered their country truly independent under ANPO.

Yoshida's political party merged with another to form the Liberal Democratic Party (LDP) in 1955. The LDP dominated politics for nearly four decades, keeping a firm hold on power with fifteen members serving consecutively as prime minister. It received millions of dollars in covert financial aid from the U.S. Central Intelligence Agency, intended to support conservative pro-American forces in Japan and undermine left-wing politics. The stability of LDP rule aided postwar financial recovery, and Japan's remarkable growth from the late 1950s to the '70s has often been called an "economic miracle." By the beginning of the '60s, Japan's gross national product (GNP) was the fifth largest in the capitalist world; before the decade was over, Japan's output was second only to that of the United States. Calling this rapid recovery a miracle, however, is something of a misnomer. Japan took longer to return to prewar levels of per capita GNP than Germany and the rest of Western Europe. Its return to the ranks of the great powers was not miraculous but based on a legacy of its prewar commercial accomplishments, shrewd state planning, individual determination to succeed, and unanticipated events that stimulated the economy.

The first significant event in Japan's recovery was the Korean War (1950–53). Japanese companies received nearly $2 billion worth of contracts for textiles, lumber, paper, steel, and vehicles to support American and United Nations forces fighting on the peninsula, spurring investment in new plants and equipment and returning the economy to full capacity. In the mid-1960s, the Vietnam War resulted in a new round of procurement orders from the United States that provided another major stimulus. In addition, because of conversion to war-related production, American manufacturing firms were unable to meet consumer demand for electronics, auto parts, chemicals, and machinery, providing Japanese companies with opportunities to increase exports.

Economic growth was also fostered by the close relationships between the LDP, bureaucracy, and big business—the so-called Iron Triangle. These three groups worked in tandem to ensure that economic growth was the nation's highest priority. A cabinet-level council of experts assessed Japan's strengths and recommended future business and import/export strategies; their reports were translated into action by other government agencies, politicians, and designated corporations. Under such coordinated direction, the level of national income doubled between 1960 and 1967. During the 1950s, the shipbuilding and steel industries were designated targets for growth; in the '60s, sectors that would enhance export trade, such as autos

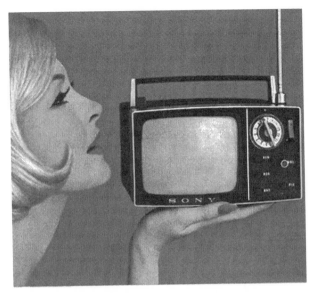

hold the future in your hand
with **SONY**

FIGURE 62. Advertisement for Sony portable TV, 1960s.

and electronics, were emphasized in economic planning. Thus, Toyota, Nissan, and other carmakers automated their factories, improved inventory control, and introduced stylish new models. The oil shock of the '70s incentivized U.S. consumers to try the smaller, more fuel-efficient Japanese autos. By 1980, Japan produced more cars than any other country; by 1989, it controlled nearly a quarter of the U.S. auto market. Electronics firms such as Matsushita and Sony began to flourish in the '50s. Matsushita teamed up with Dutch manufacturer Phillips to begin mass production of a huge line of electrical appliances for the home under the brand names National and Panasonic. They aggressively marketed refrigerators, vacuum cleaners, washing machines, and every other conceivable home appliance both domestically and abroad. The electronics giant Sony was founded by Morita Akio (1921–99), named one of the twenty most influential business geniuses of the twentieth century by *Time* magazine. Sony's first hit product was an affordable transistor radio; it has continued to produce innovative, high-quality video and audio gear over the decades, from TVs and video recorders to Walkman portable stereos and gaming consoles.

Japan's postwar economic growth was thus no miracle, but the result of multiple factors, including national prioritization and the creative efforts of major corporations. Small and medium-sized businesses, too, filled an important niche in the industrial structure as subcontractors to large firms, which could rely on supplies of high-quality parts without making additional investments. A global environment encouraging free trade also played a role in helping the Japanese economy, as did Japan's relationship with the United States. Under the security treaties, Japan spent less than 1 percent of its national budget for defense. In addition, the legacy of Japan's past was undeniably important. An educated and talented labor pool and prewar commercial experience contributed to rapid postwar growth. Finally, the domestic consumer market was critical to the success of Japanese businesses. As incomes rose, the middle-class masses acquired numerous appliances and other consumer goods deemed essential for comfortable family life.

Protest Movements

The improvement in living standards for ordinary Japanese eventually helped diffuse swelling movements of popular protest that arose in the 1960s against renewal of ANPO and in opposition to the Vietnam War. As the Diet deliberated on ratification of ANPO, leftist opposition parties staged filibusters and sit-ins to delay approval. Prime Minister Kishi Nobusuke, an indicted war criminal, resorted to heavy-handed tactics to pass the bill, ordering police to drag opponents from Diet chambers, then calling a snap vote among the remaining LDP supporters. Enraged at this disregard for democratic procedure, labor went on strike across Japan and hundreds of thousands of students swarmed the streets in protest. They developed a distinctive repertoire of protest tactics, including snake-dancing, a zigzag style of marching and chanting. The death of a young woman, crushed in a clash between students and police, unleashed even more popular anger.

Another large protest movement crystallized in opposition to the Vietnam War. A nationwide rally in June 1965 attracted over a hundred thousand, and subsequent monthly demonstrations, held until late 1973, drew up to seventy thousand protesters each. From 1967 to 1969, antiwar rallies and demonstrations involved nearly nineteen million people. One of the largest occurred in January 1968 when a U.S. nuclear-powered aircraft carrier arrived in Japan to support the war effort. In response, the generally pro-American prime minister, Satō Eisaku (1901–75), declared Japan's Three Non-Nuclear Principles: no manufacture, possession, or introduction into Japan of nuclear weapons. Satō was awarded the Nobel Peace Prize for this stance.

A second, virulent wave of anti-ANPO protest arose as the treaty approached renewal in 1970. These protests were more extensive, complex, and violent than those of 1960 and reached deeply into Japan's universities. Tactics included the secretly planned, sudden occupation of a symbolic space such as Haneda Airport or the Diet building. By the late '60s, an elite police force of twenty-nine thousand devoted most of its time to controlling student riots and gathering intelligence on student organizations.

Citizens' movements proliferated as hundreds of groups formed to protest widespread pollution and environmental damage, the result of all-out prioritization of rapid economic growth. Pro-business policies allowed factories to pollute the air and water with impunity, resulting in respiratory diseases among residents of industrial cities and exposure to chemical poisons for those living along polluted waterways. Lax oversight resulted in two major food-contamination scandals. In 1955, arsenic-contaminated powdered milk sold by the Morinaga Milk Company caused diarrhea, fever, and leukemia among some twelve thousand individuals and caused the deaths of over a hundred infants. And Minamata disease, caused by consuming mercury-tainted fish, was discovered in 1956 and afflicted over ten thousand victims, causing thousands of deaths.

Minamata Bay in southern Kyushu, famous for the abundance and variety of its fish, was home to the Chisso chemical manufacturing plant. After the war, when food production was of highest priority, Chisso's fertilizer and agricultural chemical products made it a leader in the industry. Its chemical waste was dumped without treatment into the bay. In the mid-1950s, fishermen began to notice a drastic decline in the amount and quality of their catches. Dead fish floated in the bay, and local cats began exhibiting strange, contorted movements; some threw themselves into the sea. People also began suffering from an unknown disease, with severe convulsions, intermittent loss of consciousness, lapses into insanity, and, finally, permanent coma or death. All victims had eaten large amounts of fish from Minamata Bay, and while many believed the problem was related to Chisso, it was taboo to speak of this possibility because of the community's economic dependence on the company. Chisso worked closely with the Japanese government to deny responsibility for decades. When evidence mounted, the firm consented to small amounts of compensation for victims who would pursue no further legal action. As negotiations stalled in 1971, a group of victims staged an eighteen-month sit-in, the longest and largest sit-down strike in Japanese history. The Minamata affair, still not fully resolved, provides a tragic example of how the strong bond between government and business could harm ordinary people.

FIGURE 63. Victim of Minamata disease, 1973. Source: AP Images.

Minamata was just one case of industrial pollution. In 1965, a similar mercury-poisoning case came to light in Niigata; in 1967, wide-scale chronic asthma resulted from Mitsubishi-owned plants in Mie prefecture that released sulfurous fumes; and in 1968, cadmium poisoning in Toyama prefecture contaminated water used to irrigate rice paddies. Along with Minamata, these cases are known as the "four big pollution lawsuits" and became enormously significant in spurring antipollution citizens' movements. Their activism resulted in the enactment of some of the strictest antipollution laws in the world. By 1980, Japan spent more of its GNP on antipollution measures than any other country.

Other citizens' movements involved rural resistance to industrial development and urban opposition to high-rise construction that threatened the "right to sunshine." In the '60s and '70s, farmers dramatically opposed construction of Tokyo's new international airport in the town of Narita. As authorities began to forcibly expropriate their lands, some chained themselves to their homes, built fortified encampments, and refused to leave. They were joined by students and anti–Vietnam War protesters who engaged in violent clashes with police. Narita airport was finally completed in 1978, seven years behind schedule, but its opening was delayed when a group armed with Molotov cocktails drove into the control tower. On its opening day, over six thousand protesters attacked security forces with rocks and firebombs; police responded with water cannons. The long conflict over Narita was a major factor in the decision to build Osaka's Kansai International Airport offshore on reclaimed land, instead of again trying to expropriate land in heavily populated areas.

OCCUPATION-ERA CULTURE

Material Culture

In the autumn of 1945, everything was in short supply for most Japanese, whether housing, food, medicine, or hope. The war had cost Japan one-third of its total wealth and a quarter of its housing. Meanwhile, nearly six million soldiers and civilians were returning from around the empire to a ruined economy, creating brutal competition for jobs. People survived or coped in a variety of ways, some becoming homeless drunks, others joining the yakuza—crime-syndicate families who also dealt in illegal drugs, prostitution, gambling, and protection rackets. (Yakuza remain active today and are well known for their intricate, full-body tattoos, some of which take a lifetime to complete.) Many women turned to prostitution, servicing the occupying forces. Some were widows or war orphans; others were eldest daughters working to feed their families. Rather than directly exchanging sex for money, many accepted goods, such as cigarettes or liquor, which they might barter or sell on the black market.

Deaths from starvation and malnutrition were common; around a thousand Tokyoites succumbed within three months of surrender. Food shortages became acute before the war's end, when U.S. advances cut off access to food imports from the colonies. Authorities urged people to supplement carbohydrates with acorns and sawdust and address protein deficits by eating silkworm cocoons, insects, and rodents. After surrender, conditions further deteriorated. U.S. food rations, consisting largely of wheat, supplied only one-third to one-half of required daily caloric intake. Wheat was commonly made into ramen noodles or wrappers for dumplings sold at food stalls, often run by returnees from China. Nevertheless, extreme hunger remained a constant for most Japanese until 1949. Rations could be supplemented by food purchases on the black market *(yamiichi)*, but these were exorbitantly priced and technically illegal. Over a million ordinary people were arrested annually for transactions on the black market during the first three years of the occupation. In 1947, a shocking incident demonstrated the extent of the food crisis: when a thirty-three-year-old judge responsible for prosecuting black-market offenders vowed to eat no more than his rationed allotment, he soon died of starvation. Urbanites traveled to the countryside to barter their possessions with farmers for rice or other produce. Their situation was described as a "bamboo shoot" or "onion" lifestyle because people wept while peeling off layers of their clothing, jewelry, and other valuables to trade for food.

The black market was often the only venue available to purchase food and necessary goods or to earn a living. By October 1945, seventeen thousand open-air markets existed throughout the country, mostly in the large cities, and the total value of black-market goods on offer exceeded the annual national budget. Food and drink stalls sold everything from stews made of garbage from U.S. military bases to cheap alcoholic concoctions *(kasutori)* that could blind or kill. Other stalls sold or bartered household goods or clothing. Clever entrepreneurs converted military goods into useful kitchen items, making cutlery from swords and transforming helmets into cooking pots. Former military officers and corrupt officials grew rich through sales of stolen military goods such as coal, gasoline, cigarettes, cement, and steel. Overall, the markets were tightly controlled by the yakuza.

Housing shortages affected the working classes the most, because U.S. bombings had devastated the areas where they lived, while leaving many of the wealthiest neighborhoods intact. Shantytowns housed tens of thousands of homeless families, crowded together in makeshift shacks of charred wood, corrugated tin, and other available debris. Some took shelter in burned-out trolley cars and buses, in the underground passageways of the train stations, and even in caves burrowed into urban rubble. By 1950, millions still lacked decent housing.

Disease further decimated the Japanese. In the squalor that developed following defeat, communicable diseases such as tuberculosis, cholera, dysentery, and polio burgeoned, but the health-care system had largely been destroyed, and medicine was in scarce supply. Between 1945 and 1948, some 650,000 succumbed to such diseases.

During the early weeks and months of the occupation, Allied troops terrorized the population. In Kanagawa prefecture, U.S. soldiers committed 1,336 rapes during the first ten weeks of the occupation. Perpetrators went unpunished; stories about rapes and robberies committed by soldiers were censored. Japanese officials, alarmed by the threat to female chastity, acted quickly to provide sexual services to their conquerors. The number of professional prostitutes available was insufficient, so ordinary women were recruited via a vague advertising campaign calling on "new Japanese women to participate in the great task of comforting the occupation force. Housing, clothing and food supplied."[2] Many women, unaware of the wartime system of military comfort women and desperate to survive, applied. Most left when they learned the truth about their expected duties, but 1,360 women in Tokyo initially enlisted in what would become the Recreation and Amusement Association (RAA). Like their wartime sisters, postwar comfort women were forced to service fifteen to sixty men per day, and some committed suicide or deserted in despair. Nevertheless, over thirty additional RAA centers quickly opened in Tokyo; many more were established in twenty additional cities. In all, the RAA employed up to an estimated seventy thousand women to "entertain" the occupying forces.

The RAA did not survive long. In 1946, facing antiprostitution pressure from the United States and spiking rates of venereal disease among his forces, MacArthur dismantled the RAA and outlawed prostitution. But the world's oldest profession was unlikely to disappear with a massive military occupation afoot. Brothels in red-light districts surrounding military bases continued to operate privately, and freelance streetwalkers, known as *panpan* girls, spread throughout the cities. Prostitution paid far better than most jobs then available for women, so tens of thousands took to the streets. All Japanese women were considered potential prostitutes by American military police, who periodically rounded up any females found on the streets at night, forcing them to submit to humiliating VD examinations. Most panpan girls were teenagers and were easily identified through their colorful dresses and heavy makeup. Like the modern girls of the 1920s, they were a source of both public consternation and media fascination, criticized for consorting with the Americans and for their self-indulgent eroticism and consumerism.

In the popular view, there were two main types of panpan girls: *batafurai* (butterfly), who flitted indiscriminately from client to client; and *onrii* (only), loyal to a single patron. It was no secret that many American soldiers, married or not, kept such mistresses, whom they supplied with treasured goods such as liquor, cigarettes, and chocolates, and with feminine items like lipstick and nylon stockings. Panpan girls were stereotyped in *Baby-san*, a cartoon in *Stars and Stripes*, a newspaper for U.S. military personnel in Japan. Baby-san was depicted as money-hungry and duplicitous, begging for consumer goods in her broken English, but she was also sexy, servile, and irresistible to American military men. She was the occupation's version of Madama Butterfly—a toy to be left behind in Japan, especially since many American states still enforced antimiscegenation laws criminalizing interracial marriage.

The black market and panpan girls dominated the public imagination during the occupation. In his monumental, Pulitzer Prize–winning work on

"*Joe-san! I think you have duty tonight!*"

FIGURE 64.   Bill Hume, *Baby-san*, 1952.

the era, *Embracing Defeat* (2000), John Dower notes how children's games poignantly mimicked social situations. With toys scarce, children played games of pretend; the most popular included GI and prostitute *(panpan asobi)*, mock black market *(yamiichi-gokko)*, and left-wing political demonstration *(demo asobi)*. In the train game, the designated conductor picked riders for a special train designated for occupation personnel only. Rejected players rode the "ordinary train," pushing, shoving, and crying for help.

While the Japanese lacked adequate shelter, food, and health care, and many turned to crime and prostitution for survival, American occupiers and their families lived sumptuously, in homes confiscated from purged elites or in housing complexes constructed to American standards at the Japanese government's expense. The homes were equipped with the latest modern appliances—some even had swimming pools—while the complexes contained amenities such as schools, churches, shops, clubs, and movie theaters. Military families enjoyed lifestyles far more luxurious than most could afford at home, employing one or more servants and spending their weekends at luxurious hotels throughout Japan, commandeered by the military, where they feasted on beef sukiyaki. The Americans shopped for pearls, antiques, and souvenirs in department stores declared off-limits to the natives. Restaurants, theaters, and other facilities reserved for occupation personnel enforced Jim Crow–style segregation with signs declaring "Japanese Keep Out." While some pitied Japanese impoverishment, the occupiers were usually giddy over their new entitlements, and most firmly believed that locals were inferiors who should be grateful for American benevolence. U.S. diplomat George Kennan, however, denounced them as parasites with "monumental imperviousness" to the "suffering and difficulties" of the Japanese people. He condemned occupation personnel for monopolizing "everything that smacks of comfort or elegance or luxury," and he contrasted their "idleness and boredom" with the "struggles and problems of a defeated and ruined country."[3]

Religion under the Occupation

One month after arriving, MacArthur kicked off a recruitment drive to bring two thousand American missionaries and evangelists to Japan to help fill its "spiritual vacuum." Like many Americans, the general believed wartime propaganda that the Japanese literally worshipped Hirohito as a "living god." Despite intense efforts, Christianity made little progress in Japan. At the end of the occupation, Christians numbered around half of 1 percent of the population, no more than had existed before Pearl Harbor. The postwar Japanese did not reject religion in general, however. With freedom of religion guaranteed under the postwar constitution, a flood of new religious movements emerged and several grew rapidly, with memberships reaching into the millions. One writer called the phenomenon "The Rush Hour of the Gods." SCAP authorities gave enhanced legal protections to religions to avoid the types of suppressions that had occurred against Oomoto and other groups in the 1930s and '40s. Japanese authorities, fearful of missteps in an area so important to occupation authorities, tended to take a hands-off attitude toward religious groups, allowing them to engage in questionable fundraising schemes and political activities without losing their privileged tax-free status.

Postwar new religions, like their predecessors, usually centered on charismatic personalities and often involved healing or spiritualist activity. Because of the large number of new groups, they competed fiercely to attract new members by hosting elaborate events, constructing impressive headquarters, and recruiting aggressively through extensive use of mass media. The mainstream press and general public largely held new religions in disdain, in part because of the involvement of some in tax-evasion and embezzlement scandals. Members of new religions were subjected to ridicule and discriminatory treatment. Nevertheless, several major groups succeeded in recruiting millions of people after the war, because so many were disillusioned or impoverished or had lost their entire families. Established religions and state and local agencies failed to offer real social support, but new religions provided a community with impressive activities and facilities that bespoke power and success. In many, individuals joined intimate groups for self-reflection and counseling, where they could find outlet for their daily frustrations. Thus, the new religions—though much maligned—helped many Japanese regain a sense of identity in a new and confusing era.

One infamous sect was Tenshō Kōtai Jingukyō, popularly known as the Dancing Religion. The foundress, Kitamura Sayo (1900–1967), known as Ogamisama, was a farmer's wife who claimed she was possessed by the absolute god and preached a millennial message. Her street sermons included singing and ecstatic dancing and began to attract media attention in 1947. Ogamisama was a charismatic figure who dressed in men's suits and openly denounced both the emperor and MacArthur in coarse language. Other new postwar groups were spin-offs from older sects. After the war, the Shintoist Oomoto began to recover from its 1935 suppression but was quickly outpaced by groups founded by former members who borrowed from its teachings and practices. The largest were Sekai Kyūseikyō, PL Kyōdan, and Seichō no Ie, which claimed over 1.5 million members by the late 1950s. Nichiren Buddhism (see chapter 4) was the root of several large new religions, including Reiyūkai, Risshō Kōseikai, and Sōka Gakkai.

Sōka Gakkai was founded in 1930 by educators Makiguchi Tsunesaburō (1871–1944) and Toda Jōsei (1900–1958), who wanted to reform Japan's militaristic education system into a more humanistic one. In 1943, both were sent to prison for refusing to enshrine Shinto talismans in their homes. Makiguchi died there, but Toda was released and rebuilt the organization. Sōka Gakkai engaged in militant conversion tactics known as *shakubuku* (literally, to break and flatten), harassing family and friends to join and threatening divine punishment through illness or misfortune if they refused. This approach netted the group over a million members by the time of Toda's death in 1958 but also earned it a bad reputation in mainstream society. Ikeda Daisaku (b. 1928) became the group's leader in 1960 and began a campaign stressing world peace, culture, education, and expansion abroad. Under Ikeda's leadership, the group grew to over twelve million members in 190 countries. Sōka Gakkai also became heavily involved in national politics, founding the Komeitō (Clean Government) political party in 1962, which successfully mobilized the large membership base to support candidates. Its initial platform opposed corruption and nuclear weapons, generally supporting Socialist Party positions. In 1971, the religion and the political party legally separated, but they continue to be closely associated. Over time Komeitō has moved rightward, toward social conservatism, and has been part of ruling coalitions with the LDP.

Literature and Film of the 1940s–1950s

After the war, under occupation censorship, many writers turned to expressing pacifist themes in their work; some of their novels were adapted into feature films. Michio Takeyama's 1946 novel *Harp of Burma (Biruma no tategoto)* was adapted twice by director Ichikawa Kon, in black-and-white in 1956 and in color in 1985. The novel and film depict the plight of a platoon of Japanese soldiers in Burma who surrender to the British when they learn the war has ended. Mizushima, the group's harp player, is selected to deliver the news to a group of soldiers holed up in a cave in the mountains, but they violently reject his pleas to accept defeat. When the cave is attacked, a local monk aids Mizushima. Wishing to return to his men, Mizushima steals the robes of his rescuer and disguises himself as a monk, shaving his head. On his journey, he encounters scores of Japanese corpses and resolves to remain in Burma and devote his life to burying the dead and studying Buddhism. His platoon mates suspect that their harp player has abandoned them. They train a parrot to repeat the phrase "Mizushima, let's go back to Japan together," asking a village woman to deliver the bird to a local monk they believe is their comrade in disguise. She returns with another parrot that replies, "No, I cannot go back," and a letter explaining Mizushima's new mission of peace.

Ichikawa also adapted Ōoka Shōhei's 1951 novel *Fires on the Plain* in the film *Nobi* (1959), a brutal depiction of a desperate soldier in the Philippine jungles. The protagonist, Private Tamura, has tuberculosis and is abandoned by his unit as a useless burden. He sets out on his own, stealing and killing a young Filipina girl to survive, and eventually joins a group of starving soldiers heading toward an evacuation point while trying to evade the enemy. Tamura encounters two men from his unit who claim to be surviving on "monkey meat," but he soon discovers that they have resorted to cannibalism. The film ends ambiguously, with Tamura collapsing as he walks toward fires on a distant plain, which he believes signal the evacuation site that can return him to "normal life." The bleak, grisly account of the horrors committed by individuals in the name of survival provides a disturbing, unforgettable antiwar message.

Atomic literature *(genbaku bungaku)*, written both by survivors *(hibakusha)* and nonsurvivors of the bombs, is another postwar genre. Survivors' works include testimonies, poetry, and fiction. Poet Hara Tamiki's memoir *Summer Flowers (Natsu no hana)*, written days after the bombing of Hiroshima, opens with the unvarnished claim "I was saved because I was in the toilet." The most significant writer among survivors is Ōta Yōko, who penned a quartet of angry novels about the Hiroshima bombing. The first, *City of Corpses (Shikabane no machi)*, was completed by autumn 1945 but censored by SCAP and published three years later, with many portions deleted.

It is nonsurvivors, however, who have authored the best-known works of atomic literature. Ibuse Masuji wrote the most critically acclaimed work of fiction, *Black Rain (Kuroi ame)*. This 1966 novel recounts the experience of a family of three survivors, weaving together their journal entries in a story about how the niece of a rural couple is unable to arrange a marriage because she has been exposed to radioactive black rain; the families of potential husbands fear its effects. Director Imamura Shōhei's 1989 film adaption won Best Film, Best Director, Best Actress, and several other awards from the Japanese academy. Nobel Prize–winning novelist Ōe Kenzaburō's book of essays and simple line drawings, *Hiroshima Notes (Hiroshima nōto, 1965)*, explores the humanity and heroism among survivors, such as medical personnel who labored to save others despite suffering from radiation sickness themselves, and individuals who publicly embraced their victimhood for the cause of antinuclear activism. The work most widely read by international audiences is Keiji Nakazawa's *Barefoot Gen (Hadashi no Gen)*, originally a manga comic (1973–85) but later published as a book that has sold over 6.5 million copies in a dozen languages and was adapted into a 1983 animated film. The autobiographical story opens in Hiroshima during the final months of the war, as six-year-old Gen's family is struggling to survive. After the bombing, Gen witnesses horrifying scenes of death and disfigurement, but the overall message of the work is one of hope. *Barefoot Gen* expresses a strong pacifist perspective through negative portrayals of both Japanese wartime militarism and depraved activities by occupation forces.

Another popular film inspired by antinuclear sentiment is Honda Ishirō's *Gojira* (1954), the first film about the monster better known as Godzilla. The opening scene depicts a fishing boat destroyed by an ancient creature awoken by hydrogen bomb testing, reflecting an actual incident. In March 1954, the *Lucky Dragon*, a Japanese tuna boat, was exposed to nuclear fallout from a U.S. thermonuclear device tested in Bikini Atoll, near the Marshall Islands. Its twenty-three crew members were afflicted with acute radiation poisoning, and several died. The United States tried to cover up the incident, but the tragedy gave rise to fierce grassroots antinuclear protest—with more than thirty million Japanese signing petitions opposing nuclear testing—and to the establishment of the Japan Council against Atomic and Hydrogen Bombs (Gensuikyō). In the movie, Gojira—whose name combines the words for gorilla and whale *(kujira)*—is a metaphor for the terror and destruction of the atomic bomb. Human attempts to stop Gojira are futile; he breaks through a towering electrified fence erected by the Self-Defense Forces and rampages across Tokyo. Scenes depicting the urban destruction wrought by the beast closely resemble photographs of the atomic-bomb aftermath. The first Godzilla movie was intended as a dark, somber reflection on war and the dangers of atomic weapons. It was heavily edited and reworked for American release as *Godzilla, King of the Monsters* (1956), which diluted the antinuclear and antiwar messages. In subsequent films, the monster, rather than the message, took center stage, battling other creatures like Mothra, Rodan, and the three-headed Ghidorah in a series of kitschy, low-budget features. Over thirty Japanese and U.S. feature films have starred Godzilla, including *Shin Godzilla (Godzilla Resurgence)*, Japan's highest-grossing live-action film in 2016.

Although he began making feature films in the 1930s, director Kurosawa Akira gained international prominence for *Rashōmon*, which won the Venice Film Festival in 1951 and opened foreign markets to Japanese movies for the first time. Kurosawa released a film each year through the 1950s and early '60s, including such classics as *Seven Samurai* (1954) and *Yōjimbō* (1961), and continued to create internationally acclaimed films over the following decades, earning a Lifetime Achievement Oscar in 1990. Several of Kurosawa's early postwar films, including *No Regrets for Our Youth* (1946), *Drunken Angel* (1948), *Stray Dog* (1949), and *To Live* (1952), were produced under SCAP censorship but nevertheless captured the ethos of their time. *No Regrets* provides a critique of wartime political oppression. Its protagonist, Yukie, is a young woman whose father, a college professor, is forced to resign in the 1930s for his antifascist views. She falls in love with one of his radical students, Noge, who is imprisoned and subjected to tenkō conversion by the Special Police. After Noge's death, Yukie travels to his village, where his parents are being persecuted because of their son's reputation as a traitor. After the war, Yukie's father is reinstated and Noge

FIGURE 65. Movie poster for Honda Ishirō's *Gojira*. © 1954 Toho Company.
Source: Wikimedia Commons.

is posthumously honored for his antiwar activism. *Drunken Angel* was Kurosawa's first collaboration with the dynamic Mifune Toshirō (1920–97), who portrays a young yakuza gangster with tuberculosis being treated by an older, alcoholic doctor with a feisty temper. SCAP censors prohibited films from engaging in social criticism, but Kurosawa slipped in several references to occupation-era conditions, including damning depictions of panpan girls and the black market. In *Stray Dog*, Mifune plays Murakami, a rookie detective who loses his handgun to a pickpocket. The young thief uses the pistol to commit robbery and murder. A well-known sequence employs documentary footage of war-ravaged neighborhoods to follow the detective, disguised as a destitute war veteran, as he searches for the criminal in the backstreets of Tokyo. *To Live* centers on Watanabe (Shimura Takashi), a middle-aged bureaucrat in a tedious job who learns he has terminal stomach cancer and will die within a year. Watanabe reacts by indulging in clubs and nightlife but soon realizes that such distractions are ultimately unfulfilling. After meeting a young woman exhilarated by her new job making toys, he decides to dedicate his remaining life to a single cause: getting the slow, ineffective bureaucracy to build a children's playground. In summary, Kurosawa's occupation-era films realistically convey both the pain and social dislocation experienced by ordinary Japanese and the sense of hope and opportunity under the promise of a new era.

Literature that expressed feelings of humiliation and helplessness during the occupation, often using dark humor—by writers such as Kojima Nobuo (1915–2006), Nosaka Akiyuki (1930–2015), and Ōe Kenzaburō (b. 1935)—could be published only after censorship ended. Kojima's 1948 short story "On the Train" was acceptable to SCAP, as it did not comment directly on the American presence. In this story, a teacher who lost everything during the war rides the train back from the countryside, where he had obtained some black-market rice, but is robbed by another traveler who pretends to be his friend. The tale demonstrates the selfish, dog-eat-dog world of the occupation, shattering wartime illusions of Japanese unity under propagandistic slogans like "One Hundred Million Souls Working Together." By contrast, Kojima's story "The American School" (1954) could more openly point out the economic and social disparities between Americans and Japanese during the occupation. The plot revolves around three main characters, all Japanese teachers of English, who have been ordered to visit a school for American children run by occupation personnel, requiring a long, arduous walk to the facility. The protagonist, Isa, feels inadequate in the language and wants to avoid having to speak with Americans, toward whom he feels both resentment and fear. His nemesis,

FIGURE 66. Movie poster for Kurosawa Akira's *Drunken Angel*. © 1948 Toho
Company. Source: Wikimedia Commons.

Yamada, is a nationalistic bully and sycophant who wants to curry favor with the Americans by giving lessons in English to demonstrate his proficiency. The only female in the group, Michiko, speaks the best English and receives gifts and catcalls from soldiers passing by in jeeps. The satirical story reveals mutual cultural misunderstandings and the contrast between the hardships faced by the Japanese and the relative luxuries enjoyed by their overlords.

Ōe's short story "Sheep" (1958) viscerally addresses the indignities imposed by occupation forces, compounded by the actions of other Japanese. The narrator is a young man who boards a crowded bus, also being ridden by drunken American soldiers and their boozy, disheveled Japanese female companion. She flirts with the narrator and begins to insult the occupiers in Japanese. The soldiers retaliate by forcing the narrator to drop his trousers and bend over, exposing his butt to the biting cold, and proceed to make other passengers and the driver assume the degrading pose while they chant "Sheep Killer! Sheep Killer! Bang! Bang!" over and over again. After growing tired of their game, the soldiers depart with the girl, and their victims try to regain their composure. But the unmolested passengers, led by a teacher, gather around them, expressing rage and disgust, urging the victims to report the incident to the police to "teach those bastards a lesson." The narrator comments: "Surrounding us like dogs out for the kill in a rabbit hunt, the passengers talked among themselves in loud angry voices. We sheep looked down meekly, sunk in our seats and suffered in silence."[4] As the unmolested continue to clamor for action, one sheep rises and punches the teacher in the face, draining the urgency of the spectators. The teacher returns to his seat but later follows the narrator off the bus, dragging him to a nearby police box to report the incident, where the young man refuses to talk. The teacher recounts the humiliating episode to the police, who are reluctant to get involved in matters regarding American soldiers. When the narrator runs off without revealing his identity, the teacher chases him. The story ends as the teacher threatens: "Don't worry—I'll find out who you are. . . . And I'll heap shame on both you and the soldiers so that you'll want to die. . . . You'll never get away from me."[5]

Critics have read "Sheep" as an allegory for atomic-bomb victims who wish to forget their horrific experiences but are unable to do so because of pressure by antinuclear activists. The story also illustrates the psychological scars of the occupation experienced by writers who were then teenage boys, such as Ōe and Nosaka, author of the short stories "Grave of the Fireflies," about a brother and sister who succumb to starvation during the war, and "American Hijiki," in which the protagonist, a successful TV producer in the 1960s, must face and relive the sense of inferiority and servility he felt as an adolescent during the occupation when he pimped Japanese girls to soldiers.

1950s–1970s CULTURE

Conditions improved as the occupation ended and policymakers turned their focus to economic growth, making rapid strides. The Tokyo Olympics of 1964 acted as a symbolic event demonstrating Japan's recovery from defeat and reentry onto the world stage. Olympic preparations cost over a billion yen and included major improvements to highway infrastructure; development of the bullet train *(shinkansen)* and new subway lines; installation of new systems for water supply and waste disposal, necessary for Tokyo to appear modern and hygienic; and construction of Haneda Airport and state-of-the-art broadcast facilities.

National symbols associated with imperialism, war, and defeat could be erased or transformed via association with the Olympic games, which embodied international peace and friendship. The main stadium was constructed in Yoyogi Park, on the site of a U.S. military housing project; removal of the facilities allowed Japan to expunge painful reminders of the occupation. Emperor Hirohito gave the opening address, followed by a release of doves, thus demonstrating his new postwar role as a symbol of peace. The controversial national flag *(hinomaru)* flew alongside those of other nations as a patriotic symbol of Japanese identity. At the opening ceremony, seventy-five thousand spectators filled the national stadium as jets of the Self-Defense Forces inscribed the five Olympic rings in the sky and seven thousand participants from nearly ninety nations marched onto the field. The crowd stood in reverential silence as Sakai Yoshinori, the "Atom Boy"—a nineteen-year-old college student born in a Hiroshima suburb on the day the atomic bomb was dropped—ran into the stadium bearing the Olympic torch. Who could better represent how Japan had successfully overcome its wartime defeat? The opening ceremony was broadcast live across the globe for the first time in Olympic history. Japanese citizens followed the games closely on TV, enthusiastically cheering on their nation's athletes, who won sixteen gold medals. The dramatic final match in women's volleyball, won by Japan against the Soviet Union, was watched live by 95 percent of the populace.

Six years later, Japan further demonstrated its growing affluence by hosting Expo '70 in Osaka, the first world's fair ever held in Asia. The theme of the Expo was "Progress and Harmony of Mankind"; exhibits focused on advances in science and technology and forecasts for the future. Site development and construction of a monorail and the Japan Pavilion cost a phenomenal $2 billion. Major manufacturers such as Mitsui, Toshiba, and Mazda invested additional millions for their own pavilions. The Expo attracted over sixty million visitors, over 95 percent of whom were Japanese. They came from every corner of the islands to witness the "magnificent months-long celebration of the Japanese industrial miracle" with their own eyes.[6] Expo '70 elevated the international profiles of several Japanese architects and artists. Architects Tange Kenzō (1913–2005) and Isozaki Arata (b. 1931), who designed the master plan and festival plaza, became two of the most celebrated and award-winning architects of the twentieth century. The Tower of the Sun, an anthropomorphic sculpture standing 229 feet tall by avant-garde artist Okamoto Tarō (1911–96; see below), became the symbol of the Expo.

Material Culture

The rise in the standard of living enabled by the economic growth of the 1960s gave rise to the widely accepted notion that Japan was a homogeneous, middle-class society. Surveys routinely indicated that 90 percent of the Japanese considered themselves members of the middle class. A relatively narrow income gap, with those in the top 20 percent earning under three times what the bottom 20 percent earned, accounts for this perception. High-speed economic growth accelerated the pace of urbanization as more people left rural lives as farmers, miners, and fishermen to take manufacturing or management jobs in and around urban centers. Thirty-eight percent of the population lived in cities in 1950; this percentage had almost doubled by 1972, reaching 72 percent. Nearly half the population was squeezed into just 6 percent of the country's total land area: the Kobe-Osaka-Kyoto triangle was home to more than fifteen million, while thirty-nine million were jammed into the Tokyo metropolitan area. Within those huge urban centers, the bleakness of the immediate postwar years soon gave way to a "bright life" of consumerism. From the late 1950s onward, Japan's economic boom translated into better housing and food and more fashionable clothing. With new affluence, such basic expenditures required a lower percentage of household income, meaning that more discretionary funds remained for recreational activities, travel, and education.

The population's concentration in a few urban centers resulted in serious housing problems, especially in Tokyo, where buying a single-family house remained out of reach for most families. In the mid-1950s, public housing authorities began constructing concrete apartment complexes *(danchi)* in urban suburbs. They contained modern conveniences like flush toilets, stainless steel sinks, and separate bedrooms for parents and children. The demand for the units was so enormous that people entered lotteries for the chance to move in; the odds of winning a lottery in 1957 for a danchi apartment in Chiba, a far suburb of Tokyo, were 25,000 to 1. Those determined to own single-family homes moved farther and farther away from the city and took out mortgage loans averaging ten times their annual income. Crowded commutes lasting up to two hours each way were often the breadwinner's cost of providing his family the luxury of a home.

Homes were filled with new electrical goods. Even the poorest bought radios, irons, and toasters. By 1960, most families had also purchased vacuum cleaners and electric fans, along with three appliances nicknamed the "three sacred treasures"—a refrigerator, washing machine, and black-and-white TV. They soon swapped the last of these for color models as Japan introduced color broadcasting. During the '70s, the sacred treasures evolved into a car, air conditioning, and color TV. Other household must-haves revealed the particular tastes of the domestic market, including automatic rice-cookers, introduced by Toshiba in 1955, and electrically heated low tables *(kotatsu)* to sit at during winter.

Men adopted Western-style suits as their daily work uniform during the prewar years, but the majority of women maintained traditional kimono dress throughout the war. In the postwar era, however, nearly all women adopted Western-style dress, made quickly and economically at home, and more comfortable and easier to launder than kimonos. Domestic textile industries began to recover in 1949 and cloth rationing ended in 1951, leading to a boom in Western dressmaking. In Tokyo the number of dress shops grew from around thirteen hundred in 1943 to fifteen thousand by 1955. They needed seamstresses, so dressmaking schools proliferated, teaching helpful skills to would-be brides, housewives, and those seeking paid work. Almost all households bought sewing machines. During the '50s, housewives devoted nearly three hours daily to home sewing projects. Many also engaged in home-based sewing piecework as a source of extra income that did not jeopardize their identities as full-time housewives.

Food consumption changed in significant ways. Consumption of rice, which had provided over 70 percent of daily calories for most people in the 1930s, declined significantly as eating patterns diversified, incorporating more meats, dairy, breads, and processed foods. Daily average caloric intake doubled between 1946 and the late '80s. Many households swapped rice for toast at breakfast and for sandwiches at lunch, but the formula "white rice plus three side dishes" remained the norm for most family dinners. Those side dishes, however, were increasingly available in processed or pre-prepared forms, including varieties of pickles, instant miso soups, and canned or frozen foods. Older generations often continued to consume a diet heavy on rice, vegetables, and fish, while younger people ate fewer carbohydrates and more protein. As a result, adolescents in 1989 were four inches taller than their grandparents, on average.

Momofuku Ando (1910–2007), a Taiwanese who remained in Japan following the war, invented instant ramen noodles in 1958. During postwar food shortages, authorities encouraged the populace to eat bread made from U.S. surplus wheat, but Ando believed that Japanese would favor wheat as noodles, a more familiar food. He aimed for a processed ramen product that was tasty, inexpensive, and easy to prepare, with a long shelf life. It took years of experimentation before Ando perfected a method of flash frying that created a wavy, dried noodle, easy to rehydrate and flavor with a packet of seasoning. His company, Nissin Foods, grew rapidly as instant ramen exploded in popularity. Exports were soon being shipped to Asian nations and the United States. Sales abroad grew further with Ando's next major invention, Cup Noodle, which provided instant noodles in a Styrofoam cup so that a dish was no longer necessary. Today instant ramen is a cheap commodity food, manufactured globally by a handful of companies in a dizzying variety of chemically enhanced flavors appealing to local palates, from pizza to tom yum to classic masala. In 2015, nearly a hundred billion servings were eaten worldwide. Although it's considered unhealthy for the high sodium and fat content, the poorest peoples of South and Southeast Asia often rely on instant ramen as a cheap staple food.

Another striking change in food habits was the increased frequency of dining out, especially among families. During the 1950s and '60s, dining at restaurants was considered a luxury for most middle-class families. By the '70s, greater discretionary income, increased leisure time, and widespread acquisition of automobiles made it possible for families to enjoy regular outings to family-oriented chain restaurants *(famiresu)*. One of the first was the American chain Denny's, where diners could choose from a variety of Western or Japanese favorites from large, colorful menus with pictures. Famiresu were relatively inexpensive and kid-friendly, offering children's menus and toys, making them attractive to families. American fast-food chains also quickly gained popular followings. Kentucky Fried Chicken (KFC) was the first, opening an outlet at Osaka's Expo '70, followed by a hundred others over the next two years. By 1990, there were over a thousand KFCs in cities and towns across Japan. McDonald's opened its first restaurant in Ginza in 1971 and expanded even more rapidly. Both chains

were among the first "glocalizers," catering to local tastes by altering recipes or developing special products for the Japanese markets, such as
McDonald's teriyaki and "moon-viewing" *(tsukimi)* burgers, the latter
topped with a fried egg. KFC and McDonald's have become so naturalized
in Japan that most children don't consider them "foreign" fast foods.
Another American restaurant, Shakey's Pizza, opened in Tokyo in 1973 and
became popular for its all-you-can-eat buffet *(baikingu)* lunch, a formula
adopted by many other restaurants of different genres that remains popular today. Japanese firms developed their own competing fast-food chains,
such as Lotteria and MOSBurger, both founded in 1972 and both successful
in expanding throughout East Asia. MOSBurger, the second largest fast-
food franchise after McDonald's, offers the unique rice burger: a bun made
of two compressed rice patties filled with traditional favorites like sautéed
burdock and carrot *(kinpira gobo)*.

Gender Norms

From the 1950s to the '70s, the *sarariman*, or white-collar businessman
working for a major corporation, earned iconic status as a masculine ideal,
a corporate warrior who enabled Japan to regain prosperity. University-
educated males aspired to this position more than any other. The sarariman
identity first appeared in late Meiji, but from the late '50s forward such
white-collar jobs were more available to larger numbers of men. These
careers were not easy, as the sarariman was expected to commit body and
soul to the company, working overtime daily and joining his boss and colleagues for drinks at bars and hostess clubs after work. He sometimes had
to accept temporary transfers to regional branch offices, often leaving his
family behind in Tokyo to avoid disrupting his children's education. Yet the
payoffs for his sacrifices were high: he was assured of lifetime employment
in a seniority-based system that guaranteed salary raises and promotions
independent of actual performance. The sarariman spent weekends and
holidays playing golf or vacationing with his family at company-owned
resorts. He received large annual bonuses and a sizable chunk of money at
retirement. In all, the sarariman served as a model for Japanese men because
his secure, affluent lifestyle could realistically be achieved.

 The typical sarariman hoped to marry a woman who embodied the earlier "good wife, wise mother" feminine ideal, but he wished to find a "love
match" rather than resorting to a traditional marriage arrangement. His
salary was sufficient to take care of his family's needs, allowing his spouse
to be a full-time housewife *(shufu)* tasked with providing a comfortable
home environment and serving her family. She spent her days cleaning and

doing the shopping and cooking, and was also expected to manage household expenses and pay bills, setting aside enough for savings. Since her husband was often absent, she was almost single-handedly responsible for raising the children, ideally two. The stereotypical mother earned the nickname "education mama" *(kyōiku mama)* by hovering over her children's homework at night to make certain they could scale the education ladder to a respected high school and college. The life of a middle-class housewife brought women both frustration and gratification. Many regretted that their husbands spent so much time working and commuting. Yet most mass-media accounts depicted the full-time housewife as the female gender ideal, finding satisfaction through financial security and taking pride in nurturing the future of her children.

The sons and daughters of sararimen and education mamas were expected to follow in their parents' footsteps. For boys, this meant studying hard to pass rigorous school entrance examinations, often attending cram schools *(juku)* in their free time. If they weren't successful in gaining entrance to the college of their choice, they might spend a year or more after graduation as "rōnin" (masterless samurai), studying full-time for the next year's exam. Girls usually followed a different path. Many parents considered junior college the suitable end point for girls' higher education, since few professional careers were open to women. Junior college graduates often worked as "OLs" (office ladies) who performed clerical work or menial tasks, such as serving tea or sharpening pencils, for male colleagues. Young women who wished to enhance their bridal credentials often took lessons in polite arts like flower arranging and tea ceremony, just as they had done in the prewar period.

Mass Culture: TV and Manga

The advent of television was enormously significant in Japan, providing a new forum for national consciousness about desirable lifestyles and values and helping rebuild national pride. When the first commercial TVs were produced in 1953, they were unaffordable by the vast majority. To create a viewing audience, hundreds of TV sets were installed in outdoor public spaces where crowds congregated, such as at busy stations, on the grounds of major temples and shrines, in front of department stores, and in Ueno and Asakusa, where urbanites gathered for entertainment. In addition, many of the twenty to thirty thousand small electrical-goods stores located in urban neighborhoods featured a TV in their shop windows. As many as a million people gathered around such "street TVs" for popular broadcasts, such as baseball games and, especially, professional wrestling. Rikidōzan

FIGURE 67.   Pro wrestler Rikidōzan. Photo in *Asahi gurafu,* September, 21, 1955.
Source: Wikimedia Commons.

(1924–63), a Korean-born wrestler initially trained in sumo, became Japanese TV's first superstar. In 1951, he debuted as a pro wrestler who specialized in defeating villainous American opponents with his signature "karate chop" move. Rikidōzan understood the need for theatricality in the farcical bouts and became a hero who symbolized an alternate world where Japanese could triumph over the all-powerful Americans.

By the end of the 1950s, TVs had become more affordable and moved indoors to restaurants, bars, and coffee shops, which installed them to attract customers, and into middle-class homes. Much of the early programming was imported from the United States, including shows such as *I Love Lucy*, *Father Knows Best*, and *Lassie* and cartoons like *Popeye* and *The Flintstones*. The live-action shows gave the Japanese a glimpse of attractive American lifestyles, including appliances and consumer goods considered standard for middle-class families. Public interest in the 1959 royal wedding further spurred demand for home TVs, as did the 1964 Olympics. Media frenzy arose over the engagement of Crown Prince Akihito and Shōda Michiko, a wealthy commoner whom the public embraced as "Mitchi." Over two million TVs were sold in the year before the wedding, many in anticipation of its TV coverage. The marriage procession, ceremony, and other related coverage were broadcast from 6 A.M. until 10 P.M. on the day of the wedding; many viewers watched ten or more hours of the programming on their new sets. Intense interest was attributed to public excitement over the Cinderella story of the prince's true "love match" with a modern and well-educated commoner. The marriage was thought to symbolize Japan's transformation into a progressive, democratic society. It also helped to reforge public ties of loyalty and affection to the imperial family, badly frayed by defeat and occupation.

During the 1960s, Japanese-produced programming grew in both quantity and quality. In 1961, NHK established its still-popular morning drama format, yearlong productions of serialized novels broadcast in fifteen-minute daily segments. In 1963, it began to air year-long Sunday-night dramas *(taiga dorama)* based on popular novels set in premodern times, centered around a famous historical figure. Animated programs, often based on popular manga comics, targeted not only children but the whole family. *Sazae-san*, the world's longest-running animated series, was first broadcast in 1969 and still consistently places among the top ten most-watched shows. The title character is a full-time housewife who lives in a suburban multigenerational household with her parents and siblings, along with her husband and young son. Episodes portray everyday life and problems at work, in school, or in the neighborhood, presenting a nostalgic,

FIGURE 68. Photo of the imperial family, commemorating the wedding of Crown Prince Akihito and Shōda Michiko. Supplied by the Imperial Household Agency, 1959, and printed in the *Sunday mainichi*. Source: Wikimedia Commons.

conservative vision of ideal family life, with sarariman husbands, wives devoted to family matters, and studious, polite children. Depictions of family celebrations during the New Year, cherry blossom season, summer festivals, and the beginning of spring *(setsubun)* instructed viewers on how to properly observe traditional holidays. Electrical-goods manufacturer Toshiba has been the main sponsor of the show since its inception, an appropriate arrangement since Sazae-san uses vacuum cleaners, rice-cookers, and other appliances in most episodes.

Another successful animated series that supported national values was *Astro Boy* (*Tetsuwan atomu*, 1963–66), based on a manga by the renowned Tezuka Osamu (1928–89; see below), about a boy robot built by a scientist to replace his dead son. In his battles against evil, the conscientious Astro Boy demonstrates both the power of science and the merit of more traditional values such as hard work and cooperation. *Ultraman* (*Urutoraman*, 1966–67), another science-centric series, became an international cult favorite. The story is set in the 1990s and features a benevolent alien superhero who fights off giant monsters and evil aliens that threaten the earth. Both *Astro Boy* and *Ultraman* have enjoyed numerous remakes and re-releases and spawned myriad collectible figures and other merchandise. A

FIGURE 69. Tezuka Osamu's *Astro Boy.* Courtesy of Tezuka Productions.

cartoon for young children, *Anpanman* (1973–2013), is about the exploits of a superhero whose head is made of a bun filled with sweet bean jam. While entertaining, the series also teaches children lessons in hygiene, etiquette, and interpersonal relations. Popular characters from the series, including the title character, his nemesis Bacteria Man (Baikinman), and his pals like White Bread Man (Shokupanman), adorn a vast array of children's toys, clothing, and snack foods. *Anpanman* books have sold over fifty million copies, and there are five dedicated *Anpanman* museums across Japan.

Genres and styles of manga comic books multiplied rapidly in the 1950s and '60s. Scholars debate whether manga are rooted in historical precedents—such as the *Chōjūgiga* illustrated scrolls (see Figure 20), Edo-period kibyōshi and woodblock prints, kamishibai, and Meiji-era comic strips—or whether they are a new genre of mass culture more influenced by trends in American youth culture such as Disney films and comic books. The two largest influences on the work of Tezuka Osamu, the "godfather" of modern Japanese manga and anime, were Walt Disney and Max Fleischer, who brought cartoon characters like Betty Boop, Popeye, and Superman to life. Tezuka reportedly saw Disney's *Bambi* (1942) eighty times. Like most of his mentors' creations, Tezuka's characters tend to have cute, rounded features and glistening, saucer-shaped eyes. Tezuka created more than seven hundred volumes of manga and over five hundred episodes of anime. His first best-selling manga was 1947's *New Treasure Island (Shin takarajima)*, which used exciting sound effects and cinematic techniques like close-ups, fade-outs, and montage to make the story flow across the pages. He followed up with *Kimba the White Lion (Janguru taitei*, 1950)—the purported model for Disney's *The Lion King*—which was adapted into an animated series in 1965. The iconic *Astro Boy* emerged first as a manga (1952–68); its associated animated series began in 1963. Tezuka also authored two epic manga projects: the fourteen-volume *Buddha (Budda*, 1972–83), a novelized account of the life of the historical Buddha Gautama; and *Phoenix (Hi no tori*, 1967–88), a twelve-volume work with each book set in a different era, switching back and forth between historical times and the distant future. Each volume involves a quest for immortality, which characters seek by pursuing the titular bird of fire with underlying moralistic messages about karma and reincarnation. Volume 1 takes place in the prehistoric era of Himiko, Queen of Yamatai, while the second volume leaps to the year 3404, when a young man and his alien girlfriend face nuclear war. Later volumes take place during the Nara period and the twelfth-century Genpei War between the Taira and Minamoto. Tezuka considered *Phoenix* his life's work, but it was left unfinished when he died in 1989.

Comic books of the '50s and '60s tended to target preteen boys and girls. They were (and are) commonly published in thick magazines on low-grade paper, containing up to fifteen different story lines. Some stories are drawn in cute, rounded styles, but others use a more realistic style known as *gekiga* (dramatic picture). Top magazine titles sell well over a million copies per issue. Boys' comics *(shōnen manga)* tend to focus on adventure, samurai, science fiction, gangsters, or sports. Sports comics teach boys about cooperation and teamwork and praise masculine traits like courage, perseverance, and remaining tough and cool in the face of adversity. *Star of the Giants (Kyojin no hoshi,* 1966–71) depicted actual baseball stars and Japan's favorite team, the Tokyo Giants, in a story about a young pitcher's strenuous climb to the top of the game. The boxing comic *Tomorrow's Joe (Ashita no Joe,* 1968–73) was one of the most popular sports comics of all time, following Joe's triumphant victories and heartbreaking defeats in the ring. The controversial finale, in which Joe dies during a championship bout, became a hot topic of discussion in the wider mass media.

Girls' comics *(shōjo manga)* also spanned genres like science fiction, historical dramas, and sports but were more typically romance oriented. Tezuka Osamu's *Princess Knight (Ribon no kishi,* 1953–56) was pioneering among girls' comics in the bold, martial character of its heroine, Princess Sapphire, who pretends to be a male prince to protect her kingdom and who masquerades as the crime-fighting Phantom of Night. As women manga artists came of age, girls' comics diversified and became more sophisticated. Chikako Urano's *Attack no. 1 (Atakku no. 1,* 1968–70) capitalized on Olympic fervor over women's volleyball, following the travails of a gifted young player who must negotiate rivalries among her teammates. *Attack no. 1* was adapted into the first TV anime about female sports and was subsequently made into four anime feature films and a live-action drama. It inspired numerous other manga and anime on girls in other sports, such as tennis and judo.

Manga employ certain conventions in depicting sound and style. Sound effects are indicated with onomatopoeic words boldly written across the drawn panel. For example, the word *guooo* represents a roar, like that of a fire; *agu agu* accompanies someone munching enthusiastically on food; and *shiiin* indicates silence or motionlessness. Most girls' comics use standard visual conventions, depicting their female characters as slim, long-legged beauties. Their faces are often interchangeable, characterized by pert noses, sharp chins, and especially huge eyes, often with twinkling stars inside. To distinguish between them, characters' fashions and hairstyles are often drawn with painstaking precision.

Today, people of all ages and backgrounds commonly read manga, though sales have declined somewhat from their peak in the '80s. Frederik Schodt reports that over a billion comics were published in 1984, representing about ten for every man, woman, and child in Japan.[7] New categories have evolved for different target audiences, including young men's comics *(seinen manga),* often featuring violence, pornography, or psychological distress; and ladies' comics *(josei manga)* that generally center on interpersonal

FIGURE 70. Contemporary example of a female manga
character, illustrating typical features: "Niabot, with the
reason in mind, that prudery shall not take over the world."
Source: Wikimedia Commons.

relationships, especially among beautiful gay men, but that sometimes have
dark aspects, portraying rape and violence against women.

Visual and Performing Arts

As individuals and families became more affluent, they spent their increased
discretionary income on recreational and leisure activities. Many in the
emerging middle masses took lessons in pursuit of self-improvement, studying English conversation, music, or some form of traditional art. The
numbers engaged in traditional cultural activities reached such unprece-

dented levels from the mid-1950s to the mid-1960s that these years are sometimes referred to as Shōwa Genroku, in reference to the golden age of Edo culture when urban commoners increasingly participated in the arts. Women streamed in the largest numbers to ikebana, but traditional dance (Nihon buyō), musical instruments such as the shamisen and the *koto* (a thirteen-stringed zither), and tea ceremony were also very popular. During ikebana's peak in the mid-1960s, there were over three thousand schools in Japan; the three largest had over a million students each. Men undertook different arts, such as bonsai—the art of tree miniaturization—and martial arts. Judo became especially popular after it was declared an official Olympic sport in 1964. With the invention of the karaoke machine in 1971, men also turned to singing lessons to better impress their bosses and colleagues in after-work outings. Both sexes studied calligraphy and poetry, particularly the composition of haiku.

The re-elevation of traditional culture in the postwar era was part of a conservative national "rebranding" strategy, presenting Japan as a peaceful country of culture *(bunka kokka)* and no longer an aggressive military power. Official policies and projects were launched on many fronts to support this image, including the 1948 declaration of November 3 as National Culture Day (Bunka no hi), the inauguration of prefectural Culture Festivals (Bunkasai), and the 1950 law for protection of "Living National Treasures"—that is, artists, performers, and craftspeople who preserved traditional techniques. Promotion and support of premodern culture, however, while deemed exotic and desirable by Western audiences, contrasted sharply with the contemporary daily reality of a rapidly expanding urban middle class living increasingly Americanized lifestyles.

Many modern artists attempted to merge traditional arts with modernist forms associated with artists such as Picasso, Klee, and Duchamps in attempts to make their work more relevant in the international art world. Experimental calligraphy by Hasegawa Saburō and Morita Shiryū fused script with abstract painting, giving their works recognizable Japanese qualities through the use of space and traditional materials. Yagi Kazuo and Tsuji Shindō injected the boldness and conceptuality of abstract art into ceramic pieces made using traditional techniques. Teshigahara Sōfu promoted an avant-garde approach to ikebana, incorporating non-plant materials and using unconventional objects as containers.

Other contemporary artists of the era, however, preferred to create works that expressed more originality or political and social critique. Artists such as Okamoto Tarō, Kusama Yayoi, and Yokō Tadanori; filmmakers Terayama Shūji and Ōshima Nagisa; photographers Hosoe Eikō and

Tōmatsu Shōmei; music improvisation troupe Group Ongaku; and dancers Hijikata Tatsumi and Ōno Kazuo created works that engaged with global trends while offering criticism of the Japanese condition, seen as subject to rampant capitalism and to national trauma due to overwhelming American influence in culture and politics.

In the early 1950s, painters such as Yamashita Kikuji (1890–1973) drew upon Russian Social Realism in "Reportage" murals that depicted the effects of social injustice and American imperialism, from rural poverty and urban blight to the scars of atomic victims and the tawdriness of towns near U.S. military bases. Okamato Tarō provided an influential voice calling on young artists to engage in works that communicated Japanese realities beyond the horrors and helplessness of Social Realists and beyond traditional conceptions of beauty that supported Orientalist conceptions of Japan. His surrealistic sculptures and paintings—such as *The Law of the Jungle* (1950), depicting fantastic creatures fleeing from a zipper-mouthed monster—were intentionally confrontational and grotesque.

In the 1950s and '60s, radical art collectives such as Gutai, Hi-Red Center, and Neo-Dada engaged in collaborative experiments that aimed to express original vision through original means, as exemplified in Gutai founder Yoshihara Jirō's (1905–72) famous call, "Do what no one has done before!"[8] These groups mounted "Happenings," ephemeral installations that blurred the lines between art and everyday life by incorporating junk and utilitarian objects, seeking to expand the definitions of art in postwar Japan. For instance, Hi-Red Center's *1000 Meter String* (1963) consisted of an unremarkable piece of twine that led from the Tokyo Metropolitan Art Museum through Ueno Park, ending at the Ueno train station. Other works conveyed that art was created in the interplay between an artist's bodily actions and mundane materials. Gutai members used photography to capture works created while writhing in piles of mud and jumping through large screens of paper. The "boxing paintings" of Neo-Dada's Shinohara Ushio (b. 1932) were made by randomly punching long canvases with boxing gloves dipped in ink or paint.

Obsession with sex, madness, and monstrousness among many avant-garde artists recalled prewar tastes for "erotic-grotesque nonsense" and aimed to express primal urges suppressed in conservative mainstream society. Hijikata Tatsumi (1928–86) was one originator of the *butoh* dance form, known for its torturous movements, exaggerated facial expressions, and open sexuality, which he distilled from the misery and fertility associated with his agrarian, poverty-stricken boyhood. Hijikata intended butoh to transcend both Western contemporary and stagnant traditional dance.

FIGURE 71. Yokō Tadanori, *Having Reached a Climax at the Age of 29, I Was Dead*, silkscreen, 1965, The Museum of Modern Art, New York. Source: Art Resource.

His dark, subversive works sought to assert a Japanese artistic modernity rooted in indigenous conditions and aesthetics. Graphic artist Yokō Tadanori (b. 1936) created posters for Hijikata and many other avant-garde performances and exhibitions in the 1960s. Yokō's iconic collages combined disparate images, such as Edo-period erotic shunga, nostalgic advertisements, nationalist symbols, and American icons, in decadent, psychedelic works that suggested the instability and banality of Japanese society. Nude and orgiastic happenings by Kusama Yayoi (b. 1929), along with her assemblages of polka-dotted phalli, expressed feminist outrage against the oppressive Japanese patriarchy. Diagnosed with obsessive-compulsive disorder, Kusama made works characterized by minimalistic repetitions, patterns, and accumulations to express her psychological states.

Today's contemporary art world highly esteems the groundbreaking work of such Japanese artists. Gutai and Kusama Yayoi have been the solo subjects of recent, blockbuster exhibitions in New York and Washington, D.C. Foreign spectators flock to these shows for their playful qualities and visual shock appeal; few deeply consider the social and emotional turmoil of the 1950s and '60s that inspired the works.

In summary, Japan's painful interlude of occupation by a foreign power was followed by an era of consumerist plenty, with middle-class lifestyles influenced by American norms. From the 1950s to the '70s, civil liberties granted under the postwar constitution and a sense of optimism inspired the development and growth of a variety of new religions and social movements. The variety and quantity of forms of entertainment and culture proliferated and became more accessible. At the same time, conservative forces continued to dictate ideal gender norms and continued to control politics and the economy. Their all-out prioritization of economic growth resulted in environmental damage and unrestrained industrial development that spurred popular opposition. Public resentment and violent protests also arose over Japan's continued subordination to the United States, represented by the ANPO treaties. The majority of the middle-class masses, however, contented themselves with their improved standards of living, supported through dedication to work and family.

FURTHER READING

Avenell, Simon A. *Making Japanese Citizens: Civil Society and the Mythology of the Shimin in Postwar Japan*. Berkeley: University of California Press, 2010.

Barshay, Andrew E. *The Gods Left First: The Captivity and Repatriation of Japanese POWs in Northeast Asia, 1945–1956.* Berkeley: University of California Press, 2013.

Bardsley, Jan. *Women and Democracy in Cold War Japan.* London: Bloomsbury, 2014.

Dower, John W. *Embracing Defeat: Japan in the Wake of World War II.* New York: W.W. Norton, 2000.

Francks, Penelope. *The Japanese Consumer: An Alternative History of Modern Japan.* New York: Cambridge University Press, 2009.

Gordon, Andrew. *The Wages of Affluence: Labor and Management in Postwar Japan.* Cambridge, MA: Harvard University Press, 2001.

Kushner, Barak. *Men to Devils, Devils to Men: Japanese War Crimes and Chinese Justice.* Cambridge, MA: Harvard University Press, 2015.

Munroe, Alexandra. *Japanese Art after 1945: Scream against the Sky.* New York: Harry N. Abrams, 1994.

Partner, Simon. *Assembled in Japan: Electrical Goods and the Making of the Japanese Consumer.* Berkeley: University of California Press, 2000.

Watt, Lori. *When Empire Comes Home: Repatriation and Reintegration in Postwar Japan.* Cambridge, MA: Harvard University Press, 2010.

RECOMMENDED FILMS

ANPO: Art X War. 2010. Documentary film directed by Linda Hoaglund. Chronicles public protest and artists' reactions related to ANPO.

Gate of Flesh. 1964. Feature film directed by Seijun Suzuki. Drama about a band of panpan girl prostitutes living in postwar ruins.

Giants and Toys. 1958. Feature film directed by Masumura Yasuzō. Satire about ruthless corporate competition between three manufacturers of caramels.

Minamata: The Victims and Their World. 1971. Documentary film directed by Tsuchimoto Noriaki. Award-winning work on Minamata mercury poisoning.

Tokyo Olympiad. 1965. Documentary film directed by Ichikawa Kon. Highly regarded work on the 1964 Olympics.

Tokyo Story. 1955. Feature film directed by Ozu Yasujirō. Family drama about an elderly couple who travel to Tokyo to visit their grown children. Often cited as one of the best films ever made.

Yakuza Papers: Battles without Honor or Humanity. 1973. Feature films directed by Fukasaku Kinji. Series of gritty films based on the memoirs of a member of the yakuza.

12 "Cool" Japan as Cultural Superpower

1980s–2010s

Japan's economic expansion continued in the 1980s, but its benefits were selective, serving those who fit the myth of homogeneity while consigning others to the margins. In the '90s, the economic bubble burst and Japan faced a number of serious crises, including a devastating earthquake in Kobe, domestic terrorism by a religious group, and the demographic threat of a rapidly aging society. Around the same time, however, Japanese popular culture began to attract acclaim and large, new audiences around the globe. Japan's rising influence—in arenas ranging from pop music to consumer electronics, from architecture to fashion, and from animation to cuisine— makes it look more like a cultural superpower today than it did in the '80s, when it was an economic superpower, or the late '30s, when it was a major military and imperialist power.

ECONOMIC AND SOCIAL DEVELOPMENTS

During the '80s, the Japanese economy continued to expand, especially among service industries such as banking, insurance, mass media, and real estate, which collectively employed over 60 percent of the population. Manufacturing, especially the automotive and electronics industries, also continued to prosper. Among the nation's twenty-five largest corporations, fourteen were in those two industries. Japan became the world's top producer of automobiles in 1980; between 1974 and 1989, production nearly doubled, from seven to thirteen million vehicles. Forty percent of these were exported to U.S. and European markets, damaging the sales of their domestic auto manufacturers. With the dollar strong in the early '80s, Americans snapped up Japanese cars and electronics, resulting in a chronic trade imbalance, which grew from $49 billion to $87 billion between 1985 and 1987. U.S. protectionists began to call for import restrictions to defend manufacturers against Japanese competition. As trade friction mounted, Japanese firms such as Toyota, Nissan, and Honda began to invest in factory construction in the United States and other countries to avoid trade barriers. Electrical equipment makers produced a large spectrum of goods, from industrial machinery to office equipment and household goods. In the late '70s, many successfully expanded their product lines to include computers and related equipment. They, too, began to construct many of their factories abroad to avoid market restrictions and take advantage of lower labor costs.

In the retail sector, convenience stores and superstores began to appear across the country, offering consumers shopping choices midway between the small neighborhood shop and the luxurious urban department store. Convenience stores *(konbini)*, including Seven-Eleven, Lawson, and Family Mart, are generally open 24/7 and always nearby. They offer a wide range of food and drink beyond simple snack foods and Cup Noodle, including rice balls *(onigiri)*, sandwiches, and bento meals, replenished up to nine times per day through the use of sophisticated computer inventory systems. Most konbini also sell beer, wine, sake, and whiskey; stock an assortment of daily essentials such as batteries, shampoo, and umbrellas; and offer racks of magazines and manga for customers to peruse. Today they also offer services such as tickets for movies, concerts, and other events; bill payment; photo printing; and copier/fax service. Life without konbini is simply unimaginable in contemporary Japan. Superstores such as Seiyū, Jusco, and Don Quijote are similar to Target or Walmart in the United States, selling a wide range of economically priced groceries, clothing, household furniture and appliances, and other goods. Their rapid growth, however, did not affect the more luxurious department stores or high-end boutiques, because as consumers prospered they developed an appetite for international designer brands such as Louis Vuitton, Chanel, and Gucci. Young consumers sought trendy fashions, household décor, and goods that supported their hobbies at stores that marketed a lifestyle "brand," such as Muji, Loft, and Tōkyū Hands.

In short, the '80s were a time of conspicuous consumption and differentiation of goods and services for niche markets. Newly affluent consumers indulged in luxury cars, expensive golf-club memberships, hundred-dollar melons, and sake flecked with real gold. Tanaka Yasuo's 1980 novel *Nantonaku kurisutaru (Somehow, Crystal)* captured the consumer-centered lifestyles and materialistic values of the younger generations—called the "crystal" life by the author—by depicting two weeks in the life of a college student, celebrating her unrestrained consumption. Thin on plot, it instead provided a guide to the most desirable brands and fashions

FIGURE 72. Typical variety of *bento*-style meals offered at a *konbini*. Source: Wikimedia Commons.

and the most chic restaurants and cafés. The narrator cherishes her "snobbery" and "affectation," demonstrated through acts like carrying a Courrèges shopping bag or eating her afternoon cake in a café "French style, with white wine" rather than espresso. The message of the book is ambivalent. On one hand, it seems to critique consumption as a source of identity. One character comments, "I guess in the end you have to say that we have no resistance to brand names. Our generation. Maybe it's not just our generation, maybe it's all of Japan."[1] On the other hand, the book offers several hundred detailed notes recommending brand-name goods and restaurants. It quickly sold eight hundred thousand copies and became a sensation in the media, setting off debates over changing social values.

Awash in capital, companies also made ostentatious purchases. In 1987, a Japanese insurance company bought Vincent Van Gogh's *Sunflowers* for $39.9 million, then the highest price ever paid for a work of art. Sony and Matsushita each spent billions to acquire their own Hollywood studios, Columbia Pictures and MCA Entertainment. Other Japanese firms took control of Rockefeller Center, CBS Records, and Pebble Beach golf course, site of the U.S. Open. The U.S. media reported on these acquisitions in alarmist tones, as if they constituted a Japanese invasion, but in fact,

European countries like the United Kingdom and Holland owned many more U.S. companies and real estate.

Affluence was accompanied by a new surge of nationalism—pride in a prosperous nation that had risen from the ashes of defeat to once again challenge Western nations. Some authors began to credit Japan's accomplishments to unique racial and cultural characteristics in a genre of writing known as *Nihonjinron,* or reflections on Japaneseness. Many works asserted that Western customs were "hard" and "dry," so that Westerners were unconnected, like grains of sand; whereas Japanese ways were "wet" and "soft," so that members of society stuck together like cooked rice. During the occupation, qualities such as groupism and social indulgence were deemed negative and feudal, but they were now reevaluated positively as the very values that made Japan affluent and superior to other nations. Academic versions of Nihonjinron were popularized by psychologist Doi Takeo, who asserted that Japanese society was built on indulgence of or dependence on others *(amae),* rooted in mother-child relationships; and by Tokyo University economist Murakami Yasusuke, who claimed that Japan's corporate success was rooted in the samurai family structure, a collectivist rather than individualist model that emphasized relationships and organizational skills. Pseudoscientific works of Nihonjinron sometimes made absurd claims, such as that Japanese bees are more communal than non-Japanese bees or that Japanese physiology is different from that of other humans and so Japanese cannot digest foreign beef or use birth control pills.

New national confidence was pointedly expressed by LDP politician Ishihara Shintarō, later the governor of Tokyo, in the 1989 essay "The Japan That Can Say No: Why Japan Will Be First among Equals." The title referred to the widely felt sense that the Japanese government kowtowed too much to the United States and needed to take a more independent stance in both foreign affairs and business. The essay criticized America's prejudice and predicted its decline while outlining what Japan must do in order to be the mainspring of the new world order, with claims like the following: "Americans, with their scant few centuries of history, have never experienced the transition from one major historical period to another. They emerged as the premier world power only decades ago, toward the end of the modern era. That Japan, an Oriental country, is about to supplant them in some major fields is what annoys the Americans so much."[2] This type of rhetoric was viewed by many Americans as arrogant, humiliating, and frighteningly reminiscent of Japan's imperialist days. Offended Americans did not have to worry long, however, because Japan's bubble economy and new confidence were soon to burst.

The death of Emperor Hirohito in 1989 portended a decade of decline and disaster. The reign of the Shōwa emperor, the longest in Japan's recorded history, had witnessed remarkable highs and lows. Hirohito ascended the throne in 1926 as Japan began to flex its military muscle, soon becoming capable of challenging the United States. Twenty years later, the nation was decimated and occupied militarily for the first time in its history; its future seemed bleak. But within a few decades Japan had recovered and become a leading economic power, one of the most advanced nations in the world. The emperor died after months of serious illness, during which the mass media reported minute details of his daily health and treatments in somber, honorific language. Following his death, TV networks suspended regular programming for three days to facilitate national mourning. The emperor's death sparked widespread public reflection on the question of his war responsibility and on the value of the imperial institution. His son and successor, Crown Prince Akihito, chose Heisei for the title of his reign, a classical term expressing hope for peace in the world. During his first years as monarch, however, Japan experienced political and economic turmoil as it fell into recession and the LDP lost power for the first time, while the collapse of the Soviet Union altered the Cold War landscape that had supported its American-led prosperity.

The fall into recession is often described as the "bursting of the bubble." Risky bank loans had financed much of the domestic and overseas investments of the '80s. Speculation in land and real estate had resulted in unbelievably inflated values: the grounds of the Imperial Palace in central Tokyo, occupying under three square miles, was worth more on paper than all of the real estate in California; the aggregate value of land in Japan was 50 percent greater than the value of all the land in the rest of the world. To reign in the overheated economy, the government raised interest rates in 1990, resulting in a credit crunch. When loans came due, many speculators could neither make repayments nor sell their rapidly deflating assets. The real estate market collapsed, wiping out a trillion dollars' worth of paper assets. The Nikkei stock index plummeted by over 80 percent and has never fully recovered. Corporate bankruptcies reached record rates and domestic consumption crashed as families lost their nest eggs. To help restore financial stability, major banks received $600 billion of taxpayer bailout.

In 1995 two national disasters, one natural and one man-made, compounded economic woes. On January 17, the Great Hanshin Earthquake razed a third of the city of Kobe, including much of its central business district. The quake, which measured 7.2 on the Richter scale, claimed over 6,200 lives and caused over $100 billion in damage, the equivalent of 2.5 percent of the national gross domestic product. Highways collapsed and the port and rail links were destroyed, making access difficult for emergency responders. Over 320,000 residents were forced to live in temporary evacuation shelters, some for four or more years. Early-warning systems had failed to predict the quake, and "earthquake-proof" construction techniques came to naught. Furthermore, national government agencies were slow to respond to emergency needs and even refused offers of aid from other nations. Individuals, non-governmental organizations, and corporations—in the absence of effective relief from the state—mobilized to provide aid to local residents. To the embarrassment of the government, a yakuza syndicate headquartered in Kobe was among the first groups to offer food and water to victims. New religions sent thousands of volunteers who set up local relief centers, and right-wing political activists *(uyoku dantai)* sponsored soup lines. The Japanese mass media reported selectively on the quake's aftermath, focusing on positive stories of cooperation and perseverance among victims and ignoring the looting and violence that accompanied the massive disaster. The media's censored, wishful approach to reporting disasters would be repeated in the 2011 Tohoku earthquake and nuclear disaster.

On March 20, 1995, while the nation was still reeling from the quake, a new religion called Aum Shinrikyō committed a heinous act of domestic terrorism, releasing deadly sarin gas into the Tokyo subway system. Twelve people died and over 5,500 required hospitalization. Aum's founder and guru, Asahara Shōkō (b. 1955), initially established the group as a meditation and yoga circle. Members entering the community gave up all outside ties and engaged in harsh ascetic practices. Aum arose with a wave of other new religions in the 1980s that, like their predecessors, were centered on charismatic leaders and often stressed spiritual healing. In keeping with the mood of the bubble economy, several new groups claimed the ability to make followers wealthy. Many of them mounted spectacular events and festivals to gain mass media attention and used manga and anime as a recruitment tool to reach new followers. Earlier new religions had combined beliefs and practices from a variety of religions, including Buddhism, Shinto, Confucianism, and Christianity. But many of these "new age" groups went even further, incorporating folk beliefs about ghosts and wandering spirits along with UFOs and the lost continents of Mu and Atlantis. Aum mixed Hinduism and Tibetan Tantra into its teachings.

Asahara first gained public notoriety in 1985 when a magazine photograph appeared to capture him floating in midair in the lotus position. Aum developed a series of profitable businesses, including ramen shops, a telephone dating club, a babysitting service, and computer stores, financed and staffed at no cost by members. The group launched a political party in 1990, attempting to elect twenty-five candidates, including Asahara. In its bizarre campaign, followers danced and chanted while wearing masks of the guru or the Hindu elephant deity Ganesha. They were widely mocked in the media, and none of the Aum candidates prevailed. Finding the path to political power blocked, Asahara turned increasingly to messages of violence, preaching of a coming Armageddon. The group began amassing arms and developing chemical and biological weapons in preparation. Police planned a raid on Aum headquarters after investigating the death of an accountant murdered by Aum for trying to help his sister flee the cult. The sarin gas attack was likely launched to forestall the raid. In the decade following the attack, 189 Aum members were brought to trial and eleven sentenced to death, including Asahara, although executions have been held up by legal complications. At its peak, Aum had some forty thousand members, the vast majority of whom had no knowledge of its violent activities. Most attempted to return to normal life, but over a thousand continued to live and practice the religion in insular Aum compounds.

News of the Aum attack and subsequent coverage of the group's nefarious activities dominated the mass media for months. The public was especially shocked to learn that Asahara's top lieutenants included many graduates of top universities, who might have enjoyed successful careers elsewhere but chose to join a radical cult instead. Endless essays and TV roundtable discussions obsessed over where "Japan" had gone wrong. Coming on the heels of the recession and earthquake, the events deeply shook society, which had long regarded itself as one of the world's safest, most stable nations, where disasters and crimes that occurred in other parts of the world never happened. Many called for stricter policing of religious groups. It is important to remember, however, that the Aum incident was an aberration, not attributable to something inherent in Japanese society or in new religious movements. Millennial cults are particularly prone to violence because they often believe that a catastrophic war will result in paradise on earth. Aum's path to violent crime was due to a combination of Asahara's paranoia, the weapons-making capabilities of scientists among his leading followers, and the isolation of members, reinforced by spartan communal living.

Demographic change has also created a sense of threat to Japanese society. The population is rapidly shrinking and aging; by 2025, Japan will be the world's oldest nation, with 36 percent of the populace over the age of sixty-five. The birthrate has declined steeply and continuously since the 1970s, and the population is expected to drop to one hundred million by

2050, when only 1.5 people will be working to support every person over sixty-five. The falling birth rate is due, in part, to women's growing refusal to marry because they resent and reject the heavy social expectations to act as nurturers and housewives. Many women are reluctant to have offspring because of a relative lack of child-care facilities and support mechanisms for mothers. Furthermore, childbirth is not covered by national health insurance, and the cost of raising children in Japan is very high. Low rates of childbirth are also related to the decline in Japan's marriage rate, which has fallen steadily for decades and especially steeply since 2000. While 21 percent of Japanese men in their early thirties were unmarried in 2005, this had grown to nearly half of all men in the same age group by 2015. More young women are organizing their lives around the principle that they will remain single by preparing for careers and buying condos for themselves.

The sharp population decrease has dire consequences for the economy: falling production, shrinking consumer markets, soaring taxes, and plummeting savings. The anticipated reduction of the future labor force will drive small and medium-sized businesses that depend on low-wage labor into bankruptcy. To avoid these outcomes, Japan needs to add over half a million workers every year for the next fifty years. Government officials have discussed for decades how to increase the number of workers and limit future tax burdens, but changes will require adjustments to long-standing policies and attitudes in order to allow higher rates of immigration and provide equal opportunities for women and minorities who wish to pursue professional careers.

There is a willing supply of immigrant labor to meet demand, but the government has made it difficult for most foreign individuals to work legally in Japan. Many would-be immigrants arrive as tourists and simply overstay their visas, hoping they won't be caught. Foreign workers are often employed in the lowest rungs of construction and manufacturing, in very small businesses or doing repetitive factory work. Foreign women from poorer countries often work in the sex trade or as in-home helpers for the elderly. Despite the growing need for labor, immigration is widely resisted because the general public, egged on by the media, believes that migrants are potential criminals threatening their imagined crime-free society. Furthermore, admitting foreign workers threatens to destabilize a society that views itself as racially and culturally homogeneous. With the continuing recession, people blame foreigners for taking jobs, although few Japanese would want the types of work available to immigrants.

Existing minority populations also tend to fill the "dirty, hard, and dangerous" jobs unwanted by middle-class Japanese. Minorities did not equally share in the bounty of the postwar economic miracle. Four percent of the Japanese population can be classified as members of minority groups, but their experiences are often ignored in accounts of postwar affluence. Notions of homogeneous Japaneseness ignore diverse populations such as the burakumin, Ainu, Koreans, Okinawans, and Nikkeijin (i.e., South Americans of Japanese descent who were allowed to immigrate beginning in the 1980s to fill labor needs).

The burakumin, the former outcaste group of the premodern period, are the largest minority group in Japan, numbering around three million individuals, mostly clustered in six thousand communities. Burakumin are not a racial or ethnic minority; it is only their past low-caste status that makes them the target of continued discrimination. A commission in the 1960s found that buraku communities had ghetto-like conditions, often lacking basic public services such as sewers, tap water, streetlights, and fire protection. Educational achievement in these communities was well below the national average, while unemployment rates and welfare cases were significantly above average. Legislation in the '60s established special funds to improve housing and provide educational opportunities, but various forms of illegal discrimination persist. Major companies require that applicants submit their official household registries, and they eliminate candidates from addresses in known buraku areas. Because of public perception that they are polluted or tainted, few in the minority populations can find jobs in service industries like retail or restaurants. Marriage is also an area of persistent discrimination. Families sometimes hire private detectives to ensure that their children's fiancés are not from buraku areas.

Koreans form one of the largest ethnic minority populations, with over seven hundred thousand in Japan. Second-, third-, and fourth-generation Korean residents, descended from colonials who resided in Japan before and during World War II, are referred to as *zainichi* ("stay in Japan") to differentiate them from contemporary immigrants. With the postwar dismantling of the empire, Koreans who remained in Japan were stripped of Japanese nationality; they had no right to vote, to hold public office, or to be employed as teachers in public schools. Although the majority were born in Japan and speak Japanese as their first or only language, their rights are constrained by their status as resident aliens. Japanese law determines citizenship according to the nationality of one's parents rather than one's place of birth. Koreans born in Japan must take formal steps to become naturalized citizens, but many choose not to do so for political reasons. The zainichi population is divided according to loyalties to North or South Korea. North Korean groups are especially active in trying to maintain Korean language and culture, sponsoring over a hundred private schools, including a university—necessary because graduates of Korean high schools are not allowed to take entrance examinations for most Japanese universities.

Zainichi Koreans are rarely employed as unionized or permanent workers in large Japanese firms and are barred from holding government jobs, despite being born and raised in Japan. They are disproportionately represented in the poorly paid service and entertainment industries, in small, non-unionized subcontracting companies, and as unskilled labor for the construction industry. On average, they earn 30 percent less than Japanese working in comparable jobs. In order to avoid such discrimination, many become small-business owners and are particularly known for operating barbecue restaurants, pachinko parlors, and small construction companies. Like some burakumin, some zainichi try to "pass" in Japanese society, changing their names and obscuring their ethnic origins. Since many feel fully Japanese, with no ties to Korea, they are frustrated by continuing discrimination.

The Ainu number twenty-five thousand officially but include up to two hundred thousand persons of Ainu ancestry. They represent the indigenous inhabitants of Ezo, the former name for Hokkaido, whose subsistence as hunter-gatherers began to transform under the Tokugawa shogunate. In the seventeenth century, the Ainu began to trade animal skins and fish products for Japanese tobacco, sake, rice, tools, and other items under disadvantageous terms, leading to a loss of their autonomy and exhaustion of natural resources. By the Meiji period, the Ainu were seriously weakened and unable to resist the state's demands for assimilation that imperiled their language and culture.

Ainu have never been formally recognized by the state as an indigenous people of Japan and have thus not received financial and social reparations that other industrialized countries have provided to displaced native populations. Like other minority populations, they also tend to work as construction laborers and have a lower educational profile than mainstream Japanese. Beginning in the 1960s, Ainu groups began international dialogues with other oppressed indigenous peoples, including Native Americans and the Eskimo. In recent decades they have begun to seek guaranteed political participation and rights pertaining to education, language, and culture.

Okinawans are the largest ethnic minority, with 1.3 million in the Okinawan islands and three hundred thousand in other parts of Japan. Their native language and culture are distinct from the mainland Japanese. In the early twentieth century, the Okinawan economy was not developed in the same way as the main islands, and many Okinawans emigrated, going to Hawaii, Brazil, the Philippines, and the Nan'yō to earn a living.

Okinawans have paid the highest price for Japan's postwar security. The U.S. occupation of Okinawa lasted until 1972, twenty years longer than for the rest of Japan. SCAP placed the islands under military governance and neglected the reconstruction being performed on the mainland. As fears of Cold War heightened in the 1950s, the U.S. military saw that some degree of economic and social progress was necessary to gain the popular support of Okinawans, who resented the appropriation of their land to construct foreign military bases. Today, U.S. bases still occupy a fifth of the Okinawan islands and are home to nearly fifty thousand American military troops. Residents complain that the bases cause noise and environmental pollution and hinder development. The commission of crimes by U.S. military personnel has become a controversial and emotional issue. In 1995, three soldiers were convicted of raping and beating a twelve-year-old girl they had abducted off the streets. Nearly eighty-five thousand Okinawans demonstrated in protest, and the case intensified debates about expulsion of U.S. troops. In 2010, a hundred thousand Okinawans (10 percent of the population) gathered to protest the building of a new U.S. base that would damage a fragile ecosystem and likely obliterate the population of the endangered dugong, a cousin of the manatee.

Belief in Japanese racial superiority and the myth of homogeneity is demonstrated by a 1990 government program allowing the legal immigration of South Americans of Japanese ancestry, or Nikkei, in order to help solve labor shortages. Authorities acted on convictions that Nikkei, whose families had lived abroad for generations and who knew neither the Japanese language nor culture very well, could be integrated into society more easily than immigrants from other nations. They created a visa category exclusively for foreign descendants of Japanese emigrants. Many poor farmers had left Japan in the early twentieth century and migrated to South America in search of better opportunities. In fact, the city of São Paulo, Brazil, hosts the second largest population of Japanese in the world, after Tokyo. Over 280,000 Nikkei have immigrated to Japan for work since the program was instituted.

Workers are often recruited in South America through subcontractors, many with yakuza ties. Initially, many Nikkei were hired for manufacturing jobs at large auto and electronics factories. As production increasingly moved to China and other countries with lower labor costs, the jobs available for Nikkei have become less secure and pay lower wages. By 2001, a quarter of Brazilian Nikkei in Japan were unemployed. A variety of social problems arose as South American populations settled in. Immigrant children were often academically unprepared for the Japanese school system, which did not offer the multilingual education they required. Nikkei faced discrimination in obtaining housing and access to public services. In areas with high Nikkei populations some businesses, fearing theft, prohibited their entry or limited the number allowed in shops at one time, prompting lawsuits charging discrimination.

The number of available Nikkei immigrant workers plateaued at a level that could not fill anticipated labor demand. In response, the government created special trainee programs, allowing companies to legally hire Asian workers—mostly from China, the Philippines, and Indonesia—with the goal of eventually sending trained employees back to their home countries to work for Japanese companies there. Trainees are not protected by labor standards and receive "allowances" much lower than market wages. Another category of Asians permitted to immigrate are women who agree to become the brides of rural farmers. As Japanese women are increasingly unwilling to lead the difficult lives of farm wives, local governments in rural areas are sponsoring searches abroad for Asian brides among mostly Chinese, Filipina, Korean, and Thai women.

Other disadvantaged populations in Japan ignored by the notion of a middle-class majority are day laborers and the homeless. Major cities contain pockets of poverty and homelessness, with people sleeping in underground subway passages, living in community encampments and tent cities, or gathering in seedy, skid-row neighborhoods. A huge population of day or seasonal workers continues to undergird Japanese economic strength, constituting a disposable labor force controlled largely by the yakuza. Throughout the 1950s, bankrupt farmers, war veterans, and unemployed coal miners drifted into day-labor enclaves such as the San'ya district in Tokyo. Their numbers increased dramatically in the '60s with the mammoth construction projects required by the Olympics and the Osaka Expo. The areas housing the laborers contain shabby flophouses where eight or more men share a crowded dorm room. Yakuza labor contractors operate neighborhood prostitution and gambling facilities to drain the meager finances of these men. Health problems are very common in these areas: tuberculosis rates are twice the Japanese average, advanced alcoholism afflicts over 70 percent of the residents, and many also suffer from disabilities or are mentally ill.

Gender Issues in Contemporary Japan

Around half of all women between fifteen and sixty-five engage in paid labor, constituting over 40 percent of the workforce. The Japanese labor system is structured to keep companies competitive by employing women in low-cost, dead-end jobs that receive few benefits. Much of women's labor is concentrated in service and light industries and is considered "part-time," a category that covers employees with limited working hours (usually thirty-five per week), those hired for fixed terms, and those who work at full-time, permanent jobs but don't receive benefits. To cope with chronic labor shortages, Japanese companies recruit women as supplementary, low-wage labor under unstable employment conditions. Deregulation of the labor market in response to the recession has doubled the number of such part-time workers; they now make up around a third of the total workforce. In 1985, Japan passed an Equal Opportunity Law intended to improve women's employment options. The law advocated equality between men and women in the workplace but was toothless, with no penalties for noncompliance. As a result, few companies substantially altered gendered work practices.

Full-time female employees in white-collar jobs fall into two categories. Career employees have employment paths similar to men, leading to management positions. They're expected to work overtime without pay, to accept transfers, and to work under the same conditions as their sarariman colleagues. This is a small, elite group of women with degrees from prestigious universities. Only a quarter of Japanese firms have women in these management positions. In large corporations they represent less than 3.5 percent of career-track employees. Among government officials, only 1 percent of employees at top levels are women. The second, larger category is for "ordinary" employees, often known as "OLs" (office ladies), subordinate workers with low wages and low responsibilities who performing administrative and menial tasks for their male coworkers.

Young women receive mixed messages on ideal gender roles from contemporary media, schools, and other state agencies. On one hand, they are socialized and encouraged by official ideology to perform nurturing roles as mothers, dutiful wives, and caretakers of the elderly. Yet they are also bombarded with commercial advertisements urging them to dress in the latest fashions and buy the newest gadgets despite the economic recession. At the same time, popular culture idealizes the schoolgirl, in her uniform and white socks, as a desirable sexual object. "Lolita-complex" (roricon) is the name for the common sexual obsession with young girls encouraged by popular culture and the media. Mass media has heightened teenage girls' awareness of their sexual desirability and how to use it for financial benefit. Teenage prostitution, known euphemistically as "compensated dating" (enjo kōsai), emerged as a social issue in the mid-1990s. In urban areas like Tokyo, some teenage girls engaged in this activity, seeking out middle-aged men as clients who paid up to $500 per hour. Transactions didn't always involve sex: some simply consisted of companionship while strolling about town, chatting in coffee shops, and hanging out. But most required an exchange of sexual services for money or expensive gifts. Encounters were often anonymous and random, arranged through widely advertised "telephone clubs." Teens engaged in the practice out of peer pressure to buy expensive items not covered by their allowances or part-time jobs. They were usually from middle-class homes and not considered rebellious or troubled youths; their clients were usually ordinary sararimen. Some social critics, mostly men, viewed the phenomenon as positive, a rite of passage into adulthood and mature relationships. Others saw it as an example of the shallowness and superficiality of relationships in modern Japanese society.

Since the turn of the twenty-first century, the mass media has often turned to gendered caricatures to explain the decline in marriage and birth rates. Young women reluctant to marry were dubbed "parasite singles," while young men with little desire to wed were christened "herbivores" *(sōshoku danshi)*. The majority of single women in their twenties and thirties live in their parents' homes and are accustomed to spending their disposable income on themselves: traveling, dining out, and buying expensive cosmetics and fashions. Most receive free housekeeping, laundry services, and meals from their parents. They are in no hurry to marry, as they are reluctant to give up their enjoyable lifestyles to become domestic housewives with the responsibility of nurturing everyone but themselves. Media critics and authorities blame Japan's population problems on the selfishness of these "parasite singles." Meanwhile, the number of heterosexual men in their twenties and thirties who are reluctant to pursue marriage or even sexual relations are called "herbivores" because, like grass-eating animals, they are uninterested in consuming flesh. The media has characterized herbivore men as obsessed with fashion and grooming and as quiet and submissive, traits associated with femininity. Nevertheless, unmarried men began embracing the term themselves; one 2012 survey of four hundred single men around age thirty reported that a full 75 percent self-identified as herbivores.

In the twenty-first century, the economy is still stagnant and rural towns are being decimated by population decline. Growing numbers of individuals have withdrawn from society, including youths who refuse to leave their homes or interact with others *(hikikomori)*. A general sense of insecurity, anxiety, and hopelessness seems to have become the new norm. On March 11, 2011, such feelings were further exacerbated by the Tohoku earthquake, which triggered powerful tsunami waves that led to the meltdown of nuclear reactors at the Fukushima power plant. The combined disasters claimed over sixteen thousand lives and resulted in an estimated $25 trillion in economic damage. The earthquake, with a magnitude of 9.0, was the most powerful tremor recorded in Japanese history. It generated tsunami waves over 130 feet in height that traveled up to six miles inland along a three-hundred-mile span of coastline, wiping out entire towns, such as Minami Sanriku. The damaged nuclear plants emitted 170 times the amount of radiation released by the Hiroshima bomb; over three hundred thousand individuals who lived nearby had to be evacuated from their homes, many with no hope of ever returning. The disaster reinvigorated the dormant antinuclear movement, launching massive protests through-out Japan. Government energy policy had relied heavily on nuclear power, but the post-3/11 public outcry resulted in the shutdown of the majority of nuclear reactors. In attempts to digest the causes and effects of the natural and man-made disasters, social critics called for the people to rouse them-selves from apathy and alienation and reconsider Japan's future. Tens of thousands of volunteers answered the call, traveling to the Tohoku region to help provide humanitarian relief. Some critics advocated simpler life-styles, including less dependence on consumer goods and more conserva-tion of energy and other resources. Once again, Japan faces the challenges of overcoming a cataclysmic setback. Whether the future holds another miraculous comeback or continued decline remains to be seen.

"COOL JAPAN": A NEW CULTURAL SUPERPOWER

Despite its recent challenges, Japan has remained a dominant exporter of electronics and hardware—including audiovisual components, computers, and gaming consoles—since the 1960s. Such technologies have had a tremendous impact on the everyday lives of people around the world, giving them greater choice and mobility in their consumption of media. Nevertheless, the twenty-first-century reinvention of Japan as a cultural superpower is based more on international demand for products like media, music, fashion, and food than on manufactured hardware. Although Japanese contemporary popular culture first began infiltrating world mar-kets in the 1980s, widespread use of the Internet since the early twenty-first century has accelerated global dissemination. As audiences abroad, especially youths, were exposed to Japanese manga and anime, J-pop music, trendy fashions, and high-quality ramen, new demand for Japanese goods helped reinvigorate the economy.

Government agencies began to realize the power of the "Cool Japan" brand in the early twenty-first century and created numerous programs to promote popular culture as a key component of Japanese "soft power," a term coined to describe a nation's ability to influence others noncoercively through the attractiveness of its culture and values rather than through military force or economic aid. America has long held soft power via such exports as Hollywood films, rock music, Levi's jeans, McDonald's, and Coca-Cola, many of which encode "American" values such as individualism and capitalism. American films and TV tend to feature strong, handsome heroes and beautiful heroines and usually draw clear divisions between good and evil characters. Japanese media products, in turn, focus more on cute characters, often with ambivalent morality, who frequently work in teams. They tend to encode social values such as cooperation, animism, and attention to aesthetic detail. *Kawaii*—meaning cute, sweet, adorable, and vulnerable—became an important aesthetic in popular culture in the 1970s and has since been identified as the word used most often in Japan today. Cuteness may seem like a strangely trivial source of Japanese soft power, but there's no question that a country that commands channels of communication and consumerism has more opportunities to affect preferences in other parts of the world.

Many elements of contemporary popular culture are deeply interconnected today, as they were in the Edo period. Anime, manga, and video games influence fashion and merchandise, and vice versa. Fads and fashions rise and fall rapidly, providing a steady supply of new images that inspire new media products and merchandise. While kawaii remains an aesthetic ideal, new genres of cute emerge constantly and challenge conventions of what might be considered adorable. In the late 1990s, droopy, lethargic-looking characters emerged after the commercial success of Tarepanda, an exhausted panda lying on his tummy. In the first decade of the twenty-first century, the popular manga and anime *Gegege no Kitarō*, based on folk stories about ghosts and monsters, transformed giant eyeballs and a rat-human hybrid into cute commodities. In recent years, creepy-cute *(kimo-kawaii)* and grotesque-cute *(gurokawaii)* aesthetics came into vogue. Examples include Gloomy Bear, a pink bear with blood spattered on his face and paws from attacking and eating humans; and Kobitodukan, tiny creatures with the skin of plants, such as mushrooms and peaches, and disturbing human faces. Pop superstar Kyary Pamyu Pamyu (b. 1993; see below) embraces this aesthetic, claiming in an interview: "I love grotesque things. My concept is scary things that become traumatic with their cuteness. There are so many 'just cute' things in the world, so I add grotesque, scary and even shocking materials like eyeballs and brains to balance out the cuteness."[3]

Literature

Murakami Haruki (b. 1949) and Yoshimoto Banana (b. 1964) emerged as literary sensations in the 1980s, developing mass followings in Japan and abroad. Their critically acclaimed works manage to blur distinctions between "high" and "popular" literature and share a sense of casual intimacy and accessibility that appeals to a broad range of readers.

Banana is the pen name of Yoshimoto Mahoko, daughter of an influential leftist philosopher. *Kitchen* (1988), her first published work, struck a chord with the public, raising questions about gender identities in modern Japan and the pressures faced by young women. The novel sold over ten million copies, and the term "Bananamania" was coined to capture her hordes of fans. It has had over sixty printings in Japan alone and has been translated into thirty-nine languages. Mikage, the novel's protagonist, is a young woman grieving her recently lost grandmother, who raised her after her parents were killed. She seeks solace in the familiar objects and smells of her grandmother's kitchen but is afraid to stay alone in the large apartment. Yūichi, a young male friend of her grandmother, suggests that Mikage move in with his family. There she throws herself into cooking for Yūichi and his transsexual mother, Eriko. Drawn to Yūichi, who already has a girlfriend, Mikage decides to move out, taking a job as an assistant to a cooking teacher. In the following passage, she compares herself to the types of mainstream, middle-class women taking cooking courses:

> These women lived their lives happily. They had been taught, probably by loving parents, not to exceed the boundaries of their happiness regardless of what they were doing. But therefore they could never know real joy. Which is better? Who can say? Everyone lives the way she knows best. What I mean by 'their happiness' is living a life untouched as much as possible by the knowledge that we are really, all of us, alone. That's not a bad thing. Dressed in their aprons, their smiling faces like flowers, learning to cook, absorbed in their little troubles and perplexities, they fall in love and marry. I think that's great. I wouldn't mind that kind of life. Me, when I'm utterly exhausted by it all, my skin breaks out, on those lonely evenings when I call my friends again and again and nobody's home, then I despise my own life—my birth, my upbringing, everything. I feel only regret for the whole thing.[4]

At the end of the novel, when Mikage learns that Eriko has been murdered by a boyfriend disturbed to learn of her sex change, she returns to comfort Yūichi with her home-cooked foods.

Since *Kitchen*, Banana has produced eleven novels and seven collections of essays, but none have recaptured the excitement of her debut. Her works deal with heavy themes like death, violence, and loneliness but enfold these within the healing details of everyday life. She and her characters appear to be unconcerned with global issues or domestic politics, seeming to prefer manga, pop music, pulp fiction, and food as sources of diversion. Banana herself is an enigmatic figure who shuns publicity and photographs. Unlike most female celebrities in Japan, she usually appears without makeup and in simple clothing. She also maintains that marriage is unnecessary, although she is in a long-term relationship. Most of Banana's characters similarly enjoy unconventional relationships and lead atypical Japanese lives. Some critics suggest that the key to her popularity is wishful thinking among young Japanese women who dream of leading different lives but face pressures from family and peers to conform to social expectations.

Murakami's remarkable output—over a dozen best-selling novels, four collections of short stories, and numerous nonfiction works—has been translated into fifty languages and won scores of prizes, and he ranks among the greatest and best-known writers living in the world today. He is sometimes labeled postmodern for his experimentation in the structure and style of his novels, which frequently contain elements of magical realism, surrealism, and dystopia. Loss, alienation, loneliness, and memory are frequent themes, and his protagonists are often indecisive young men suffering from ennui, surrounded by strong, energetic wives or female friends. The rich and convoluted plots of Murakami's novels defy easy synopsis. *Norwegian Wood* (1987), a spare coming-of-age story about a young college student's relationships with two very different women, propelled Murakami to celebrity status. Another major work, *The Wind-Up Bird Chronicle* (1994–95), published in three volumes in Japan, established his reputation as a dominant literary figure. This complex novel follows Toru, an unemployed thirty-something man, on his quest for a missing cat and then his missing wife. It uses a variety of forms—such as dream sequences, letters, and transcripts from Internet chats—to weave together story lines that address romantic disappointment, the emptiness of contemporary politics, and the legacy of Japan's wartime aggression, related in two harrowing stories about Japanese soldiers' actions in Mongolia and Manchukuo.

The first printing of Murakami's *1Q84* (2009–10), a dystopian novel about parallel worlds and an abusive religious cult, sold out the day of release, and sales reached one million within a month. The following passage—which discusses the meaning of literature for one of the main characters, Tengo, an unpublished novelist who works as a math tutor—provides insights into Murakami's own feelings toward his craft:

While math was like a magnificent imaginary building for Tengo, literature was a vast magical forest. Math stretched infinitely upward toward the heavens, but stories spread out before him, their sturdy roots stretching deep into the earth. In this forest there were no maps, no doorways. As Tengo got older, the forest of story began to exert an even stronger pull on his heart than the world of math. Of course, reading novels was just another form of escape—as soon as he closed the book, he had to come back to the real world. But at some point he noticed that returning to reality from the world of a novel was not as devastating a blow as returning from the world of math. Why was that? After much thought, he reached a conclusion. No matter how clear things might become in the forest of story, there was never a clear-cut solution, as there was in math. The role of a story was, in the broadest terms, to transpose a problem into another form. Depending on the nature and the direction of the problem, a solution might be suggested in the narrative. Tengo would return to the real world with that suggestion in hand. It was like a piece of paper bearing the indecipherable text of a magic spell. It served no immediate practical purpose, but it contained a possibility.[5]

Anime

Anime are often considered Japan's chief contemporary cultural export. The value of Japanese animation and manga abroad has grown rapidly in the twenty-first century, from $75 million for both categories in 1996 to $200 million for manga alone in 2006 and $2.7 billion for anime in 2009. The advent of the Cartoon Network cable channel in the United States in the early 1990s helped many American viewers discover Japan's most popular anime series. These series are now carried by major on-demand streaming-video services, such as Netflix and Hulu, rather than just by niche specialists like Crunchyroll and Funimation. Anime conventions around the world attract mass followings; 2014's Anime Expo Convention in Los Angeles drew eighty thousand fans, making it the eleventh largest convention in the world that year.

The world of anime is so vast that our discussion must be limited to a few iconic films and TV series. The anime feature film *Akira* (1988), directed by Ōtomo Katsuhiro and based on his manga of the same name, was pioneering in its use of cutting-edge techniques and targeting of adult audiences. The dystopian film is set in 2019 in Neo-Tokyo, rebuilt after the government dropped an atomic bomb on the city in 1988 after psychic experiments on children spun out of control. Akira, the most powerful psychic child, was cryogenically sealed in the Olympic Stadium. Neo-Tokyo is now rife with gang violence and domestic terrorism. Kaneda, the leader of a biker gang, attempts to save his friend Tetsuo, who has been subjected to military experiments that gave him psychic powers. Kaneda and members of his gang must battle various groups and prevent Tetsuo from freeing Akira and unleashing uncontrollable psychic abilities that will result in Neo-Tokyo's destruction. The high quality of *Akira's* art and animation, including super-fluid motion and detailed, realistic backgrounds of a futuristic Tokyo, earned critical acclaim. The film gained a worldwide cult following and is considered by many to be one of the best animated films of all time. It was seminal in prompting wider demand for sophisticated anime outside of Japan.

Two other important anime in the science fiction genre are the 1995 film *Ghost in the Shell*, directed by Oshii Mamoru and based on a popular manga, and *Neon Genesis Evangelion* (1995–96). *Ghost in the Shell* follows the members of a counter cyber-terrorism group called Section 9, led by the cyborg Kusanagi. The action takes place at a time when people are at least partially cyborg, with brains that can interface with computer networks or prosthetic body parts. Section 9 battles hackers, especially the Puppet Master, who takes control of cyberbrains in order to turn their owners into slaves. The well-received film was followed by a TV series and by film sequels released in 2004 and 2015. Hollywood's remake in 2017 received mixed reviews; many fans criticized the casting of Scarlett Johansson in the lead as "whitewashing."

Like *Akira*, *Neon Genesis Evangelion* is set in a futuristic Tokyo several years after an apocalyptic event. Specially selected teenage pilots operate giant robotic machines, synchronized to their nervous systems, to fight against a race of beings known as Angels that can wipe out humanity. The main character is a teenage pilot named Shinji who is tormented by self-doubt. The series explores his emotions and relationships with other pilots, delving deep into psychoanalytic concepts. It employs imagery and mythology from a number of religious traditions, from the Jewish Kabbalah to Shinto mythology and the biblical story of creation. *Evangelion* gained critical acclaim at home and abroad. In Japan it became the topic of widespread media discussion, especially after the airing of the finale, a confusing mélange of imagery meant to represent Shinji's inner psychological states as he contemplates the fate of mankind. Public outcry against the finale was so strong that the film *End of Evangelion* (1997) was released a year later to explain the events in it. Nevertheless, the series overwhelmingly won first place in the "Best Loved Series" category of the Anime Grand Prix awards in 1996 and 1997 and was ranked the most popular anime of all time in a 2006 survey. Subsequent *Evangelion* films, manga, and merchandise, including products like cell phones and laptops targeted at adult consumers, have earned over $1.3 billion in domestic and overseas sales.

Among anime targeted toward children, several have become major hits in international markets. Space limitations permit mentioning only a few iconic examples. *Doraemon* was one of the first overseas smash hits. It follows the adventures of a blue robot cat from the future that uses high-tech gadgets, such as "memory bread" and a (prescient) 3-D printer, to help his ten-year-old friend Nobita. The series first aired in Japan in 1979 and can now be seen in over thirty countries. *Dragon Ball Z* premiered in the United States in a dubbed version in 1996 and attracted an entire generation of young boys. Its protagonist, an extraterrestrial named Goku sent to conquer Earth as a child, forgets his mission after a head injury. As an adult, Goku protects Earth, fighting intergalactic aliens and androids. *Sailor Moon*, a '90s series about ordinary teenage girls who morph into sexy warriors to battle evil, is an example of the "magical girl" genre. The manga underpinning the series is one of the most popular of all time, selling thirty-five million copies in over fifty countries. *Naruto* (2002–7), named for its title character, centers on a teenage ninja possessed by the spirit of a powerful fox kami. Dubbed versions began export to the United States and other markets in 2005. Finally, *One Piece*, a humorous pirate anime based on the best-selling manga series in history, began airing in Japan in 1998, reaching American markets in 2007. It recounts the adventures of Monkey D. Luffy and his crew on his quest to become King of the Pirates. In addition to the TV series, thirteen *One Piece* animated feature films have been released since 2000. These and many other anime series have spurred tens of billions of dollars in sales of video games, trading cards, figurines, and other merchandise.

Any discussion of Japanese anime must include the work of director Miyazaki Hayao (b. 1941), founder of Studio Ghibli and creator of beloved feature films such as *My Neighbor Totoro* (1988), *Princess Mononoke* (1997), and his masterpiece *Spirited Away* (2001), which won Best Picture at Japan's Academy Awards and Best Animated Feature at the U.S. Academy Awards. Miyazaki's films span a wide variety of genres in a multitude of geographic and historical settings, from apocalyptic futures to European fantasies to family dramas in modern Japan. Recurring themes within most of his works include animism, the power of nature, and the need for humankind to protect the environment; the depiction of flight and various means of aircraft as a source of agency; and strong, plucky girls as heroines. Miyazaki's remarkable girl heroes are one reason for his popularity. In contrast to gender norms that encourage girls to be cute and act submissively,

FIGURE 73. A cosplayer portraying Sailor Moon at FanimeCon 2010 in San Jose, California. © 2010 BrokenSphere/Wikimedia Commons.

Miyazaki's heroines are bold, courageous, and independent; they are often orphaned or neglected by parents. Unlike the voluptuous warriors of magical girl genres like *Sailor Moon* or *Cutey Honey,* they do not need to morph into sexualized bodies to feel empowered.

In his early career, Miyazaki worked for several different TV and film animation studios and earned acclaim for works in European settings such as *Heidi, Girl of the Alps* (1974) and *The Castle of Cagliostro* (1979). The first feature that he both wrote and directed was *Nausicaä of the Valley of the Wind* (1984). The film takes place in a postapocalyptic world where bioweapons called Giant Warriors have destroyed civilization and created a Toxic Jungle, inhabited by dangerous mutant insects and large armored creatures called Ohm. The heroine, Nausicaä, is a princess of the Valley of the Wind who defies warnings about the dangers of the Jungle, using her jet glider to explore the forests in search of a way for her people to reinhabit the land. She learns to communicate with the creatures of the forest and discovers possibilities for producing clean water and soil. The militaristic Tolmekians, however, want to destroy the Jungle by using a Giant Warrior embryo. They kill Nausicaä's father, the king, and manipulate the Ohm into stampeding into the Valley. Nausicaä calms the herd but is injured in the process. The Ohm surround her with healing golden tentacles, revealing that she is the savior of Earth, as foretold in a prophecy. *Nausicaä* thus first expressed many of Miyazaki's major thematic concerns.

Following *Nausicaä's* success, Miyazaki established Studio Ghibli in 1985. Its first release was *Laputa: Castle in the Sky* (1986), about two orphans seeking a magical kingdom that floats in the sky. In 1988 he made the beloved *Totoro,* which told the story of Mei, a headstrong girl who moves to a large house in the country with her father and older sister while her mother is hospitalized in a nearby sanitorium. She befriends Totoro, a giant nature spirit that appears to be a cross between a bear and a cat, who lives in a large tree adjacent to her home. Like Shinto kami and *Nausicaä's* Ohm, Totoro is an ambiguous character of nature, sometimes gentle and kind but capable of ferocity and great power. In *Princess Mononoke,* a historical fantasy about a young woman raised by wolves who fights against human destruction of the forest with the help of a young warrior from an indigenous tribe, a giant magical stag represents another such kami, the god of the forest.

Spirited Away is Studio Ghibli's largest critical and financial success to date and is frequently named one of the greatest animated films of all time. The ten-year-old heroine, Chihiro, is forced to take a job at a magical bathhouse for kami and spirits run by the witch Yubaba. She must do so to free

FIGURE 74. Image from Miyazaki Hayao's *My Neighbor Totoro,* produced and distributed by Studio Ghibli. Source: Alamy stock photo.

her parents, who were turned into pigs when they gorged on food after unknowingly entering the spirit world. The film presents a colorful world of unforgettable characters, drawing deeply on Japanese myths and legends. Among its many messages are the redemptive powers of hard work and love and the hazards of overconsumption—clearly a critique of Japan's consumer-oriented society.

Miyazaki's genius has opened doors for Japan's feature-length animated films abroad. In recent years many anime features by other directors have achieved worldwide success, including *The Tale of the Princess Kaguya* (2013) and *Miss Hokusai* (2015). *Your Name* (2017) by director Shinkai Makoto became the highest-grossing anime film worldwide and the fourth-highest-grossing film of all time in Japan. Based on a novel of the same name, it is the story of Mitsuha, a teenage girl living in a rural mountain town, who begins to swap bodies with Taki, a high school boy in Tokyo living three years in Mitsuha's future. Through their growing relationship, they are able to save Mitsuha's town from destruction by a comet.

Cute Commodities

Children's culture has become a globalized market, and Japan is a new center for the production of commodities targeted toward children, thus challenging the U.S. hegemony over this market, as best represented by Disney.

FIGURE 75. Ribbon-cutting ceremony for Hello Kitty's Kawaii Paradise. Source: Alamy stock photo.

Japanese toys and games are first conceived, produced, and marketed domestically and then "glocalized" (i.e., adapted for specific overseas markets). Cute characters *(kyara)* are an important component of this market, with an appeal that is not limited to children. Even serious businesses such as banks feature cartoon mascots like Miffy the Bunny or Disney characters; many sararimen adorn their cell phones or other possessions with their favorite characters. Some observers believe that the appeal of cute characters for the Japanese is due, in large part, to the attraction of childhood and the feeling of never wanting to grow up, perhaps because Japanese adulthood means heavy responsibilities and pressures to conform. Cute characters often display elements of helplessness and vulnerability. They frequently lack a mouth and have undersized or rounded stumps as limbs.

Japan's most visible symbol of cute is Hello Kitty, introduced by Sanrio in 1974 and imported to the United States in 1976. Kitty is a white cat with a giant head and red bow. Products bearing her image sell briskly in more than thirty countries and were worth about $7 billion in sales in 2014. Unlike other characters that originated in manga or anime, Kitty was designed specifically to sell merchandise. Although she was originally aimed at preteen girls, Hello Kitty's fans now include many adult consumers. Her image is found on products ranging from school supplies to diamond jewelry. Diehard enthusiasts can buy Hello Kitty–themed cars and condos or hold Hello Kitty weddings. Sanrio licenses her image to makers of twelve to fifteen thousand products and will grant licensing rights for almost anything except weapons or hard liquor.

Sanrio has an entire stable of cute characters designed to suit different tastes and personalities, whose images are also emblazoned across a wide range of merchandise, available at dedicated Sanrio stores located in shopping malls around the world and from many other retail outlets. Sanrio's large staff of graphic artists design hundreds of potential characters each year, but the normal life span of a new character adopted by the firm is only a few years. Fifteen or so core characters have remained in circulation much longer than average, like Kitty. For instance, Kero Kero Keroppi is a big-eyed frog created in 1987; Bad Batz Maru, released in 1993, is a naughty penguin with spiky hair; and Pompompurin, a roly-poly golden retriever in a brown beret, was introduced in 1996. Favorite characters can be visited at Sanrio's theme park, Puroland, in the Tokyo suburbs. Built in 1990, it is one of Japan's most popular attractions, visited by twenty thousand every weekend.

In addition, there are hundreds of non-Sanrio characters, usually from domestic or foreign anime, that have generated their own lines of merchandise. Favorites include Totoro, Doraemon, and foreign characters like Miffy, Snoopy, and Moomin. Underneath Tokyo's main railroad station, amid a warren of shops and restaurants, one can visit the recently opened Character Street, with over twenty stores dedicated to these beloved—and enormously profitable—characters.

Unique characters are also designed to act as mascots, primarily for towns and cities, but also for festivals, businesses, and governmental or non-governmental agencies. Local mascots try to embody some aspect of the area they represent, whether a famous product, historical figure, or geographical feature. Since 2007, the number of such characters has boomed; an online database lists three thousand local mascots. Many have their own signature song and dance and compete in an annual Grand Prix to select the most popular. The 2011 winner, Kumamon, a lumpy black bear with red cheeks created by Kumamoto prefecture to commemorate the opening of a new high-speed rail line, has generated hundreds of millions of dollars in sales of merchandise ranging from snack foods to fake nails to actual teddy bears created by the famous German toymaker Steiff. Other, more idiosyncratic characters also attract a large fan base. Funassyi, the unofficial mascot of Funabashi city, is a freckled pear. Unlike most mascots that remain silent and make cute, awkward movements, Funassyi speaks

FIGURE 76. ANA Pokemon 747 jet at Haneda Airport, 2007. Photo by Kouhei 14915, via Japanese Wikimedia.

and jumps around hyperactively. He appears frequently on TV, and four stores have been launched to sell Funassyi-related merchandise.

Pokemon represents a globally significant export of Japanese children's culture. The massive franchise began as a game for Nintendo's Game Boy in the early 1990s and has grown to an empire that includes hundreds of toys, billions of trading cards, animated TV series broadcast in sixty-five countries, and nineteen animated feature films. In the virtual world of the game, players must acquire and train fantastic creatures, called Pokemon ("pocket monsters"), which they place into battle with other creatures to gain new powers. The number of Pokemon has grown from around a hundred and fifty to over eight hundred species. Among the most popular are Mew, a pink cat with psychic powers; Charizard, a flame-breathing dragon; and Pikachu, the iconic yellow mouse-like creature with a lightning-bolt tail. Pikachu has its own Macy's Thanksgiving Parade balloon and is painted on airplanes in the fleet of the Japanese airline ANA. Anthropologist Anne Allison has analyzed how Pokemon targets children for endless consumerist acquisition and teaches that commodities can act as companions.

Other Japanese video games, such as Pac-Man and Space Invaders, first became global hits as arcade games in the early 1980s. In the '90s, game companies Sega, Nintendo, and Sony competed fiercely for market share in home consoles and handheld games. Nintendo's Super Mario Brothers is one of the top games of all time, popular since its release in the mid-1980s. According to one survey, Mario is better known among American children than Mickey Mouse. Other games that earned large followings abroad include Nintendo's Legend of Zelda, Sega's Sonic the Hedgehog, and Capcom's Street Fighter. The Japanese video game industry earned $9.6 billion in 2014. Over the past five years, mobile games for smartphones have accounted for a growing portion of that market.

Fashion

Japanese fashion designers began to attract international reputations for innovative haute couture in the 1980s. Avant-garde designers Issey Miyake (b. 1938), Yohji Yamamoto (b. 1943), and Rei Kawakubo (b. 1942) of Comme des Garcons, known for monochromatic, asymmetrical looks, opened studios and premiered collections in Paris, as did Hanae Mori (1948–96), who created more conventional looks that incorporated Japanese motifs like kanji characters and cherry blossoms. In the 1990s, at the opposite end of the couture scale, youth street fashion became a source of media obsession with the emergence of the *kogyaru* (high school gal). The look began simply as modifications to standard schoolgirl uniforms—hiking up plaid skirts to micromini levels and sporting baggy white knee socks and Burberry scarves. The term *gyaru* was then applied to super-trendy teenagers who wore platform boots up to ten inches high along with a very distinctive look, including dyed blonde hair, dark tan makeup, white rings around the eyes, and heavy black eyeliner. Several fashion magazines, such as *Egg* and *Cawaii!*, were dedicated to the latest in gyaru makeup, accessories, and clothing. Most gyaru were simply indulging in trendy fashions, but some took the look to extremes, resulting in variations such as blackface *(ganguro)* and *yamamba* (mountain hag—with witchy, messy hair). Some girls and social analysts claimed that such new variations were a parody of the social pressure to be cute, representing rejection of male-dominated society's ability to dictate girls' looks and their lives.

Gyaru fashion declined in the late '90s as street fashion associated with Tokyo's trendy Harajuku district gained popularity. New looks captured international attention through *FRUiTS* magazine, established by photographer Aoki Shōichi, who published photos of fashion-forward youths with detailed captions describing their ensembles. Aoki had noticed how trendy youths were crafting unique, fun outfits that disregarded fashion conventions. Many fashionistas mixed different styles—incorporating elements of traditional dress like kimono or obi sashes with modern wear—or refashioned secondhand clothing into handmade designs. Others adopted a head-to-toe "Lolita" style that came in variations like Sweet Lolita *(ama rōri)*, characterized by pastel colors, lace, and ribbons; or Gothic Lolita *(gosu rōri)*, all-black looks with lace and ruffles modeled on Victorian clothing. The Lolita look became even more prevalent through frequent representation in manga and anime, video games, and feature films. Other fashion genres

FIGURE 77.   Harajuku street fashions, including Decora, Sweet Lolita, and Gothic Lolita. Photo by Peter Van den Bossche, via Wikimedia Commons.

captured in the magazine's pages included Cyber, Punk, and Decora, a style achieved by copious accessorizing with cheap plastic jewelry and barrettes.

Cosplay ("costume play") is a form of fashion performance originating in Japan that demonstrates the interconnections between different forms of popular culture. Cosplayers wear costumes and fashion accessories to represent a specific character from a movie, TV series, book, manga, video game, or musical band (see fig. 73). Some cosplayers also try to mimic the mannerisms, body language, and speech patterns of the characters they portray. The practice has been growing rapidly since the 1990s in Japan and more recently in other parts of the world. Cosplayers congregate at sci-fi, anime, and manga conventions as well as at their own dedicated conventions and competitions.

J-Pop Music

While contemporary popular music spans a wide number of genres, from glam-rock *(bijuaru kei)* to hip-hop to nostalgic ballads *(enka)*, the varieties most often associated with "Cool Japan" are pop idols, who first emerged in the late 1960s and early '70s. Girl idols are "manufactured" and heavily managed by talent and promotion agencies that often identify and recruit them through talent shows and mass auditions. In contrast to European and American singers, who become stars on the basis of their talents or looks,

Japanese idols are deliberately selected for girl-next-door qualities, with average voices and slightly above-average looks. Above all, they should be cute—speaking and acting in an innocent, adorable manner. Their photos capture coy expressions, with eyes opened widely and crooked-toothed smiles, considered kawaii.

Matsuda Seiko (b. 1962) debuted in the 1980s and earned the nickname "eternal idol" for her string of twenty-four consecutive number-one hits stretching into the first decade of the twenty-first century. She has often been compared to Madonna for her ability to continuously reinvent her look and capture media attention. Matsuda epitomizes the typical girl idol who acts cute and innocent, even well into adulthood. Such idols intentionally project vulnerability in order to promote feelings of protectiveness among fans who will want to support their efforts in fan clubs. This ploy is illustrated through one of Matsuda's statements: "Seiko is so happy to meet you!! As a singer and an 18-year-old girl, I feel for the first time that I can become independent. Please watch over me warmly forever!!"[6]

Japanese idols became very popular across East Asia, selling millions of records and appearing frequently in the foreign media. Nations like Taiwan, South Korea, Hong Kong, and Vietnam adopted Japanese business models for producing and promoting their own national idols, often collaborating with Japanese companies. By the mid-1990s, taste for cute but mediocre performers began to wane and better performers with more mature, confident images began to emerge. Okinawan singer Amuro Namie (b. 1977) has been compared to Madonna and to Janet Jackson for her "hip-pop" musical style, blending hip-hop and pop. The sexy, funky, tattooed Namie is nothing like the sweet teenagers of earlier decades. She has sold over thirty-five million records in Japan and has a major fan base throughout Asia. But, like Seiko Matsuda, she was unable to successfully break into the mainstream American music market.

Among the first to do that was Puffy AmiYumi (known as PUFFY in Japan), a girl duo paired by Sony talent scouts in the mid-1990s. Their debut single, "Asian Purity" ("Ajia no junshin"), became a phenomenon. Its lyrics suggest the importance of Asian markets for J-pop idols:

Open the door, flow out now and there's Asia
Lining up any and every white panda
Pure hearts twinkle in the night sky as if it's about to burst
Like a spark.[7]

Japanese fans were swept up in "Puffymania," and the duo soon had their own weekly TV series that featured foreign guests such as Lenny Kravitz,

Sylvester Stallone, and Harrison Ford. They next landed an American-Japanese animated series on the Cartoon Network, *Hi Hi Puffy AmiYumi* (2004–6). Although their characters were voiced by American actresses, the show contained live-action segments featuring the original singers and their music.

One format for girl idols that has remained popular is large groups of high-school-age girls, pioneered by Onyanko Club (Kitty Club), which had fifty-two members and disbanded in 1987. Morning Musume, with thirteen members, emerged in 1997 and is still performing today. These groups maintain a teenage lineup by recruiting new members through nationwide auditions and "graduating" members in their twenties. The most famous girl group is AKB48, formed in 2005 and named after the Akihabara area in Tokyo, where the group performs daily in its own theater, plus the number of members originally planned. Akihabara is strongly associated with the geeky subculture of *otaku*—individuals obsessed with computers or particular aspects of popular culture, often possessing limited social skills. AKB48 are among the highest-earning musical performers in Japan; their thirty-two latest singles have topped the charts. They are a media marvel, with spin-off manga, an anime series, and a video game that allows fans to simulate dating favorite members. In 2012, the national post office even issued an AKB48 commemorative stamp.

There are currently 130 members of AKB48, split into several teams that allow the group to perform in several venues simultaneously. Sister groups have been established in China and Indonesia and are planned for the Philippines, Taiwan, and Thailand. AKB48 perform daily at their Akihabara home theater so that fans always have the opportunity to see them live. There they stage simple, synchronized dances to fast-paced pop songs while audience members cheer in tandem and sing along with the choruses. The audience is roughly 95 percent male but also includes many prepubescent girls. After performances, fans can interact with the members, taking pictures or shaking their hands. Members are not allowed to date, however, and have strict behavior guidelines that, if violated, can result in expulsion.

Singer Kyary Pamyu Pamyu, known as the "Harajuku Pop Princess," is the latest J-pop phenomenon. She cites Gwen Stefani, Katy Perry, and Lady Gaga as her inspirations in both music and fashion. Like Gaga, Kyary uses unusual fashions to attract media attention. The video for her 2011 debut single, "Pon Pon Pon," went viral on YouTube, with over a hundred million views, becoming an international smash hit. The colorful, imaginative video included graphics of eyeballs, skeletons, donuts, and psychedelic animals flying around a pink room piled with toys while a beribboned Kyary dances

FIGURE 78. AKB48 performing in Beijing in December 2016. Photo by Imaginechina, via AP Images.

and sings and a large-bodied dancer in blackface, pink tutu, and platinum blonde wig mirrors her moves in the background. Follow-up songs and videos, including "Candy, Candy," "Ninja Re Bang Bang," and "Fashion Monster," similarly feature Kyary in adorable outfits surrounded by unsettling graphic elements. The faces of backup dancers are often eerily obscured with numbers, letters, or blank masks. Such weird and wacky features inevitably appealed to foreign markets long infatuated with Japan's exotic Otherness, and Kyary was soon profiled in Western fashion and art magazines and even in the *Wall Street Journal*. In 2013, MTV called her "the coolest girl on the planet." Tokyo's posh Roppongi Hills complex held a month-long exhibition in March of that year showcasing all the costumes from her music videos and live performances. In early 2017, Kyary had over 4.4 million followers on Twitter, making her the most followed female celebrity in Japan.

In 2007, Crypton Future Media introduced a virtual pop idol, Hatsune Miku, a sixteen-year-old android girl with long, turquoise pigtails. She performs in concert tours as an animated projection with a voice provided by a singing synthesizer application. An English-language version of Hatsune was released in 2013, and she completed a ten-city tour of the United States in 2016. A more recent trend in J-pop is "kawaii metal" by groups like

Babymetal and Ladybaby, in which girl idols are backed by heavy metal instrumentation. The latter was established by an Australian pro wrestler known as Ladybeard, who wore outfits matching those of his two teenage, kawaii bandmates and added guttural screams to their pop numbers.

Japanese Cuisine

Japanese cuisine has been rising in international esteem since the 1980s, when sushi first became prominent in the West. Until the '70s, most Westerners were repulsed by the idea of eating raw fish. The first U.S. sushi bar opened in 1972, when Americans were beginning to look for alternatives to a heavy, meat-and-potatoes diet. High-quality fresh fish with rice and vegetables became an attractive and exotic dining alternative in many major cities. From the '70s to the '80s, the idea of sushi moved from an icky ethnic specialty to a cool, popular staple. Today sushi is globally embraced as a healthy, sophisticated food widely available in restaurants, supermarkets, and even convenience stores and stadiums. During the bubble years, the sushi business boomed in Japan; imports of fresh bluefin tuna, the most popular fish for sushi, quintupled between 1984 and 1993. The average wholesale price of a bluefin peaked in 1990 at $33 per pound, making a 500-pound tuna worth around $17,000. When the economic bubble burst, demand for tuna managed to survive because of sushi's growing global popularity.

Increasing international familiarity with sushi added to Japan's reputation for "cool" and opened people's minds to trying its other characteristic foods. In recent years, Japanese cuisine has reached new heights of global gourmet popularity, with the number of Japanese restaurants outside of Japan doubling between 2003 and 2013, when UNESCO recognized *washoku* (Japanese dietary culture) as an intangible cultural treasure of the world. The elite Michelin guide to the world's best restaurants began rating Tokyo restaurants in 2008 and gave more stars to its establishments than to those in Paris and New York combined. At the other end of the culinary scale, professionally prepared ramen has now achieved cult status across America and in many cities around the world, with long lines outside popular establishments. In the 1970s, as domestic tourism boomed among the Japanese, so did ramen. Local variations—such as Sapporo's miso-based broth, Kumamoto's thick, pork-based tonkotsu style, and Iwate's light chicken broth—became available nationwide. Ramen quickly emerged as Japan's most popular object of lowbrow culinary connoisseurship, a trend that expanded even further with the advent of the Internet and social media. In the United States today, high-quality ramen represents an affordable, yet exotic and "authentic," gourmet experience, just as sushi did in the '80s and '90s.

Visual Arts

The Superflat art movement arose in the late 1990s in response to the pervasiveness of cute consumerism. Its founder, Murakami Takashi (b. 1962), formulated an aesthetics and theory of contemporary art that he labeled Superflat, referring simultaneously to the two-dimensional, cartoonish forms that dominated pop culture; the flat composition of traditional Japanese paintings, which are devoid of the illusion of depth and perspective; and the two-dimensionality of Japanese modern life—the shallow emptiness of its consumer culture. Superflat represented a challenge to the Western hegemony of fine art by reasserting Japanese-centric standards for creating and appreciating art and by collapsing false hierarchies between "high" art and "low" mass media and between art and commerce.

Murakami initially studied traditional Japanese painting, earning a doctorate in 1993. On a trip to New York, he first saw the pop, erotic sculptures of Jeff Koons and met many artists' collectives engaging in "fun" forms of artistic activity that were quite unlike those of the staid Japanese art establishment. He subsequently developed a new style depicting playful, child-like, and humorous images using traditional painting and printmaking techniques. Murakami asserts that this kind of contemporary art is rooted not in Western pop art but in the stylized, colorful works of Edo-period ukiyo-e and Meiji-period nihonga artists. The subject matter is drawn from the contemporary native otaku culture of anime, manga, and collectible figurines, frequently including young girls, monsters, and apocalyptic imagery.

Murakami's view of the U.S.-Japan relationship echoes that of postwar avant-garde artists. He asserts that the atomic bombings, the humiliating defeat, and postwar dependence on the U.S. security arrangement left Japan infantilized, impotent, deformed, and apolitical. Its hybrid postcolonial culture was thus distressingly shallow, childish, and consumeristic. But following the bursting of the economic bubble, Superflat artists, facing national instability and uncertainty, engaged in social critique by depicting the sexual fetishism and consumerism that dominated popular culture. In a long 2005 essay on the state of popular culture in Japan, Murakami wrote:

> Japan may be the future of the world. And now, Japan is Superflat. From social mores to art and culture, everything is super two-dimensional. *Kawaii* culture has become a living entity that pervades everything. With a population heedless of the cost of embracing immaturity, the nation is in the throes of a dilemma. . . .

FIGURE 79. Murakami Takashi, three-panel painting of Mr. DOB, 1996. Source: Alamy stock photo.

> These monotonous ruins of a nation-state, which arrived on the heels of an American puppet government, have been perfectly realized in the name of capitalism. Those who inhabit this vacant crucible spin in endless, inarticulate circles. . . . We Japanese still embody "Little Boy," nicknamed, like the atomic bomb itself, after a nasty childhood taunt.[8]

Some of Murakami's most recognizable characters include Mr. DOB, a circular head with Mickey Mouse–like ears, huge, lashed eyes, and a disturbing grimace; Mr. Pointy (Tongari-kun), a rounded white creature with a rainbow horn; and Miss Ko2 (pronounced "ko ko"), a voluptuous, long-legged waitress. These and other images are produced in mass quantities on watches, t-shirts, purses, and other consumer goods at Murakami's Kaikai Kiki factory. Like the Factory, established by Andy Warhol, Kaikai Kiki employs teams of young artists to help Murakami realize his visions. They make extensive use of computer technology, utilizing clip art for his recurring motifs like anthropomorphic flowers and mushrooms. Murakami does not distinguish between art and commerce and has collaborated with fashion houses such as Marc Jacobs and Louis Vuitton, which sold his limited-edition handbags for $5,000.

Another Superflat artist who achieved international stardom is painter and sculptor Nara Yoshitomo (b. 1959), known for works depicting chil-

FIGURE 80.   Nara Yoshitomo, *Punch Me Harder,* exhibited at London Art Fair Preview, 2016. Source: AP Images.

dren, many of whom bear surprisingly threatening, angry, or cruel facial expressions. They sometimes hold weapons such as knives or chainsaws. The images are simple but psychologically complex, conveying vulnerability, loneliness, and aggression. Yoshitomo's work, like that of author Yoshimoto Banana, garnered a massive fan base among young women aged eighteen to twenty-five who seemed otherwise uninterested in art or literature. The pair have subsequently collaborated on illustrated books.

Other artists associated with Superflat include Aoshima Chihō (b. 1974), who uses computer-generated imagery in large, all-digital murals featuring waifish girls who seem both innocent and sexually knowing amid apocalyptic or sublime dreamscapes. The plastic figurines of Ōshima Yūki (b. 1974) similarly explore the tensions between innocence and eroticism, with posed, prepubescent girls that female consumers find cute and adult male otaku find arousing.

In summary and conclusion, throughout its long history Japan has engaged in interactions with other nations that have deeply influenced its society, culture, and economy. In ancient and premodern times, contacts with Korean and Chinese civilizations brought profound changes in religion, philosophy, and theories of governance; imported technologies of agriculture, craft, medicine, and written and artistic expression enriched the lives of commoners and elites alike. These borrowings were inevitably tempered by indigenous tastes and values, resulting in a rich mélange of cultural forms and social practices that were unquestionably Japanese. Beginning in the sixteenth century, European nations became a new source of information on developments in science, art, and geopolitics. With the Meiji Restoration, Japan turned definitively toward Western imperialist models to guide its path to modern wealth and power, but borrowings from the West were markedly transformed to suit Japanese circumstances and preferences. Japanese identity remained hybrid; its modernity was not a simple copy of a universal "modern" patterned on Western norms.

As Japan developed and gained confidence in the early twentieth century, many grew to resent Western hegemony, leading the nation to a disastrous war, the legacy of which continues to haunt its relationship with its East Asian neighbors, Korea and China. Defeat and occupation by the United States meant that American lifestyles and democratic values would take center stage as the main sources of international influence in postwar society and culture. Today Japan continues to rely on its strong relationship with the United States for assistance with regional defense and diplomacy, but with the end of the Cold War, as accelerating forces of globalization have shifted economic and cultural relationships with other nations, America has become somewhat less of a role model. The Chinese economy surpassed Japan's in the early twenty-first century, making China the leading economic and military power in Asia and Japan's largest trading partner. Nevertheless, new technologies such as the Internet and the growth of global mass media have allowed Japan to emerge as East Asia's leading cultural power, admired and emulated around the world. Foreign audiences idolize both Japan's new pop culture and more traditional forms, epitomized by samurai, geisha, and tea ceremony. Manga, films, art, and other current cultural products often feature or reference these older traditions, keeping them alive in the imaginations of younger generations.

In the twenty-first century, Japan faces numerous challenges, brought into sharp focus by the 2011 nuclear disaster. Its scarcity of natural and energy resources has dictated reliance on trade and nuclear energy to meet the needs of the citizenry. But overwhelming public opposition to nuclear power following the disaster raises questions about how Japan can safely meet its long-term economic needs, which are further jeopardized by the rapid graying of its population. Public suspicion of officials—and of their collusion with scientific communities and mainstream media—has recently deepened, and an air of hopelessness and anxiety over national decline seems to prevail. Yet is this sense of despair truly warranted? Japan can boast that it has one of the cleanest environments and one of the lowest crime rates in the world. Its residents have the world's longest life expectancies, thanks in part to strong safety nets in health care and elder support.

Japan's cultural and consumer-goods industries create innovative, vibrant products at every price level that are considered fashionable and desirable around the globe. Japan may not be the most powerful or the wealthiest nation in the world, but there is no doubt that it is one of the coolest.

FURTHER READING

Allison, Anne. *Millennial Monsters: Japanese Toys and the Global Imagination.* Berkeley: University of California Press, 2006.

————. *Precarious Japan.* Durham, NC: Duke University Press, 2013.

Condry, Ian. *Hip-Hop Japan: Rap and the Paths of Cultural Globalization.* Durham, NC: Duke University Press, 2006.

Field, Norma. *In the Realm of a Dying Emperor: Japan at Century's End.* New York: Vintage, 1993.

Iwabuchi, Koichi. *Recentering Globalization: Popular Culture and Japanese Transnationalism.* Durham, NC: Duke University Press, 2002.

Lie, John. *Multiethnic Japan.* Cambridge, MA: Harvard University Press, 2004.

Monden, Masafumi. *Japanese Fashion Cultures: Dress and Gender in Contemporary Japan.* London: Bloomsbury, 2015.

Napier, Susan J. *Anime: From Akira to Howl's Moving Castle.* New York: Palgrave MacMillan, 2005.

Reader, Ian. *Religious Violence in Contemporary Japan: The Case of Aum Shinrikyō.* Honolulu: University of Hawaii Press, 2000.

Yano, Christine R. *Pink Globalization: Hello Kitty's Trek across the Pacific.* Durham, NC: Duke University Press, 2013.

RECOMMENDED FILMS

A and A2. 1998, 2011. Documentary films directed by Mori Tatsuya. An inside look at Aum Shinrikyo's response following the 1995 sarin attack and its sequel, filmed several years later as the sect was dissolving.

After Life. 1998. Feature film directed by Kore-eda Hirokazu. Quirky story of how the recently deceased must make a film about the happiest moment in their life before moving on to Heaven.

Kamikaze Girls. 2004. Feature film directed by Nakashima Tetsuya. Tale of friendship between two teenagers, a girl biker and a Lolita.

Kids Return. 1996. Feature film directed by Kitano Takeshi. Two high school dropouts seek direction in life; one becomes a boxer, the other a yakuza.

Tampopo. 1985. Feature film directed by Itami Jūzō. This "foodie" comedy about a ramen restaurant includes many food-related subplots.

The Great Happiness Space. 2006. Documentary film directed by Jake Clennell. Life in an Osaka host club.

The Kingdom of Dreams and Madness. 2013. Documentary film directed by Sunada Mami. Follows the daily lives of Miyazaki Hayao and other directors at Studio Ghibli.

Notes

CHAPTER 1. EARLY JAPAN

1. Wm. Theodore de Bary et al., eds., *Sources of Japanese Tradition, vol. 1: From Earliest Times to 1600*, 2nd ed. (New York: Columbia University Press, 2001), 8.

2. Ibid., 14. Adapted from W.G. Aston, trans., *Nihongi: Chronicles of Japan from the Earliest Times to A.D. 697, vol. 1* (London: Kegan Paul, Trench, Trübner & Co., 1896), 10–14.

3. W.G. Aston, trans., *Nihongi: Chronicles of Japan from the Earliest Times to A.D. 697, vol. 2* (London: Kegan Paul, Trench, Trübner & Co., 1896; repr., New York: Paragon, 1956), 66.

CHAPTER 2. FORGING A CENTRALIZED STATE

1. Wm. Theodore de Bary et al., eds., *Sources of Japanese Tradition, vol. 1: From Earliest Times to 1600*, 2nd ed. (New York: Columbia University Press, 2001), 42.

2. Ibid., 51.

3. Ibid.

4. Joan R. Piggott, "The Last Classical Female Sovereign: Kōken-Shōtoku Tennō," in *Women and Confucian Cultures in Premodern China, Korea, and Japan*, ed. Dorothy Ko, JaHyun Kim Haboush, and Joan R. Piggott (Berkeley, CA: University of California Press, 2003), 60.

5. Ibid., 64.

6. Steven D. Carter, trans., *Traditional Japanese Poetry: An Anthology* (Stanford, CA: Stanford University Press, 1991), 46.

7. Edwin Cranston, *A Waka Anthology, vol. 1: The Gem-Glistening Cap* (Stanford, CA: Stanford University Press, 1993), 362–363.

8. Donald Keene, *Anthology of Japanese Literature: From the Earliest Era to the Mid-Nineteenth Century* (New York: Grove Press, 1955), 40.

9. Ibid., 53.

10. Nihon Gakujutsu Shinkōkai, trans., *The Manyōshū: One Thousand Poems* (New York: Columbia University Press, 1965), 281.

11. Ibid., 283.

12. Earl Miner, *An Introduction to Japanese Court Poetry* (Stanford, CA: Stanford University Press, 1948), 48–49.

CHAPTER 3. THE RULE OF TASTE: LIVES OF HEIAN ARISTOCRATS

1. Geoffrey Bownas and Anthony Thwaite, trans., *The Penguin Book of Japanese Verse* (London: Puffin, 1986; repr., London: Penguin, 1998), 75.

2. Murasaki Shikibu, *Murasaki Shikibu Nikki,* ed. Mochizuki Seikyo (Tokyo: Kobundo, 1929), 113–114. Quoted in Ivan Morris, *The World of the Shining Prince: Court Life in Ancient Japan* (New York: Kodansha America, 1994), 206.

3. Edward Seidensticker, trans., *The Gosammer Years: The Diary of a Noblewoman of Heian Japan* (Tokyo: Charles E. Tuttle, 1964; repr., Tokyo: Tuttle, 2011), 44.

4. Bownas and Thwaite, *Penguin Book of Japanese Verse,* 68.

5. Ibid., 70. The final couplet was omitted.

6. Ibid., 71.

7. Helen McCullough, trans., *Kokin wakashū: The First Imperial Anthology of Japanese Poetry* (Stanford, CA: Stanford University Press, 1985), 3–5.

8. Ivan Morris, trans., *The Pillow Book of Sei Shōnagon* (New York: Columbia University Press, 1991), 71, 69, 83.

9. Ibid., 117. Quoted in Haruo Shirane, ed., *Traditional Japanese Literature: An Anthology, Beginnings to 1600* (New York: Columbia University Press, 2012), 155–156.

10. Janet R. Goodwin, *Selling Songs and Smiles: The Sex Trade in Heian and Kamakura Japan* (Honolulu: University of Hawaii Press, 2006), 16.

11. Morris, *Pillow Book of Sei Shōnagon,* 260.

CHAPTER 4. THE RISE AND RULE OF THE WARRIOR CLASS

1. G.B. Sansom, *Japan: A Short Cultural History* (New York: Century, 1931; repr., Stanford, CA: Stanford University Press, 1978), 353.

2. Donald Keene, *Anthology of Japanese Literature: From the Earliest Era to the Mid-Nineteenth Century* (New York: Grove Press, 1955), 197.

3. Kōun Yamada, *The Gateless Gate: The Classic Book of Zen Koans* (New York: Simon and Schuster, 2005), https://books.google.com/books?id = VUA6AwAAQBAJ (accessed May 11, 2017).

4. Dōgen and Kosho Uchiyama Roshi, *How to Cook Your Life: From the Zen Kitchen to Enlightenment* (Boston: Shambhala, 2005), https://books .google.com/books?id = IKOvrBtWJHUC (accessed May 11, 2017). Note that

the six flavors are bitter, sour, sweet, hot, mild, and salty; the three qualities are light, clean, and dignified.

5. Paul Varley, *Japanese Culture*, 4th ed. (Honolulu: University of Hawai'i Press, 2000), 116.

6. Donald Keene, *Nō and Bunraku: Two Forms of Japanese Theatre* (New York: Columbia University Press, 1990), 32.

7. Quoted in Wm. Theodore de Bary et al., eds., *Sources of Japanese Tradition, vol. 1: From Earliest Times to 1600*, 2nd ed. (New York: Columbia University Press, 2001), 204.

8. Keene, *Anthology of Japanese Literature*, 196.

9. de Bary et al., *Sources of Japanese Tradition, vol. 1*, 271.

10. Edwin O. Reischauer and Joseph K. Yamagiwa, *Translations from Early Japanese Literature* (Cambridge, MA: Harvard University Press, 1972), 301–302. Quoted in de Bary et al., *Sources of Japanese Tradition, vol. 1*, 275.

11. Royall Tyler, trans., *The Tale of the Heike* (New York: Penguin, 2012), 504.

12. Helen McCullough, trans., *The Tale of the Heike* (Stanford, CA: Stanford University Press, 1988), 23.

CHAPTER 5. DISINTEGRATION AND REUNIFICATION

1. Wm. Theodore de Bary et al., eds., *Sources of Japanese Tradition, vol. 1: From Earliest Times to 1600*, 2nd ed. (New York: Columbia University Press, 2001), 433.

2. Ibid., 445–446.

3. Ibid.

4. Ibid., 439–440. Numerals of the clauses have been omitted.

5. Ibid., 467.

6. Ibid., 468–469.

7. Michael Cooper, *They Came to Japan: An Anthology of European Reports on Japan, 1543–1640* (Berkeley, CA: University of California Press, 1982), 134–135.

8. Geoffrey Bownas and Anthony Thwaite, trans., *The Penguin Book of Japanese Verse* (London: Puffin, 1986; repr., London: Penguin, 1998), 100.

9. Dennis Hirota, *Wind in the Pines: Classic Writings of the Way of Tea as a Buddhist Path* (Asian Humanities Press, 2002), 217.

10. Kawasaki Momoto, *Hideyoshi to bunroku no eki* (Tokyo: Chūō kōron-sha, 1979), 60–61.

11. Donald Richie, *The Masters' Book of Ikebana: Background & Principles of Japanese Flower Arrangement* (Tokyo: Bijutsu Shuppan-sha, 1966), 56.

12. Quoted in Richie, *The Masters' Book of Ikebana*, 57.

13. Wm. Theodore de Bary et al., eds., *Sources of Japanese Tradition, vol. 2: 1600 to 2000*, 2nd ed. (New York: Columbia University Press, 2005), 180–181.

14. N. Murakami and K. Murakawa, eds., *Letters Written by the English Residents in Japan, 1611–1623, with Other Documents on the English Trading*

Settlement in Japan in the Seventeenth Century (Tokyo: The Sankosha, 1900), 23–24. The spelling has been modernized.

CHAPTER 6. MAINTAINING CONTROL: TOKUGAWA OFFICIAL CULTURE

1. Constantine N. Vaporis, *Tour of Duty: Samurai, Military Service in Edo, and the Culture of Early Modern Japan* (Honolulu: University of Hawaii Press, 2009), 62–101.

2. Constantine N. Vaporis, *Voices of Early Modern Japan: Contemporary Accounts of Daily Life during the Age of the Shoguns* (Westview Press, 2013), 90–91.

3. E. S. Crawcour, "Some Observations of Merchants: A Translation of Mitsui Takafusa's Chōnin Kōken Roku," in David J. Lu, ed., *Japan: A Documentary History, vol. 1* (Armonk, NY: M.E. Sharpe, 1997), 230–231.

4. Wm. Theodore de Bary et al., eds., *Sources of Japanese Tradition, vol. 2: 1600 to 2000*, 2nd ed. (New York: Columbia University Press, 2005), 186–187.

5. Ibid., 193–194.

6. Ibid., 326–330.

7. Basil Hall Chamberlain, *Things Japanese* (London: John Murray, 1890; repr., Cambridge, UK: University of Cambridge Press, 2015), 371–374.

8. de Bary et al., *Sources of Japanese Tradition, vol. 2*, 571–572.

9. Nam-lin Hur, *Prayer and Play in Late Tokugawa Japan: Asakusa Sensōji and Edo Society* (Cambridge, MA: Harvard University Asia Center, 2000), 87.

CHAPTER 7. EDO POPULAR CULTURE: THE FLOATING WORLD

1. Mary Elizabeth Berry, *Japan in Print: Information and Nation in the Early Modern Period* (Berkeley: University of California Press, 2007), 15.

2. Howard Hibbett, *The Chrysanthemum and the Fish: Japanese Humor since the Age of the Shoguns* (New York: Kodansha America, 2002), 54.

3. Ibid., 56.

4. Donald Keene, *World within Walls: Japanese Literature of the Premodern Era, 1600–1867* (New York: Columbia University Press, 1999), 189.

5. Ihara Saikaku, *Five Women Who Loved Love*, trans. W. Theodore de Bary, in Donald Keene, *Anthology of Japanese Literature: From the Earliest Era to the Mid-Nineteenth Century* (New York: Grove Press, 1955), 336–337.

6. Wm. Theodore de Bary et al., eds., *Sources of Japanese Tradition, vol. 2: 1600 to 2000*, 2nd ed. (New York: Columbia University Press, 2005), 348.

7. Geoffrey Bownas and Anthony Thwaite, trans., *The Penguin Book of Japanese Verse* (London: Puffin, 1986; repr., London: Penguin, 1998), 125–127.

8. Matsuo Bashō, *Narrow Road to the Interior*, trans. Sam Hamill (Boston: Shambhala, 2006), 1.

9. Ibid., 50–51.

10. Karen Brazell, ed., *Traditional Japanese Theater: An Anthology of Plays* (New York: Columbia University Press, 1999), 357.

11. Cecilia S. Seigle, *Yoshiwara: The Glittering World of the Japanese Courtesan* (Honolulu: University of Hawaii Press, 1993), 35.

CHAPTER 8. FACING AND EMBRACING THE WEST

1. Harold S. Williams, *Tales of the Foreign Settlements in Japan* (Tokyo: C.E. Tuttle, 1958), 33.

2. Wm. Theodore de Bary et al., eds., *Sources of Japanese Tradition*, vol. 2: *1600 to 2000*, 2nd ed. (New York: Columbia University Press, 2005), 672.

3. Kanagaki Robun, "The Beefeater," in *Modern Japanese Literature: From 1868 to the Present Day*, ed. Donald Keene (New York: Grove Press), 31–32.

4. Steven Ericson, *The Sound of the Whistle: Railroads and the State in Meiji Japan* (Cambridge, MA: Harvard East Asian Monographs, 1996), 54.

5. E. Patricia Tsurumi, *Factory Girls: Women in the Threadmills of Meiji Japan* (Princeton, NJ: Princeton University Press, 1990), 93.

6. Ibid.

7. Ibid., 98.

8. Fukuzawa Yukichi, "An Outline of a Theory of Civilization," in de Bary et al., *Sources of Japanese Tradition*, vol. 2, 703.

9. Ibid., 706.

10. Natsume Sōseki, *Kokoro*, trans. Edwin McClellan (Washington, DC: Regnery Gateway, 1957), 128–129.

11. de Bary et al., *Sources of Japanese Tradition*, vol. 2, 747.

12. Uchimura Kanzō, "Two Js," in de Bary et al., *Sources of Japanese Tradition*, vol. 2, 1167.

CHAPTER 9. MODERNITY AND ITS DISCONTENTS

1. Thomas C. Smith, *Native Sources of Japanese Industrialization, 1750–1920* (Berkeley: University of California Press, 1988), 242.

2. Akira Kurosawa, *Something Like an Autobiography* (New York: Knopf Doubleday, 2011), 48.

3. William J. Tyler, ed., *Modanizumu: Modernist Fiction from Japan, 1913–1938* (Honolulu: University of Hawaii Press, 2008), 19.

4. T. Philip Terry, *Terry's Japanese Empire* (New York: Houghton Mifflin, 1914), 368.

5. Junichirō Tanizaki, *Naomi*, trans. Anthony H. Chambers (New York: Alfred Knopf, 1985; repr., New York: Vintage, 2001), vii–viii.

6. Yasunari Kawabata, *The Scarlet Gang of Asakusa*, trans. Alisa Freedman (Berkeley: University of California Press, 2005), 30.

7. Ibid., 120.

8. Ibid., xxxix.

9. Gennifer Weisenfeld, *MAVO: Japanese Artists and the Avant-Garde, 1905–1931* (Berkeley: University of California Press, 2001), 95.

10. Okakura Kakuzō, *The Ideals of the East,* in Wm. Theodore de Bary et al., eds., *Sources of East Asian Tradition, vol. 2: The Modern Period* (New York: Columbia University Press, 2008), 549.

11. Okakura Kakuzō, *The Book of Tea* (Boulder, CO: Shambhala, 2003 reprint), 72.

12. Ibid., 93.

13. Sōetsu Yanagi, *The Unknown Craftsman: A Japanese Insight into Beauty* (Tokyo: Kodansha, 1972), 107.

14. Ronald A. Morse, ed., *Folk Legends from Tono: Japan's Spirits, Deities, and Phantastic Creatures* (London: Rowman & Littlefield, 2015), 85.

15. Jun'ichirō Tanizaki, *In Praise of Shadows* (New Haven, CT: Leet's Island Books, 1977), 5–6.

CHAPTER 10. CULTURES OF EMPIRE AND WAR

1. Maria Rosa Henson, *Comfort Woman: A Filipina's Story of Prostitution and Slavery under the Japanese Military* (Lanham, MD: Rowman & Littlefield, 1999), 36–37.

2. Louise Young, "Colonizing Manchuria: The Making of an Imperial Myth," in *Mirror of Modernity: Invented Traditions of Modern Japan,* ed. Stephen Vlastos (Berkeley: University of California, 1998), 102.

3. Faye Yuan Kleeman, *Under an Imperial Sun: Japanese Colonial Literature of Taiwan and the South* (Honolulu: University of Hawaii Press, 2003), 30.

4. Jiwon Shin, "Recasting Colonial Space: Naturalist Vision and Modern Fiction in 1920s Korea," *Journal of International and Area Studies* 11, no. 3 (2004): 51–74. Another translation of the story is available in Sunyoung Park and Jefferson J.A. Gattrall, trans., *On the Eve of the Uprising and Other Stories from Colonial Korea* (Ithaca, NY: Cornell University Press, 2010).

5. Michael Baskett, *Attractive Empire: Transnational Film Culture in Imperial Japan,* (Honolulu: University of Hawaii Press, 2008), 23.

6. Noriko Aso, *Public Properties: Museums in Imperial Japan* (Durham, NC: Duke University Press, 2013), 114.

7. Kenneth J. Ruoff, *Imperial Japan at Its Zenith: The Wartime Celebration of the Empire's 2,600th Anniversary* (New York: Columbia University Press, 2014), 121.

CHAPTER 11. DEFEAT AND RECONSTRUCTION

1. Wm. Theodore de Bary et al., eds., *Sources of Japanese Tradition, vol. 2: 1600 to 2000,* 2nd ed. (New York: Columbia University Press, 2005), 1016.

2. John W. Dower, *Embracing Defeat: Japan in the Wake of World War II* (New York: W.W. Norton, 2000), 127.

3. Michael Schaller, *The American Occupation of Japan* (New York: Oxford University Press, 1985), 125.

4. Kenzaburō Ōe, "Sheep," trans. Frank T. Motofuji, *Japan Quarterly* 17, no. 2 (April–June 1970): 171.

5. Ibid., 177.

6. Angus Hone, "Expo '70: A Japanese Fair," *Economic and Political Weekly* 5, no. 38 (September 1970): 1564–1565.

7. Frederik L. Schodt, *Manga! Manga! The World of Japanese Comics*, 2nd ed. (New York: Kodansha USA, 2012), 17.

8. Ming Tiampo and Alexandra Munroe, eds., *Gutai: Splendid Playground* (New York: The Guggenheim Foundation, 2013), 45.

CHAPTER 12. "COOL" JAPAN AS CULTURAL SUPERPOWER

1. Norma Field, "Somehow: The Postmodern as Atmosphere," in *Postmodernism and Japan*, ed. Masao Miyoshi and Harry Harootunian (Durham, NC: Duke University Press, 1989), 178.

2. Shintarō Ishihara, *The Japan That Can Say No*, trans. Frank Baldwin (New York: Simon & Schuster, 1991), 30.

3. Rachel B., "Kimokawaii: Both Cute and Gross at the Same Time," *Tofugu*, June 18, 2013, https://www.tofugu.com/japan/kimokawaii/.

4. Yoshimoto Banana, *Kitchen* (New York: Grove Press, 1988), 59.

5. Haruki Murakami "Town of Cats," *New Yorker*, September 5, 2011, http://www.newyorker.com/magazine/2011/09/05/town-of-cats.

6. Quoted in Hiroshi Aoyagi, "Pop Idols and the Asian Identity," in *Japan Pop! Inside the World of Japanese Popular Culture*, ed. Timothy J. Craig (M.E. Sharpe, 2000), 313.

7. Ibid., 309.

8. Murakami Takashi, "Earth in My Window," in *Little Boy: The Arts of Japan's Exploding Subculture*, ed. Murakami Takashi (New York: Japan Society, 2005), 100–101.

Index

Made in the USA
Columbia, SC
22 August 2023

21998956R00269